STRATEGIC MANAGEMENT ACCOUNTING

Dr. Kamatam Srinivas
M.Com., M.B.A., M. Phil., Ph.D.
Department of Commerce,
Nizam College, Osmania University,
Hyderabad.

Himalaya Publishing House
MUMBAI • NEW DELHI • NAGPUR • BENGALURU • HYDERABAD • CHENNAI • PUNE
• LUCKNOW • AHMEDABAD • ERNAKULAM • BHUBANESWAR • KOLKATA

First Edition : 2016

Published by : Mrs. Meena Pandey for **Himalaya Publishing House Pvt. Ltd.,**
"Ramdoot", Dr. Bhalerao Marg, Girgaon, **Mumbai - 400 004.**
Phone: 022-23860170/23863863, Fax: 022-23877178
E-mail: himpub@vsnl.com; Website: www.himpub.com

Branch Offices :

New Delhi : "Pooja Apartments", 4-B, Murari Lal Street, Ansari Road, Darya Ganj, New Delhi - 110 002. Phone: 011-23270392, 23278631; Fax: 011-23256286

Nagpur : Kundanlal Chandak Industrial Estate, Ghat Road, Nagpur - 440 018. Phone: 0712-2738731, 3296733; Telefax: 0712-2721216

Bengaluru : Plot No. 91-33, 2nd Main Road Seshadripuram, Behind Nataraja Theatre, Bengaluru-560020. Phone: 08041138821, 9379847017, 9379847005

Hyderabad : No. 3-4-184, Lingampally, Besides Raghavendra Swamy Matham, Kachiguda, Hyderabad - 500 027. Phone: 040-27560041, 27550139

Chennai : New-20, Old-59, Thirumalai Pillai Road, T. Nagar, Chennai - 600 017. Mobile: 9380460419

Pune : First Floor, "Laksha" Apartment, No. 527, Mehunpura, Shaniwarpeth (Near Prabhat Theatre), Pune - 411 030. Phone: 020-24496323/24496333; Mobile: 09370579333

Lucknow : House No 731, Shekhupura Colony, Near B.D. Convent School, Aliganj, Lucknow - 226 022. Phone: 0522-4012353; Mobile: 09307501549

Ahmedabad : 114, "SHAIL", 1st Floor, Opp. Madhu Sudan House, C.G. Road, Navrang Pura, Ahmedabad - 380 009. Phone: 079-26560126; Mobile: 09377088847

Ernakulam : 39/176 (New No: 60/251) 1st Floor, Karikkamuri Road, Ernakulam, Kochi – 682011. Phone: 0484-2378012, 2378016; Mobile: 09387122121

Bhubaneswar : 5 Station Square, Bhubaneswar - 751 001 (Odisha). Phone: 0674-2532129, Mobile: 09338746007

Kolkata : 108/4, Beliaghata Main Road, Near ID Hospital, Opp. SBI Bank, Kolkata - 700 010, Phone: 033-32449649, Mobile: 7439040301

DTP by : **Vani Graphics, Hyderabad.**

Printed at : M/s Sri Sai Art Printer Hyderabad. On behalf of HPH.

PREFACE

Strategic Management Accounting is a recent addition to the finance and accounting specialization and offered by many universities in the country to the post-graduate students of business management and commerce to enhance their decision-making skills in the area of finance and accounting. In nutshell, strategic management accounting is a form of management accounting in which emphasis is placed on information which relates to factors external to the firm, as well as non-financial information and internally generated information. It helps the student in tools and techniques in the collection of management accounting information about a business and its competitors for use in developing and monitoring the business strategy. The emphasis of the subject is placed upon relative levels and trends in real costs and prices, volume, market share, cash flow and stewardship of the resources available to the business.

However, the choice of text books available to the students in the subject is very limited. Hardly, there are very few books which struck a right balance between theory and practical aspects of the subject.

The present book is an attempt to fill this gap as it discusses the core concepts of strategic management accounting in a lucid manner by combining theory with a lot of practical examples in a student-friendly manner. The book covers the contemporary issues pertaining to the subject such as life cycle cost accounting, customer profitability accounting, competitor accounting and analysis, activity based costing, responsibility accounting and target costing. The book not only helps the student in acquiring the conceptual clarity in the subject but also provides practical knowledge of various business situations, which would help them to use the knowledge in the actual business situation. This book is also useful for students of professional courses such as C.A., ICSI, ICWA as it covers a large number of solved problems and exercises. I sincerely feel that the book provides a good academic support to the teachers in providing clarity on various dimensions of the subject to the students.

The syllabi of **M.B.A., M.Com.** and **MHRM** of Osmania University contain the subject of Strategic Management Accounting as a finance specialization paper. The present book has been written according to the syllabus prescribed for the same and contains well-defined chapters.

I thank my teachers for motivating and guiding to complete this book – Prof. A. Sudhakar, Registrar, Dr. B.R.O.U, Prof. R. Nageshwar Rao, Director Academic Audit and OSD Osmania University, Prof. S.V. Satyanarayana, Head, Department of Commerce and former OSD Osmania University, Prof. V. Shekhar, Principal, OUCC&BM, Prof. P.V. Ramana Rao, Principal, KGR Institute of Technology and Management and member in Higher Education Telangana State, Prof. Akbar Ali Khan, Former Vice Chancellor, Telengana University, Prof. H. Venkateshwarlu, Director PGRRCDE, Prof. K. Achalapathi,

Director Placement, Osmania University, Prof. Vidyadhar Reddy, Prof. V. Appa Rao, Prof. Anand Kumar, B.O.S. Department of Commerce, Prof. Prashanta Athma, Prof. K. Shankaraiah, Prof. G. Laxman, Dean, Faculty of Commerce, Prof. M. Usha, Prof. Krishna Kumar, Prof. D. Chenappa and Dr. M. Gangadhar Vice Principal, Nizam College.

I thank my friends for encouraging me to complete this book – Dr. G. Naresh Reddy, Assistant Professor, Osmania University, Dr. S. Vijay Laxmi, Associate Professor, KGR Institute of Technology and Management, Dr. J. Ravi Kumar, Assistant Professor, Osmania University, Dr. R. Sampath Kumar, Assistant Professor, Osmania University, Dr Y. Jahangir, Assistant Professor, Osmania University, Dr. Patric, Assistant Professor, Osmania University, Dr. K. Sudersan, Associate Profesor, IIM Kozhikode, Dr. Rachappa. Associate Profesor IIM Kozhikode , Dr. S. Narsimulu, Dr. L. Srinivasa Reddy, Principal, Einstein PG College, Dr. Ranjani, Head Department of Commerce, Nizam College and Dr. P. Srinivas Reddy, Assistant Professor.

My special thanks to Prof. T.L.N. Swamy, Principal, Nizam College and Sri K. Govinda Reddy, Chairman, KGR Institute of Technology & Management for giving me sufficient time for completing the book.

I express my deep hearted thanks to my family especially my wife Subhashini, sons Dhanush and Kalyan without their constant support and encouragement, the book would not have possible.

I thank my colleague Mr. P.V. Narsh for this useful co-operation in taking up the typing work. I also thank the publisher for the timely publication and my special thanks are to Mr. Krishna Poojari, Br. Manager, Hyderabad Branch and Mr. G. Anil Kumar, ASM for the keen interest taken by them in bringing out this book.

Dr. K. Srininvas

CONTENTS

Chapter -1
Strategic Management Accounting

Introduction

Business environment has become increasingly dynamic and competitive; it has become increasingly important for managers to develop internally coherent, and logically consistent business strategies. The tools and models which provide useful information to support strategic decision making, planning and control. In response to these needs, there have been many important developments in both management accounting research and practice. The traditional management accounting system lacks relevance in this direction as it focuses more on short-term and internal sources of information, hence the need for strategic management accounting. Strategic management accounting is an outward looking and future oriented accounting system designed by management in the provision of information for the formulation, implementation and evaluation of strategy to cope with environmental demands. There are different forms of strategic management accounting practices. These include competitor accounting , strategic pricing, strategic costing, attribute costing, quality costing, target costing, life cycle costing, value chain costing, brand value monitoring, brand value budgeting, responsibility accounting, customer account profitability, transfer pricing and activity-based costing.

Depending on the strategic positioning of the firm, which could be a choice of different generic strategies like cost leadership, differentiation, speed and market focus. It achieves sustainable competitive advantage a defender firm competes through efficient operations in terms of cost, quality and service leadership while a prospector firm competes through new product innovations and market development. Hence, defender firm tends to place a greater emphasis on the use of financial measures of performance. The prospector firm stresses the need for non-financial measures of performance. Irrespective of the strategic positioning, the role of strategic management accounting is to provide with relevant, accurate and reliable information on the firm's critical success factors within and outside the organization for a long-term period. The management of business organization is advised to consider the strategic management accounting which is more useful in today's competitive environment.

Meaning

Management accounting is the context of business strategies being planned and implemented by an organization. Strategy is the way that a firm positions and distinguishes itself from its competitors. These business strategies must be developed in the context of the internal and external environments so that they are practical. It is also important that business strategies are developed at the appropriate levels within an organization. An overall corporate strategy is needed for the organization in total with separate but linked competitive strategies for each division of the business which is competing in different markets with different products.

Back in 1981, *Ken Simmonds*, says it is the collection of management accounting information about a business and its competitors for use in developing and monitoring the business strategy. The emphasis was placed upon relative levels and trends in real costs, prices, volume, market share, cash flow and stewardship of the resources available to the business.

Bromwich pointed out that adding the strategic perspective to traditional management accounting required the role of accounting to extend in two directions. First, costs need to be integrated into strategy through strategic cost analysis and thus align costs with strategy. Secondly, to ascertain, even though in a fairly general way, the cost structure of competitors and to monitor the changes over time.

Strategies

Strategies are the means by which long-term objectives will be achieved. "A strategy is a unified, comprehensive and integrated plan that relates the strategic advantages of the firm to the challenges of the environment. It is designed to ensure that the basic objectives of the enterprise are achieved through proper execution by the organization" (*William F. Glueck*, and *Lawrence R. Jauch*). The role of strategy is to identify the general approaches that the organization utilize to achieve its organizational objectives. Hence the choice of strategy is so central to the study and understanding of strategic management.

Need of Strategic Management Accounting

A number of reasons are given by authors to as why organizations should engage in strategic management accounting. These studies show both financial and nonfinancial benefits which can be derived from a strategic-management approach to decision making. Organizations measure both financial and nonfinancial benefits through strategic management accounting. It considers information which relates to external factors and internally generated information.

Financial Benefits

All organization engages in strategic management accounting looking at the relationship between strategic management and performance evaluation.

Eastlack and *McDonald* (1970), in his research indicate that formalized strategic planning does result in superior performance by organizations. He was able to provide conceiving evidence of the profitability of strategy formulation and implementation. The formalized strategic management process does make a difference in the recorded measurements of profits, sales and return on assets. Organizations that adopt a strategic management approach can expect that the new system will lead to improved financial performance.

Nonfinancial Benefits

Strategic management is needed to cope with and manage uncertainty in decision making. The following are the nonfinancial benefits of strategic management accounting.

1. It provides a way to anticipate future problems and opportunities.
2. It provides employees with clear objectives and directions for the future of the organization.

3. It results in more effective and better performance compared to non-strategic management organizations.
4. It increases employee satisfaction and motivation.
5. It results in faster and better decision making and
6. It results on cost savings.

It offers the following process and personal benefits:

1. It allows for identification, prioritization and exploitation of opportunities.
2. It provides an objective view of management problems.
3. It represents a framework for improved coordination and control of activities.
4. It minimizes the effects of adverse conditions and changes.
5. It allows major decisions to better support established objectives.
6. It allows more effective allocation of time and resources to identified opportunities.
7. It allows fewer resources and less time to be devoted to correcting erroneous or *ad hoc* decisions.
8. It creates a framework for internal communication among personnel.
9. It helps to integrate the behavior of individuals into a total effort.
10. It provides a basic for the clarification of individual responsibilities.
11. It gives encouragement to forward thinking.
12. It provides a cooperative, integrated and enthusiastic approach to tackling problems and opportunities.
13. It encourages a favourable attitude towards change.
14. It gives a degree of discipline and formality to the management of a business.

Finally strategic management accounting is an integral and important function of organization life. However, successful organizations are successful for using adequate resources and producing good products and services.

Evolution of Strategic Management Accounting

The systems can be grouped into four distinctive stages of evolution that were responsive to the progressively decreasing familiarity of events and decreasing visibility of the future:

1. **Management by control of performance,** which was adequate when change was slow.
2. **Management by extrapolation,** when change accelerated but the future could be predicted by extrapolation of the past.

3. **Management by anticipation**, when discontinuities began to appear but change, while rapid, was still slow enough to permit timely anticipation and response.

4. **Management through flexible/rapid response**, which is currently emerging, under conditions in which many significant challenges develop too rapidly to permit timely anticipation.

Developing the Strategic Management Accounting Process

Frederick W. Glueck, suggested that strategic planning in many organizations must evolve through four sequential phases.

Phase 1 Basic financial planning. Organizations in phase 1 emphasize preparing and meeting annual budgets. Financial targets are established and revenues and costs are carefully monitored. The emphasis is short-term and the primary focus is on the functional aspects of the organization. Most organizations in this phase exhibit few other characteristics relating to the future.

Phase 2 Forecast-based planning. Organizations in phase two usually extend the time frames covered by the budgeting process. Managers tend to seek more sophisticated forecasts and to become aware of their external environment and its effect on their organizations. Therefore, organization in phase two has more effective resource allocation and more timely decisions relating to organization's long-range competitive position.

Phase 3 Externally-oriented planning. Phase three is characterized by the attempt to understand basic marketplace phenomena. Organization begins to search for new ways to define and satisfy customer needs. Moreover, phase three differs from the earlier phases that the corporate planners are expected to generate a number of alterative courses of action for top management. Top management begins to evaluate strategic alternatives in a formalized manner to planning and actions.

Phase 4 Strategic Management. Phase four is characterized by the merging of strategic planning and management into a single process. This integrated approach is accomplished through the presence of three elements: pervasive strategic thinking (managers all levels have learned to think strategically), comprehensive planning process and supportive value system.

It is a further development of management accounting. It starts with formulation of the plans to execution of products or services and evaluation of performance based on activities, divisions or whole organization. Strategic management accounting provides information for taking the decisions of long period as well as short period.

Scope of Strategic Management Accounting

The management processes and decisions which determine the long-term structure and activities of the organization. the primary objective of strategic management accounting is to serve the management in its functions of planning, directing and controlling and to serve the management. It makes use of tools and techniques of various disciplines including accounting, costing and management accounting. It helps the management accountant to discharge his duties and responsibility satisfactorily, may be considered as falling within the scope of strategic management accounting. Consequently, it is very difficult task to specify the scope of a growing subject like, strategic management accounting. However, the following tools, systems, techniques, etc., definitely fall within the scope of strategic management accounting.

1. **Structure of the Organization :** An organization is managed by people within a structure. The decisions which result from the way that managers work together within the structure can result in strategic change.

2. **Activities of the Organization :** This is potentially for identifying various areas of study and we normally shall centre upon all activities which affect the organization.

3. **Financial Accounting :** Strategic Management Accounting gathers maximum data from Financial Accounting. Because, the annual reports which include, among others, the financial statements provide voluminous data. Though Financial Accounting generates only the historical data, they are useful for planning, directing and controlling purposes. Because all these cases, historical financial data are used as the base and they act as guidelines for the future. With the help of financial analysis tools, the management accountant analyses and interprets the financial data to get a greater insight into the company's performance and position etc. Hence financial accounting is considered as falling within the scope of strategic management accounting.

4. **Cost Accounting :** Cost Accounting has been considered as an integral part of strategic management accounting due to two important reasons. The first reason is financial accounting; cost accounting also generates voluminous data about the primary activity of the company, *viz.*, cost of production and selling the goods and services. The second reason is also the revenue from the activity of the company, it also provides a number of sophisticated analytical tools like, marginal costing, standard costing, budgetary control, inter firm comparison, etc., which are widely being used by the management accountant to discharge his duties and responsibilities. Hence, cost accounting falls within the scope of strategic management accounting.

5. **Tools and Techniques of Financial Analysis :** Financial Statements are analyzed and interpreted to get an idea about the company's performance and prospects. A number of tools are used to accomplish this objective. The different tools are comparative financial statements, common–size financial statements, trend ratios, ratio analysis and statements of changes in financial position. All these are subject matters of management accounting but it is part of strategic management accounting.

6. **Control Accounting :** Controlling means to measure the variation if any between actual and the standard results and taking corrective measures to remove the variation. Management accounting is the essential part of control accounting; budgetary control, inventory control and equality control are some of the important techniques of strategic management accounting for control accounting.

7. **Management Reporting :** Collection of facts and figures, analysis and classification of the same are done with the sole objective of reporting to the management. The reports are important as they identify the achievements and failures, the strong and weak areas, the positive and the negative aspects of the company. Frequency format contents of the reports differ from one report to another. Management reviews the performance of the company and each of the divisions or departments on continuous basis of these reports and takes appropriate action. The management reports which are also called internal reports are the subject matter of strategic management accounting.

Strategic Importance of Management Accounting

The planning, controlling, coordinating, organizing, motivating and communicating are the six important managerial functions. Management accounting helps the managerial personnel to perform each one of these functions more effectively and profitably by providing relevant information at the right time. They collect the information from different sources and analyses them systematically to find out their relevance to the decision under consideration. It provides the relevant information to the management to take proper decisions. The work of the management is made easy by the management accountant. They carry out a comprehensive evaluation of all the possible and available alternatives and suggest the best alternative. Management accounting renders a very valuable service to the management in all its fields of activity.

1. **Helps in Planning and Forecasting :** Management is assisted to a better extent by the management accountant in its plans for different departments and operations. It provides the relevant information pertaining to different products, markets, departments, etc. Accordingly it is possible for the management to plan for each segment and also for the whole organization. Further forecasting is made easy by the use of management accounting tools along with statistical tools.
2. **Helps in Decision Making Process :** Management has to take a number of decisions such as pricing, revision of prices, product diversification, dropping a product, sell or process further, replacement of existing capital assets, mechanization, expansion, etc. Management accountant identifies alternatives, collects all the necessary details, evaluates the alternatives, identifies the optimal alternative, and prepares and submits report to the management incorporating his analysis, and suggestion. The report submitted by the management accountant helps the management in selecting a suitable alternative and in taking appropriate decisions.
3. **Measurement and Evaluation of Performance** : With the help of budgetary control, standard costing, marginal costing, etc., the management accountant is able to measure and evaluate the performance of departments, products, functions etc., and also the overall performance of the company. Standards or budgets set and actually accomplished are compared to find the deviations, and to evaluate the performance. Further, Contribution, P/V Ratio, etc., are also used to assess the performance as objectively as possible. Based on this exercise a number of appropriate decisions are taken by the management to improve the overall profitability.

4. **Efficient Management Control :** Since the Management Accountant makes use of the Budgetary Control, Standard Costing, etc., it is possible to set the standards or targets and compares them with the actual accomplished. The comparison enables to identify the areas wherein the company has failed to reach the targets. As the management Accountant, in his reports to different levels of management, draws the management's attention to these areas, it helps the management to have management by exception and to take immediate actions.
5. **Customer Welfare :** A part of whole of the benefits of cost control exercises can be passed on by the company to its customers in the form of reduction in prices. Further, the companies lay emphasis on the quality of their product and the employees are made quality conscious. Hence, the customers, interest is protected through the supply of quality goods at reasonable prices.
6. **Maximization of Profitability :** The emphasis of management accounting is improving efficiency of each individual and segment cost control and maximization of revenue. Budgetary control, standard costing, marginal costing, responsibility accounting, etc., are used for segment or activity or product to minimize its cost and contribute more towards the overall contribution and profit of the company.

Elements of Strategic Management Accounting

Strategic management accounting includes strategic planning, strategic control and decision making. Strategic planning describes the periodic activities undertaken by organizations to cope with changes in their external environments (*Lester A. Digman*) it involves formulating and evaluating alternative strategies for selecting a strategy and developing detailed plans for putting the strategy into practice. Strategic planning consists of formulating strategies from which overall plans for implementing the strategy are developed. Strategic control consists of ensuring that the chosen strategy is being implemented properly and that it is producing the desired results or not.

Based on *Robert Anthony's* framework, three types of planning and control are required by organizations :

1. **Strategic Planning and Control** : The process of deciding on changes in organizational objectives, the resources to be used for attaining these objectives. The policies are governing for acquisition and use of these resources and attaining the objectives. Strategic planning and control involve actions that change the character or direction of the organization.

2. **Management Planning and Control** : The process of ensuring that resources are obtained and used efficiently in the accomplishment of the organization's objectives. It is carried on within the framework recognized by strategic planning and is similar to operating control.

3. **Technical Planning and Control** : The process of ensuring efficient acquisition and use of resources. The optimum relationship between outputs and resources can be accurately estimated through financial accounting and quality controls.

Another key term in the study of strategic management accounting is long-range planning. It is absolutely reasonable to have long-range operating or technical plans that are not strategic. However, it should be noted that the majority strategic decisions have long-term ramifications.

Management Control

A management control system consists of a process and structure. The process is the set of measures that take place and the collection is the organizational arrangement and information constructs that facilitate this process. A management function designed at achieving clear goals within an established schedule, and more often than not understood to have three components are setting standards, measuring actual performance and taking action. Management control services under the supervision of the management accountant are responsible for the related accounting, reporting, budgetary and financial activities.

It covers the whole process of translating strategy into objectives and finally monitoring the results actually achieved. Management accountant's report is now produced for internal use on a monthly basis and covers details together of accountancy and budget issues. Financial manager is expressing a second view on certain aspects of the bank's financial policies and their execution. It covers all the bank's activities whose data streams have an important impact on the EIB's financial position such as credit risk, performance indicators, the administrative budget and asset and liability management. Accountant is liable for general accounting and for preparing the bank's financial statements. The financial manager analyzing financial management instruments as well as the associated systems.

Managers

Management control is the communication of managers with one a different and with subordinates. It is a people oriented method and line managers are the important points in management control. They are the persons whose judgments are incorporated in the approved plans and they are the persons who must power others and whose performance is considered. Staff people collect, review and present information that is helpful in the process and they make calculations that interpret management judgments into the plans. Control department is often the head staff department in a company.

However the significant decisions are made by the line managers, not by the staff. Since managers are human beings, psychological considerations are leading in management control. Activities such as communication, persuading, exhorting, inspiring and criticizing are a significant part of the process.

Goals

The goals of an organization are set in the strategic planning process in the management control process these goals are generally taken as given. The management control process is planned to facilitate the achievement of these goals.

The broad strategies and polices that have been decided on in the strategic planning process are also taken as given in the management control process.

Efficiency and Effectiveness

By effectiveness, we mean how healthy an organization unit does its job; that is, the extent to which it produces the expected results. Efficiency is used in its manufacturing sense; that is, the amount of output per unit of input.

A well-organized machine is one which produces a given quantity of outputs with a minimum consumption of inputs which produces the largest possible output from a given quantity of inputs.

Effectiveness is always associated to the organizations goals, efficiency is related to goals. Efficient organization unit is one which is the lowest consumption of resources, but if what it does is an inadequate contribution to the success of the organizations goals, it is unproductive.

Benefits of strategic management accounting

1. Strategic management accounting can also conclude if a company needs to drop certain business lines to recover its profit margin and cut inefficient operations
2. Using strategic management accounting to build up cost leadership strategies and strong economic forecasts can help companies improve its market share in the economic marketplace.
3. Companies may also be able to create a distinct competitive advantage over competitors in its business industry or sector.
4. Company earns more profits and the opportunity to expand its operations or enter new business markets.

Limitations of strategic management accounting

1. Implementing strategic management accounting can be a difficult and expensive process for companies.
2. Accountants are generally trained to only collect financial information, input the information into the accounting software and prepare financial reports.
3. Strategic management accounting attempts to change this approach by including management accountants in the strategic planning and decision making process of the company.
4. This change goes against decades of traditional accounting training, requiring companies to develop new business thought processes in their accountants.

Management Control Systems

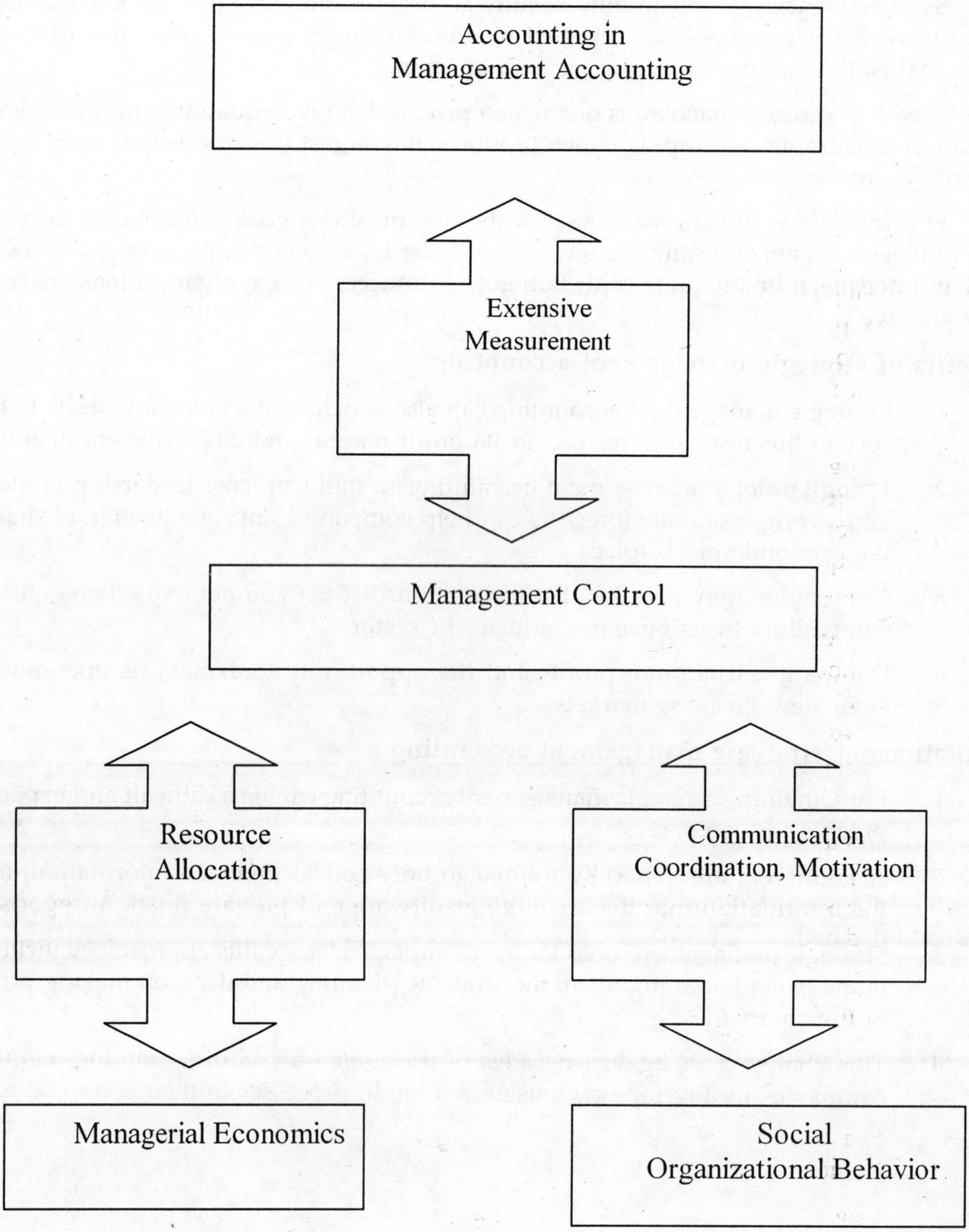

Management Control System

A **management control system** is a system which gathers and uses information to assess the performance of diverse organizational resources like human, physical, financial and also the organization as a whole considering the organizational strategies. Lastly, MCS influences the behaviour of organizational resources to implement organizational strategies and it might be formal or informal.

Robert N. Anthony (2007) says Management control is the process by which managers influence other members of the organization to implement the organization's strategies. Management control systems are tools to aid management for steering an organization toward its strategic objectives and competitive advantage. Management controls are only one of the tools which managers use in implementing desired strategies. However strategies get implemented through management controls, organizational structure, human resources management and culture.

Anthony & Young (1999) explained management control system as a black box. The term black box is used to explain a process whose precise nature cannot be observed. MCS involves the behavior of managers and these behaviours cannot be expressed by equations.

According to *Horngren* management control system is an integrated technique for collecting and using information to motivate employee behaviour and to estimate performance. According to *Simon*'s management control systems are the formal, information-based routines and measures, managers use to maintain or alter patterns in organizational activities.

Chenhall (2003) says that the terms management accounting, management accounting systems, management control systems and organizational controls are sometimes used interchangeably. It refers to a collection of practices such as product costing. But management accounting systems refers to the systematic use of management accounting to achieve some goal and MCS is a broader term that encompasses management accounting systems and also includes other controls such as personal controls. According to Maciariello management control is concerned with coordination, resource allocation, motivation and performance measurement. The practice of management control and the design of management control systems describe a number of academic disciplines. Management control involves extensive measurement and it requires contributions from accounting especially management accounting. Second, it involves resource allocation decisions and requires contribution from economics especially managerial economics. Third, it involves communication, and motivation which means it is related to contributions from social psychology especially organizational behavior.

Management control systems use many techniques such as

1. Balanced scorecard
2. Total quality management (TQM)
3. Kaizen (Continuous Improvement)
4. Activity-based costing
5. Target costing
6. Benchmarking and Bench trending
7. JIT

8. Budgeting
9. Capital budgeting
10. Program management techniques, etc.

The Nature of Management Control Systems

Basic Concepts :

Elements of a control system consist of the following concepts :

1. A detector
2. An assessor
3. An effector
4. A communication network

A detector or sensor : It is a device that measure what is actually happening in the process being controlled.

An assessor : It is a device that determines the significance of what is actually happening by comparing it with some standards or expectations of what should happen.

An effector (feedback) : It is a device that alters behavior if the assessor indicates the need to do so.

A communications network : It consists of devices that transmit information between the detector and the assessor and between the assessor and the effector.

Example : You are driving a car

- Detectors = Your eyes
- Assessor = Your brain
- Effector = Your foot
- Communication network = Your nerves system

Your eyes (detectors) measure actual speed by observing the speedometer. Your brain (assessor) compares actual speed with desired speed (standard: the highest speed is 80 km/hour) to detect a deviation from standard. Your brain (assessor) directs your foot (effector) to ease up the accelerator if actual speed (90 km/hour) is faster than the standard speed (80 km/hour), press down the accelerator if the actual speed (70 km/hour) is slower than standard speed (80 km/hour). And, your nerves (communication network) form the communication system that transmits information from eyes (detectors) to brain (assessor) and brain (assessor) to foot (effector).

Boundaries of Management Control :

1. Strategy formulation is the process of deciding on the goals of the organization and the strategies for attaining these goals.
2. Management control (*Anthony* and *Govindarajan*, 2004): is the process by which managers influence other members of organization to implement the organization's strategies.
3. Task control is the process of ensuring that specified tasks are carried out effectively and efficiently.

Short Question and Answers

1. Define Strategy?
2. Explain the following terms
   (a) A detector
   (b) An assessor
   (c) An effector
   (d) A communication network
3. What is the Management Control?

Essay Type Question and Answers

1. Explain the meaning and need of strategic management accounting?
2. Explain the importance and evolution of strategic management accounting?
3. Process of developing the strategic management accounting?
4. What is the strategic management accounting and explain the scope?
5. Explain the strategic importance of management accounting?
6. Explain the elements of strategic management accounting?
7. Explain the benefits of strategic management accounting?
8. Explain the limitations of strategic management accounting?
9. Explain the management control systems and the nature of management control systems?

❖ ❖ ❖

Chapter - 2

Cost Concepts and Behaviour

Cost means an amount of money, given up in exchange for something else, usually goods or services. All expenses are costs, but not all costs are expenses. Cost is to estimate the amount of money needed to produce a product or perform a service.

According to *ICWA*, London : " Cost accounting is the process of accounting for cost from the point at which expenditure is incurred or committed to the establishment of its ultimate relationship with cost centers and cost units. In its widest usage, it embraces the preparation of statistical data, the application of cost control methods and the ascertainment of the profitability of activities carried on as planned.

***J.E. Brett & A.G. Tralton* defines** : "Cost accounting which is an indispensable part of the costing system, afford the desired measurement of the manufacturing and business operations from the point of cost and consequently in addition to their value as an aid to measurement to provide the basic information necessary for price fixing."

Features of Cost Accounting

The following are the features of cost accounting :

i) It is a process of accounting for costs.

ii) It is concerned with cost ascertainment and cost control.

iii) It records income and expenditure relating to product of goods and services.

iv) It prepares budgets and standards so that actual costs may be compared to find out deviations and variances.

v) It provides statistical data on the basis of which future estimates are prepared and quotations are submitted.

vi) It involves the preparation of right information to the right person at the right time so that it may be helpful to the management for planning, control and decision making.

vii) Cost accounting is the special part of financial accounting.

viii) Total cost or cost per unit of goods manufacture can be ascertained by cost accounting.

ix) Under this cost of incomplete work is also ascertained.

x) It is complementary of financial accounting.

(xi) Cost accounting is both science and art.

Objects of Cost Accounting

The following are the key objects of cost accounting :

1. **Cost Ascertainment :** The primary objective of the cost accounting is to find out the cost of each product, process, job, operation or service rendered. Cost accounting provides the cost that is necessary to be sacrificed for a thing or service.

2. **Cost Control :** Cost accounting aims at controlling cost by setting standards and compared with the actual, the variation between two is identified and necessary steps are taken to control them. It helps in attaining aim of controlling cost by using various techniques such as budgetary control, standard costing and inventory control. Each item of cost like material, labour and expense is budgeted at the beginning of the period and actual expense incurred is compared with the budget. It increases the efficiency of the enterprise.

3. **Basis for operating policy :** Cost accounting helps in planning groundwork and policy formulation for the management. It provides daily, weekly or monthly statement of units produced, accumulated cost with analysis. It also provides instant information regarding stock of raw material; semi-finished and finished goods. It helps in providing information for managerial decisions for formulating effective policies.

Cost Concepts

1. Cost

It is the amount of resources given up in exchange for some goods or services. The resources given up are expressed in monetary terms. Cost is the amount of expenditure incurred on or attributable to a given thing or to ascertain the cost of a given thing. The committee on cost terminology of the *American Accounting Association* has defined cost as the foregoing in monetary terms, incurred or potentially to be incurred in the realization of the objective of management which may be manufacturing of a product or rendering of a service.

Thus cost is that which is given or is sacrificed to obtain something. The cost of an article consists of ascertained charges incurred in its production and sale. Cost is a generic term and it is always worthwhile to qualify the word cost to show closely what means is prime cost, factory cost; sunk cost, etc., cost is also different from value, as cost is measured in terms of money whereas value is measured in terms of usefulness on an article.

A cost must always be studied with reference to its purpose and conditions. Different costs may be ascertained for different purposes and under different conditions. For the valuation of work in progress, factory cost is used, but for valuation of finished goods, cost of production is used. If the purpose of the study of cost is the same, different conditions may lead in variation in cost.

2. Cost Centre

A cost centre is the smallest segment of activity for which costs are accumulated. Typically cost centres are departments but in some instances, a department may contain several cost centres. These cost centres are the departments or sub-departments of an organization with reference to which cost is collected for cost ascertainment and cost control. For example an assembly department may be supervised by one foreman, it may contain several assembly lines. Sometimes each assembly line is regarded as a separate cost centre with its own assistant foreman. A cost centre can be a location, i.e., an area such as department, store yard or sales area or an item of equipment like lathe machine, delivery vehicle or a person like salesman, foreman.

The determination of a suitable cost centre is very important for ascertainment and cost control of cost. The manager is incharge of a cost centre is held responsible for control of cost of his cost centre. It enables the accumulation of all such costs at one place for which a common base of recovery may be used.

Types of Cost Centres

Cost Centres may be classified as under :

(a) **Personal and impersonal cost centres** : Personal cost centre is one which consists of a person or a group of persons. On the other hand, impersonal cost center consists of a machine, a department or plant.

(b) **Operation and process cost centres** : Operation cost consists of those persons or machines carrying out the same kind of operation. On the other hand a center which has a continuous sequence of operations is called process cost centre.

(c) **Product and service cost centers** : Product centre refers to a centre through which a product passes and generally corresponds to a product department. In such centres, raw materials are converted into finished goods. Service Center is a center which incurs direct and indirect costs but does not work directly on products. Maintenance department is the general factory office. Such centres are ancillary and render service to production centres to enable them to carry out the work of production smoothly. The number of cost centers varies from organization to organization. In engineering industry, the cost centres may be (i) Machine shop, (ii) Welding shop, (iii) Assembly shop, (iv) Maintenance department, (v) General administrative department ; (i) to (iii) centres are production centres whereas (iv) and (v) centers are service cost centers.

3. Profit Centre

A profit centre is that segment of activity of a business which is responsible for both revenue and expenses and discloses the profit of a particular segment of activity. Profit centres are created to delegate responsibility to individuals and measure their performance. Profit center is different from cost centre.

The following are the main difference between a cost centre and profit centre :

(a) Cost centre is the smallest unit of activity of responsibility for which costs are collected whereas a profit centre is that segment of activity of a business which is responsible for both revenue and expenses.

(b) Cost centres are created for accounting conveniences of costs and their control whereas a profit center is created because of decentralization of operations, i.e., to delegate responsibility to individuals who have greater knowledge of local conditions etc.

(c) Cost centres are not autonomous whereas profit centres are autonomous.

(d) A cost center does not have target costs but efforts are made to minimize costs, but each profit centre has a profit target and enjoys authority to adopt such policies as are necessary to achieve its targets.

(e) The selection of suitable cost centres for which costs are to be ascertained in an undertaking depends upon the organisation of the factory condition and incidence of cost, requirements of costing.

4. Conversion Cost

It is the sum of direct wages, direct expenses and overhead costs of converting raw material from one stage of production to the next. In other words, conversion costs is works costs minus the cost of direct materials.

Cost Classification

Classification of cost means, the grouping of costs according to their common characteristics. The important ways of classification of costs is of importance in order to indentify the cost with cost centres or cost units. The costs are classified by different ways of costs depending upon the purpose to be achieved and requirement of a particular concern.

The following are the important ways of classifications :

(1) By nature or elements

(2) By functions

(3) By degree of traceability to the product

(4) By changes in activity or volume

(5) By controllability

(6) By normality

(7) By relationship with accounting period (Capital and Revenue)

(8) By time

(9) According to planning and control

(10) By association with the product

(11) For managerial decisions.

1. **By Nature or Elements or Analytical Classification :** The costs are divided based on nature is three categories, i.e., Materials, Labour, and Expenses. It can be further sub-classification of each element; for example, materials into raw material components, spare parts, consumables stores, packing materials etc., this classification is important as it helps to find out the total cost.

2. **By Functional Classification :** According to this classification costs are divided in the different aspect of basic managerial activities involved in the operation of a business undertaking. It leads to grouping of cost according to the broad divisions or functions of a business undertaking, i.e., production, administration, selling and distribution.

According to this classification costs are divided as follows:

a) ***Manufacturing and Production Cost :*** This is the total of costs involved in manufacture, construction and fabrication of units of production.

b) ***Commercial Cost :*** This is the total of costs incurred in the operation of a business undertaking other than the cost of manufacturing and production. Commercial cost is subdivided into administrative cost and selling and distribution cost.

3. **By Degree of Traceability to the Product (Direct and Indirect) :** Based on this classification total cost is divided into direct costs and indirect costs.

a) ***Direct costs*** are those which are incurred for conveniently identified with a particular cost centre or cost unit. Materials used and labour employed in manufacturing in a particular process of production are examples of direct costs.

b) ***Indirect costs*** are those costs which are incurred for the benefit of a number of cost centres or cost units and cannot be identified with a particular cost centre or cost unit. Examples of indirect costs include rent of building, management salaries, machinery depreciation, etc., The nature of the business and the cost unit chosen will determine which costs are direct and which are indirect. For example, the hire of a mobile crane for use by a contractor at site would be regarded as a direct cost but if the crane is used as a part of the services of a factory. The hire charges would be regarded as a direct cost but if the crane is used as a part of the probably benefit more than one cost centre. The importance of the difference of costs into direct and indirect lies in the fact that direct costs of a product or activity can be exactly determined while indirect costs have to be apportioned on certain assumptions as regards their incidence.

4. **By Change in Activity or Volume :** Costs are classified according to their behaviour in relation to changes in the level of activity or volume of production. On this basis costs are classified into three types, i.e., fixed, variable and semi-variable cost.

(a) ***Fixed Costs*** are usually described as those which remain fixed in total amount with increase or decrease in the volume of output for a given period of time. Fixed cost per unit decreases as production increases and increases as production declines. Examples of fixed costs are rent, insurance of factory building, factory manager's salary, etc., these fixed costs are constant in total amount but fluctuate per unit as production changes. These costs are

known as period costs because these are dependent on time rather than on output. Examples factory rent of Rs. 50,000 per month remaining same for every month irrespective of output of every month.

(b) *Variable Costs* are those which vary in total in directly proportion to the volume of output. These costs per unit remain constant with changes in production. Thus, variable costs fluctuate in total amount but tend to remain constant per unit as production activity changes. Examples are direct material costs, direct labour costs, power, repair, etc., such costs are known as product costs because they depend on the quantum of output rather than on time.

(c) *Semi- variable Costs.* Semi-variable costs are partly fixed and partly variable. The distinction between fixed and variable costs is a suitable way of categorizing business costs, in certainty there are some costs which are fixed in nature but which increase when output reaches certain levels. These are largely related to the overall "scale" and/or complexity of the business. For example, when a business has relatively low levels of output or sales, it may not require costs associated with functions such as human resource management. However, as the scale of the business grows (e.g., output, number people employed, number and complexity of transactions) then more resources are required. If production rises suddenly then some short-term increase in warehousing and transport may be required. Other examples like telephone expenses include a fixed portion of annual charge plus variable charge according to calls, depreciation, repairs and maintenance of building and plant.

5. **By Controllability** : Costs are classified according to whether or not they are influenced by the action of a given member of the undertaking. On this basis cost is classified into two categories.

(i) **Controllable costs** are those which can be influenced by the action of a specified member of an undertaking. An organisation is divided into a number of responsibility centres and controllable costs incurred in a particular cost centre can be influenced by the action of the manager responsible for the centre. Generally all direct costs including direct materials, direct labour and some of the overhead expenses are controllable by lower level of management.

(ii) **Uncontrollable costs** are those which cannot be influenced by the action of a specified member of an undertaking. Most of the fixed costs are uncontrollable. For example, rent of the building is not controllable and salaries. Overhead cost, which is incurred by one service section and is apportioned to another which received the service, is also not controllable by the later.

The distinction between controllable and uncontrollable is sometimes left to individual judgment and is not sharply maintained. It is only in relation to a particular level of management or an individual manager that we may say whether a cost is controllable or uncontrollable. A particular item of cost which may be controllable from the point of view of one level of management may be uncontrollable from another point of view. Moreover, there may be an item of cost which is controllable from long-term point of view and uncontrollable from short-term point of view. This is partly so in the case of fixed costs.

6. **By Normality** : Based on normality costs are classified into two categories Normal Cost and Abnormal cost. Whether these are costs which are normally incurred at a given level of output in the conditions in which that level of activity is normally attained.

   (a) ***Normal Cost :*** It is the cost which is normally incurred at given level of output in the conditions in which that level of output is normally attained. It is a part of cost of production.

   (b) ***Abnormal cost :*** It is the cost which is not normally incurred at a given level of output in the conditions in which that level of output is normally attained. It is not a part of cost of production and charged to costing profit and loss account.

7. **By Relationship with Accounting Period (Capital and Revenue) :** The cost which is incurred in purchasing assets either to earn income or increasing the earning capacity of the business is called capital cost, for example the cost of a rolling machine in case of steel plant. Such costs are incurred at one point of time but the benefits spread over a number of accounting years. If any expenditure is done in order to maintain the earning capacity of the concern such as cost of maintaining an asset or running a business it is revenue expenditure, e.g., cost of materials used in production, labour charges paid to convert the material into production, salaries, deprecation, repairs and maintenance charges, selling and distribution charges etc. The difference between capital and revenue items are important in costing as all items of revenue expenditure are taken into consideration and while calculating cost whereas capital items are completely ignored.

8. **By Time :** Costs can be classified as historical cost and predetermined cost.

   Historical Cost : The costs which are ascertained after being incurred are called historical costs. Such costs are available only when the production of a particular thing has already been done. Such costs are only of historical value and not at all helpful for cost control purposes.

   Characteristics of historical costs are :

   (a) They are based on recorded facts.

   (b) They can be verified because they are always supported by the evidence of their occurrence.

   (c) They are mostly objective because they relate to happenings which have already taken place.

Predetermined cost : Such costs are estimated costs, i.e., computed in advance of production taking into consideration the previous periods costs and factors affecting such costs. Predetermined cost determined on scientific basis becomes standard cost. Such costs when compared with actual costs will give the reasons of variance and will help the management to fix the responsibility and to take remedial action to avoid its repetition in future.

Historical costs and predetermined costs are not mutually exclusive but they work together in the accounting system of an organization. In competitive age it is standards. So that after comparison with the actual, the management may be able to take stock of the situation to find out as to how far the standards fixed by it have been achieved and take suitable action in the light of such information. Therefore, even in a system when historical costs are used, predetermined costs have a very important role to play because a figure of historical cost by itself has no meaning unless it is related to some other standard figure to give meaning information to the management.

9. **According to Planning and Control :** Planning and control are two important functions of management. Cost accounting furnishes information to the management which helpful in the due discharge of these two functions. According to this, costs can be classified as budgeted costs and standard costs.

Budgeted costs : Budgeted costs represent an estimate of expenditure for different phases of business operations. These costs are manufacturing, administration; sales, research and development, etc., are coordinated in a well conceived framework for a period of time. In future which subsequently becomes the written expression of managerial targets to be achieved. Various budgets are prepared for various phases, such as raw material cost budget, labour cost budget, cost of production budget, manufacturing overhead budget, office and administration overhead budget etc. It is useful for continuous comparison of actual performance with that of the budgeted cost and reports the variations from the budgeted cost to the management for corrective action.

Standard Costs : Budgeted costs are translated into actual operation through the instrument of standard costs. The *Chartered Institute of Management Accountants*, London defines standard cost as "the predetermined cost based on a technical estimate for materials, labour and overhead for a selected period of time and for a prescribed set of working conditions" thus; standard cost is a determination in advance of production o what should be the cost.

Budgeted costs and standard costs are similar to each other to the extent but both of them represent estimates for cost for a period of time in future. In spite of this they differ in the following aspects:

1. Standard costs are scientifically predetermined costs of every aspect of business activity whereas budgeted costs are mere estimated made on the basis of past actual financial accounting data adjusted to future trends. Thus budgeted costs are projection of financial accounts whereas standard costs are projection of cost accounts.

2. The primary emphasis of budgeted costs is on the planning function of management whereas the main force of standard costs is on control because standard costs lay emphasis on what should be the cost.

3. Budgeted costs are extensive whereas standard costs are intensive in their application. Budgeted costs represent a macro approach of business operations because they are estimated in respect of the operations of a department. Divergent to this standard costs are concerned with each and every aspect of business operation carried in a department. Thus budgeted costs deal with aggregates whereas standard costs deal with individual parts which make the aggregate. For example, budgeted costs are calculated for different functions of the business, i.e., production, sales, purchases, etc., whereas standard are compiled for various elements of costs, i.e., materials, labour and overhead.

10. **By Association with the Product :** Under this classification, cost can be product costs and period costs.

Products costs are those costs which are traceable to the product and are included in inventory valuation. It comprises direct material, direct labour and manufacturing overheads in case of manufacturing concerns. These are used for valuation of inventory and are shown in the balance sheet till they are sold. The product cost of goods sold is transferred to the cost of goods sold account.

Period costs are incurred on the basis of time such as rent, salaries, etc., these may relate to administration and selling costs essential to keep the business running. Though these are not associated with production and are necessary to generate revenue but cannot be assigned to a product. These are charged to the period in which these are incurred and treated as expense.

The net income of a concern is influenced by both product and period costs product costs are included in the cost of production and do not affect income till it is sold, period costs are charged to the period in which these are incurred.

11. **For Managerial Decisions**

On the basis of managerial decisions the costs are classified into the following ways:

(a) *Marginal cost :* Marginal cost is the total of variable cost, i.e., prime cost plus variable overheads. It is based on the difference between fixed and variable costs. Fixed costs are ignored and only variable costs are taken into consideration for determining the cost of products, value of work in progress and finished goods.

(b) *Out of pocket costs :* It is the portion of the costs which involve payment to outsiders. It gives rise to cash expenditure as opposed to such costs as depreciation, which does not involve any cash expenditure. Such costs are relevant for price fixation during recession or when make or buy decision is to be made.

(c) **Differential cost :** The change in cost due to change in the level of activity is known as differential cost. If the change increases the cost, it will be called incremental cost. If there is decrease in cost resulting from decrease in output, the difference is known as decremental cost.

(d) **Sunk cost :** Such costs are not relevant for decision making and are not affected by increase or decrease in volume. Thus, expenditure which has taken place and is irrecoverable in a situation is treated as sunk cost. For taking managerial decisions with future implications, a sunk cost is an irrelevant cost. If a decision has to be made for replacing the existing plant, the book value of the plant less salvage value will be a sunk cost and will be irrelevant cost for taking decision of the replacement of the existing plant.

(e) **Imputed or notional costs :** Notional cost is imputed cost these cost are notional in nature and do not involve any cash outlay. The *Chartered Institute of Management Accountants*, London, defines notional cost as the value of a benefit where no actual cost is incurred even though such costs do not involve any cash outlay but are taken into consideration while making managerial decisions. Example of such costs are notional rent charged on business premises owned by the proprietor, interest on capital for which no interest has been paid. When alternative capital investment projects are being evaluated it is necessary to consider the imputed interest on capital before a decision is arrived to which is the most profitable project.

(f) ***Opportunity cost*** : It is the maximum possible alternative earning that might been earned if the productive capacity had been put to some alternative use. In other words, it is the advantage in measureable terms which has been foregone due to not using the facility in the manner originally planned. For example if an owned building is proposed to be used for a project the likely rent of the building is the opportunity cost which should be taken into consideration while evaluating the profitability of the project.

(g) ***Replacement cost :*** It is the cost at which there could be purchase of an asset or material identical to that which is being replaced. It is the cost of replacement at current market price.

(h) ***Avoidable and Unavoidable cost*** : Avoidable costs are those which can be eliminated if a particular product or department is directly related and discontinued. For example salary of the clerks employed in a particular department can be eliminated, if the department is discontinued. Unavoidable cost is that cost which will not be eliminated with the discontinuation of a product or department. For example salary of factory manager or factory rent cannot be eliminated even if a product is eliminated.

Other terms :

(a) **Carrying cost** : It is also known as holding costs. It means the maintenance of inventory, money locked up in the inventory, inventory obsolescence, storage space rent and cost of stores operation.

(b) **Out of stock cost** : This cost takes place when a stock shortage occurs and includes loss of sales, loss of goodwill on account of disgruntled customers and employees ill will and cost of idle machines.

(c) **Ordering cost :** These costs are incurred each time an order for the purchase of material is placed and are expressed as rupee cost per order and include the cost of getting an item into the firm's inventory.

(d) **Development cost** : It is the cost of the process which begins with the implementation of the decision to produce a new or improved method and ends with the commencement of formal production of the product.

(e) **Policy cost** : It is the cost which is in addition to normal requirement incurred in accordance with the policy of an undertaking.

(f) **Discretionary costs** : Discretionary costs also known as managed costs or programmed costs. It includes fixed costs that arise from periodic appropriate decision that directly reflected top management policies.

(g) **Idle facilities cost :** It is the cost of abnormal idleness of fixed assets or available services.

(h) **Expired cost** : It is the cost which is related to the current period as an expense or loss.

(i) **Incremental cost :** It reflects the difference in cost between two alternatives. While making an assessment of profitability of a proposed alternative, incremental revenues are compared with incremental costs.

(j) **Added value** : It is the change in market value resulting from an alternation in the form, location or availability of a product or service excluding the cost of bought out materials or services. Unlike conversion cost it includes profit.

(k) **Urgent costs** : These costs are to be incurred instantly in order to avoid the hampering of production line. These are entirely essential and their shifting to future period will have adverse effect on the efficiency of operation in hand.

(l) **Postponable costs :** Such costs can be postponed or shifted to the future period without any effect on the efficiency of current operations. It is a postponement of cost and not avoiding altogether.

Practice Questions

1. What are the behavioral costs and explain?
2. Explain the various methods of classification of costs?
3. Explain the objectives of cost accounting?
4. Explain cost concepts based on managerial decisions?
5. What are important features of cost accounting?
6. Explain cost concepts and various types cost centres?

7. Explain the following terms?
   i. Conversion cost
   ii. Controllable costs
   iii. Uncontrollable costs
   iv. Cost centre
   v. Direct costs
   vi. Indirect costs
   vii. Fixed costs
   viii. Variable costs
   ix. Semi-variable costs
   x. Normal cost
   xi. Abnormal cost
   xii. Historical cost
   xiii. Predetermined costs
   xiv. Budgeted costs
   xv. Standard costs
   xvi. Products costs
   xvii. Period costs
   xviii. Marginal cost
   xix. Out of pocket costs
   xx. Differential cost
   xxi. Sunk cost.

❖ ❖ ❖

Chapter - 3
Marginal Costing

Introduction

Marginal Costing is a technique of costing in which only variable manufacturing costs are considered for calculating the cost of production and also for valuation of inventory. This technique is based on the fundamental principle, in which the total costs can be divided into fixed and variable. The total fixed costs remain constant at all levels of production and the variable costs are changing with the production level. Variable cost will increase if the production increases and decrease if the production decreases. The technique of marginal costing helps in supplying the relevant information to the management to facilitate them to take decisions.

Definitions

Marginal Cost : According to *ICMA*, London "marginal cost is the amount for any given volume of output by which aggregate costs are changed if the volume of output is increased or decreased by one unit".

Marginal Costing : Marginal costing is the technique of applying the concept of marginal cost in decision making process. It is a technique that distinguishes between fixed and variable costs. The marginal cost of a product is its variable cost.

Importance of Marginal Costing

Marginal costing is a useful tool for management because of the following applications and merits :

1. **Cost control :** Marginal costing divides the total cost into fixed and variable cost. Fixed cost can be controlled by the top management and that to a limited extent. Variable costs can be controlled by the lower level of management. Marginal cost by concentrating all efforts on the variable costs can control and thus, provide a tool to the management for control of total cost.

   In marginal costing fixed costs are not eliminated at all. These are shown separately as a deduction from the contribution instead of merging with cost of sales and inventory. This helps the management to have a control on fixed costs.

2. **Profit planning :** Marginal costing helps the profit planning, i.e., planning for future operations in such a way as to maximize the profits to maintain a particular level of profit. Absorption costing fails to bring out the correct effect of change in sale price, variable cost are product mix on the profits of the concern but that is possible with the help of marginal costing.

Profits are increased or decreased as a result of fluctuations in selling prices, variable costs and sales quantities in case there is fixed capacity to produce and sell.

3. **Evaluation of performance :** The different products, departments, markets and sales divisions have different profit earning potentialities. Marginal cost analysis is very useful for evaluating the performance of each division of a concern. Performance evaluation is better done if distinction is made between fixed and variable expenses.

4. **Decision making :** The information provided by the total cost method is not sufficient in solving the management problems. Marginal costing technique is used in providing assistance to the management in vital decision making, especially in dealing with the problems requiring short-term decisions where fixed costs are excluded.

Features of Marginal Costing

The distinguishing features of marginal costing are as follows :

1. Marginal costing is not a separate method of costing but it is a technique of costing based on variable cost.
2. It is distinct from the traditional costing which is also called as 'Absorption Costing'.
3. In marginal costing, costs are segregated into fixed and variable.
4. Only variable costs are charged to the production, i.e., included in the cost of production.
5. Fixed costs are not included in the cost of production, which means that they are not absorbed in the production.
6. Fixed cost is ignored into consideration at all but while computing the final profit or loss by debiting them to the costing profit and loss account.
7. The reason follow the skip over fixed costs from cost of production is that fixed costs do not remain fixed on per unit basis.
8. On per unit basis, the fixed cost will increase if the production decreases while it will decrease if the production increases.
9. Thus fixed cost per unit are always variable. In view of this some basis they should be charged to the product, there is a problem of under and over absorption of fixed overheads.
10. Fixed cost should be eliminated from the cost of production but should be taken into consideration while calculating profit.
11. Another feature of marginal costing is the preparation of income statement. The income statement is prepared in a different manner as compared to the statement prepared under traditional costing, i.e., absorption costing.

Income Statement under Marginal Costing of X Ltd.'s Product P

Particulars	Amount Rs.	Amount Rs.
Sales		XXXXX
Less: Variable Costs		XX
Contribution		XXX
Less: Fixed Costs		X
Profit		XX

12. If the company is producing more than one product, the contribution from each product is combined as a pool from which the total fixed cost is deducted. Fixed cost is not charged to each product unless it is identifiable with a product.

Marginal Costing and Absorption Costing

The meaning and features of marginal costing, it is easy to understand that marginal costing is a technique of costing which advocates that only variable costs should be taken into consideration. While working out the total cost of production and valuing the inventory the variable costs should be taken into the calculation. Fixed costs should not be absorbed in the cost of production but should be charged to the Costing Profit and Loss account.

Absorption Costing: Absorption costing deals with the allocation of all manufacturing costs like fixed and variable cost to the production. It also values unsold stocks at the total cost of manufacture. The term of absorption costing is generally used in production cost and cost of all functions. Absorption costing fixed costs as well as variable costs are allotted to cost units and total overheads are absorbed to activity level.

Absorption costing is based on the progressive reapportionment of costs through cost centers until all non-production costs are identified with production centers. These costs can be absorbed into the cost of saleable products or services.

Features of absorption costing :

The following are the features of absorption costing :

(a) Costs apportioned into a cost center should be reported separately from those costs incurred by the manager of that cost center. Only the latter category of costs is controllable by him in the short-term and it is only in relation to such costs that his performance should be judged. If this is not done, a disproportionate part of that manager's time may be spent in disputing the apportioned costs rather than in running his department.

(b) The amounts apportioned should for control purposes at budgeted amounts, any excess or saving compared with budget should be recognized as the responsibility of the manager of the department where the costs were incurred.

(c) At the time of setting budgets there should be a complete analysis of cost apportionment proposals.

Limitations of absorption costing :

1. It is based random apportionment of overheads; hence the cost data for control propose become insignificant.
2. It fails to observe matching principle of accounting. Fixed cost relating to closing stock carrying forward to the next year.
3. At the same time the fixed cost relating to opening stock is charged to current year in place of previous year.
4. All the fixed costs are not charged against the revenue of the year in which they are incurred.
5. It is incapable to develop sound process for collection and presentation of cost data.
6. It fails to develop consistent behavior framework for costs.

Difference between Marginal Costing and Absorption Costing

Marginal Costing	Absorption Costing
1. Variable cost is considered for calculating product cost and inventory value.	1. Fixed cost and variable cost both are considered for calculating product cost and inventory value.
2. Fixed cost is not considered for decisions but it is a period cost and profitability of different products is judged by P/V ratio.	2. The fixed cost is charged to cost of production. Each product is to be charged by a reasonable share of fixed cost and profitability of product is affected by subjective apportionment of fixed overheads.
3. Total contribution and contribution from each product is presented with the help of data analysis.	3. Cost data is presented on conventional pattern. Net profit of each product is calculated after deducting fixed overheads.
4. Unit cost of production is not affected by the difference in the magnitude of opening stock and closing stock.	4. Unit cost of production is affected by the difference in the magnitude of opening stock and closing stock.
5. Net profit is arrived at by deducting fixed expenses from contribution.	5. Net profit is arrived at by deducting administration, selling and distribution expenses from gross profit.
6. Inventory is valued at variable cost and no part of fixed cost is applied to the inventory. Thus, the influence of production on profit is totally eliminated. Profits of both the periods remain unaffected by the inventory holding.	6. Inventory is valued at factory cost, which includes production overheads, both fixed and variable. A part of production overhead is, therefore, carried to the next accounting period with work-in-progress and finished goods. As a result, profits of both current period as well as next period are influenced by the inventory value.

Calculation of Income under Marginal and Absorption Costing

It is possible that net profit under marginal costing and absorption costing may be the same or it may be different. The main reason behind the difference in net profit is due to the basis of inventory valuation. Valuation of finished goods and work in progress under marginal costing is based on variable cost. But, in absorption costing closing stocks are valued at total costs. Necessary format for calculating of net profit is given below :

Income Statement under Absorption Costing

Sales	--------
Production Costs:	
Direct materials consumed	--------
Direct Labour Cost	--------
Variable manufacturing overheads	--------
Fixed manufacturing overheads	--------
Cost of production	
Add : Opening stock of finished goods	
(valued at production cost of current period)	--------
Less : Closing stock of finished goods	--------
(valued at production cost of current period)	--------
Cost of Goods Sold	
Add : (or less) under (or over) absorption of fixed manufacturing Overhead	--------
Add : Selling and distribution costs	--------
Administration costs	--------
Total Cost	--------
Profit (Sales - Total Cost)	--------

Income Statement under Marginal Costing

Sales	--------
Variable Manufacturing Costs	--------
Direct Manufacturing Costs	--------
Direct Labour	--------
Variable manufacturing overheads	--------
Cost of Goods Produced	--------
Add : Opening stock of finished goods (Valued at variable cost of previous period)	--------
Less : Closing stock of finished goods(valued at current variable cost)	--------
Cost of Goods Sold	--------
Add : Variable adm., selling and dist. overhead	--------
Total Variable Cost	--------
Contribution (Sales - Total Variable cost)	--------
Less : Fixed Costs (Production, adm., selling and distribution)	--------
Net profit	--------

Problem 1 :

Raman Ltd. can produce 4,00,000 units of a product per annum at 100% capacity. The variable production costs are Rs. 40 per unit and the variable selling expenses are Rs. 12 per sold unit. The budgeted fixed production expenses were Rs. 24,00,000 per annum and the fixed selling expenses were Rs. 16,00,000. During the year ended 31st March, 2008 the company worked at 80% of its capacity. The operating data for the year are as follows;

Production	3, 20,000	units
Sales @ Rs. 80 per unit	3, 10,000	units
Opening stock of finished goods	40,000	units

Fixed production expenses are absorbed on the basis of capacity and fixed selling expenses are recovered on the basis of period.

You are required to prepare statements of cost and profit for the year ending 31st March, 2008;

(i) On the basis of marginal costing

(ii) On the basis of absorption costing. *(CA, Inter, Nov, 2008)*

Solution :

Statement of Cost and Profit under Marginal Costing for the year ending 31st March, 2008

Particulars	Amount ₹	Amount ₹
Sales: 3,10,000 units @ Rs. 80		2,48,00,000
Less: Marginal Cost/Variable Cost:		
Variable cost of production (3,20,000 x Rs.40)	1,28,00,000	
Add: Opening stock 40,000 units @ Rs. 40 = 16,00,000	16,00,000	
	1,44,00,000	
Less: Closing Stock (3,20,000 + 40,000 - 3,10,000)@ Rs. 40 50,000 units @ Rs. 40	20,00,000	
Variable cost of production of 3,10,000 units	1,24,00,000	
Add: Variable selling expenses @ Rs. 12 per unit	37,20,000	1,61,20,000
Contribution (Sales - Variable cost)		86,80,000
Less : Fixed production cost	24,00,000	
Fixed selling expenses	16,00,000	40,00,000
Actual profit under marginal costing		46,80,000

ii. Statement of Cost and Profit under Absorption Costing for the year ending 31st March, 2008.

Particulars	*Amount (Rs.)*	*Amount (Rs.)*
Sales: 3, 10,000 units @ Rs. 80		2, 48,00,000
Less: Cost of Sales		
Variable cost of Production (3, 20,000 @ Rs. 40)	1, 28,00,000	
Add: Fixed Cost of production absorbed 3, 20,000 units @ Rs. 6	19, 20,000	
	1, 47,20,000	
Add: Opening Stock: $40{,}000 \times \frac{1{,}47{,}20{,}000}{3{,}20{,}000}$	18,40,000	
	1, 65,60,000	
Less: Closing stock: $50{,}000 \times \frac{1{,}47{,}20{,}000}{3{,}20{,}000}$	23,00,000	
Production cost of 3, 10,000 units	1, 42, 60,000	
Selling expenses:		
Variable: Rs. 12 x 3, 10,000 units	37, 20,000	
Fixed	16, 00,000	1, 95, 80,000
Unadjusted profit		52, 20,000
Less: Overheads underabsorbed		4, 80,000
Fixed production overheads		
Actual profit under absorption costing		47,40,000

Workings:

1. Absorption rate or fixed cost of production $= \frac{Rs. 24,00,000}{4,00,000\ units}$ = Rs. 6 per unit

2. Fixed production overhead under absorbed = Rs. (24,00,000 – 19,20,000) = Rs. 4,80,000

Problem 2

From the following data compute the profit under Marginal costing and Absorption costing and reconcile the difference in profits.

Selling price per unit : Rs. 8

Variable cost per unit : Rs. 4

Fixed cost per unit : Rs. 2

Normal volume of production is 26 000 units per quarter.

The opening and closing stocks consisting of both finished goods and equivalent units of work in progress are as follows :

Particulars	Quarter I [Units]	Quarter II [Units]	Quarter III	Quarter IV	Total
Opening stock	-	-	6,000	2,000	-
Production [Units]	26,000	30,000	24,000	30,000	1,10,000
Sales [Units]	26,000	24,000	28,000	32,000	1,10,000
Closing stock [Units]	-	6,000	2,000	-	-

ICWA

Solution :

Calculation of Profit/Loss under Marginal Costing

Particulars	Quarter I ₹	Quarter II ₹	Quarter III ₹	Quarter IV ₹	Total ₹
A] Sales @ Rs.8 *	2, 08,000	1, 92,000	2, 24,000	2, 56,000	8, 80,000
B] Marginal costs Opening Stock @ Rs. 4	–	–	24,000	8,000	
Production @ Rs. 4	1,04,000	1,20,000	96,000	1,20,000	4,40,000
Total [Opening stock + Production]	1,04,000	1,20,000	1,20,000	1,28,000	4,40,000
Less: Closing Stock @ Rs.4	–	24,000	8,000		
Cost of goods Sold	1,04,000	96,000	1,12,000	1,28,000	4,40,000
C] Contribution [A – B]	1,04,000	96,000	1,12,000	1,28,000	4,40,000
D] Fixed Cost	52,000	52,000	52,000	52,000	2,08,000
E] Profit [C – D]	52,000	44,000	60,000	76,000	2,32,000

- Sales value is computed by multiplying the number of units sold in each quarter by the selling price per unit of Rs.8

II] Statement of Profit under Absorption Costing

Particulars	Quarter I ₹	Quarter II ₹	Quarter III ₹	Quarter IV ₹	Total ₹
A] Sales @ Rs.8	2, 08,000	1, 92,000	2, 24,000	2, 56,000	8, 80,000
B] Opening Stock @ Rs.6	–	–	36, 000	12,000	
C] Cost of Production @ Rs.6	1, 56, 000	1, 80, 000	1, 44, 000	1, 80, 000	6, 60, 000
D] B + C	1, 56, 000	1, 80, 000	1, 80, 000	1, 92, 000	7, 08, 000
E] Closing Stock @ Rs.6	–	36, 000	12, 000	–	–
F] Cost of Sales [Actual] D – E	1, 56, 000	1, 44, 000	1, 68, 000	1, 92, 000	6, 60, 000
G] Profit before adjustment of under or over absorbed fixed cost [A – F]	52, 000	48, 000	56, 000	64, 000	2, 20, 000
Add: Over absorbed fixed overheads	–	8, 000	–	8, 000	16, 000
Less: Under-absorbed fixed overheads	–		4, 000	–	4, 000
Profit	52, 000	56, 000	52, 000	72, 000	2, 32, 000

The total cost of production is 6, which, consists of ₹ 4 variable cost, and ₹ 2 fixed cost per unit at the normal volume of production. The opening stock cost of production and closing stock values are computed by same.

Over absorption of fixed overheads is computed by multiplying the excess production than the normal volume by the fixed overheads per unit i.e. ₹ 2. Under absorption of overheads is computed by multiplying the units produced below the normal volume of production by the fixed overheads per unit i.e. ₹ 2.

III] Reconciliation of Profit

Particulars	Quarter I ₹	Quarter II ₹	Quarter III ₹	Quarter IV ₹	Total ₹
Profit as per absorption costing	52, 000	56, 000	52, 000	72, 000	2, 32, 000
Less: Higher fixed cost in closing stock [6000 x ₹2]		12, 000	—	—	12, 000
Add: Higher fixed cost in opening stock *			8, 000	4, 000	12, 000
Profit as per marginal costing	52, 000	44, 000	60, 000	76, 000	2, 32, 000

* In quarter III: [6000 – 2000] x ₹ 2 = ₹ 8, 000. Quarter IV = 2, 000 x ₹ 2 = ₹ 4, 000.

Marginal Cost Equation

This is fundamental equation in marginal costing. It plays an important role in profit projection and wider application in managerial decisions.

- Sales – Marginal cost = Fixed cost + Profit (or Loss)

Sales (S) = Variable cost (V) + Fixed cost (F) + Profit (P) / - Loss (L)

Contribution = Sales – Variable (Marginal) Cost

Contribution = fixed costs + Profit (- Loss)

The sales and marginal costs fluctuate directly with the number of units sold or produced. The difference between sales and marginal cost is contribution. The ratio of contribution to sales remains constant at all levels and it is called profit volume.

$$\text{P/V Ratio (or C/S Ratio)} = \frac{\text{Contribution (C)}}{\text{Sales (S)}}$$

It is expressed in terms of percentage

P/V ratio = (C/S) x 100.

Contribution

Contribution is the difference between sales and variable cost or marginal cost. It is the excess of selling price over variable cost per unit. Contribution is called as contribution margin and gross margin. Contribution is the amount that is contributed towards fixed expense and profit.

Contribution = Sales – Variable (Marginal) Cost (or)

Contribution = Fixed Costs + Profit (- Loss)

Advantages of Contribution :

The concept of contribution is helpful in making managerial decisions. The advantages of contribution are explained below:

1. It helps the management in the fixing of selling price.
2. It assists in formative the break-even point.
3. It helps management in the selection of a suitable product mix for profit maximization.
4. It helps in choosing from among alternative methods of production.
5. It helps the management in deciding make or buy decision.
6. It helps in taking a decision with adding a new product in the market.

Cost Volume Profit (CVP) Analysis

It is a technique for studying the relationship between cost, volume and profit. A profit of an enterprise depends upon a large number of factors. But the most important of these factors are the cost of manufacture, volume of sales and the selling prices of the products. The most significant single factor in profit planning of the average business is the relationship between volume of business, costs and profits. The CVP relationship is an important tool used for the profit planning.

Analyzing CVP, its three components, i.e., costs, volume and profit are interconnected and dependent on one another. Profit depends upon sales. The selling price of an organization depends upon cost and cost depends upon volume of production. It aims to analyze the relationship between variations in cost with variations in volume. It observed that in marginal costing, marginal cost varies directly with the volume of production or output. On the other hand, fixed cost remains unchanged in spite of the volume of output within the scale of production already fixed by management. If cost behavior is related to sales income, it shows cost-volume-profit relationship. If volume is changed, variable cost varies as per the change in volume. In this situation selling price and fixed cost remains fixed and then there is a change in profit. The concept of Cost-Volume-Profit (CVP) is relevant to virtually all decision making areas, particularly in the short run. The relationship among cost, revenue and profit at different levels may be expressed in graphs such as break-even charts, profit volume graphs.

Profit depends on a large number of factors, most important of which are the cost of manufacturing and the volume of sales. Both these factors are interdependent. Volume of sales depends upon the volume of production and market forces which in turn is related to costs. Management has no control over market. In order to achieve certain level of profitability, it has to exercise control and management of costs, mainly variable cost. This is because fixed cost is a non-controllable cost. But then, cost is based on the following factors:

- Volume of production
- Product mix

- Internal efficiency and the productivity of the factors of production
- Methods of production and technology
- Size of batches
- Size of plant

Cost-volume-profit analysis can answer a number of analytical questions. Some of the questions are as follows:

1. What is the break-even revenue of an organization?
2. How much revenue does an organization need to achieve a budgeted profit?
3. What level of price change affects the achievement of budgeted profit?
4. What is the effect of cost changes on the profitability of an operation?

Cost-volume-profit analysis can also answer many other "what if" type of questions. Cost-volume-profit analysis is one of the important techniques of cost and management accounting. It is a simple and powerful tool for planning of profits of commercial operations. It provides an answer to "what if" theme by telling the volume required producing.

Following are the three approaches to a CVP analysis :

- Cost and revenue equations
- Contribution margin
- Profit graph

Objectives of Cost-Volume-Profit Analysis :

1. It helps to estimate profit accurately.
2. It is useful in setting up flexible budgets which indicate costs at various levels of activity.
3. It assists in evaluation of performance for the purpose of control.
4. It also assists in formulating price policies by showing the effect of different price structures on costs and profits.
5. It helps to know the amount of overhead costs to be charged to the product cost at various levels of operations.

Assumptions of CVP Analysis :

The following are the assumptions of CVP analysis

(a) All costs can be divided into fixed and variable costs

(b) Fixed costs remain constant whereas the variable costs vary with a change in output.

(c) Selling price remains constant

(d) The number of units produced and sold will be one and the same

(e) There will be no change in the operating efficiency.

(f) There is linear relationship between revenue and cost.

(g) The theory of CVP is based upon the production of a single product.

(h) The analysis either covers a single product or assumes that the sales mix sold in case of multiple products will remain constant as the level of total units sold changes.

(i) All revenue and cost can be added or compared without taking into account the time value of money.

(j) The theory of CVP is based on the technology that remains constant.

(k) The theory of price elasticity is not taken into consideration.

Managers and management accountants should assess whether the simplified CVP relationships generate sufficiently accurate information for predictions of total revenue and total cost. However different complex situations to which the theory of CVP would rightly be applicable in order to help managers to take appropriate decisions under different situations.

Limitations of Cost-Volume Profit Analysis :

The CVP analysis is generally made under certain limitations and with certain assumed conditions, some of which may not occur in practice. Following are the major limitations in the cost-volume-profit analysis:

1. It assumed that the production facilities anticipated for the purpose of cost volume profit analysis no change. It gives ambiguous results if expansion or reduction of capacity takes place.
2. Total fixed cost increase if range increased but it assumed constant.
3. With changes in demand, the sales mix also change and the constant sales mix assumption is not good.
4. It is assumed that variable costs are variable at all levels of activity and fixed cost remains constant throughout the range of volume being considered.
5. Under the concept of absorption costing principle, profits change with production and sales while under marginal costing profits vary with sales.
6. Inflationary conditions and political factors also influence costs and not just volume.

Profit Volume Ratio (P/V Ratio)

The ratio of contribution to sales is P/V ratio or C/S ratio. It is the contribution per rupee of sales and since the fixed cost remains constant in short term period, P/V ratio will also measure the rate of change of profit due to change in volume of sales. The P/V ratio may be expressed as follows:

$$\text{P/V ratio} = \frac{Contribution \times 100}{Sales}$$

Contribution = Sales - Variable (Marginal) Cost

Contribution = Fixed Costs + Profit (- Loss)

A change in fixed cost does not affect P/V ratio. The concept of P/V ratio helps in determining the following :

- Break-even point
- Profit at any volume of sales
- Sales volume required to earn a desired quantum of profit
- Profitability of products

The following ways for improving the P/V ratio :

- Increasing selling price
- Reducing marginal costs by effectively utilizing men, machines, materials and other services
- Selling more profitable products, thereby increasing the overall P/V ratio.

Break-even Point

Break-even point is the volume of sales or production where there is neither profit nor loss. Hence, the contribution margin is equal to fixed cost.

Break-even analysis

Introduction : Break-even analysis is a technique widely used by production management and management accountants. It is based on categorizing production costs between those which are "variable" (costs that change when the production output changes) and those that are "fixed" (costs not directly related to the volume of production).

Total variable and fixed costs are compared with sales revenue in order to determine the level of sales volume, sales value or production at which the business makes neither a profit nor a loss is known as break-even point.

The break-even point easy to calculated with the help of fundamental marginal cost equation, P/V ratio and contribution per unit.

Marginal Cost Equation

$$\text{Break-even Point Sales Value (Rs)} = \frac{\text{Fixed Cost} \times \text{Sales}}{\text{Sales} - \text{Variable Cost}}$$

Using P/V Ratio

$$\text{Break-even Sales Value (Rs)} = \frac{\text{Fixed Cost}}{\text{P/V Ratio}}$$

Using Contribution per unit

$$\text{Break-even Point Units} = \frac{\text{Fixed Cost}}{\text{Contribution per Unit}}$$

Break-even Sales Value (Rs) = Breakeven Point Units x Selling Price per Unit

Assumptions of Break-even Analysis

The following are the assumptions of break-even analysis :

1. All costs can be divided into fixed and variable costs.
2. Total fixed costs remain constant whereas the total variable costs vary with a change in output.
3. Selling price and variable cost per unit remains constant.
4. The number of units produced and sold will be one and the same.
5. There will be no change in the operating efficiency.
6. There is linear relationship between revenue and cost.
7. There will be no change in the general price level.
8. The analysis either covers a single product or assumes that the sales mix sold in case of multiple products will remain constant as the level of total units sold changes.
9. The theory of BEP is based upon the production of a single product.
10. The theory of price elasticity is not taken into consideration.

Advantages of Break-even Analysis

The following are the advantages of break even analysis :

1. It helps to determine the break-even point.
2. It helps in determining the selling price which will give the desired profit.
3. It helps to determine the most profitable mix and controlling the cost.
4. It helps in the determination of comparative profitability of each product line.
5. It helps in determining cost and revenue at various levels of output.
6. It helps to study the effect of price change in different markets.
7. It assists the management in decision making.
8. It shows the impact of increase or decrease of fixed and variable costs on profits.
9. It offers suggestions for shift in sales unit.

Limitations of Break-even Analysis

1. Break-even analysis is only a supply side or costs only analysis, as it tells you nothing about what sales are actually likely to be for the product at these various prices.

2. It assumes that fixed costs (FC) are constant. But it is true in the short run; an increase in the scale of production is likely to cause fixed costs to rise.

3. It assumes average variable costs are constant per unit of output, at least in the range of likely quantities of sales *i.e.* linearity.

4. It assumes that the quantity of goods produced is equal to the quantity of goods sold (i.e., there is no change in the quantity of goods held in inventory at the beginning of the period and the quantity of goods held in inventory at the end of the period).

5. In multi-product companies, it assumes that the relative proportions of each product sold and produced are constant, *i.e.*, the sales mix is constant.

Break-even Analysis Graphical Presentation

Break-even chart is a device which shows the relationship between sales volume, marginal costs, fixed costs and profit or loss at different levels of activity. It also shows the effect of change of one factor on other factors and exhibits the rate of profit and margin of safety at different levels. A breakeven chart contains, *inter alia*, total sales line, total cost line and the point of intersection called breakeven point. It is also called break-even chart because it shows clearly break-even point at this point there is no profit or no loss. Profit graph is a development of simple break-even chart and shows clearly profit at different volumes of sales.

Construction of a Break-even Chart

The construction of a break-even chart involves the drawing of fixed cost line, total cost line and sales line as follows :

1. Select a scale for production on horizontal axis and a scale for costs and sales on vertical axis.

2. Plot fixed cost on vertical axis and draw fixed cost line passing through this point parallel to horizontal axis.

3. Plot variable costs for some activity levels starting from the fixed cost line and join these points. This will give total cost line. Alternatively, obtain total cost at different levels; plot the points starting from horizontal axis and draw total cost line.

4. Plot the maximum sales volume and draw sales line by joining zero and the point so obtained.

Solved Problems Break-even Point

The concept of 'Break-even Point' is important for decision making in the organisation. This concept is based on the behaviour of costs, i.e., fixed cost and variable costs. The fixed costs are those costs that remain constant irrespective of the changes in the volume of production. On the other hand, variable costs are the costs that vary with the level of production. While fixed cost per unit is always variable, variable cost per units is always fixed. In addition to these two types of costs, there are semi-variable costs that are partially fixed and partially variable. Semi variable costs thus have the features of both types of costs. They remain fixed up to a certain level of production and after crossing that level, they become variable.

The Break-even Point is a level of production where the total costs are equal to the total revenue, i.e. sales. Thus at the break-even level, there is neither profit nor loss. Production level below the break-even-point will result into loss while production above break-even point will result in profits. This concept can be better understood with the help of the following table.

Suppose, the selling price of a product is Rs.10 per unit, variable cost ₹ 6 per unit and fixed cost ₹ 30,000, the break-even level can be found out with the help of the following table.

Number of Units	Sales Value [₹100 per unit] ₹	Variable Cost [₹60 per unit] ₹	Fixed Cost [₹30000] ₹	Total Cost [Variable + Fixed] ₹	Profit/Loss [Sales value – total cost] ₹
250	25,000	15,000	30,000	45,000	(-) 20,000
500	50,000	30,000	30,000	60,000	(-) 10,000
750	75,000	45,000	30,000	75,000	Nil
1000	1,00,000	60,000	30,000	90,000	10,000
1250	1,25,000	75,000	30,000	1,05,000	20,000
1500	1,50,000	90,000	30,000	1,20,000	30,000

The above table shows that at the production level of 750 units, the total costs are equal to the total revenue and hence it is the break-even level. Production and sales level below the break-even level results into loss as shown in the table while above the break-even level will result in profits.

If the above table is analyzed, it will be seen that, when the production level was 250, the revenue from sales was not sufficient to cover the total cost i.e. variable + fixed. When the production level starts rising, the sales level starts rising but the total cost does not rise in the proportion as the fixed cost remain the same. Consequently the amount of loss starts decreasing and the trend continues till the break- even level is reached. After the break-even level is crossed, the sales revenue exceeds the total costs and hence it results in profits.

Break-even Chart :

Break-even point can also be shown on the graph paper. It is the simplest form; the break-even chart is a graphical representation of costs at various levels of activity shown on the chart as the variation of income (sales revenue) with the same variation in activity. The point at which neither profit nor loss is known as the "break-even point" and is represented on the chart below by the intersection of the two lines :

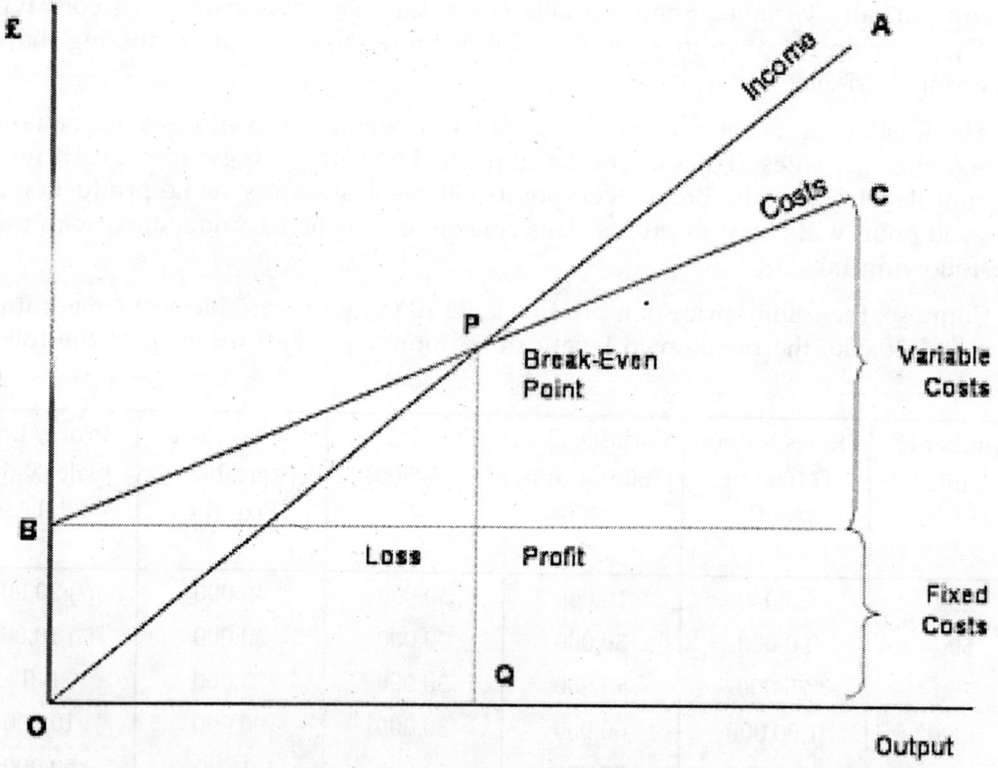

From the above diagram the line OA represents the variation of income at varying levels of production activity. OB represents the total fixed costs in the business. As output increases, variable costs are also increased hence the total cost (fixed + variable) also increase. At low levels of output, costs are greater than income. At the point of intersection point "P" costs are exactly equal to income hence no profit no loss it is called break-even point..

Uses of Break-even Chart :

A break-even chart can be used to show the effect of changes in any of the following profit factors :

- Volume of sales
- Variable expenses
- Fixed expenses
- Selling price

Break-even chart is used by management as an efficient tool in marginal costing, i.e., in forecasting, decision making, long-term profit planning and maintaining profitability. The margin of safety shows the soundness of business whereas the fixed cost line shows the degree of mechanization. The angle of incidence is an indicator of plant efficiency and profitability of the product under consideration. It helps a monopolist to make price discrimination for maximization of profit.

Limitations of Break-even Chart

If a company sells different products having different percentages of profit to turnover, the original combined break-even chart fails to give a clear picture when the sales mix changes. In this situation we are necessary to draw up a break-even chart for each product or a group of products. A break-even chart does not take into account capital employed which is a very important factor to measure the overall efficiency of business. Fixed costs may increase at some level whereas variable costs may sometimes start to decline. For example, with the help of quantity discount on materials purchased, the sales price may be reduced to sell the additional units produced, etc. These changes may result in more than one break-even point it indicate higher profit at lower volumes or lower profit at still higher levels of sales.

Multiple Product Situations

Actually most of the firms turn out many products. Here also, there is no problem with regard to the calculation of BEP. The assumption has to be made that the sales mix remains constant. This is the relative proportion of each product's sale to total sales. It could be expressed as a ratio such as 2 : 4 : 6 or as a percentage as 20%, 40% and 60%.

The calculation of breakeven point in a multi-product firm follows the same pattern as in a single product firm. While the numerator will be the same fixed costs, the denominator now will be weighted average contribution margin. The modified formula is as follows:

$$\text{Breakeven point (in units)} = \frac{\text{Fixed costs}}{\text{Weighted average contribution margin per unit}}$$

One should always remember that weights are assigned in proportion to the relative sales of all products. Here, it will be the contribution margin of each product multiplied by its quantity.

Profit Graph

Profit graph is an improvement of a simple break-even chart. It clearly exhibits the relationship of profit to volume of sales. The construction of a profit graph is relatively easy and the procedure involves the following:

1. Selecting a scale for the sales on horizontal axis and another scale for profit and fixed costs or loss on vertical axis. The area above horizontal axis is called profit area and the one below it is called loss area.

2. Plotting the profits of corresponding sales and joining them it is called profit line.

Margin of Safety (MOS)

Every organization tries to know how much sales are there; above they are from the breakeven point. It is known as margin of safety. It is calculated the difference between total actual sale and the break-even sales. It expressed in monetary terms or as a number of units. It can be expressed as profit / P/V ratio. A large margin of safety indicates the soundness and financial strength of business.

Margin of safety can be improved by lowering fixed and variable costs, increasing volume of sales or selling price and changing product mix. Hence it improves contribution and overall P/V ratio.

Margin of Safety = Total Actual Sales – Sales at BEP

$$\text{Margin of Safety} = \frac{\text{Profit}}{\text{P/V ratio}}$$

$$\text{P/V Ratio} = \frac{\text{Contribution} \times 100}{\text{Sales}}$$

The size of margin of safety is an extremely valuable guide to the strength of a business. If it is large, there can be substantial falling of sales and yet a profit can be made. On the other hand, if margin is small, any loss of sales may be a serious matter. If margin of safety is unsatisfactory, to take the possible steps for rectify the causes of mismanagement in commercial activities.

Angle of Incidence

This is the angle formed at which the sales lines cut the total cost line. The angle indicates the rate at which profits are being made at a higher rate. The small angle indicates a low rate of profit and suggests that variable costs form a major part of cost of production. A large angle of incidence with a high margin of safety indicates the most favourable position of a business and even the monopoly conditions.

Problem 1

X Ltd earned a profit of ₹ 30,000 during the year 2012-13. Marginal cost and selling price of a product are ₹ 8 and Rs. 10 per unit respectively. Find out the P/V Ratio and margin of safety.

Solution :

$$\text{P/V Ratio} = \frac{\text{Contribution} \times 100}{\text{Sales}}$$

P/V Ratio = [(10-8)/10] x 100 = 20%

$$\text{Margin of Safety} = \frac{\text{Profit}}{\text{P/Vratio}}$$

Margin of Safety = 30000/0.20 = Rs 1,50,000.

Problem 2

Sales ₹ 5,00,000; Fixed Cost Rs. 1, 00,000; Profit ₹ 1,50,000;

Find out the following (i) P/V Ratio (iii) BEP (iv) MOS

Solution :

P/V Ratio = Contribution / Sales

Sales = ₹5,00, 000,

Fixed Cost = ₹ 1,00,000

Profit = ₹1,50,000

Contribution = Sales – Variable Cost (OR) Fixed Cost + Profit

Contribution = 1,00,000 + 1,50,000 = 2,50,000

P/V Ratio = 2, 50, 000 / 5, 00, 000 = 0.5 or 50%

P/V Ratio = 50%;

BEP = Fixed Cost / P/V Ratio

Fixed Cost = ₹1, 00, 000;

P/V Ratio = 50%;

BEP = 1,00,000 / 50%

BEP = Rs 2, 00, 000

Margin of Safety (MOS) = Total Sales – Break-even Sales

= 5,00,000 – 2,00,000 = 3,00,000.

Problem 3

SV Ltd, a multi product company, furnishes you the following data relating to the year 1979;

Particulars	First half of the year	Second half of the year
Sales	Rs. 45,000	Rs. 50,000
Total Cost	Rs. 40,000	Rs. 43,000

Assuming that there is no change in prices and variable costs and that the fixed expenses are incurred equally in the two half years periods, calculate for the year 2012.

Calculate

(a) P V ratio

(b) Fixed expenses

(c) Break-even sales

(d) Margin of safety

(C.A. Inter, May, 1980)

1. The first step is to find out the PV ratio

Formula for PV Ratio = $\frac{\text{Change in Profit}}{\text{Change in Sales}} \times 100$

To indentify the change in profit, the profits of the two different periods should be known.

Profit = Sales - Total cost

Profit of the first half of the year = ₹ 45,000 – ₹ 40,000 = ₹ 5,000

Profit of the second half of the year = ₹ 50,000 – ₹ 43,000 = ₹ 7,000

Change in profit = ₹ 7,000 – ₹ 5,000 = ₹ 2,000

Change in sales = Rs, 50,000 – ₹ 45,000 = ₹ 5,000

PV Ratio = $\frac{Rs. 2{,}000}{Rs. 5{,}000}$ x 100 = 40 %

2. To find out, fixed expenses the contribution should be initially found out

Contribution = Sales × PV ratio

= ₹ 50,000 x 40 % = ₹ 20,000

The fixed expenses are to be found out through the following equation:

Contribution – Fixed expenses = Profit

₹ 20,000 – ₹ 7,000 = ₹ 13,000 = Fixed expenses

The fixed expenses found only for six months; hence for the entire year

= ₹ 13,000 x 2 = ₹ 26,000

3. BEP Sales

$= \frac{\text{Fixed Expenses}}{\text{PV ratio}} = \frac{\text{Rs. } 26{,}000}{40\%} = 65{,}000$

4. Margin of Safety

= Total Sales – BEP sales

The next component to be found out is the total sales.

Total sales = Sale of the first half of the year + Sale of the second half of the year

= ₹ 45,000 + ₹ 50,000 = ₹ 95,000

Margin of Safety = ₹ 95,000 - ₹ 65,000 = ₹ 30,000

Margin of safety in percentage of sales = $\frac{₹\ 30{,}000}{₹\ 95{,}000}$ x 100 = 31.57%

Problem 4

The following figures are available from the records of Sai Ltd as on 31st March 2012.

Figures : ₹ in Lakhs.

Particulars	*2011*	*2012*
Sales	300	400
Profits	60	100

Calculate :

a) Profit/Volume ratio and total fixed expenses

b) Break-even Sales

c) Sales required to earn a profit of ₹ 80 lakhs

d) Profit/Loss that would arise if the sales were ₹ 580 lakhs

Solution :

a) **Calculation of PV Ratio :**

Particulars	*2011*	*2012*	*Change*
Sales	300	400	100
Profits	60	100	40

Profit / Volume Ratio = (Change in profit/Change in sales) × 100

₹ 40/ ₹100 × 100 = 40%

Fixed Expenses : We can take the sales of any one year, suppose we take the sales of the year ended on 31st March 2011, the amount is ₹300 lakhs

The profit/volume ratio is 40% which means that contribution is 40% of sales

Contribution = 40% of ₹ 300 lakhs = ₹ 120 lakhs.

The amount of profit is ₹ 60 lakhs.

Contribution = Fixed Cost + Profit,

Fixed Cost = ₹ 120 lakhs – ₹ 60 lakhs,

Fixed cost is ₹ 60 lakhs

b) **Break-even Sales**

= Fixed Cost/PV Ratio

= ₹60 lakhs/40% = ₹ 150 lakhs

c) **Sales required to earn a profit of ₹ 80 lakhs :**

Sales = (Fixed Cost + Profit) /PV Ratio

Sales = (₹60 lakhs + ₹80 lakhs) /40%

Sales = ₹140 lakhs/40% = ₹350 lakhs

d) Profit / Loss if sales are ₹580 lakhs,

Sales = Fixed Cost + Profit /PV Ratio

Sales × PV Ratio = Fixed Cost + Profit

= ₹ 580 lakhs x 40% = (₹ 60 lakhs + Profit)

= ₹ 262 lakhs – ₹ 60 lakhs = ₹172 lakhs

Problem 5

Swarna Ltd. maintains a margin of safety of 40% with an overall contribution to sales ratio of 50%. Its fixed costs amount to ₹ 4,00,000. Calculate the following :

1. Break-even Sales
2. Total Sales
3. Total Variable Sales
4. Current Profits
5. New 'Margin of Safety' if the sales volume is increased by 8%

Solution :

1. Break-even Sales = Fixed Cost/Profit Volume Ratio = ₹4, 00,000/50%

   = ₹8, 00,000

2. Total Sales = Break-even Sales + Margin of Safety

   Margin of Safety = Actual Sales – Break-even Sales

   Let the actual sales be 100, Margin of Safety is 40 (hence 40%)

   Therefore Break-even sales will be ₹ 60

   Now, if the Break-even sales are ₹ 60, actual sales are ₹100, hence if Break-even sales are ₹8 lakhs, actual sales will be (100/60) X ₹8 lakhs = ₹13.33 lakhs

3. Contribution = Sales – Variable Cost. As the contribution is 50% of sales, the variable cost is 50% of sales and so variable cost will be 50% of Rs13.33 lakhs, i.e., ₹6.66 lakhs.

4. Current Profits = Sales – [Fixed Cost + Variable Cost]

   = ₹13,33,333 – [₹4,00,000 + ₹6,66,666]

   = ₹2,66,667

5. New Margin of Safety is the sales volume is increased by 8 % New Sales Volume

   = ₹ 13,33,333 + 8% of ₹ 13,33,333 = ₹14,40,000

   Hence, New Margin of Safety

   = ₹ 14,40,000 – BEP Sales ₹ 8,00,000 = ₹6,40,000

   New Margin of Safety = ₹ 6,40,000

Problem 6

Dhanush Company has two plants at Locations A and B, operating at 100% and 75% of their capacities respectively. The company is considering a proposal to merge the two plants at one location to optimize

Particulars	Plant A	Plant B
Sales [Rs.in lakhs]	300	225
Variable Costs [Rs. in lakhs]	210	162
Fixed Cost [Rs. in lakhs]	35	20

For decision making purposes, you are required to work out the following information,

I. The capacity at which the merged plan will break-even.

II. The profit of the merged plant working at 80% capacity

III. Sales required if the merged plant is required to earn an overall profit of ₹30 lakhs.

Solution :

After merging the plants, the total of sales, variable costs and fixed costs will have to be taken. The capacity utilization of plant at Plant B will have to be made 100%. Accordingly the figures at 75% are converted into figures at 100%. Fixed cost is the exception for this, as it will remain the same at 100% capacity utilization also. The statement prepared on the table is on the basis of 100% capacity utilization of both plants.

Comparative Performance of Plant at 100% Capacity ₹ in lakhs

Particulars	Plant Location A	Plant Location B	Total Merged Plant
Capacity Levels [%]	100	100	100
Sales	300	225	525
Less: Variable Cost	210	162	372
Contribution	90	63	153
Less: Fixed Costs	35	20	55
Profit	55	43	98
Profit/Volume Ratio: Contribution/Sales	90/300 = 30%	63/225 = 28%	153/525 = 29.14%
Break-even Sales: Fixed Cost/ PV Ratio			55/29.14% = ₹ 188.74 lakhs

I] Capacity of the merged plant at break-even = (188.74 /525) X 100 = 35.95%

II] Computation of the profitability of the merged plan at 80% capacity

Particulars	Amount [Rs. in lakhs]
Sales 80% of Rs.525	420.00
Less: Variable Cost = 70.86% of sales	297.60
Contribution	122.40
Less: Fixed Cost	55.00
Profit	67.40

III] Computation of sales required to earn desired profit of ₹30 lakhs Sales = (Fixed Cost + Desired Profit)/PV Ratio

= (₹55 lakhs + ₹30 lakhs)/29.14% = ₹291.69 lakhs

Problem 7

Subhashini Ltd sells its products at ₹20 per unit. In a period, if it produces and sells 8000 units, it incurs a loss of ₹5 per unit. If the volume is raised to 20 000 units, it earns a profit of ₹4 per unit. Calculate Break Even Point both in terms of rupees as well as units.

Solution :

The basic marginal cost equation is S –V = F + P

Where S = Sales, V = Variable Cost, F = Fixed Cost and P = Profit.

Let us assume that variable cost = x Say

Fixed cost = y Say

We can form the following simultaneous equations under various situations.

₹20 × 8000 - 8000x = y – 40,000 [loss of ₹5 per unit × 8000 units] - Plan I

₹20 × 20,000 – 20,000x = y + 80,000 – Plan I

Or, 1,60,000 – 8000x = y – 40,000 (3)

And 4, 00,000 – 20,000 x = y + 80,000 (4)

By solving both the equations, we get x = ₹10

i.e., variable cost per unit is ₹10 and y = ₹1, 20,000, i.e., fixed cost ₹1, 20,000

Profit Volume Ratio = (Contribution/Sales) X 100

= (₹20 – ₹10/₹20) X 100 = 50%

Break-even Point = Fixed Cost/PV Ratio = ₹1, 20,000 / 50% = ₹2, 40,000

Break-even Point [Units] = Fixed Cost/Contribution per unit = ₹1, 20,000/₹10 = 12000 units

Practice Questions

1. What do you understand by Marginal Costing?
2. Define Marginal Costing. Briefly explain the features of marginal costing.
3. What are the difference between Absorption Costing and Marginal Costing?
4. What is meant by Differential Costing?
5. Compare and contrast Marginal Costing and Differential Costing.
6. What are the important decision making areas of Marginal Costing?
7. Briefly explain the advantages and limitations of Marginal Costing.
8. What do you understand by Cost Volume Profit Analysis?
9. Briefly explain the objectives of cost volume profit analysis.
10. Explain Marginal Cost equation.
11. What is Contribution? How it is computed?
12. What do you understand by Break-even Analysis?
13. Write short notes on :

    (a) Profit Volume ratio; (b) Margin of Safety; (c) Break-even Chart, (d) Angle of Incidence
14. Briefly explain the advantages and limitations of Break-even chart
15. Briefly explain the relationship between Angle of Incidence, Break-even Sales and Margin of Safety.
16. From the following particulars, you are required to find out : (a) Contribution (b) Break-even Point Units (c) Margin of Safety and (d) Profit

Total Fixed Cost	₹ 4.500
Total Variable Cost	₹ 7,500
Total Sales	₹ 15,000
Units Sold	5000 units

Also calculate the volume of sales to earn profit of Rs 6,000

[Ans : (a) Contribution ₹ 7,500 (b) Break-even Points in Units Rs 3,000 units (c) Margin of Safety ₹ 6,000 (d) Profit Rs 3,000]

17. From the following data, calculate :

    (a) P/V Ratio.

    (b) Profit when sales are ₹ 40,000

    (c) New break-even point if selling price is reduced by 20%

(d) Fixed Expenses ₹ 8,000

(e) Break-even point Rs 10,000

[Ans: (a) profit Volume ration 40%. (b) Profit when sales are ₹ 40,000 is 8,000 (c) New break-even point if selling price is reduced by 20% is Rs 32,000]

18. From the following particulars you are required to calculate: (a) P/V ratio, and (b) Break-even point :

Present sales ₹ 2, 00,000

Variable Cost ₹ 1, 20,000

Fixed Expenses ₹ 40,000

Ascertain the effect of 10% reduction of selling price on (a) P/V ratio, and (b) Break-even point also calculate the sales required to maintain the profit at the present level.

[Ans: (a) P/V Ratio 40% ; New P/V Ratio = 33%

(a) Break-even point ₹ 1,00,000 ; New BEP = Rs 1,20,000

(b) Sales required to maintain the profit at the present level. Present profit ₹ 20,000. Required sales ₹ 1,81,820]

19. The following are the cost information in relation to the manufacture of a product : Selling price – Rs 10, per unit, Trade discount – 5% of selling price, Material Cost – Rs 3 per unit Labour – Rs 2 per unit

Overheads : Fixed ₹ 10,000 Variable 100% of labour cost,

Calculate:

(a) BEP

(b) Profit if sales are 15% above break-even volume

[Ans : BEP – 4,000 units; Profits ₹ 1,5000, volume 4,600 units.]

20. Sales price – Rs 20 unit

Variable manufacturing cost Rs – 11 per unit. Variable selling cost – Rs 3 per unit. Fixed factory overheads Rs 5,40,000 per year. Fixed Selling costs – Rs 2, 52,000 per unit.

Calculate

(a) BEP Volume and Value.

(b) Sales required to earn a profit of ₹ 60,000

(c) Sales required to earn a profit of 10% of Sales.

[Ans: (a) BEP Volume – 1,32,000 units ; Value – Rs 26,40,000 (b) Sales – 1,42,000 units; Value – Rs 28,40,000 (d) Sales – Rs 1,98,000 units; Value – Rs 39,60,000 (11.88.000; 3,96,000)]

21. From the following data, find out how many units should be sold to earn a net profit of 10% on sales. Selling price per unit ₹ 20

Variable cost per unit Rs 14

Fixed Cost (total) ₹ 7, 92,000

[Ans: Sales in Units 1, 98,000]

22. A company estimates that next year it will earn a profit of Rs 50,000. The budget fixed costs and sales are ₹ 2,50,000 and ₹ 9,93,000 respectively. Find out the break even point for the company.

[Ans : BEP in sales Rs 8,27,500]

23. Plant I produces a product which cost Rs 3 per unit when produced in quantities of 10,000 units and ₹ 2.50 per unit when produced in quantities of 20,000 units. You are asked to estimate total fixed costs.

[Ans : Fixed Cost Rs 10,000]

24. The following are the budgeted data of a company.

Sales	Rs 6, 00,000
Variable Cost	Rs 3, 00,000
Fixed Cost	Rs 1, 80,000

Find out the break even point at

(i) The budget data

(ii) Assuming 20% increase in variable cost.

[Ans: Break-even point Rs 3,60,000; New Break-even point at 20% increase in variable costs Rs 4,50,000]

25. Calculate No. of Units to be sold to earn a profit of ₹ 60,000 a year

Sale price	Rs 20 per unit
Variable manufacturing Cost	Rs 11 per unit
Variable selling price	Rs 3 per unit
Fixed factory overhead	Rs 5, 40,000 per year
Fixed Selling Costs	Rs 2, 52,000 per year

[Ans : No of Units to be sold is 1,42,000 units]

26. Present production and sales : 80,000 units

Selling price per unit Rs 20

Direct labour Rs 2.50

Variable overhead Rs 100% of direct labour cost

Direct materials Rs 5

Fixed costs Rs 40,000

Find output:

(a) P/V Ratio

(b) Sales required to break-even point, and

(c) Margin of safety

[Ans: P/V ratio 50% ; BEP Rs 80,000; Margin of Safety ₹ 80,000]

27. The P/V ratio of Gupta & Co is 60% during 2003. Sales were ₹ 1,50,000 and the fixed cost Rs 15,000.

Calculate :

(a) Total Variable expenses

(b) Total Contribution

(c) Profit, and

(d) Profit if sales are increased to Rs 2,25,000

[Ans: (a) Total Variable cost ₹ 60,000 (b) Total Contribution Rs 90,000 (c) Profit ₹ 75,000; (d) Profit Rs 1, 20,000]

28. The projected capacity of a plant, when sold, would return Rs 70,000 in sales income to the company. The variable costs for this production volume were determined to be ₹ 30,000. The fixed costs are Rs 20,000. Determine the following:

(1) The break-even point of the business

(2) The profit or loss to the business on sales of Rs 49,000; Rs 28,000

(3) The amount of sales that will enable the business to earn a net profit of ₹ 28,000

[Ans: (i) break-even point ₹ 35,000; (2) if sales of Rs 49,000 the profit is Rs 8,000; if sales of Rs 28,000 the loss is Rs 4,000 (3) the amount of sales Rs 80,500]

29. From the following data, find out the break-even point; P/V ratio and margin of safety ratio. Fixed ratio

Fixed Costs	6,00,000	30%
Variable costs	12,00,000	60%
Net profit	2,00,000	10%
Sales	20,00,000	100%

[Ans: P/V ratio 40%; BEP Rs 15,00,000; Margin of Safety Ratio 25%]

30. A Company budgets for a production of 1,50,000 units, the variable cost per unit is Rs 14 an fixed cost is Rs 2 per unit. The company fixes its selling price to fetch a profit of 15% on cost.

(a) What is the break-even point ?

(b) What is the profit volume ratio ?

(c) If it reduces its selling price by 5%, how the revised selling price affect the break -even point and the profit volume ratio ?

(d) If a profit increase of 10% is desired more than the budtget, what should be the sales at the reduced prices ?

[Ans : (a) Break-even point (in Rs) 12,54,549 (b) P/V ratio 23.91% (c) New break-even point in units 86,207 units new P/V ratio 19.90% (d) Sales for desired profit ₹ 34,96,000]

31. The following information regarding the operations of 2003 has been made available from the records of the AAA Corporation.

Sales	Rs 1,00,000
Direct materials used	Rs 40,000
Direct labour	Rs 15,000
Fixed manufacturing overheads	Rs 20,000
Fixed Selling and administrative expenses	Rs 10,000
Gross profit	Rs 20,000
Net loss	Rs 5,000

There are no openings or closing inventories. It is require to calculate;

(1) Variable selling and administrative expenses

(2) Contribution margin in rupees

(3) Variable factory overhead

(4) Break even point in rupee sales

(5) Factory cost of goods sold.

[Ans: Variable factory overheads ₹ 5,000; variable selling and administrative expenses ₹ 15,000; Contribution Margin ₹ 25,000; Break-even point ₹ 1,20,000 Factory cost of goods sold ₹ 80,000]

32. The data below related to a company which makes and sells computers.

Sales (units) Production	March 5.000 10,000	April 10,000 5,000
Selling price per unit	100	100
Variable production cost per unit	50	50
Fixed production overhead incurred	1,00,000	1,00,000
Fixed Production overhead cost, per unit being the pre-determined overhead absorption rate	10	10
Selling, distribution and administration cost (all fixed)	50,000	50,000

You are required to present comparative profit statements for each month using (i) absorption costing (ii) marginal costing.

(I.C.W.A, Inter, Dec 1989)

❖ ❖ ❖

Chapter - 4
Decision Making

Introduction

The total cost method is not adequate in solving the management problems. Marginal costing technique is used in providing assistance to the management in vital decision making in dealing with the problems requiring short-term decisions where fixed costs are excluded. The following are important methods used for decision making:

1. Key or Limiting factor
2. Effect of change in sales price
3. Make or Buy decisions
4. Selection of a suitable product mix
5. Fixation of selling price
6. Diversification of products
7. Maintaining desired levels of profits
8. Alternative methods of production
9. Closing down or Suspending activities
10. Alternative course of action
11. Level of activity planning
12. Capital investment decisions

1. Key or Limiting Factor Analysis

Marginal costing helps in budgeting and the company faces the problem of non availability of input factors in adequate quantities it is called key or limiting factor. *CIMA* define limiting factor as "The factors in activities of an undertaking which at a particular point in time or over a period will limit the volume of output". It gives consideration to factory affecting the production system most. It helps the management to determine the profit maximizing budget. It also facilitates in formulation of when one or more factors of production or other business resources are in short supply.

A key factor is that factor which puts a limit on production and profit of a business. Usually this limiting factor is sales' a concern may not be able to sells as much as it can produce. But sometimes a concern can sell all it produces but production is limited due to the shortage of materials, labour, plant capacity or capital. In such a case decision has to be taken regarding the choice of the product whose production is to be increased, reduced or stopped. Suppose no limiting factor then the choice of the product will be on the basis of the highest profit volume ratio. But when there are scarce or limited resources, the selection of the product will be on the basis of contribution per unit of scarce resource.

For example material is limited in supply but same is used for product A and B. The usage of materials for four units for producing product A and six units for product B. Suppose further contribution per unit is ₹ 16 in case of product A and ₹ 18 in case of product B. In this case contribution per unit of materials is ₹ 4 $\left(\text{i.e. } \frac{₹\,16}{4}\right)$ for product A and ₹ 3 $\left(\text{i.e. } \frac{₹\,18}{6}\right)$ for product B. Hence the available materials should first be used for manufacturing product A up to limit of demand for it and then the balance of materials used for product B because product A yields more contribution per unit of scarce resources.

Usually limiting factor is sales and in addition to limiting factor from the production side, it may also be difficulty in selling the items produced. In such a case ranking of items produced will be based on relative contribution per unit of limiting factor of production. But the number of units of a product to be produced getting rank one will be restricted to the number of units as per demand for that product and then the production of the other product getting rank will be done but restricted to sales demand and balance of limiting factor is available.

If the limiting factors are more than one and the ranking given by contribution per unit of limiting factor conflicts with that given by the contribution per unit of another limiting factor, the problem of taking decision becomes complicated. In such a case use the linear programming.

Problem 1

The following particulars are extracted from the records of Ujwala Ltd.

Particulars	*Product A*	*Product B*
Sale price per unit	₹ 200	₹ 240
Consumption of material	4 kg	6 kg
Material cost	₹ 20	₹ 30
Direct labour cost	30	20
Direct expenses	10	12
Machine hours used	4	3
Fixed overheads per unit	₹ 10	₹ 20
Variable overheads per unit	30	40

Direct labour per hour is ₹10. Comment on the profitability of each product [both use same raw material] when [a] total sales potential in units is limited [b] total sales potential in value is limited [c] raw material is in short supply [d] production capacity [in terms of machine hours] is limited.

Assuming raw material as the key factor, availability of which is 10,000 kg and maximum sales potential of each product being 3500 units find out the product mix which will yield maximum profits.

Solution :

Calculation of Contribution

Particulars	*Product A*	*Product B*
Selling price per unit	₹ 200	₹ 240
Less: Variable cost per unit		
Direct materials	₹ 20	₹ 30
Direct labour	₹ 30	₹ 20
Direct expenses	₹ 10	₹ 12
Variable overheads	₹ 30	₹ 40
Total variable cost per unit	₹90	₹102
Contribution [Selling price per unit – Variable cost per unit]	₹110	₹138
Profit/volume ratio: (Contribution/Sales) x 100	(110/200) x 100 = 55%	(69/120) x 100 = 57.5%
Contribution per machine hour: Contribution/ Machine hours per unit	₹110/4 = 27.5	₹138/3 = ₹46
Contribution per kg of direct material = Contribution/kg of material per unit	₹110/4 kg = ₹ 27.5	₹ 138/6 kg=₹ 23

Profitability of each product in each of the following situations :

a) Total sales potential in units is limited: In this situation, the product with higher contribution per unit will be preferred as it will be more profitable to promote the same. Product B earns higher contribution per unit than product A hence it will be more profitable.

b) Total sales potential in value is limited: Product with higher profit/volume ratio will be more profitable. Product B will be more profitable as its profit volume ratio is higher than that of product A.

c) Raw material is in short supply: Product A will be more profitable in such situation as it earns higher contribution per kg of raw material.

d) Production capacity in machine hours is limited: In such case, product B will be more profitable as it earns higher contribution per machine hour.

Problem 2

From the following particulars, find the most profitable product mix and prepare a statement of profitability of that product mix of Nagaraj Ltd.

Particulars	Product A	Product B	Product C
Units budgeted to be produced and sold	1,800	3,000	1,500
Selling price per unit	₹ 60	₹ 55	₹ 50
Requirement per unit			
Direct Materials	5 kg.	3 kg.	4 kg
Direct Labour	4 hrs.	3 hrs.	2 hrs
Variable Overheads	₹ 7	₹ 13	₹8
Fixed Overheads	₹ 10	₹ 10	₹ 10
Cost of direct materials per kg	₹ 4	₹ 4	₹ 4
Direct Labour hours rate	₹ 2	₹ 2	₹ 2
Maximum Possible Units of Sales	4,000	5,000	1,500

All the three products are produced from the same direct material using the same type of machines and labour. Direct Labour, which is the key factor and limited to 18,600 hours.

(CA, Inter, May, 1990)

Solution :

Calculation Contribution per Direct Labour Hour

Product	A	B	C
A. Selling price per unit	60	55	50
B. **Variable Cost per Unit**			
Direct Materials	20	12	16
Direct Labour	8	6	4
Variable Overheads	7	13	8
Total	35	31	28
(i) Contribution per unit (A) - (B)	25	24	22
(ii) No. of direct hours per unit	4	3	2
Contribution per direct labour hour (i) / (ii) (Rs.)	6.3	8	11
Ranking	III	II	I

Allocation of Direct Labour Hours to Products based on its Ranking

Product	No. of Units	Labour hours	Total hours
C	1,500	2	3,000
B	5,000	3	15,000
A	150	4	600 (Balance)
		Total	18,600

Statement of Profit

		Rs.
Contribution		
A (150 x 25)	3,750	
B (5,000 x 24)	1,20,000	
C (1,500 x 22)	33,000	1,56,750
Less: Fixed Cost		
A (1,800 x 10)	18,000	
B (3,000 x 10)	30,000	
C (1,500 x 10)	15,000	63,000
	Profit	93,750

2. **Profit Planning :**

Marginal Costing technique helps the management in profit planning because long run it is uncertain and highly unpredictable. It will maximize profit in the long run with the help of following steps :

(i) By increasing volume

(ii) By increasing selling price

(iii) By decreasing variable costs

(iv) By decreasing fixed costs

Problem 3

The chief Accountant of Ramesh Limited found to his surprise that the actual profit for the period ending 30th June 2012 was the same as budgeted in spite of realizing 10% more than the budgeted selling prices. The following were the result:

Particulars	Budget ₹	Actuals ₹
Sales	5,00,000	8,25,000
Variable cost	3,00,000	5,75,000
Fixed Costs	1,00,000	1,50,000
Profit	1,00,000	1,00,000

You are required to assist the Chief Cost Accountant in preparing the necessary explanations as to why the profit remained the same despite an increase in sales.

(ICWA, Inter, June, 2002)

Solution :

	₹	₹
Factors contributing the increase in profit		
(i) Increase in sales revenue	82,500	
Due to increased selling price (Working note 1)		
(ii) Increase in contribution on Account of increased sales volume (Working Note 4)	97,000	1,79,500
Factors contributing to the increase in cost		
(i) Increase in variable cost (working note 5)	1,29,500	
(ii) Increase in fixed cost	50,000	1,79,500

Working Notes :

1. Increase in sales revenue due to price increase (10 % more than Budgeted)

$$= \frac{\text{Rs. } 8,25,000 \times 10}{100} = \text{Rs. } 82,500$$

2. Increase in sales volume :

= Actual Sales – [Sales Revenue due to increased selling price + Budgeted Sales]

= ₹ 8, 25,000 – [₹ 82, 500 + 5,00,000]

= ₹ 2, 42,500

3. Budgeted P/V Ratio $= \frac{\text{Budgeted Contribution} \times 100}{\text{Budgeted Sales}}$

$$= \frac{₹\,5,00,000 - ₹\,3,00,000}{₹\,5,00,000} \times 100$$

$= 40\ \%$

4. Increase in contribution due to higher sales volume from calculation (2) and (3) we have = ₹ 2, 42,500 x 40 % = ₹ 97,000

5. Budgeted proportion of variable cost (on the sale of ₹ 500000 + 2,42,500 = 7,42,500)
   = [Budgeted Costs/Budgeted Sales] × Actual Sales Volume
   = (₹ 3, 00,000/ ₹ 5, 00,000) x ₹ 7, 42,500
   = ₹ 4, 45,500

   Increase in variable cost = (Actual Variable Cost – Budgeted proportion of Variable Cost)
   = ₹ 5, 75,000 – ₹ 4, 45,500
   = ₹ 1, 29,500

From the above calculation the listed factors that shows the profit of M/s Ramesh Ltd. has increased by ₹ 1,79,500 due to increase in selling price (₹ 82,500) and the contribution on increased volume (₹ 97,000). The cost of the concern has also increased to the tune of ₹ 1,79,500 due to increase in variable cost (₹ 1,29,500) and fixed cost (₹ 50,000). As the increase in profit equals the increase in cost, therefore the profit of the concern has remained the same as shown in the budget.

Problem 4

Raju Limited expected to reveal a profit of ₹ 14, 00,000 after charging fixed cost of ₹ 10, 00,000 for the year ended 31st March, 2013. The selling price of the product is ₹ 50 per unit and variable cost per unit is ₹ 20. The market investigations suggest the following responses to the price changes :

Alternatives	**Selling price reduced by**	**Quantity sold increased by**
I	5%	10%
II	7%	20%
III	10%	25%

Evaluate these alternatives and state which of the alternatives, on profitability consideration, be adopted for the forthcoming year. *(C.S, Inter June, 2001)*

Solution :

Alternatives	I	II	III
Selling price per unit (₹)	47.50 (₹ 50 -5% of ₹ 50)	46.50 (₹ 50 -7% of ₹ 50)	45.00 (₹ 50 -10% of ₹ 50)
Less: Variable cost per unit (₹)	20.00	20.00	20.00
Contribution per unit (₹)	27.50	26.50	25.00
Revised quantity of units to be sold (Working note 3)	88,000	96,000	1,00,000
Total Contribution (₹)	24,20,000 (88,000 units x ₹ 27.50)	25,44,000 (96,000 units x ₹ 26.50)	25,00,000 (1,00,000 units x ₹ 25)

Conclusion : From the above calculations of three alternatives on profitability consideration clearly shows that the alternative II is the best as it gives maximum contribution and hence more profitable adopt the alternative II.

Working Notes :

1. Contribution per unit = ₹ Selling price per unit – Variable Cost per unit

   = ₹ 50 – ₹ 20 = ₹ 30

2. Expected quantity of units to be sold

	₹
Profit	14, 00,000
Add : Fixed Costs	10, 00,000
Total Contribution	24, 00,000

$$\text{Quantity of units sold} = \frac{\text{Total Contribution}}{\text{Contribution per unit}}$$

$$= \frac{₹\ 24,00,000}{₹\ 30 \text{ per unit}}$$

= 80,000 units

3. Revised quantity of units to be sold

Alternatives	Units to be sold
I	80,000 units + 10 % of 80,000 units = 88, 000 units
II	80,000 units + 20 % of 80,000 units = 96, 000 units
III	80,000 units + 25 % of 80,000 units = 1,00,000 units

Problem 5A

Richa Industries engaged in manufacturing Lunch Boxes is working to 50% capacity and produces 15,000 Lunch Boxes per annum. The present cost break up for one Lunch Box is as under :

Material 25; Labour; 20 and Overheads : 15 (60% variable).

The selling price is ₹ 75 per Lunch Box.

If it is decided to work at 60% capacity, the selling price falls by 2%. At 80% capacity, the selling price falls by 10% accompanied by a similar fall in the price of material but labour rate increasesby 10%

You are required to find out the most profitable capacity level amongst 50%, 60% and 80% capacity levels and also calculate the Break-even Point (in units) at above said levels.

(ICWA June 2012)

Solution :

Working Notes :

(i) Fixed overheads per unit = 100 – 60 variable = 40% of 15 = 6.

Total fixed overheads = 6 × 15,000 units = 90,000

(ii) Variable cost per unit :

At 50 % capacity - (25 + 20 + 60% of 15) = (25 + 20 + 9) = 54

At 60% capacity = Same at 50% capacity = 54

At 80% capacity = (90% of 25 + 110% of 20 + 60% of 15) = (22.50 + 22 + 9) = 53.50

(iii) Selling price :

At 50% capacity = 75

At 60% capacity = (98% of 75) = 73.50

At 80% capacity = (90% of 75) = 67.50

Statement showing profit at 50%, 60% & 80 % Capacity levels

	50%	60%	80%
Output and Sales (units)	15000	18000	24000
	Rs	Rs	Rs
Selling price per unit	75	73.50	67.50
Less: Variable Cost	54	54.00	53.50
Contribution per unit	21	19.50	14.00
Total contribution (Units x Cost per unit)	315000	351000	336000
Less: Fixed Cost	90000	90000	90000
Profit	225000	261000	246000

Hence, on the basis of above calculations the 60% capacity is most profitable capacity level.

		50% capacity	60% capacity	80% capacity
BEP (in units) =	Fixed cost / Contribution per unit	90,000 / 21	90,000 / 19.50	90,000 / 14
	BEP units	4286 units (approx.)	4615 units (approx.)	6429 units (approx.)

Problem 5B

KLR manufactures producing a single product and selling price of product is ₹ 100 per unit. Currently the capacity utilization is 60 % with the sales turnover of ₹ 12 lakhs. The company proposes to reduce the selling price by 20 % but desires to maintain the same profit position by increasing the output. Assuming that the increased output could be made and sold determine the level at which the company should operate to achieve the desired objectives.

The following further data are available :

(i) Variable cost per unit ₹ 20

(ii) Semi variable cost (including a variable element of ₹ 5 per unit) ₹ 80,000.

(iii) Fixed cost of ₹ 2, 00,000 will remain constant up to 80% level. Beyond this an additional amount of ₹ 40,000 will be needed.

Solution :

Current Sales turnover	₹ 12,00,000
Selling price per unit	₹ 100
Current sales in units (Rs. 12,00,000/Rs. 100)	12,000 units
Current Capacity utilization	60%
Capacity at 100 % (12,000 units x 100/60)	20,000 units

Calculation of profit at current 60 % (i.e., 12,000 units) capacity utilization

	₹
Variable cost for 12,000 units @ ₹ 20 per unit	2,40,000
Variable cost included in semi-variable cost for 12,000 units @ ₹ 5 per unit	60,000
Fixed cost included in semi-variable cost (Total ₹ 80,000 - ₹ 60,000) = 20,000	
Variable cost included therein 20,000 other fixed costs 2,00,000	2,20,000
Total cost for 12,000 units	5,20,000
Profit (Balancing figure)	6,80,000
Sales (given)	12,00,000

Thus, profit at 60 % capacity utilization is ₹ 6,80,000. This profit is to be maintained even if the selling price is reduced by 20 %. Fixed expenses up to 80 % capacity utilization will remain same. Let us see whether profit of ₹ 6,80,000 earned at 60 % capacity utilization can be earned below 80 % capacity utilization.

Present selling price	₹ 100
Less: 20 % reduction	₹ 20
	₹ 80

$$\text{Sales in units} = \frac{\text{Fixed Expenses} + \text{Profit}}{\text{Selling Price per Unit - Variable Cost per Unit}}$$

$$= \frac{₹\,2,20,000 + ₹\,6,80,000}{₹\,80 - ₹\,25}$$

$$= ₹\,9,00,000 \,/\, ₹\,55 = 16,364 \text{ units}$$

% Capacity utilization = 16,364 units / 20,000 units x 100 = 81.82 %

Capacity utilization is more than 80 %, therefore fixed expenses will increase by ₹ 40,000. Keeping in view increase in fixed expenses, the desired sales will have to be calculated again.

$$\text{Sales in units} = \frac{\text{Revised Fixed Expenses} + \text{Desired Profit}}{\text{Selling Price - Variable Cost}}$$

$$= \frac{\text{Rs. } 2,60,000 + \text{Rs. } 6,80,000}{\text{Rs. } 80 - \text{Rs. } 25} = 17,091 \text{ Units}$$

Revised Fixed Expenses = Present fixed expense + Increased amount

= ₹ 2, 20,000 + ₹ 40,000 = ₹ 2, 60,000

Percentage of Capacity utilization = 17,091 units / 20,000 units x 100 = 85. 45%

3. Make or Buy Decision

It indicates the choice between making a product within the company or purchasing it from the outside suppliers. Such a problem will arise when the firm has the idle capacity and the technical capacity of manufacturing the component parts. In arriving at such a make or buy decision, qualitative and quantitative factors are involved in make or buy decision. The quantitative factors to be considered are the differential costs of the make and buy alternatives and the consequences of the alternative uses of the idle capacity which exists in the firm. The relevant cost of buying the component part will include the purchase price and other costs related to purchasing the component part similarly, costs relevant for make decision will include the variable cost of making the component and fixed cost which are avoidable if the component is not made.

Fixed costs which are not expected to change would be ignored being irrelevant in the make or buy decision. Management should compare the differential cost of the two alternatives and follow the cheaper one. The firm may use the idle capacity for the more profitable alternative and buy the component part from outside. For example the total cost of making a component part comes to ₹ 8 consisting of Rs 6 as variable cost and ₹ 2 as fixed cost. Suppose further an outside supplier is ready to supply the same component part at ₹ 7. On the basis of total cost method, it appears that it is cheaper to buy the component. But on the basis of marginal cost, the offer of the outside supplier should be rejected because the acceptance will mean that the total cost of the purchased part from the outside supplier will come to ₹ 9, i.e., ₹ 7 (Suppliers price) plus ₹ 2 (Fixed cost which cannot be saved even if the component is purchased from outside source). Hence, make the product in the factory.

The following factors are generally taken into account at the time of taking a make or buy decision :

(i) Quality of goods supplied by the supplier

(ii) Uninterrupted supply by the supplier meeting the delivery dates.

(iii) If secrecy is to be maintained and manufacturing know-how is not to be passed on to the supplier of the component part, the decision will be better to manufacture the component part though the manufacturing cost may be more than the price to be charged by the supplier.

(iv) Any adverse effect on labour relations if it is decided to buy from outside.

(v) The differential cost of making or buying the item.

(vi) The impact of decision to make the item on aggregate volumes, an increase in which should contribute to overhead recovery and facilitate the balancing of demand and operations capacity over time.

(vii) The level of variable overheads which are charged to the part or article.

Problem 6

Hero Cycles Ltd purchases 40,000 bells per annum from an outside supplier at ₹ 5 each. The management feels that these be manufactured and not purchased. A machine costing ₹ 50,000 will be required to manufacture the item within the factory. The machine has an annual capacity of 60,000 units and life of 5 years. The following additional information is available.

Marginal cost per bell will be	₹ 2.00
Labour Cost	₹ 1.00
Variable Overheads	₹ 100 % of labour cost

You are required to advice whether the company should continue to purchase the bells from the outside supplier or should make them in the factory and the company should accept an order to supply 10,000 bells to the market at a selling price of 4.50 per unit?

(C.S. Inter, Dec. 1990)

Solution :

Working Notes :

Calculation of Depreciation per unit

Depreciation p.a = ₹ 100,000 / 5 years = ₹ 20,000 p.a

Depreciation per unit = ₹ 20,000/40,000 units =₹ 0.50 per unit

Calculation of Cost of Production per bell

Particulars	Amount
Variable Cost :	
Material	2.00
Labour	1.00
Variable Overhead (100 % of labour)	1.00
Variable Cost	4.00
Add: Fixed Cost – Depreciation	0.50
Cost of Production per Bell	4.50

Purchase cost of bell from outside = 5.00

Annual saving in production of bells (40,000 bells x (₹ 5 – ₹ 4.50) = ₹ 10,000

1. Hence make the bells in the factory which increases profitability.
2. Accept the order of Ten thousand bells which selling price of ₹ 4.50. It is more than the variable cost equal to the total cost.

4. Selection of Suitable Production Mix

When a factory manufactures more than one product a problem is faced by the management to which product mix will give the maximum profits. The best product mix is that which yields more profits. It also helps in management about discontinuance of non-profitable products and lines of activity which are unable to cover its variable costs.

Problem 7

From the following particulars find the most profitable product mix and prepare statement of profitability of that product mix of XYZ Ltd.

	Product A	Product B	Product C
Units budgeted to be produced and sold	18,000	3,000	1,200
Selling price per unit ₹	65	60	55
Requirement per unit			
Direct Materials	5kg	3kg	4kg
Direct Labour	4hrs	3hrs	2hrs
Variable Overheads	₹ 12	₹ 18	₹ 13
Fixed Overheads	₹ 10	₹ 10	₹ 10
Cost of Direct Material per kg	₹ 4	₹ 4	₹ 4
Direct Labour Hour Rate	₹ 2	₹ 2	₹ 2
Maximum Possible Units of Sales	10,000	5,000	1,500

All the three products are produced from the same direct material using the same type of machines and labour. Direct labour, which is the key factor, is limited to 18,600 hours.

(ICWA, Inter, Dec, 2003)

Solution :

Calculation of Profitable Product Mix of XYZ Ltd

Products	A ₹	B ₹	C ₹
Selling Price per unit (i)	65	60	55
Variable cost			
Direct Material	20	12	16
Direct Labour	8	6	4
Variable Overhead	12	18	13
Total Variable Cost (ii)	40	36	33
Contribution per unit [(i) – (ii)]	25	24	22
Contribution per hour (Refer to Note 12)			
Ranking of most profitable product mix	III	II	I

	A	B	C	Total
Ranking	III	II	I	
Units produced and sold (Refer to Note 2)	150	5,000	1,500	
Contribution per unit (₹)	25	24	22	
Total Contribution on units sold (Rs)	₹ 3,750 (150 x ₹25)	₹ 1,20,000 (5000 x ₹24)	₹ 33,000 (1,500 x ₹22)	1,56,750
Less: Fixed Cost (₹) Note 3				60,000
Profit (Rs)				96,750
Note 1				
Products	A	B	C	
A. Contribution per unit (₹)	25	24	22	
B. Direct Labour Hours per unit	4	3	2	

Contribution per hour $\frac{25}{4}=6.25$ $\frac{24}{3}=8$ $\frac{22}{2}=11$

(2) Here direct labour hour is the key factor and only 18,600 hours are available to produce the three products. The available 18,000 hours are utilized in the order of the ranking assigned i.e. first of all product C then product B lastly product A will be produced.

The number of units of each product to be produces will depend upon the maximum possible sale of each product. The details of the products to be produced, keeping in view of available hours and their ranking are as below :

		Total hours utilized
Product C	1,500 units x 2 hrs	3,000
Product B	5,000 units x 3 hrs	15,000
Product A	150 units x 4 hrs	600
	Total hours	18,600

(3) Calculation of fixed overheads

	Products			
	A	B	C	Total
Budgeted units to be produced and sold:	18,00	3,000	12,00	
Fixed overheads (Rs.) per unit	10	10	10	
Total fixed overheads (Rs.)	18,000	30,000	12,000	6,000

Problem 8

A decision is to be taken by the management of a company relating to the possible introduction of a new product. There can be three models of this product, aimed at different sections of the consumer market. The relevant figures as follows :

	Model I ₹	Model II ₹	Model III ₹
Variable Cost (per unit) :			
Materials	1.54	1.22	0.86
Labour	1.06	0.96	0.58
Varialbe Overheads	0.40	0.33	0.31
Total Variable cost	3.00	2.50	1.75
Selling Price (per units)	4.25	3.50	2.50
Expected Sales volume per month (unit)	800	2000	4000
Capital expenditure before product production can commerce (finance by bank overdraft at 5% per annum)	₹ 800	₹ 3,000	₹ 4,000
Fixed overhead per month attributable to new model (including depreciation on capital expenditure but excluding Interests)	280	850	1,100

You are required to prepare a statement of relative profitability and determined for each model the percentage of net profit to selling price at the expected sales volume.

(ICWA, inter, Dec. 2004)

Solution :

Comparative Profitability Statement

Particulars	Model I (800 units)		Model II (2000 units)		Model III (4000 units)	
	Per unit	Total	Per unit	Total	Per unit	Total
	₹	₹	₹	₹	₹	₹
Sales	4.25	3400	3.50	7000	2.50	10,000
Less: Varialbe Cost	3	2400	2.50	5000	1.75	7000
Contribution	1.25	1,000	1.00	2,000	0.75	3,000
Less: Fixed Overheads (Excluding bank interest)	0.35	280	0.425	850	0.275	1,100
Net Profit	0.90	720	0.575	1,150	0.475	1,900
Percentage of Net Profit on Selling price		21.2%		6.4%		19.0%

Problem 9A

From the following data which product would you recommend to be manufactured in a factory?

	Per Unit of Product A	Per Unit of Product B
Direct Materials	24	14
Direct Labour @ Rs. 1 per hour	2	3
Variable Overhead at Rs. 2 per hour	4	6
Selling price	106	116
Standard Time to Produce	2 hours	3 hours
Output Units	3,500	2,500

Solution :

Calculation of Contribution per hour

		Product A per unit		Product B per unit
		₹		₹
Selling price		106		116
Less: Marginal Cost	₹		₹	
Direct Materials	24		14	
Direct Labour	2		3	
Variable Overhead	4	30	6	23
		76		93
Standard Time to produce		2 hours		3 hours
Contribution per hour		76/2 = ₹ 38		93/3 = ₹ 31

Product A is more profitable and is recommended to be manufactured.

Problem 10

P Ltd. manufactures and sells children's toys of high quality over an extensive market utilizing the services of skilled artists who are paid at an average rate of ₹ 30 per hour. The total number of skilled hours available in a year is only 28000. The details of planned production for 2011-12; estimated cost and unit selling prices are given below:

Product [Toy]	Production Planned [Units]	Direct Materials Per Unit Rs.	Direct Labour Per Unit Rs.	Fixed Overheads Per Unit Rs.	Selling Price Per Unit Rs.
A	6000	40	20	30	140
B	8000	48	24	36	184
C	8000	64	24	36	190
D	6000	80	32	48	220
E	4800	120	40	60	360

Variable overheads costs amount to 50% of the direct labour cost. The company has estimated the following maximum and minimum demands for each product.

Particulars	A	B	C	D	E
Maximum - Units	10,000	6,000	12,000	8,000	4,000
Minimum - Units	2,000	2,000	2,000	1,000	1,000

You are required to work out profit as per the production plan of the company and also compute the optimum profit in the given situation.

Solution :

In this problem the direct labour hour is the key factor. The availability of labour hours is only 28000 hours and hence the priority of the products will have to be decided as all the product cannot be produced equal to the maximum quantity. The contribution per direct labour hour will be criteria for determining the priority.

Particulars	Product A ₹	Product B ₹	Product C ₹	Product D ₹	Product E ₹
I] Selling price per unit	140	184	190	220	360
II] Variable cost per unit					
Direct materials	40	48	64	80	120
Direct labour	20	24	24	32	40
Variable overheads [50% of direct labour]	10	12	12	16	20
III] Total variable cost	70	84	100	128	180
IV] Contribution per unit [I - III]	70	100	90	92	180
V] Direct labour hours per unit *	.67	.8	.8	1.06	1.33
VI] Contribution per direct labour hour [V / VI]	₹52.23	₹62.5	₹56.25	₹43.39	₹67.66
VII] Priority	IV	II	III	V	I

* Direct labour hours for each product is computed by dividing the direct labour cost per unit of each product by direct labour rate per hour, which is ₹ 30

The next step in the problem is to work out the amount of profit as per the production plan prepared by the company.

2] Statement showing amount of Profits as per the Production Plan of the Company

Particulars	Product A	Product B	Product C	Product D	Product E	Total
I] Number of units to be sold	6,000	8,000	8,000	6,000	4,800	32,800
II] Contribution per unit [As per statement number 1]	₹70	₹100	₹90	₹92	₹180	
III] Total ₹ contribution [I X II]	4,20,000	8, 00,000	7, 20,000	5, 52,000	8, 64,000	33, 56,000
IV] Total fixed cost	1,80, 000	2,88,000	2,88,000	2,88,000	2,88,000	13, 32,000
V] Profit [III -IV]	2,40, 000	5,12, 000	4,32,000	2,64,000	5,76,000	20, 24, 000

3] Statement Showing Production Plan with optimum product mix

Product in order of priority	Sales Units	Number of hours required	Contribution Per Unit	Total Contribution
E	4000 Max	5320	Rs. 180	Rs. 3, 60,000
B	6000 Max	4800	Rs. 100	Rs. 3, 00,000
C	12000 Max	9600	Rs. 90	Rs. 1, 49,895
A	10000 Max	6700	Rs. 70	Rs. 35, 000
D	1491 (Bal.)	1580	Rs. 92	Rs. 23, 000
Total		28, 000		Rs. 8, 67, 895

Amount of maximum profit = Total Contribution – Total Fixed Cost

= ₹ 8, 67,895 – ₹ 13, 32, 000 = ₹ 5, 34, 895

Problem 11

XY Ltd. is manufacturing three household products, A, B and C and selling them in a competitive market. Details of current demand, selling price and cost structure are given below.

Particulars	A	B	C
Expected Demand [units]	9000	13,000	20, 000
Selling price per unit ₹	21	17	11
Variable cost per unit :			
Direct materials ₹10 per kg (₹)	6	4	2
Direct labour ₹1.5 per hour (₹)	3	3	1.50
Variable overheads	3	2	2

The company is frequently affected by acute scarcity of raw material and high labour turnover. During the next period, it is expected to have one of the following situations:

The total fixed cost is ₹ 1,40,000

I] Raw material available will be only 12,100 kg

II] Direct labour hours available will be only 50,000 hrs.

III] It may be possible to increase sales of any one product by 25% without any additional fixed costs but by spending ₹20,000 on advertisement. There will be no shortage of materials or labour.

Suggest the best production plan in each case and the resultant profit that the company would earn according to your suggestion.

Solution :

The following statement is prepared to compute the contribution per unit and for deciding best production plan in each case. There are limiting factors like raw material and direct labour. For deciding the best production plan, priority of the products will have to be decided by computing the contribution per unit of the key factor. Accordingly the following statements are prepared.

I] Raw Material availability is 12,100 kg

Statement Showing Contribution per kg of Raw Material

Particulars	Product A ₹	Product B ₹	Product C ₹
I] Selling price per unit	21	17	11
II] Variable cost per unit			
Direct materials	6	4	2.0
Direct labour	3	3	1.50
Variable overheads	3	2	2
III] Total variable cost per unit	12	9	5.5
IV] Contribution per unit [I – III]	9	8	5.50
V] Raw material requirement per unit (₹ 10 per kg.)	.6	.4	.2
VI] Contribution per kg of raw material: Contribution / Raw material requirement per kg	9 / . 6 = ₹ 15	8/ .4 = ₹ 20	₹5.50 / .2 = ₹ 27.50
Priority	III	II	I

II] Statement of Production Plan: Raw Material is the key factor

Products Order of Priority	Production Units	Raw Materials per unit kg	Total Raw Materials kg	Contribution Per Unit ₹	Total Contribution ₹
C	20 000	0.2	4000	5.50	1, 10,000
B	13 000	0.4	5200	8.00	1,04, 000
A	4833	0.6	2900 *	9.00	43, 497
Total			12 100		2, 57,497
Less: Fixed Cost					1, 40,000
Profit					1, 17,497

* Total availability of raw material is 12 100 kg as given in the problem. Total 9200 kg are consumed for producing the maximum production of C and B and hence the balance quantity of 2900 kg is used to produce 4833 kg of product A.

III] Statement Showing Contribution Per Direct Labour Hour :

Particulars	Product A ₹	Product B ₹	Product C ₹
Contribution per unit as per statement I	9	8	5.50
Labour hrs per unit (₹ 1.50 per kg.)	2	2	1
Contribution per labour hour [Contribution per unit/ labour hour per unit]	9/2 = ₹4.5	8/.2 = ₹4	5.50/1 = ₹5.5
Priority	II	III	I

IV] Statement of Best Production Plan: Direct Labour Hour Key Factor

Product as per Priority	Production Units	Labour Hours Per Unit	Total Labour Hours	Contribution Per Unit	Total Contribution
C	20, 000	1	20,000	₹5.50	₹ 1,10,000
A	9, 000	2	18,000	₹9.00	₹ 81,000
B	6, 000	2	12,000	₹8.00	₹ 48,000
Total			50,000		₹ 2,39,000
Less: Fixed Cost					₹ 1,40,000
Profit					₹ 99,000

* Balance labour hours after producing C and A to the maximum possible extent

V] Statement Showing Profit/Volume Ratio:

Particulars	Product A	Product B	Product C
I] Selling price per unit	Rs.20	Rs.17	Rs.11
II] Contribution per unit [As shown in earlier statements]	Rs.9	Rs.8	Rs.5.50
III] Profit/Volume Ratio: (Contribution / Sales) × 100	(9/20) × 100 = 43%	(8/17) × 100 = 47%	(5.50/11) × 100 = 50%
IV] Priority	III	II	I

VI] Best Production Plan When Sales of One Product Can Be Increased By Spending ₹20,000 on Advertising

Product	Production Units	Contribution Per Unit ₹	Total Contribution ₹
A	9, 000	9.00	81, 000
B	13, 000	8.00	1,04, 000
C	25, 000 *	5.50	1, 37, 500
Total			3, 22, 500
Less: Fixed Cost			1, 60, 000
Profit			1, 62, 500

* Sales of any one product can be increased by 25% by spending additional amount on advertising ₹20, 000. In such situation, the product with highest profit/volume ratio can be promoted and hence production and sales of product C should be increased by 25% as the profit/volume ratio for the same is highest. Thus the production and sale units will be 25% higher, i.e. 20 000 + 25% of 20 000 = 25 000 units.

Problem 12

A company has compiled the following data for the preparation of its budget for the year 2008-09

Particulars	Product P	Product Q	Product R
Sale per month - units	10, 000	5, 000	8, 000
Selling Price	₹50 per unit	₹100 per unit	₹135 per unit
Direct Materials	₹25 per unit	₹60 per unit	₹50 per unit
Direct Labour:	10	20	40
Department 1 ₹10 per hour	16	8	24
Department II ₹8 per hour			
Variable Overheads	₹5 per unit	₹5 per unit	₹9 per unit
Fixed Overheads:			
₹1,50, 000 per month			

After the budget was discussed, the following action plan was approved for improving the profitability of the company.

I] Direct labour in department 1, which is in short supply, should be increased by 20, 000 hours by spending fixed overheads of ₹10, 000 per month.

II] To boost sales, an advertisement program should be launched at a cost of ₹20, 000 per month.

III] The selling price should be reduced by: P: 2.5%, Q: 8.75%, R: 1%

IV] The sales target have been increased and the sales department has confirmed that the company will be able to achieve the following quantities of sales P: 16,000 units, Q: 10,000 units, R: 14,000 units

Required :

1. Present the original budget for the year 2011-12
2. Set an optimal product mix after taking into the action plan into consideration and determine the monthly profit or Loss

Solution :

The original budget for the year 2011-12 is prepared as shown below. Original Monthly Budget for the Year 2008-09

Particulars	Product P	Product Q	Product R	Total
I] Sales for the month - units	10,000	5,000	8,000	
II] Selling price per unit	₹50	₹100	₹135	
III] Variable cost per unit				
Direct material	₹25	₹60	₹50	
Direct labour [Dept 1]	₹10	₹20	₹40	
Direct labour [Dept 2]	₹16	₹8	₹24	
Variable overheads	₹5	₹5	₹9	
IV] Total variable cost per unit	₹56	₹93	₹123	
V] Contribution per unit [II – IV]	₹4	₹7	₹12	
VI] Total contribution [I X V]	₹40,000	₹35,000	₹96,000	₹1,71,000
VII] Fixed cost				₹2,00,000
VIII] Profit [VI – VII]				₹29, 000

5. Price Fixation

Marginal costing helps in setting sale price. In this case, fixed cost is ignored and prices are determined on the basis of marginal cost. Marginal cost is the change in total costs that results from production of additional unit of a product or service. Each and every increase in production is to be justified in terms of price increase or decrease.

Although prices are more controlled by market conditions and other economic factors than by decisions of the management, now fixation of selling price is one of the most important functions of management. This function is to be performed with following ways.

(a) Under normal circumstances.

(b) In times of competition

(c) In time on trade depression.

(d) In accepting additional orders for utilizing idle capacity

(e) In exporting and exploring new markets

(f) Quotation in jobbing undertaking

In normal circumstances, the price fixed must cover total cost as otherwise profits cannot be earned. It can also be fixed on the basis of marginal cost by adding a high margin to marginal cost which may be sufficient to contribute towards fixed expenses and profits. But under other circumstances, product may have to be sold at a price below total cost , if such cases necessary to meet that situation arising due to competition, trade depression, additional orders for utilizing spare capacity, exploring new markets etc,. Thus, in special circumstances, price may be below the total cost and it should be equal to marginal cost plus a certain margin.

Pricing in depression : Prices fall during depression and the product may be sold below the total cost. In case there is a serious but temporary fall in demand on account of depression leading to the need for a drastic reduction in prices temporarily and the minimum selling price should be equal to the marginal cost. If the selling price at which the goods can be sold is equal to marginal cost or more than marginal cost then the product should be continued. Fixed expenses will be incurred even if the product is discontinued during depression for a short period. If the product can be sold at a price which is a little more than marginal cost, loss on account of fixed expenses will be reduced because price will recover fixed expenses to some extent.

Selling price below the marginal cost

1. When a new product is introduced in the market. The new product is sold at a very low price to make is popular. This is done with the hope that sales will increase with the passage of time and cost of production will come down as a result of increase in sales. Ultimately cost of production will be in line with the selling price and the concern will start earning profit from the new line of production.

2. When foreign market is to be explored to earn foreign exchange. Government sometimes allows import quotas against foreign exchange earned and profits from import quotas may be much more that the loss on exporting the product at a price below the marginal cost.

3. When the concern has already purchased large quantities of materials. It is better to convert the material into finished. goods and sell these at a price below the marginal cost if the sale of material will give rise to loss which is more than the loss incurred if the production is done

4. When closure of business may mean breaking of business connections and connections may be re-established by a heavy expenditure on advertisement and sales promotion. In such a case it is better to continue the production and sell the product at a price below the marginal cost.

5. When the sales of one product at a price below the marginal cost it will push up the sales of other profitable products. The loss in one product will be made up by profits of other products.

6. When employees cannot be retrenched. In such a case, it is better to maintain the products. Even if the price is below the marginal cost. Then competitors are to be eliminated from the market.

7. When the goods are of perishable nature it is better to sell the goods at a price below the marginal cost; otherwise these goods will perish and nothing will be realized.

Accepting Additional orders, exploring additional markets and exporting

When additional orders are accepted or additional markets explored at a price below normal price to utilize idle capacity, it should be carefully study that they will not affect the normal market and goodwill of the company. The order from local merchant should not be accepted at a price below normal price because it will affect relationship of the other customers purchasing the goods at normal price. In case of foreign markets, goods may be sold at a price below normal price keeping in view the direct and indirect benefits of exporting such as import quotas, subsidies of Government, prestige of exporting etc.

Problem 13

Sonu Ltd engaged in manufacturing is working to 40% capacity and produces 8,000 products per annum. The present cost break up for one product is as under,

Material ₹20

Labour ₹6

Overheads ₹10 [60% fixed]

The selling price is ₹50 per product.

If it is decided to work the factory at 50% capacity, the selling price falls by 3%. At 90% capacity, the selling price falls by 4% accompanied by a similar fall in the price of material.

You are required to calculate the profit at 50% and 90% capacities and also show break-even points for the same capacity production.

Solution :

Statement showing Profit and Break-even Point at 50% and 90% Capacity

Particulars	50% Capacity	90% Capacity
Production – units	10, 000	18, 000
A] Sale Price per Unit	₹49	₹48
B] Variable Cost per Unit		
Material	20.00	19.20
Labour	6.00	6.00
Variable Overheads	4.00	4.00
C] Total Variable Cost Per Unit	30.00	29.20
D] Contribution per Unit [A – C]	19	18.80
E] Total Contribution [Units X D]	1,90, 000	3,38,400
F] Fixed Costs ₹3 per unit at 30% capacity, i.e. 7, 500 units	48, 000	48,000
G] Profits [E – F]	1,42, 000	2,90,400

Break-even Sales at 50% capacity

= Fixed Cost/Contribution per unit

= ₹48,000/₹19 = 2527 units: ₹1,23,823 (approx)

Break-even Sales at 90% capacity

= Fixed Cost/Contribution per unit

= ₹ 48, 000/₹18.80 = 2554 units: ₹1,22,592/

Problem 14

KGR manufactures a single product with a capacity of 1,00,000 units per annum. The summarized profitability statement for a year is as under:

Particulars	Amount ₹	Amount ₹
Sales: 1 00 000 units @ ₹15 per unit		15, 00,000
Less: Cost of Sales		
Direct materials	3, 00,000	
Direct labour	2, 00,000	
Production overheads – variable	60,000	
Production overheads – fixed	3,00,000	
Administrative overheads – fixed	1, 50,000	
Selling and distribution overheads- fixed	1,50,000	
Selling and distribution overheads- variable	90,000	
Total cost of sales		12, 50,000
Profit		2, 50,000

You are required to evaluate the following options:

1) What will be the amount of sales required to earn a target profit of 25% on sales, if the packing is improved at a cost of Re.1 per unit?
2) There is an offer from a large retailer for purchasing 30,000 units per annum subject to providing a packing with a different brand name at a cost of ₹2 per unit. However, in this case there will be no selling and distribution expenses. Also this will not in any way affect the company's existing business. What will be the break-even price for this additional offer?
3) If an expenditure of ₹3, 00,000 is made on advertising, the sales would increase from the present level of 1,00,000 units to 1,20,000 units at a price of ₹18 per unit. Will that expenditure be justified?
4) If the selling price is reduced by ₹2 per unit, there will be 100% capacity utilization. Will the reduction in selling price be justified? ICWA

Solution :

Working Note No. 1

Statement Showing Total Contribution and Contribution per Unit

Particulars		Amount [₹]
Sales: 1, 00,000 units @ ₹15 per unit		15, 00,000
Less: Variable Costs:		
Direct materials:	3, 00,000	
Direct Labour:	2, 00,000	
Variable overheads [prod.]	60,000	
	90,000	
Total Variable Cost		6, 50,000
Contribution [Sales – Total Variable Cost]		8, 50,000
Variable Cost Per Unit		6, 50,000 / 1, 00,000 = ₹6.50
Contribution Per Unit		8, 50,000 / 1, 00,000 = ₹8.50

Additional cost of improvement in packing	=	₹ 1.00
Revised variable cost per unit	=	₹ 7.50
Revised contribution per unit	=	₹ 7.50
Profit/volume ratio	=	(₹ 7.50/₹ 15)/100 = 50%

Working Note No. 2

Total Fixed Cost :

Production overheads:	₹ 3,00,000
Administration overheads:	₹ 1,50,000
S & D Overheads:	₹ 1,50,000

1) Amount of sales required to earn a target profit of 25% on sales after improving the packing:

Present variable cost per unit [Working Note No.1] = ₹6.50

Revised variable cost per unit = ₹6.50 + ₹1.00 = Rs 7.50

Let be the amount of sales to earn desired profit, the amount of sales will be computed with the help of the following formula

S = (Fixed Cost + Desired Profit) /Profit Volume Ratio

= (₹6, 00,000 + 15,00,000*25%)*/50% = ₹19,50,000.

Sales = ₹19,50,000

2) Evaluation of purchase offer by a large retailer: 30 000 units, additional packing cost of ₹ 2 per unit

Present variable cost per unit: ₹6.50

Less: S & D Overheads: ₹.90

Add: Packing expenses: ₹2.00

Revised variable cost per unit: ₹7.60

The current selling price is ₹15 per unit and after considering the revised variable cost, the contribution per unit works out ₹15 - ₹7.60 = ₹7.40. Since the fixed costs are not going to increase, there will be additional contribution of 30 000 units x ₹7.40 = ₹2, 22,000 which will the additional profit and hence the offer can be accepted. The break-even price for this offer will be ₹7.60 per unit, which is equal to the variable cost per unit.

3) Evaluation of proposal for incurring additional advertising expenses of ₹3, 00,000

Particulars		Amount [₹]
Revised Selling Price per unit		18.00
Less: variable cost [working note no.1] per unit		6.50
Contribution per unit		11.50
Total contribution : 1, 20,000 × ₹11.50		13,80,000
Less: Fixed cost : Current	₹ 6, 00,000	
Addl. Expenditure on Advertising	₹ 3, 00,000	9,00,000
Profit		4,80,000

Since the amount of profit has increased from the present ₹2, 50,000 to ₹4, 80,000, the expenditure on advertising is justified.

4) Reduction in selling price for increasing capacity utilization to 100%

Particulars	Amount ₹
New selling price per unit	13.00
Less: variable cost per unit	6.50
Contribution per unit	6.50
Total Contribution 1, 50,000 units × ₹6.50	9,75,000
Less: Fixed cost	6,00,000
Profit	3,75,000

It can be seen that the existing profit can increase by reducing the selling price up to ₹13 per unit and thus increasing the capacity utilization to 100% and hence the proposal is justified.

Problem 15

Noveena industries Ltd has received an export for its only product that would require the use of half of the factory's present capacity of 400,000 units per annum. The factory is currently operating at 60 % level to meet the demand of its domestic market.

As against current price of ₹ 6.00 per unit, the export order offers @ ₹4.50 per unit, which is less than the cost of production, the details of which are given below:

- Direct Materials ₹ 2.50 per unit.
- Direct Labour ₹ 1.00 per unit.
- Direct Expenses ₹ 0.50 per unit
- Fixed Overheads ₹ 1.00 per unit.

The condition of the export is that it has either to be accepted in full or totally rejected.

A. Accept the order and keep domestic sales unfulfilled to the excess demand for the same.

B. Increase factory capacity by installing a few balancing machinery and equipments and also by working extra time to meet the balance of the required capacity this will increase fixed overheads by ₹ 20,000 annually and the additional cost of overtime will work out to ₹ 40,000 per annum.

C. Outsource the production of additional requirement by supplying direct materials and paying charges of ₹ 1.75 per unit to a small converter, and engaging one supervision at a cost of ₹ 3,000 per month to look after quality, packing and dispatch.

D. As a Management Accountant you are required to make comparative analysis of various proposals and suggest which of the alternative proposals is the most attractive to Noveena industries Ltd. *(ICWA, Inter, June, 2006)*

Solution :

Analysis of four alternative proposals of Noveena Industries Ltd.

Proposal A: (Accept export order & domestic sale of 20,000 units) ₹

Export Sales -	2,00,000 Units @ ₹ 4.50 P.U	9, 00,000
Domestic Sales -	2,00,000 Units @ ₹ 6.00 P.U	12,00,000
Total	4,00,000 Units	21,00,000
Less : Direct Cost of sales (variable)@ ₹ 4		16,00,000
Contribution		5,00,000
Less : Fixed Cost (60 % level ie, 2,40,000 units x 1)		2,40,000
Profit		2,60,000

Proposal B:

		₹
Export Sales –	2,00,000 Units @ ₹ 4.50 P.U/	9,00,000
Domestic Sales –	2,40,000 Units @ ₹ 6.00 P.U	14,40,000
Total -	4,40,000 Units	23,40,000
Additional Cost of overtime = ₹ 17,60,000		
	₹ 40,000	
		18,00,000
Contribution		5,40,000
Less : Fixed overhead (2, 40,000 + Additional 20,000)		2,60,000
Profit		2,80,000

Proposal C

Export Sales –	2,00,000 Units @ ₹ 4.50 P.U /	9,00,000
Domestic Sales –	2,40,000 Units @ ₹ 6.00 P.U	14,40,000
	4, 40,000 Units	Total 23,40,000

Less : Direct Cost of sales (variable) 4,00,000 x 4 = ₹ 16,00,000

Direct Material Cost of 40,000 units x 2.50 = ₹ 1,00,000

Conversion charges @ 40,000 units x 1.75 = ₹ 70,000

Supervision cost 3,000 × 12 = ₹ 36,000

Total	18,06,000
Contribution	5,36,000
Less : Fixed Overheads	2,40,000
Profit	2,96,000

Proposal D : (Rejecting Export Order & remaining with domestic market)

	₹
Domestic Sales, 2,40,000 units @ ₹ 6.00 P.U	14,40,000
Less : Direct Cost of Sales (2,40,000 x 4)	9,60,000
Contribution	4,80,000
Less : Fixed Overheads	2,40,000
Profit	2,40,000

Decision on making comparative analysis of four alternatives proposals (A,B,C,D), it is revealed that for accepting export order proposal – C is most profitable and should be accepted by Noveena Industries Ltd.

Problem 16

A company currently operating at 80 % capacity has the following particulars:

	₹
Sales	32,00,000
Direct Materials	1,00,000
Direct Labour	4,00,000
Variable Overhead	2,00,000
Fixed Overheads	13,00,000

In export order has been received that would utilize half the capacity of the factory. The order cannot be split, i.e it has either to be taken in full and executed at 10 % below the normal domestic prices, or rejected totally.

The alternatives are available to management is:

(1) Reject the order and continue with the domestic sales only ; (as at present), or

(2) Accept the order, split capacity between overseas and domestic sales and turn away excess domestic demand, or

(3) Increase capacity so as to accept the export order and maintain the present domestic sales by:

(a) Buying equipment that will increase capacity by 10 %. This will result in an increase of ₹ 1,00,000 in fixed costs, and

(b) Work overtime to meet balance of required capacity. In that case labour will be paid at one and a half times the normal wage rate.

Prepare a comparative statement of profitability and suggest the best alternative.

(ICWA, Inter, Dec, 2006)

Solution :

Statement of Comparative Profitability

	I ₹	II ₹	III ₹
Sales domestic [working Note 1 (i)]	32,00,000	20,00,000	32,00,000
Sales export [working note 1(ii)]	-	18,00,000	18,00,000
Total Sales: (A)	32,00,000	38,00,000	50,00,000
Direct Materials (Working Note 2)	10,00,000	12,50,000	16,25,000
Direct Labour (Working Note 3)	4,00,000	5,00,000	7,00,000
Variable Overhead (working Note 4)	2,00,000	2,50,000	3,25,000
Total Variable Cost: (B)	16,00,000	20,00,000	26,50,000
Contribution (A- B)	16,00,000	18,00,000	23,50,000
Fixed Overheads	13,00,000	13,00,000	14,00,000
Profit	3,00,000	5,00,000	9,50,000

Suggestion : Alternative III is the best as it would give the highest profits.

Working Notes :

1. (i) Sales revenue at 100 % Capacity

$$= \text{Sales Revenue at 80 \% capacity} \times \frac{100}{80}$$

= ₹ 32, 00,000 x = ₹ 4, 00,000

(ii) Sales revenue from export order at 50 % capacity

= ₹ 20, 00,000 – 10 % of ₹ 20, 00,000

= ₹ 20, 00,000 – ₹ 2, 00,000 = ₹ 18, 00,000

2. (i) Direct Material cost at 100 % Capacity

$$= \frac{\text{Direct Material Cost at 80\% Capacity}}{80} \times 100$$

$$= ₹\ 10,00,000 \times \frac{100}{80} = ₹\ 12,50,000$$

(ii) Direct Material Cost at 130 % capacity

$$= ₹\ 10{,}00{,}000 \times \frac{130}{80} = ₹\ 16{,}25{,}000$$

3. (i) Direct Labour Cost of 100% capacity

$$= ₹\ 4{,}00{,}000 \times \frac{100}{80} = ₹\ 5{,}00{,}000$$

(ii) Direct labour cost of 130% capacity

Direct labour cost of 110% capacity at normal wage rate + direct labour cost of 20 % capacity at 1.5 times the normal wage rate.

$$= ₹\ \frac{5{,}00{,}000}{100} \times 110 + ₹\ 5{,}00{,}000 \times 20\% \times 1.5$$

$$= ₹\ 5,\ 50{,}000 + ₹\ 1,\ 50{,}000 = ₹\ 7,\ 00{,}000$$

4. (i) Variable Overhead at 100 % capacity

$$= ₹\ 2,\ 00{,}000 \times \frac{100}{80} = ₹\ 2,\ 50{,}000$$

(ii) Variable Overhead at 130 % Capacity

$$= ₹\ 2,\ 00{,}000 \times \frac{130}{80} = ₹\ 3,\ 25,\ 000$$

Problem 18

S. Ltd. manufactures and markets a single product. The following information is available.

	₹ Per Unit
Materials	8.00
Conversion costs (variable)	6.00
Dealer's margin	2.00
Selling price	20.00
Fixed cost	2,50,000
Capacity utilization : 60%	80,000 units

There is acute competition. Extra efforts are necessary to sell. Suggestions have been made for increasing sales: (i) by reducing sales price by 5 %; and (ii) by increasing dealer's margin by 25% over the existing rate. Which of the two suggestions would you recommend if the company desires to maintain the present profit? Give reasons. *(CS, Inter, June, 2005)*

Solution :

1. Present Marginal cost per unit :

	₹
Material	8.00
Conversion costs	6.00
Dealer's margin	2.00
Total	16.00

Contribution per unit = Selling price – Marginal Cost

= ₹ 20.00 – ₹ 16.00 = ₹ 4.00

Total Contribution = ₹ 4 x 80,000 = 3, 20,000

Profit = Contribution - Fixed Cost

= ₹ 3, 20,000 – ₹ 2,50,000 = ₹ 70,000

The present profit can be maintained by keeping total contribution at present level ₹ 3, 20,000.

(i) Reducing sales price by 5 %

Now sales price = (₹ 20.00 – Re. 1) = ₹ 19.00

New dealers margin = 10% of ₹ 19.00 = ₹ 1.90

Variable costs = ₹ 8 + ₹ 6 + ₹ 1.90 = ₹ 15.90

Contribution per unit = ₹ 19.00 – ₹ 15.90 = ₹ 3.10

Sales (units) required to maintain the present level of profit

$$= \frac{\text{total contribution}}{\text{Contribution per unit}} = \frac{\text{Rs. } 3{,}20{,}000}{\text{Rs. } 3.10} = 1,\ 03{,}226 \text{ units}$$

(ii) Increasing dealer's margin by 25 %

New dealer's margin = ₹ 2 +25 % = ₹ 2.50

New variable cost = ₹ 8 + ₹6 + ₹ 2.50 = 16.50

Contribution = ₹ 20 –₹ 16.50 = ₹ 3.50

Sales (units) required to maintain the present level of profit =

$$= \frac{\text{Total Contribution}}{\text{Contribution per unit}}$$

$$= \frac{3{,}20{,}000}{3.50} = 91{,}1429 \text{ units}$$

The second proposal is recommended because the contribution per unit is higher and the sales (in units) are lower. Lower sales efforts would be required in implementing the proposal.

6. Discontinuance or Diversification of Product Line

Marginal costing is useful in taking decisions regarding whether to continue the production of a product or discontinue the product. Similarly, diversification of a particular product is also decided on the basis of marginal cost data. Thus, if the profit of the product is not good then the production of that product should be discontinued. Non availability of contribution is generally used as a basis for discontinuance. of products. The introduction of a new product into the market, is also depends on the ability of the product to recover at least its variable cost. If contribution is available in excess of variable cost then it also justifies that new product is viable one. It will improve the overall profitability of business.

Problem 19

Swagath industry unit manufactures three joint products. A, B, but C has no realizable value unless it undergoes further processing after the point of separation. The cost details of C are as follows:

	Per Unit
Up to point of Separation :	₹
Marginal Cost	15
Fixed Cost	10
After point of separation :	
Marginal cost	6
Fixed cost	3
Total Cost	34

'C' can be sold at ₹ 18 per unit and no more. Would you recommend discontinuing product C?

Would your recommendation be different if A, B and C is not joint products?

(CA, Inter, May, 2004)

Solution :

As a joint product :	₹	
Revenue from further processing of product C per unit	18	
Less- Marginal Cost after point of separation	6	
Contribution	12	
Less - Fixed Cost	3	
Net Revenue	9	
(ii) Not as a joint product	₹	
Revenue from the product C after processing	18	₹ 18
Less - Marginal Costs	₹	
Upto point of separation	15	
After point of separation	6	₹ 21
Contribution (₹)		-3

Problem 20

The following are the present cost and output data of manufacture :

Product	Price	Variable Cost per unit	% of Sales
	₹	₹	
Tables	120	80	40
Chairs	60	40	35
Book Cases	80	60	25
Total fixed cost ₹ 40,000			
Last year's sales was ₹ 2,00,000			

The manufacture is considering dropping the line of book cases and replacing with Chairs. His estimates for the new scheme are as follows.

Product	Price	Variable Cost per unit	% of Sales
	₹	₹	
Tables	120	80	40
Chairs	60	40	40
Book Cases	150	100	20
Total fixed cost ₹ 40,000			
Last year's sales was ₹ 2,50,000			

(CA, Inter, Nov, 2006)

Solution :

Calculation of present profit

Product	Selling price	Variable Cost per unit	Contribution per unit (2) - (3)	P/V Ratio (4) / (2) x 100	% of Sales	Total Sales 2,00,000	Contribution (7) X (5)
1	2	3	4	5	6	7	8
	₹	₹	₹			₹	₹
Tables	120	80	40	$33\frac{1}{3}$%	40%	80,000	26,667
Chairs	60	40	20	$33\frac{1}{3}$%	35%	70,000	23,333
Book Cases	80	60	20	25%	25%	50,000	12,500
Total						2,00,000	62,500
Less: Fixed Cost							40,000
Profit							22,500

Calculation of profit for the new scheme

Product	Selling price	Variable Cost per unit	Contribution per unit (2) - (3)	P/V Ratio (4) / (2) x 100	% of Sales	Total Sales 2,00,000	Contribution (7) X (5)
1	2	3	4	5	6	7	8
	₹	₹	₹			₹	₹
Tables	120	80	40	$33\frac{1}{3}$%	40%	1,00,000	33,333
Chairs	60	40	20	$33\frac{1}{3}$%	40%	1,00,00	33,333
Book Cases	150	100	50	$33\frac{1}{3}$%	20%	50,000	16,667
Total						2,00,000	83,333
Less: Fixed Cost							40,000
Profit							43,333

From the above tables, it is evident that the change is worth undertaking as it will increase present profit of ₹ 22,500 to ₹ 43,333.

Maintaining Desired Levels of Profits

Marginal Costing techniques can be applied for profit planning and it involves the planning of future operations to achieve more profits or maintain a desired level of profits. The change in the sale price variable cost and product mix affect the profitability of a concern.

Problem 21

XYZ Ltd budgets for a production of 15000 units. The variable cost per unit is ₹12 and fixed cost per unit is ₹2 per unit. The company fixes the selling price to fetch a profit of 15% on cost. Required,

A] What is the break-even point?

B] What is the profit/volume ratio?

C] If the selling price is reduced by 5%, how does the revised selling price affects the Break-even Point and the Profit/Volume Ratio?

D] If profit increase of 10% is desired more than the budget, what should be the sales Value?

Solution :

A] Break-even Point (Units) = Fixed Cost / Contribution Per unit

= ₹2 x 1 5,0 00 units = ₹30,000 /

Selling Price per unit = Total Cost + 15% on cost

= (12+2) + (14 X15/100)

Selling Price per unit = 16.10

Contribution = Selling Price - Variable cost = ₹16.10 – ₹12.00

Contribution = ₹ 4.10

Break-even Point (Units) = ₹30,000 / ₹4.10 = 7,317 units.

B] Profit/Volume Ratio = (Contribution Per Unit/Selling Price Per Unit) × 100

= (₹4.10 /₹16.10) X 100 = 25.47%

C] Reduction in selling price by 5%: Reduced selling price = ₹16.10 – 5% of ₹16.10 = ₹15.30,

Revised contribution = ₹15.30 – ₹12.00 = ₹3.30

Break-even Point (Units) = Fixed Cost /Contribution Per Unit = ₹30,000 /₹3.30

Break-even Point (Units) =9,091 units

D] Desired profit per unit = ₹2.10 + 10% of ₹2.10 = ₹2.31 per unit

Total Desired Profit = ₹2.31 x 1 5,000 units = ₹34,650

Total Fixed Costs = ₹30,000

Desired Sales = (Fixed Cost + Profit) /P/V Ratio

= (30,000 + 34,650)/25.47%

= 64650/25.47% = ₹ 2,53,828

Alternative Methods of Production (Replacement of machine)

Problem 22

Kalyan Ltd wants to buy a new machine to replace one, which is having frequent breakdown. It received offers for two models, X and Y. Further details regarding these two models are given below

Particulars	Machine-X	Machine-Y
Installed Capacity [Units]	25,000	25,000
Fixed overheads per annum	₹ 5,00,000	₹ 2,20,000
Estimated profit at the above capacity	₹ 4,00,000	₹ 2,50,000

The product manufactured using this type of machine, X or Y, is sold at ₹90 per unit.

You are required to determine,

1. Break-even level of sales for each model.
2. The level of sales at which both the models will earn the same profit.
3. The model suitable for different levels of demand for the product.

Solution :

Calculation of variable cost and contribution :

Particulars	Amount [₹]
Installed capacity – 25,000 units	
Fixed overheads	5,00,000
Estimated profits	4,00,000
Total contribution [Fixed overheads + Estimated profits]	9,00,000
Sales value: 20000 units X ₹100	22,50,000
Variable cost [Sales – Contribution]	13,50,000
Variable cost per unit	54
Contribution per unit	36
Profit/Volume Ratio: Contribution/Sales X 100	40%

$$\text{Break-even Sales} = \text{Fixed Cost} / \text{P/V Ratio} = ₹\ \frac{5,00,000}{40\%} = ₹\ 12,50,000$$

$$\text{Break-even Sales} = \frac{12,50,000}{90} = 13,889 \text{ units}$$

Sometimes the management has to choose from among alternative methods of production like machines or workers. The same product may be produced either by employing machine X or machine Y and the management may be confronted with the problems of choosing one among them. In such cases, the technique of marginal costing is used and which gives the highest Contribution can be accepted

Calculation of Break-even Level, Variable Cost and Contribution

Particulars	Amount [₹]
Installed capacity – 25000 units	
Fixed overheads	2, 20,000
Estimated profits	2, 50,000
Total contribution [Fixed overheads + Estimated profits]	4, 70, 000
Sales value: 20000 units X ₹100	22, 50, 000
Variable cost [Sales – Contribution]	17, 80, 000
Variable cost per unit	71.20
Contribution per unit	18.80
Profit/Volume ratio: Contribution/Sales X 100	21%

Break-even Sales: Fixed Cost/Profit Volume Ratio

= ₹2, 50,000 /21% = ₹11,90,476

Break-even Units = 13, 228

2. The level of sales at which both the machines will earn the same profit for computation of the above, the following formula can be used, Level of sales at which both machines will earn the same profit = Difference in fixed cost/ Difference in variable cost

= (₹5,00,000 – ₹2, 50,000) /(₹71.20 – ₹54)

= ₹2,50,000 /₹17.2 = 14,535 units

Thus, at 14,535 units, the total costs of both the machines will be same and hence they will earn the same amount of profits.

3. Model suitable for different levels of demand of the product: If the cost structure of both the machines is observed, it can be seen that the machine Y has lower break-even point and lower fixed cost, and so this machine X will be suitable in case of lower demands. On the other hand, machine X will be more suitable in case of higher demand because of higher profit volume ratio.

Closing Down or Suspending Activities

In some situations firm temporarily suspend or close the activities of a particular product, department or factory as a whole due to trade recession. The decision to close down or suspend its activities will depend on contribution. If the products are making a contribution towards fixed costs, it is preferable not to close business or suspend its activities to minimize the losses. If the business is closed down there may be certain fixed costs which could be avoided but there will be certain expenses which will have to be incurred at the time of closing the operation like redundancy payments, necessary maintenance of plant or overhauling of plant on reopening, training of personnel, etc., such costs are associated with closing down of the business and must be taken into consideration before taking any decision.

In addition to cost consideration, there may be some non-cost consideration which may weigh in taking the decision to close down or suspend its activities or not. The following non-cost considerations are relevant in this respect:

(i) Once the business is closed down, competitors may establish their products and our business may be lost. It may be difficult to recapture the lost market again; heavy advertisement charges may have to be incurred to recapture it.

(ii) If workers are discharged it may be difficult to get experienced and skilled workers again restart to the business.

(iii) Plant may become obsolete with the closure of the business and heavy capital expenditure may have to be incurred on restart of the business.

(iv) Reputation of the firm may suffer if some activities are closed down or suspended.

(v) Temporary closing down or suspending activities may not be desirable if the relationship with the suppliers is adversely affected.

(vi) Fear of non-collection of dues from customers in case of close of business.

Problem 23

Supreme Ltd. which manufactures the component EXCEL, has achieved a turnover of ₹ 6, 00,000 for the calendar year 2002. The manager of the company has worked at a profit volume ratio of 25 % and margin of safety of 20 % but he feels due to severe competition, the selling price is to be reduced to maintain the same volume of sales for the year 2003. He does not expect any change in variable costs. He expects that due to cost reduction programme, the profit volume ratio and margin of safety will be 20 % and 30 % respectively and considerable saving in fixed cost for 2003.

Even if the company prefers to shut down its operations for 2003, it expects to incur a minimum fixed cost of ₹ 60,000 you are required to.

(i) Present the comparative statement for the years 2002 and 2003 showing under marginal costing.

(ii) What will be minimum sales required, if it decided to shut down its unit in 2003?

(C.A. Final, Nov, 2003)

Solution :

Some Basic Calculations

Sales of the year 2002	₹ 6,00,000
Profit Volume Ratio (given)	25%
Contribution on ₹ 6,00,000 turnover @ 25%	₹ 1,50,000
Variable costs : Sales - Contribution	₹ 4,50,000
Margin of Safety	20%
Margin of Safety in ₹ Sales (₹ 6, 00,000 x 20 %)	₹ 1,20,000
Break-even Sales : Turnover - Margin of Safety	
= 6,00,000 – 1,20,000	₹ 4,80,000

$$\text{Break-even Sale} = \frac{\text{Fixed Expenses}}{\text{P / V Ratio}}$$

$$= \frac{\text{Fixed Expenses}}{25\%}$$

= ₹ 4,80,000

$$\text{Fixed Expenses} = ₹\ 4,\ 80,000 \times \frac{25}{100} = ₹\ 1,\ 20,000$$

Computation of Sales, Break-even Sales and Fixed Cost for the year 2003

Let the Sales revenue for the year 2003 be X say, variable cost for the year will be ₹ 4, 50,000, same as it was last year.

Contribution = Sales - Variable Cost

= X - ₹ 4,50,000

P/V Ratio for the year = 20 % (given)

$$\text{Sales} = \frac{\text{Contribution}}{\text{P / VRatio}}$$

$$\text{Sales} = \frac{\text{X} - \text{Rs. } 4,50,000}{20\%}$$

$$\text{X} = \frac{\text{X} - \text{Rs. } 4,50,000}{20/100} = \left(\frac{20}{100}\right) \text{X} = \text{X} - ₹\ 4,50,000$$

$$= \frac{20\text{X}}{100} - \text{X} - ₹\ 4,50,000$$

$$= \frac{20\text{X} - 100\text{X}}{100} = - \text{Rs. } 4,50,000$$

$$= \frac{80\text{X}}{100} = \text{Rs. } 4,50,000$$

$$\text{X} = 4,50,000 \times \frac{100}{80} = ₹\ 5,62,500$$

Margin of Safety = 30% (given)

Therefore, break-even sales occurs at 70 % of turnover for the year 2003

$$\text{Break-even Sales} = \frac{70}{100} \times ₹\ 5,62,500 = ₹\ 3,93,750$$

$$\text{Break-even Sales} = \frac{\text{Fixed Expenses}}{\text{P / V Ratio}}$$

$$₹\ 3,93,750 = \frac{\text{Fixed Expenses}}{20\%}$$

$$\text{Fixed Expenses} = ₹\ 3,93,750 \times \frac{20}{100} = ₹\ 78,750$$

Comparative Statement of Sales and Profit under Marginal Costing

	2002 Rs.	2003 Rs.
Sales	6,00,000	5,62,500
Less: Variable Costs	4,50,000	4,50,000
Contribution	1,50,000	1,12,500
Less: Fixed Expenses	1,20,000	78,750
Profit	30,000	33,750

(i) Minimum Sales Required (if the firm decides to shut down its unit in 2003)

$$\text{Minimum Sales Required} = \frac{\text{Avoidable Fixed Cost}}{\text{P / V Ratio}}$$

$$= \frac{₹\,78{,}750 - ₹\,60{,}000}{20\%} = ₹\,93{,}750$$

Alternative Course of Action

When deciding between alternative courses of action, it shall be kept in mind that whatever course of action is adopted, certain fixed expenses will remain unaffected. The course of action which yields the greatest contribution is the most profitable to be followed by the management.

Problem 24

Veeresh Ltd. manufactures and sells only two types of products X and Y. An increase in the sale of one depresses sales of the other on a unit basis and *vice-versa*. The following data in respect of a period are presented to you.

	Per Unit	
	X	Y
	₹	₹
Sales Price (₹)	50	60
Fixed Overheads (₹ 5,10,000 allocated on 1:2 basis)	5	10
Variable Cost of Sales (₹)	30	36
Sales Commission (20 % of Sales)	10	12
Net profit (₹)	5	2

Required : (a) Work out the number of units X and Y used in the above cost data (b) Show clearly the actual operating results (c) State, with arguments whether the management should increase the sales of X or Y (d) if the units of X actual sold are increased by 20% or alternatively decreased by 10 % how would this increase or decrease affect the quantum of profit or loss?

Solution :

		X	Y
		₹	₹
(a)	Fixed Overheads (allocated on 1:2 basis)	1,70,000	3,40,000
	Fixed Overheads per unit	5	10
	No. of units used	34,000	34,000

(b) and (c)

Statement of Operating Results of Veeresh Ltd

	Units 34,000 X		Units 34,000 Y		Total
	Per Unit ₹	Total (₹ In Lakhs)	Per Unit ₹	Total (₹ In Lakhs)	(Rs in Lakhs)
Sales Price	50	17.00	60	20.40	37.40
Less: Commission	10	3.40	12	4.88	7.48
Net Sales Revenue	40	13.60	48	16.32	29.92
Less: Variable Cost of Sales	30	10.20	36	12.24	22.44
Contribution	10	3.40	12	4.08	7.48
Less: Fixed Cost		1.70		3.40	5.10
Profit		1.70		0.68	2.38

From the above it is clear that the contribution of Y is higher, so management should increase the sales of Y.

	Case - I		Case - II	
	Product X	Product Y	Product X	Product Y
Sales (Units)	40,800	27,200	30,600	37,400
Contribution Per Unit (Rs.)	10	12	10	12
Total Contribution (Rs.)	4,08,000	3,26,400	3,06,000	4,48,800

Calculation of Profit

Particulars	Case I	Case II
	₹	₹
Total Contribution of X and Y in each case	7,34,400	7,54,800
Less : Fixed Costs	5,10,000	5,10,000
Profit	2,24,400	2,44,800

Profit is more in case II, therefore decrease of sale of product X by 10 % and increasing the sale of product Y Correspondingly by 3,400 units would be recommended.

Level of Activity Planning

It is used for planning the level of activity where maximum contribution at a particular level of activity that gives maximum profitability. This will be explained with the following illustration.

Problem 25

KTR Engineering Company has received an export order for its sole product that would require the use of half of the factory's total capacity which is estimated at 6,00,000 units per anum. The factory is currently operating at 50% level to meet the demand of its domestic customers only. As against the current price of ₹12.00 per unit the export offer is for ₹ 9 per unit which is less that the total cost of production, the breakdown of which is given below.

Variable Cost	₹ 8.00 per unit
Fixed overhead	₹ 2.00 per unit
Total Cost	₹ 10.00 per unit

The condition of the export order is that it has either to be accepted in full or totally rejected. The following alternatives are available for decision making:

I] Accept the order and keep domestic sales unfulfilled to the extent of excess demand for the same.

II] Increase factory capacity by installing a few balancing machines and equipments and also by working overtime to meet the balance of the required capacity. This will increase the additional cost for overtime work will be ₹ 50,000 per annum. The domestic demand increased by 40,000 units.

III] Reject the order and remain with the domestic market only.

Prepare Statements indicating the alternatives and suggesting the proposal which would be most convenient to the company.

Solution :

	I		II		III
	Domestic	Export	Domestic	Export	Domestic
Units (in Lakhs)	3.00	3.00	3.40	3.00	3.40
	₹	₹	₹	₹	₹
	(Lakhs)	(Lakhs)	(Lakhs)	(Lakhs)	(Lakhs)
Sales (A)	36.00	27.00	40.8	27.00	40.80
Less: Variable cost	24.00	24.00	27.20	24.00	27.2
Overtime			0.50		
Total Variable Cost (B)	8.00	8.00	27.70	8.00	9.60
Contribution	12.00	03.00	13.1	3.00	13.6
	I	II	III		
Total Contribution for each Alternative	15.00	16.10	13.6		
Less: Fixed Costs	3.60	3.75	3.60		
Net profit	11.40	12.35	10.00		

From the above, it is clear that alternative II is the best as it yields the highest net profit. The profit in II alternative is more by ₹ 75,000 as compared to alternative I. As alternative II requires purchase of machinery and equipment and increase the fixed cost also so it is worth while only if the demand for domestic increase in future or the equipment and machinery purchased can gainfully be utilized in some other work also.

Capital Investment Decisions

The techniques of marginal costing help the management in taking capital investment decisions. This is important to the top management for preparing future plans this is relevant to capital budgeting in financial management.

Problem 26

Chandu Accountant now spends ₹ 1.00 per kilometre on taxi fares for his client's work. He is considered two other alternatives, the purpose of a new small car or an old bigger car. The estimated cost figures are:

Items	New Small Car ₹	Old Bigger Car ₹
Purchase Price	40,000	25,000
Sale Price, after 5 years	20,000	15,000
Repairs & Servicing (per annum)	1,200	1,300
Taxes & Insurance, per annum	1800	800
Petrol Consumption, per litre	10km	7 km
Petrol price ₹ 3.50 per litre		

He estimates that he does 10,000 km. annually. Which of the alternatives will be cheaper? If his practice expands and he has to do 19,000 km per annum, what should be the decision? At how many km per annum will the costs of the two cases break-even and why? Ignore interest and income tax.

Solution :

Comparative Cost Statement

	New Small Car ₹	Old Bigger Car ₹	Taxi ₹
Purchase Price	40,000	25,000	
Less: Sale Price (after 5 yrs)	20,000	15,000	
Depreciation for 5 years	20,000	10,000	
Depreciation for one years	4,000	2,000	
Repair and Servicing	1,200	1,300	
Taxes & Insurance	1,800	800	
Fixed Cost, Per annum	7,000	4,100	
Variable Cost per annum:			
(i) Petrol for 10,000 km.			
New Small Car @ ₹ 3.50 for 10 km	3,500	5,000	
Old Big Car @ ₹ 3.50 for 7 km			
(ii) Petrol for 19,000 km	6,650	9,500	
Total Cost (Fixed + Variable)	10,500	9,100	10,000
for 10,000 km (i)			(10,000 x 1)
for 19,000 km (ii)	13,650	13,600	19,000
			(19,000 x 1)

Conclusion : For present practice requiring 10,000 km and practice expands to 19,000 km the old bigger car is the cheapest as the annual cost is ₹ 9,100 and ₹ 13,600 respectively which is the lowest of the three alternatives.

Calculation of km at which the cost of the two cars will break-even:

Variable cost of new small car, for 10,000 km ₹ 3,500

Variable cost of new small car, per km = $\frac{3{,}500}{1000}$ = ₹ 0.35

Variable cost of old bigger car, for 10,000 km = ₹ 5,000

Variable cost of bigger car, per km = $\frac{5{,}000}{1000}$ = ₹ 0.50

Difference in the variable cost of two cars = 0.50 – 0.35 = ₹ 0.15

Difference in the fixed cost of two cars = ₹ 7000 – 4100 = 2900

Hence, Break-even Point = $\frac{\text{Differential in fixed cost}}{\text{Difference in variable cost per km}} = \frac{2900}{15} \times 100 = 19{,}333$ km

Proof.

At 19,333 km the total cost of two cars is as :

		New Car ₹		Old Car ₹
Fixed Cost		7,000		4100
Variable Cost	(19333 x 0.35)	766.50	(19333x0.50)	9666.50
Total cost		13,766.50		13766.50

PRACTICE PROBLEMS

Problem 1

Aruna Industries Ltd manufactures and sales five different products using one common raw material which is available according to requirements at ₹ 8 per kg. but the skilled labour required for production is in short supply and is currently limited to 35,000 hours per month at ₹ 15 per hour. Variable production overhead is ₹ 5 per labour hour and fixed production cost amounts to ₹ 1,00,000 per month. Variable selling and distribution overhead is 10% of sales value while fixed selling distribution and administration cost is ₹ 80,000 per month, further details regarding production and sales of these products are as follows:

Product	Current Demand	Selling price per unit (₹)	Raw Materials required per unit (kg)	Direct Labour hours require per unit (kg)
A	6,000	40	1.0	1.0
B	4,000	60	1.5	1.4
C	5,000	80	2.0	1.8
D	4,800	90	2.5	2.0
E	4,500	100	3.0	2.4

Required (a) Optimum product mix would you recommend. (b) Profit earned as per mix in (a). (c) The company has just received an urgent export order for 5,000 units for E to be supplied within a month. The company proposes to accept the order and if confirmed by the customer, thinks of executing the same by engaging labour on over time, paying double the normal rate. An extra amount of ₹ 10,000 has to be incurred on production overhead. If the company wants 10 % profit on sales, what price shall it quote?

Problem 2

A Ltd, operating at 75 % level of activity produces and sells two products X and Y. the cost sheets of these two products are as under :

	Product X	Product Y
Units Produced and Sold	3,000	2,000
	Per unit	Per unit
	₹	₹
Direct Material	10	20
Direct Wages	20	20
Factory Overheads (40 % Fixed)	25	15
Administration and selling overheads(60 %) fixed	40	25
Total cost per unit	95	80
Selling price per unit	115	95

Factory Overheads are absorbed on the basis of machine hour which is the limiting factor. The machine hour rate is ₹ 10 per hour.

The company receives an offer from japan for the purchase of Product X at a price of ₹ 87.50 Per unit. Alternatively the company has another offer from Bangkok for the purchase O product Y at a price of Rs 77.50 per unit. In both the cases, a special packing charge of ₹ 2.50 per unit has to be borne by the company. The company can accept either of the two export orders by utilizing the balance of 25% of its capacity.

Advice the company with detailed working as to which proposals should be accepted and prepares the statement showing the overall profitability of the company after incorporating the suggested by you. *(ICWA, Inter, June, 2003)*

3. PH Ltd. manufactured and sold two products during 1981 as per particulars given below.

	Product A	Product B
Quantity (Units)	6,00,000	3,00,000
	Rs/ Unit	Rs/ Unit
Selling price	6.00	10.00
Direct Materials	1.00	2.00
Direct Wages	1.20	2.60
Other Overheads (50% variable)	1.00	0.60

Variable factory overheads are absorbed as a percentage of direct wages. The summarized statement of profitability for 1981 is as under.

	In lakhs
Sales	66.00
Direct Materials	12.00

Direct Wages	15.00
Factory Overheads	13.50
Other Overheads (50 % fixed)	7.80

For the year 1982, due to fall in demand, the production and sales of product A will be reduced by 20% and of product B by 40%. It is therefore decided to introduce a new product C, the cost particulars of which are as under.

Production and Sales : 2,00,000 units

	Rs, Per Unit
Selling Price	7.00
Direct Materials	1.40
Direct Wages	2.40

Other variable overheads: Same as in product A

The fixed overheads will remain the same and the variable overheads will continue to be incurred at the same rate as in 1981. You are required to:

(i) Prepare a product wise and overall budget for 1982 and

(ii) State what conclusion can be drawn from the budget for 1982 by using Marginal Costing Technique. *[ICWA (Final), December 19814]*

Ans : Contribution from A = Rs 12,96,000 ; B = Rs 6,84,000 and from C = Rs 3,00,000; profit = Rs 12,90,000 (if diversified) and Rs 9,90,000

4. The Himalayan House Ltd. Is a large retailer in mountaineering equipment. The company's profit and Loss Account for the year ended 31st March 1983 is given below.

Sales	₹ 24,00,000	
Less: Cost of goods Sold	15,00,000	
Gross margin	9,00,000	
Less : Operating expenses :		
Selling expenses	₹ 3,00,000	
Administration expenses	1,50,000	4,50,000
		4,50,000

The selling expenses are 90% variable and the administrative expenses are 20% variable. You are required to rewrite the profit and loss account in the "Contribution" format and also to calculate the break even sales. *[ICWA (Inter), June 1983]*

5. Merry Manufacturer Ltd has supplied you the following information in respect of one of its products.

Total Fixed Costs	₹ 18,000
Total Variable Costs	₹ 30,000
Total Sales	₹ 60,000
Sales Volume (units)	20,000

Find out (a) contribution per unit (b) break even point (c) margin of safety (d) profit and (e) volume of sales to earn a profit of ₹ 24,000. *[ICWA (Inter)]*

6. Mikado Engineering Company has received and export order for its sole product that would require the use of half of the factory's total capacity which is estimated at 4, 00,000 units per annum. The factory is currently operating at 60% level to meet the demand of its domestic customers only. As against the current price of ₹ 6 per unit, the export offer is ₹ 4.5 per unit which is less that the total cost of current production, the break-down of which is given below.

Variable cost	₹ 4 per unit.
Fixed Overhead	₹ 1 per unit.
Total Cost	₹ 5 per unit.

The condition of the export order is that is has either to be accepted in full or totally rejected. The following alternatives are available for decision making.

a. Accept the order and keep domestic sales unfulfilled to the extent of excess demand for the same.

b. Increase factory capacity by installing a few balancing machines and equipment and also by making overtime to meet the balance of the required capacity. This will increase fixed overhead by ₹ 15,000 annually and the additional cost for overtime work will be ₹ 40,000 per annum.

c. Reject the order and remain with the domestic market only.

Prepare statements indicating the alternatives and suggesting the proposal which would be most convenient to the company. *[ICWA (Final), June 1981]*

7. As a prelude to finalizing the plans for the coming year, the executives though it advisable to have a look at the product wise performance during the current year just completed. The following information is furnished.

Particulars	Product A (₹)	Product B (₹)	Product C (₹)
Unit selling price	80	60	36
Direct Material	28	24	16
Direct labour	20	12	12
Factory Overhead : Variable	8	6	4
Fixed	8	6	1.28
Cost Production	64	48	33.28
Selling, Distribution and general administration expensess			
Variable	4	2	2
Fixed	4	6	1.52
Unit Cost (loss)	72	56	36.80
	8	4	0.80
Sales Volume (units)	10,000	15,000	15,000
	80,000	60,000	12,000

For the coming period, the selling prices and the costs of the three products are expected to remain unchanged. There will be an increase in sales of product 'A' by 1,000 units and the increase of sales of product 'C' is expected to be 8,000 units. The sales of product 'B' will remain unchanged. Sufficient additional capacity exists to enable the increased demand to be met without incurring additional fixed costs. Some among the executives contend that it will be unwise to go for additional Production and sale of product C, since it is already losing at ₹ 0.80 per unit. The suggestion is that product 'C' should be eliminated altogether. Do you agree? Substantiate with necessary analysis and determine the product - wise and overall profits for the coming year. *[ICWA (Final), December 1982]*

8. The present output details of a manufacturing department are as follows.

Average output per week: 48,000 units

Saleable value of output ₹ 60,000

Contribution made by output towards fixed expenses and profit ₹ 24,000.

The directors plan to introduce more mechanization into the department at a capital cost of ₹ 16,000. The effect of this will be reduce the number of employees from the existing strength of 160 to 120. but to increase the output per individual employee by 60 %. To provide the necessary incentive to achieve the increased output, the directors intend to offer a 1% increase in the existing piece work price of ₹ 0.10 per article for every 2% increase in average individual output achieved. To sell the increased output, it will be necessary to decrease the selling price by 4% Calculate the extra weekly contribution resulting from the proposed change and evaluate the worth of the proposal.

9. Mega Corporation manufactures and sells three products to the automobile industry. All the products must pass through a machining process the capacity of which is limited to 20,000 hour per annum both by equipment design and government regulation. The following additional information is available.

Particulars	Product A	Product B	Product C
Selling Price per unit (Rs)	1,900	2,400	4,000
Variable Cost per unit (Rs)	700	1,200	2,800
Machining requirement (hours per unit)	3	2	1
Maximum Possible sales (units)	10,000	2,000	1,000

Required: A statement showing the best possible production mix which would provide the maximum profit for Mega Corporation together with supporting workings.

[CS (Final), June 1984]

10. A company manufactures three products A, B, and C. There are no common processes and the sale of one product does not affect prices or volume of sales of any other. The company's budgeted profit/loss for 1976 has been abstracted thus:

Particulars	Total (₹)	A (₹)	B (₹)	C (₹)
Sales	3,00,000	45,000	2,25,000	30,000
Production Cost, Variable	1,80,000	24,000	1,44,000	12,000
Production Cost, Fixed	60,000	3,000	48,000	9,000
Factory Cost	2,40,000	27,000	1,92,000	21,000
Selling and Administration Costs:				
Variable	24,000	8,100	8,100	7,800
Fixed	6,000	2,100	1,800	2,100
Total Cost	2,70,000	37,200	2,01,900	30,900
Profit	30,000	7,800	23,100	-900

On the basis of the above, the Board had almost decided to eliminate product "c" on which a loss was budgeted. Meanwhile they have sought your opinion. As the company's cost accountant, what would you advicse? Give reasons for your answer.

[ICWA (Inter), June 1975]

11. SG Ltd produces four products in its factory. The volume of production and sales achieved is considerably lower than normal and so there has been substantial under recovery of overheads. The Sales and cost particulars are as under.

Particulars	Product (Rs Lakhs)				
	A	B	C	D	Total
Sales	160	200	80	40	480
Costs: Direct Materials	24	32	16	3	75
Direct Wages	40	48	32	8	128
Factory Overheads	48	64	40	8	160
Selling and Administration expenses (15% of Sales)	24	30	12	6	72
Total	296	174	100	25	435
Profit	24	26	20	15	45
Under recovery of overheads					24
Profit before tax					21

40% of factory overheads is variable at normal volume and the selling and administration overheads are variable to the extend of 5% of sales 20% of sales of product C is done in conjunction with product A in as much as the discontinuance of product C can be reduced to 20% of the present level to maintain the sales of product A. in view of the loss reported for product C, the management has for its consideration three proposal, *viz.*

a. Discontinue product C. in that event the company can save a sum of Rs 8 Lakhs per annum in fixed expenses.

b. Maintain the sales of product C to the extent of 20% of the present sales as service to product A. in that event, the reduction of fixed expenses will be Rs 3 lakhs per annum.

c. Discontinue product C totally and increase the sales of product D for which demand is available to the extent of Rs 40 lakhs. This can be done without any change in fixed expense.

Draft a report to the management bringing out the financial implications of the aforesaid three proposals as compared with the present annual operating results generating a profit before tax of Rs 21 lakhs. Suggest a course of action to be followed by the management.

[ICWA (Final), June 1981]

12. An industrial concern which had no costing system appointed a cost accountant. After installing a system of collection of cost data, the cost accountant observed that out of the three products which are produced independent of each other, loss is being incurred in product B. He immediately decides to advice management to discontinue manufacture of this product supported by the following tabulation.

Particulars	Products		
	A	B	C
Sales	100000	65000	490000
Variable manufacturing cost	52000	26000	140000
Fixed manufacturing overheads (apportioned)	6500	19000	105000
Variable selling and administration costs	18000	1700	18000
Fixed selling and administration costs	4600	4600	4000
Total Cost	81100	66000	267000
Net profits	18900		223000
Net Loss		1600	

Do you agree with the cost accountants conclusions? Argue your own views on the basis of data. *[ICWA (Inter), June 1977]*

13. A division of your company has now been operating at an uneconomic level of trading for some time and consideration is being given to a temporary shut down until the current trade recession has passed. On the basis of the following information, prepare a statement for the Board of Directors in such a way as to indicate whether or not it is desirable to close the division on a temporary basis. You should also write a brief report giving reasons for your recommendations using any other assumed information you may desire to use.

Production Capacity Costs	50% ₹	70% ₹	90% ₹	100% ₹
Direct Labour	70,000	98,000	1,26,000	1,40,000
Direct Material	50,000	70,000	90,000	1,00,000
Production Overheads	40,000	48,000	56,000	60,000
Administration and Selling Overheads	30,000	34,000	38,000	40,000
	1,90,000	2,50,000	3,10,000	3,40,000

Present revenue (for 1983) from sales at 60% capacity (at reduced prices) = ₹ 1, 75,000 per annum. If the directors close the division for, say, a year (1984), it is estimated that,

a. Closing down costs would amount to ₹ 20,000

b. Present fixed costs would be reduced by ₹ 18,000 per annum,

c. Plant maintenance during shut down would be ₹ 2,000 per annum, and

d. On re-opening, that cost of overhauling plant, training and engagement of new personnel would be ₹ 10,000.

It is estimated that in about 1985, it may be possible to work at 80% capacity with revenue from sales amounting to ₹ 3, 10,000. Fixed content of the overhead element in production and administration/selling/distribution overheads is assumed to be same at all levels of activity. *[ICWA (Final), June 1983]*

14. All Play Ltd are specialists in the manufacture of dolls for children. They manufacture and market four types of dolls patented under the names Dolly, Molly, Jolly, Polly and a doll-dress sewing kit. They require your assistance as a cost accountant for determining the appropriate sales and product mix of their products for the coming year. From the production standards established, market forecasts and pricing policies, you get the following data.

Doll's Name	Estimated Demand for next Year	Standard Material Cost per unit (₹)	Standard Labour Cost Per Unit	Established Net Price Per Unit
Dolly	50,000	1.40	0.80	5.20
Molly	42,000	0.70	0.50	2.40
Jolly	35,000	2.70	1.40	8.50
Polly	40,000	1.00	1.00	4.00
Sewing Kit	3,25,000	0.60	0.40	3.00

(i) To promote sales of the sewing kit, there is a 15% discount offered in the established price of a kit, purchased at the same time along with a doll and it is expected that all customers will avail this benefit.

(ii) The labour rate of Rs 2 per hour is expected to continue without change in the next year. The plant has an effective capacity of 1,30,000 labour hours on a single shift basis. Present equipment can produce all of the products. Overtime works is paid at double the normal rate.

(iii) Next year's fixed cost is estimated as Rs 30,000 in the factory, Rs 20,000 in administration and Rs 50,250 in selling and distribution.

(iv) Variable costs will be equivalent to 50% of standard direct labour cost.

(v) The company has a very small inventory of its products that can be ignored.

(a) You are required to draw a conservative estimate for next year of the total contribution that would be made by each product line and the net income that would be earned by the company.

(b) The company is at present having some industrial relation problems and if this continues in the next year. It would not then be possible to arrange for overtime work. Anticipating that eventuality, you are required to suggest a product mix that would absolutely minimize the drop in the income already envisaged. With that product mix, work out product-wise contribution and the new income that would be earned as a result.

[ICWA (Final), December 1982]

15. The standard unit cost of the product manufactured by Now where manufacturing company is as follows.

Direct Material	₹ 11.20
Direct Labour	₹ 3.00
Variable factory overheads	0.85
Total direct cost	15.05

Fixed overheads is budgeted at ₹ 5,500 for a normal sales volume of 8,000 units. Factory production capacity is 10,000 units. Administration and sales overheads are budgeted at ₹ 2,500. Average capital employed is equal to 25% of sales for current assets and ₹ 43,000 for fixed assets. It is anticipated.

(a) Direct material price will increase by ₹ 0.80 per unit.

(b) An unfavorable labour variance of approximately 5% has been the experience of the past years.

Required: Unit sales price to yield return of 15% on capital employed

[ICWA (Final), June 1978], (ICWA, Inter, june,1999)

❖ ❖ ❖

Chapter - 5

Strategic Planning and Control

Introduction

Strategic planning is the process by which an organization envisions its future and develops the necessary procedures and operations to achieve those future goals. The basic steps of the strategic planning process includes information gathering and analysis, identification of critical issues facing the organization, development of a strategic vision, mission review/revision and the development of strategic goals and strategies. In order to resolve the direction of the organization, it is necessary to understand its current position and the possible avenues through which it can pursue a particular course of action.

Every organization occasionally has to make some important decisions that affect the entire destiny of the organization for years into the future. These decisions are designed to address the really biggest and most important issues facing an organization issues so significant we might call them 'strategic elephants'. So the strategic planning must have something about big decisions.

Such decisions are not simply about small adjustments to activity levels but the kind of decisions that may lead to a substantially different organizational structure. It changes the relationships among key stakeholders, competitive positions and strategic partners of the organization. The outside world forces may change the major shifts in the market, big changes in government policy and radical moves by competing organizations. Technological change driving new methods of carrying out its work or weakening of its financial structure or a change in the senior management of the organization requiring a large reorganization it is the example of internal forces. Organizations have always faced such pressures to make huge decisions. Such a process is variously and sometimes confusingly described as: corporate planning, strategic planning, business planning, and variations. Other labels make the subject more industry specific such as military strategic planning, hospital strategic planning and in some jurisdictions what others know as urban and regional planning is called strategic planning. It will focus primarily on 'strategic planning' by this, we have in mind any plan which looks forward several years and which is concerned with massive factors only. The focus of the decisions in the plan are the organization as a whole in its environment.

Strategic Planning is Different from Business Planning : The definition of strategic planning must be based on understanding that a strategic plan differs from a Business Plan in three ways;

- It looks much further ahead;
- It consists largely of words with just a few figures to indicate the scale of the planners' intentions. A Business Plan on the other hand consists largely of figures

but these are often unreliable away from a few months, managers are unwilling to look ahead as far as they may need to. Strategic plans can look further ahead because so few figures are employed, and also;

- What few figures they do contain are tested by risk analysis techniques.

Definition of Strategic Planning : A systematic documented process for deciding what is the handful of key decisions that an organization viewed as a corporate whole. We must get right in order to thrive over the next few years. The process results in the production of a corporate strategic plan.

Strategic Plan : A set of statements describing the purpose and ethical conduct for an organization together with the specific strategies designed to achieve the targets set for each of these.

Components of Strategic Planning

The key components of 'strategic planning' include an understanding of the firm's vision, mission, values and strategies. The vision and mission are often captured in a Vision Statement and Mission Statement.

- **Vision :** Outlines what the organization wants to be or how it wants the world in which it operates best way. It is a long-term view and concentrates on the future. It can be emotive and is a source of inspiration. For example, a charity working with the poor might have a vision statement which reads "A World without Poverty."
- **Mission :** The fundamental purpose of an organization concisely describing why it exists and what it does to achieve its vision. For example, the charity above might have a mission statement as "providing jobs for the homeless and unemployed".
- **Values :** Beliefs that are shared among the stakeholders of an organization. Values drive an organization's culture and priorities and provide a framework in which decisions are made. For example, "Knowledge and skills are the keys to success" or "give man bread and feed him for a day, but teach him to farm and feed him for life". These example values may set the priorities of self-sufficiency over shelter.
- **Strategy :** Strategy means the art of the General. A combination of the goals for which the firm is determined and the policies by which it is seeking to get there. A strategy is sometimes called a roadmap which is the path chosen to work towards the end vision. The most important part of implementing the strategy is ensuring the company is going in the right direction which is towards the end vision.

The Strategic Planning Process

Competitive business environment requires budget-oriented planning methods for a large corporation to survive and prosper. The firm must engage in strategic planning it clearly defines objectives and assesses both the internal and external situation to formulate strategy, implement the strategy, evaluate the progress and make adjustments as necessary to stay on track.

A simplified view of the strategic planning process is shown by the following diagram:

The Strategic Planning Process

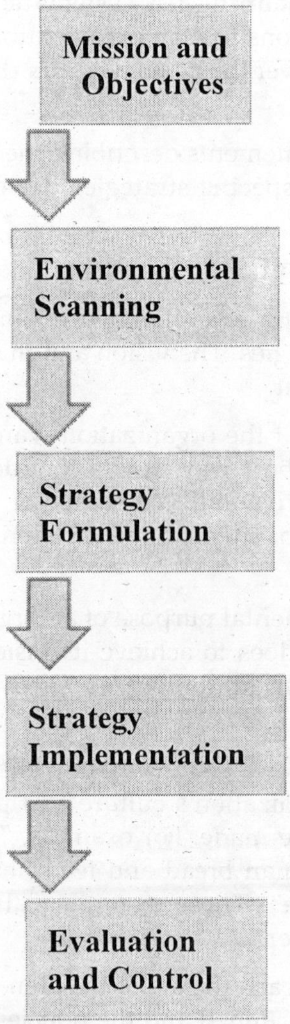

Mission and Objectives : The mission statement describes the company's business vision, including the unchanging values and purpose of the firm and forward-looking creative thinker goals that guide the search of future opportunities.

Guided by the business vision, the firm's leaders can define quantifiable financial and strategic objectives. Financial objectives involve measures such as sales targets and earnings growth. Strategic objectives are related to the firm's business position and may include market share and reputation.

Environmental Scaning : The environmental scaning includes the following components:

- Internal analysis of the firm
- Analysis of the firm's industry
- External micro-environment

The internal analysis can identify the firm's strengths and weaknesses and the external analysis reveals opportunities and threats. A profile of the strengths, weaknesses, opportunities and threats is generated by means of a SWOT analysis.

An industry analysis can be performed using a framework developed by Michael Porter known as Porter's five forces. This framework evaluates entry barriers, suppliers, customers, substitute products, and industry rivalry.

Strategy Formulation : Given the information from the environmental scaning, the firm should match its strengths to the opportunities that it has identified, while addressing its weaknesses and external threats. To attain profitability the firm seeks to develop a competitive advantage over its rivals. A competitive advantage can be based on cost or differentiation.

Strategy Implementation: The selected strategy is implemented by means of programs, budgets and procedures. Implementation involves organization of the firm's resources and motivation of the staff to achieve objectives.

The way in which the strategy is implemented can have a significant impact on whether it will be successful. In a large company, those who implement the strategy will likely be different people from those who formulated it. For this reason, care must be taken to communicate the strategy and the reasoning behind it. Otherwise the implementation might not succeed if the strategy is misunderstood and lower-level managers resist its implementation because they do not understand why the particular strategy was selected.

Evaluation and Control : The implementation of the strategy must be monitored and adjustments made as needed.

Evaluation and Control consists of the following steps:

1. Define parameters to be measured
2. Define target values for those parameters
3. Perform measurements
4. Compare measured results to the pre-defined standard
5. Make necessary changes

Control

Controlling is one of the managerial functions like planning, organizing, staffing and directing. It is an important function because it helps to check the errors and to take the corrective action, so that deviation from standards are minimized and stated goals of the organization are achieved in a desired manner.

According to modern concepts, control is a foreseeing action whereas, earlier concept of control was used only when errors were detected. Control in management means setting standards, measuring actual performance and taking corrective action. Thus, control comprises these three main activities.

Management Controls

Management controls are used daily by managers and employees to accomplish the identified objectives of an organization. Simply put, management controls are the operational methods that enable work to proceed as expected. Most controls can be classified as preventive or detective. Preventive controls are designed to discourage errors or irregularities. For example:

- A manager's review of purchases prior to approval prevents inappropriate expenditures of office funds.
- A computer program which asks for a password prevents unauthorized access to information.

Detective controls are designed to identify an error or irregularity after it has occurred. Examples include the following:

- An exception report that detects and lists incorrect or incomplete transactions.
- A manager's review of long distance telephone charges will detect improper or personal calls that should not have been charged to the account.

Often, management controls are documented in terms of policies and procedures. However, sometimes as an organization undergoes structural and functional changes, people within the organization create or adopt ways of ensuring that work proceeds normally. Many times, these methods (controls) are not documented. The purpose of a Management Control Review (MCR) is to evaluate the entire system or management controls to help your unit operate more efficiently and effectively, and to provide a reasonable level of assurance that the process and products for which you are responsible are adequately protected.

A MCR provides a variety of benefits which promote sound management, including the following:

- Ensuring that administrative, financial, and programmatic risks have been adequately addressed.
- Eliminating excessive controls that may have accumulated over the years, allowing for more efficient operations.
- Increased confidence that responsibilities are being carried out according to plan.

Review Process : NOAA (National Oceanic and Atmospheric Administration) describes that the following management control review process be utilized in order to conduct a MCR that adheres to the general accounting office standards for management controls. This link provides a listing of the tasks and estimated accomplishment times. These tasks are discussed in detail in the following section.

Analysis of the General Control Environment : The general control environment is the context in which selected processes occur. It is difficult to understand the importance of context when interpreting a spoken statement. The same is true when it comes to processes. Processes should not be analyzed apart from the environment in which they take place. For example, poor training or a lack of adequate delegation of authority may negate the effectiveness of even the best control system. Therefore, a MCR begins with an analysis of the general control environment.

Description of Functional Area : A functional statement relating the unit's organizational responsibilities should be provided. This document may be already in existence in the NOAA Organizational Handbook. If a functional statement does not already exist then one must be created for MCR purposes.

GAO General Management Control Standards : The general control environment should be assessed by determining the degree to which General Accounting Office (GAO) standards for management controls are incorporated into the strategies, plans, guidance and procedures that govern programs and operations. The following general standards must be addressed:

1. **Compliance with Law :** Do all program operations, obligations and costs comply with applicable law and regulation? Are resources efficiently and effectively allocated for duly authorized purposes?
2. **Reasonable Assurance and Safeguards :** Do management controls provide reasonable assurance that assets are safeguarded against waste, loss and misappropriation? Are management controls logical, applicable, reasonably complete, effective and efficient in accomplishing management objectives?
3. **Integrity, Competence and Attitude :** Is personal integrity encouraged among managers and employees? Are all personnel obligated to support agency ethics programs? What efforts are made to maintain a level of competence that allows employees to accomplish their assigned duties? Is there effective communication within and between offices?

GAO Specific Management Control Standards : In addition to the general standards, the following specific control standards must be addressed:

1. **Delegation of Authority and Organization :** The management ensured that appropriate authority, responsibility and accountability are defined and delegated to accomplish the mission of the organization. Organizational structure in place to effectively carry out program responsibilities, controls and related decision making authority in the hands of line managers and staff.
2. **Separation of Duties and Supervision :** The key duties and responsibilities in authorizing, processing, recording and reviewing official agency transactions separated among individuals. The managerial oversight to ensure that individuals do not exceed or abuse their assigned authorities.
3. **Access To and Accountability for Resources :** What measures are in place to limit access to resources and records to authorized individuals? How is accountability for the custody and use of resources assigned and maintained?

4. **Recording and Documentation :** In this transactions are promptly recorded, properly classified and accounted for in order to prepare timely and reliable reports. The documentation for transactions, management controls and other significant events must be clear and readily available for examination.
5. **Resolution of Audit Findings and Other Deficiencies :** Management's response to known deficiencies, reported audit and other findings and recommendations. It is useful for corrective actions completed within established time frames.

Determination of Risks : Control systems are developed in response to risks that exist within the processes being reviewed. All administrative and program areas have some degree of risk. Risks are negative events or situations that would occur if all or a part of the selected process was not carried out as planned. Determining the risks that exist within the processes being reviewed is one of the most important phases of the MCR.

Operating Control

Operational control systems are designed to ensure that day - to - day actions are consistent with established plans and objectives. It focuses on events in a recent period. Operational control systems are derived from the requirements of the management control system. Corrective action is taken where performance does not meet standards. This action may involve training, motivation, leadership, discipline or termination.

Distinctions between strategy formulation and management control

Management control is the set of measurement, analysis and action decisions required for the timely management of the continuing operation of a process.

Characteristics	Strategy Formulation	Control Management
System design	It is unsystematic, strategic decision may be made at any time.	It is predetermined procedures and periodic.
Number of persons involved	Strategy formulated through few people.	Strategy formulated through many people.
Information	Tailored-made two faced problems, more external and predictive and less accurate results.	Integrated, more internal and historical and more accurate results.
Time horizon	Tend to long-term duration.	Tend to short-term duration.
Communication of information	Communication of information is easy.	Communication of information is difficult.
Involved people	It involves top management and staffs.	It involves top management and line managers.
Mental activity	It requires creative and analytical.	It requires administrative and persuasive.

End products	The final results are goals and strategies.	The final result is strategy implementation.
Discipline	Strategy formulation discipline is economics.	Strategy formulation discipline is social psychology.

Distinctions between control management and task control

Characteristics	Control Management	Task Control
Mental activity	It requires administrative and convincing.	It requires follow direction or none.
Discipline	Control management discipline is social psychology.	Task control disciplines are economics and physics.
Time horizon	It tends to time horizon like weekly, monthly and annually.	It tends to time horizon like daily.
Type of cost	The type of cost is discretionary costs.	The type of cost is engineered costs.

Practical Questions :

1. How is the strategic planning different from business planning?
2. Define strategic planning? Explain the components of strategic planning?
3. Explain GAO general and specific management control standards?
4. Explain management control and operating control?
5. What are the differences between strategy formulation and management control?
6. What are the differences between control management and task control?
7. Explain the strategic planning process?
8. Explain the following terms:
   a) Vision
   b) Mission
   c) Values
   d) Strategy

❖ ❖ ❖

Chapter - 6

Budgeting and Budgetary Control

Introduction

A budget is a plan for the future. The budgets are planning tools and they are generally prepared prior to the current period. However, the relationship of the budget to actual results provides valuable information about performance. Hence, budgets are both planning tools and performance evaluation tools. For a manufacturing company, it measures the output of units of each product produced and production cost. The retailer will prepare sales budget to know each products and area wise sales. The act of planning as to how the amount should be spent is known as budgeting. The business plan sets out how the managers should achieve the organization goals. The first important task in front of the management is to have clearly defined objectives. Objectives are short-term as well as long-term and they should be clearly defined. It is necessary to prepare a comprehensive plan to transform these objectives into reality and planning without controlling will not be effective. Hence, there is a need of effective control system helps an organization to work systematically towards the goals. Controlling helps to review the progress made and to monitor whether the work is progressing as per the plan or not. Budgeting is one such technique that helps in planning as well as controlling. It is a technique of cost accounting with the twin objectives of facilitating planning and controlling.

Definition

Budget has been defined by CIMA U.K. as 'A financial and quantitative statement prepared prior to a defined period of time of the policy to be pursued during that period for the purpose of achieving a given objective.' The following are the features of budget.

(1) A budget is a statement it is prepared prior to a defined period of time. This means that budget is always prepared for future period and not for the past. For example, a budget for the year 2012-13 regarding the sales will be prepared in the year 2011-12. Another important point is that the time for which it is prepared is certain. Thus, a budget may be prepared for next 5years/2years/1year/6 months/1 month or even for a week, but the point is that the time frame for which it is prepared is certain. It cannot be prepared for indefinite period of time.

(2) Budget is prepared either in quantitative details or monetary details or both. This means that budget will show the planning in terms of rupees or in quantity or both. For example, a production budget will show the production target in number of units and when the target units are multiplied by the anticipated production cost, it will be a production cost budget that is expressed in terms of money. Similarly purchase budget is prepared in quantity to show the anticipated

purchases in the next year and when the quantity is multiplied by the expected price per unit, it will become a purchase cost budget that is expressed in monetary terms. Some budgets are prepared only in monetary terms, for example, cash budget, capital expenditure budget, etc.

(3) Every organization has well defined objectives, which are to be achieved in a particular span of time. It is of vital importance that there should be systematic efforts to bring them into reality. As a part of these efforts, it is necessary to formulate a policy and it is reflected in the budget. Thus, if a firm has to launch a massive drive for recruitment of people, this policy will be reflected in the manpower planning budget as well as other relevant budgets. Thus, the policy to be pursued in future for the purpose of achieving well-defined objectives is reflected in the budget.

Budgetary control is actually a means of control in which the actual results are compared with the budgeted results so that appropriate action may be taken with regard to any deviations between the two. Budgetary control has the following stages.

Budget, Budgeting and Budgetary Control

A budget is a blue print of a plan expressed in quantitative terms. Budgeting is technique for formulating budgets. Budgetary control process is the principles, procedures and practices of achieving given objectives through budgets.

Rowland and William have differentiated the three terms as: "Budgets are the individual objectives of a department, etc., whereas budgeting may be said to be the act of building budgets. Budgetary control embraces all and in addition includes the science of planning the budgets to affect an overall management tool for the business planning and control.

Steps in Budgetary Control

Developing Budgets : The first stage in budgetary control is developing various budgets. It will be necessary to identify the budget centers in the organization and budgets will have to be develops for each one of them. Thus, budgets are developed for functions like purchase, sale, production, manpower planning, cash, capital expenditure, machine hours and labour hours. The factors affecting the planning should be studied with awareness and budgets should be developed after a thorough learns of the factors.

Recording Actual Performance : There should be a proper system of recording the actual performance achieved. This facilitates the comparison between the budget and the actual. An efficient accounting and cost accounting system help to record the actual performance effectively.

Comparison of Budgeted and Actual Performances : One of the important aspects of budgetary control is the comparison between the budgeted and the actual performances. The objective of such comparison is to find out the variation between the two and provide the base for taking remedial action.

Decision Making : Taking appropriate corrective action on the basis of the comparison between the budgeted and actual results is the essence of budgeting. A budget is always prepared for future and hence, there may be a variation between the budgeted and actual results. There is a need for investigation of the same and take appropriate action so that the deviations will not repeat in the future. Responsibilities can be fixed on proper persons so that they can be held responsible for any such deviations.

Objectives of Budgeting

Any business organizations success depends on its planning and budgeting. The budgeting system has the following objectives, which are of more importance in the overall efficiency and effectiveness of the business organization. The following three are the important objectives:

Control : Planning is looking ahead while controlling is looking back. Preparation of budgets involves detailed planning about various activities like purchase, sales, production and other functions like marketing, sales promotion, manpower planning. But planning alone is not sufficient. There should be a proper system of controlling which will ensure that the work is progressing as per the plan. Budgets provide the basis for such controlling in the sense that the actual performance can be compared with the budgeted performance. Any deviation between the two can be found out and analyzed to ascertain the reasons behind the deviation so that necessary corrective action can be taken to rectify the same. Thus, budgeting helps immensely in controlling function.

Planning : Planning is the first step in budgetary control. It is necessary for doing any work in a systematic manner. A sound prepared plan helps the organization to use the scarce resources in an efficient manner and thus, achieving the pre-determined targets becomes easy. A budget is always prepared for future period and it lays down targets regarding various aspects like purchase, production, sales, manpower planning, etc.

Coordination : Setting the objectives, planning and coordination is essential for good results because coordination between the departments is most important. Budgeting facilitates coordination in the sense that budgets cannot be developed in isolation. For example, while developing the production budget, the production manager will have to consult the sales manager for sales forecast and purchase manager for the availability of raw material. Production budget cannot be developed in isolation. Likewise, the purchase and sales budget as well as other functional budgets, cash, capital expenditure, manpower planning, etc., cannot be developed without considering other functions.

Requisites for a Successful Budgetary Control System

While preparing a budgetary control system the following are the requisites:

(1) **Clarifying objectives :** The budgets are used to realize objectives of the business. The objectives should be clearly spelt out so that budgets are properly prepared. In the absence of clear goals, it is unrealistic.

(2) **Proper delegation of authority and responsibility :** Budget preparation and control is done at entry level of management. Even though budgets are finalized at top level but involvement of persons from lower levels of management is

essential for their success. It necessitates proper delegation of authority and responsibility.

(3) **Proper communication system :** An effective system of communication is required for a successful budgetary control. The flow of information regarding budgets should be quick so that these are implemented. The upward communication will help in knowing the difficulties in implementation of budgets. The performance reports of various levels will help top management in budgetary control.

(4) **Budget Education :** The employees should be properly educated about the benefits of budgeting system. They should be educated about their role in the success of this system. Budgetary control must not be taken only as a control device by the employees but it should be used as a tool to improve their efficiency.

(5) **Participation of employees :** Budgeting is done for every segment of the business. It will also require the active participation and involvement of all employees. In practice the budgets are to be executed at lower levels of management. Those for whom the budgets are framed should be actively associated with their preparation and execution. The employees on the basis of their past experience may give more practical and useful suggestions. The success of budgetary control system depends upon the participation of all employees of the organization.

(6) **Flexibility** : Flexibility in budgets is required to make them suitable under changed circumstances. Budgets are prepared for the future, which is uncertain. While budgets are prepared by allowing for the future possibilities but still some occurrences later on may require positive adjustments. Flexibility will make the budgets more suitable and practical.

(7) **Motivation :** Budgets are to be implemented by human beings. Their successful implementation will depend upon the interest shown by the employees. All persons should be motivated to improve their working so that budgeting is successful. A proper system of motivation should be introduced for making this system a success.

Essentials of Budgetary Control

The following are the essentials of budgetary control:

(1) **Budget Committee :** For successful implementation of budgetary control system, there is a need of a budget committee. In small or medium size organizations, the budget-related work may be carried out by the Chief Accountant only. Due to the size of the organization, there may not be too many problems in implementation of the budgetary control system. However, in large size organization, there is a need of a budget committee consisting of the chief executive, budget officer and heads of main departments in the organization. The main functions of the budget committee is to get the budgets prepared and then scrutinize the same, to lay down broad policies regarding the preparation of budgets, to approve the budgets, to suggest for revision, to monitor the implementation and to recommend the action to be taken in a given situation.

(2) **Budget Centers :** Establishment of budget centers is another important pre-requisite of a sound budgetary control system. A budget center is a group of activities or a section of the organization for which budget can be developed. For example, manpower planning budget, research and development cost budget, production and production cost budget, labour hour budget and so on. Budget centers should be defined clearly so that preparation becomes easy.

(3) **Budget Period :** A budget is always prepared prior to a defined period of time. This means that the period for which a budget is prepared in advance. Thus a budget may be prepared for five years, two years, one year, six months, one month or even for one week. The point is that the period for which the budget is prepared should be certain and decided in advance. Generally it can be said that the functional budgets like sales, purchase, production, etc., are prepared for one year and then broken down on monthly basis. Budgets like capital expenditure are generally prepared for a period from 1 year to 5 years. Thus depending upon the type of budget, the period of the same is decided and it is important that it is decided well in advance.

(4) **Preparation of an Organization Chart :** There should be an organization chart that shows clearly defined authorities and responsibilities of various executives. The organization chart will define clearly the functions to be performed by each executive relating to the budget preparation and his relationship with other executives. The organization chart may have to be adjusted to ensure that each budget center is controlled by an appropriate member of the staff.

Budget Manual : A budget manual is defined by CIMA as 'a document which sets out the responsibilities of the person engaged in, the routine of and the forms and records required for budgetary control'. The budget manual is thus a schedule, document or booklet, which contains different forms to be used, procedures to be followed, budgeting organization details and set of instructions to be followed in the budgeting system. It also lists out details of the responsibilities of different persons and the managers involved in the process. A typical budget manual contains the following.

- Objectives and managerial policies of the business concern.
- Internal lines of authorities and responsibilities.
- Functions of the budget committee including the role of the budget officer.
- Budget period
- Principal budget factor
- Detailed programme of budget preparation
- Accounting codes and numbering
- Follow-up procedures.

VI. **Principal Budget Factor or Key Factor :** A key factor or a principal budget factor also called as constraint is the factor, the extent of whose influence must first be assessed in order to prepare the functional budgets. Normally, sales are the key factor or principal budget factor but other factors like production, purchase and skilled labour may also be the key factors. For example, a company has production capacity to produce 40,000 units per annum but if the sales forecast tells that the market can absorb only 40,000 units, there is no point in producing 30,000 units. Hence, the sale is the key factor in this situation. On the other hand, if the company has capacity to produce 40,000 units and the market has the capacity to absorb the entire production which means that sales is not the key factor but if raw material is available in limited quantity so that only 35,000 units can be produced, the raw material will become the key factor. The key factor puts restrictions on the other functions and hence, it must be considered carefully in advance. So, continuous assessment of the business situation becomes necessary in all conditions and the key factor is the starting point in the preparation of budgets. The following are the important key factors.

1. **Sales :** Consumer demand, shortage of sales staff, inadequate advertising
2. **Material :** Availability of supply, restrictions on import
3. **Labour :** Shortage of skilled labour
4. **Plant :**Availability of capacity, bottlenecks in key processes
5. **Management :** Lack of capital, pricing policy, shortage of efficient executives, lack of know-how, faulty design of the product, etc.

III. **Adequate Accounting Records :** It is essential that the accounting system should be able to record and analyze the transactions involved. A chart of accounts or accounts code should be maintained which may correspond with the budget centers for establishment of budgets and finally, control through budgets.

Benefits of the budget

Budgeting plays an important role in planning and controlling. It helps in directing the scarce resources to the most productive use and thus, ensures overall efficiency in the organization. The benefits derived by an organization from an effective system of budgeting can be summarized as given below.

1. Budgeting facilitates planning of various activities and ensures that the working of the organization is systematic and smooth.
2. Budgeting is a coordinated exercise and hence, combines the ideas of different levels of management in preparation of the same.
3. Any budget cannot be prepared in isolation and therefore, coordination among various departments is facilitated automatically.
4. Budgeting helps planning and controlling income and expenditure so as to achieve higher profitability and also act as a guide for various management decisions.
5. Budgeting is an effective means for planning and thus, ensures sufficient availability of working capital and other resources.

6. It is really necessary to evaluate the actual performance with predetermined parameters. Budgeting ensures that there are well defined parameters and thus, the performance is evaluated against these parameters.
7. As the resources are directed to the most productive use, budgeting helps in reducing 'the wastages and losses.

Limitations of Budgetary Control

1. The top management should give full support for budgetary control, if any time there is a lack of support then this system will collapse.
2. Budgets are prepared based on assumptions but future is uncertain. Hence, frequent revision of budgets will reduce value and involve huge expenditure.
3. In this system, targets are given to every person in the organization. So budgets may serve as constraints on managerial initiatives.
4. The future uncertainties reduce the ability of budgetary control system.
5. Problem of coordination between the departments effect the performance.
6. Budget implementing is expensive; hence, small organizations cannot bear this amount.

Classification and Types of Budgets

The budgets are classified according to their nature. The following are the types of budgets which are commonly used.

(A) Classification According to Time

1. Long-term budgets
2. Short-term budgets
3. Current budgets

(B) Classification on the Basis of Functions

1. Operating Budgets
2. Financial Budgets
3. Master Budget

(C) Classification on the Basis of Flexibility

1. Fixed budget.
2. Flexible budget.

(A) Classification According to Time

1. **Long-term Budgets** : The budgets are prepared for long-term planning of the business. The period of long-term budgets varies between five to ten years. The long-term plans prepared by the top level management; it is not generally known

to lower levels of management. Long term budgets are prepared for some sectors of the concern such as capital expenditure, research and development, long-term finances, etc. These budgets are useful for those industries where gestation period is long, i.e., machinery, electricity, engineering, etc.

2. **Short-term Budgets :** These budgets are generally for one or two years only and it is prepared in the form of monetary terms. The consumer goods industries like soaps, pharmaceuticals, textile, etc., use short-term budgets.

3. **Current Budgets :** The period of current budgets are short period like months and weeks only. These budgets are related to the current activities of the business. According to I.C.W.A London. "Current budget is a budget which is established for use over a short period of time and is related to current conditions.

(B) Classification on the Basis of Functions

1. **Operating Budgets :** It is related to the different activities or operations of a firm. The number of such budgets depends upon the size and nature of business. The commonly used operating budgets are:

   (a) Sales Budget
   (b) Production Budget
   (c) Production Cost Budget
   (d) Purchase Budget
   (e) Raw Materials Budget
   (f) Labour Budget
   (g) Plant Utilization Budget
   (h) Manufacturing Expenses or Works Overhead Budget
   (i) Administrative and Selling Expenses Budget, etc.

   The operating budget for a firm may be constructed in terms of programmes or responsibility areas and hence, may consist of:

   (1) Programme Budget, and
   (2) Responsibility Budget.

(i) **Programme Budget** : It consists of expected revenues and costs of various products that are termed as the major programmes of the firm. Such a budget can be prepared for each product line or project showing revenues, costs and the relative profitability of the various programmes. Programme budgets are useful in locating areas where efforts may be required to reduce costs and increase revenues. They are also useful in determining imbalances and inadequacies in programmes so that corrective action may be taken in future.

(ii) **Responsibility Budget** : When the operating budget of a firm is constructed in terms of responsibility areas it is called the responsibility budget. Such a budget shows the plan in terms of persons responsible for achieving them. It is used by the management as a control device to evaluate the performance of executives who are incharge of various cost centres. Their performance is compared to the targets set for them and proper action is taken for adverse results, if any. The kinds of responsibility areas depend upon the size and nature of business activities and the organizational structure. However, responsibility centres may be classified under three broad categories:

(a) Cost/Expense Centre

(b) Profit Centre

(c) Investment Centre.

(a) **Cost centre :** A cost centre is the centre where inputs are measured in monetary terms. In cost centre of responsibility, the accounting system records only the cost incurred in the centre. Performance of cost centre is measured by the monetary terms of input only, where the cost of operating the division is directly traceable to it.

Performance of the cost centre manager will be judged on the basis of the cost incurred in his centre. Compare actual inputs to come predetermined level that represents efficient utilization. The variance between the actual and the budget would be indicative of the efficiency of the division.

Examples of cost centers are production department, service department, marketing department, sales region and sales representatives.

(b) **Profit Centre :** Responsibility centers may have both inputs and outputs. The inputs are taken as costs and outputs are taken as revenues. Managers of profit centers have control over both the costs and the revenues because profit is the difference between the revenues and the costs. The main purpose of a profit centre is to earn profit. Management decided to make a responsibility centre as a profit centre when it thinks that the outputs are capable of beings measured in monetary terms and that it would be beneficial to do so. A division of the company which produces and markets the products may be called a profit centre.

(c) **Investment Centre :** It is a division of an organization wherein, its performance is assessed by considering not only its costs and revenues but also by establishing a relationship between the profit (difference between revenues and costs), capital invested or employed and revenue. It is responsible for both profits and investments. When only top management takes the decision regarding the capital expenditure decision, i.e., capital budgeting decision, there will be only one investment centre covering the entire organization. Whereas, when such decision making is delegated to the divisional heads, there will be more number of investment centers. Thus, the number of investment centers will be fewer compared to profit or cost centres. Therefore all the investments centres are normally profit centers and cost centres but not all profit centres are investment centres. The performance of a division is measured by establishing a relationship between its net income and total capital employed in that division.

2. **Financial Budgets :** Financial budgets are concerned with cash receipts and disbursements, working capital, capital expenditure, financial position and results of business operations. The commonly used financial budgets are:

   1. Cash Budget
   2. Working Capital Budget
   3. Capital Expenditure Budget
   4. Income Statement Budget
   5. Budgeted Balance Sheet or Position Statement Budget.

2. **Master Budget.** Various functional budgets are integrated into one budget is called as master budget. This budget is prepared by the ultimate integration of separate functional budgets. According to ICWA London, "the master budget is the summary budget incorporating its functional budges master budget is prepared by the budget officer and it remains with the top level management. This budget is used to coordinate the activities of various functional departments and also to help as a control device.

(C) Classification on the Basis of Flexibility

1. **Fixed Budget :** The fixed budgets are prepared for a given level of activity; the budget is prepared before the beginning of the current year. If the financial year starts in April then the budget will be prepared a month or two earlier, i.e., March or February. The changes in expenditure arising out of the anticipated changes will not be adjusted in the budget. There is a difference of about twelve months in the budgeted and actual figures. According to ICWA London, "Fixed budget is a budget which is designed to remain unchanged irrespective of the level of activity actually attained." Fixed budgets are suitable under static conditions. If sales, expenses and costs are forecasted with accuracy then this budget can be useful.

1. **Flexible Budgets :** It consists of a series of budgets for different level of activity. This varies with the level of activity attained. A flexible budget is the budget which by recognizing the difference among fixed, semi-fixed and variable costs are designed to change in relation to the level of activity. It will be useful where level of activity changes from time to time. If the forecasting of demand is uncertain and the undertaking operates under conditions of shortage of materials, labour, etc., then this budget will be more useful.

DIFFERENCE BETWEEN A FIXED AND FLEXIBLE BUDGET

Fixed Budget	Flexible Budget
A fixed budget remains the same irrespective of situations. It remains inflexible even if volume of business is changed.	A flexible budget is recast to suit the changed circumstances. Suitable adjustments are made if the situations increase or decrease.
A fixed budget assumes that conditions will remain constant.	This budget is changed if level of activity varies.
In fixed budgets costs are not classified according to their nature.	The costs are studied as per their nature, i.e., fixed, variable and semi variable.
If the level of activity changes then budgeted and actual results cannot be compared because of change in basis.	The budgets are redrafted as per the changed volume and a comparison between budgeted and actual figures will be possible.
Forecasting of accurate results is difficult.	It shows the impact of expenses on operations and it helps in making accurate forecasts.
Under changed circumstances cost cannot be ascertained	The costs can be easily ascertained under different levels of activity. This helps in fixing prices.

Problem 1 : [Flexible Budget]

GK factory engaged in manufacturing plastic toys is working at 40% capacity and produces 20,000 toys per month. The present cost break-up for one toy is as under.

Material: ₹ 20

Labour: ₹ 6

Overheads: ₹ 10 [60% fixed]

The selling price is ₹ 40 per toy. If it is decided to work the factory at 50% capacity, the selling price falls by 2%. At 90% capacity, the selling price falls by 5% accompanied by a similar fall in the price of material. You are required to prepare a statement showing the profits/losses at 40%, 50% and 90% capacity utilizations.

Solution :

Flexible Budget

At 40%, 50% and 90% Capacity Utilization

Particulars	40% Capacity Utilization	50% Capacity Utilization	90% Capacity Utilization
Production – Units	20,000	25,000	45,000
Selling Price per Unit	₹ 40	₹ 39.20	₹ 38
Sales Value [units × selling price per unit]	₹ 8,00,000	₹ 9,80,000	₹ 17,10,000
Variable Costs:			
Material ₹20 per Unit	₹ 4,00,000	₹ (2500 x 19.6) 4,90,000	₹ (4500 x 19) 8,55,000
Labour ₹6 per Unit	₹ 1,20,000	₹ 1,50,000	₹ 2, 70,000
Overheads ₹4 per Unit	₹ 80,000	₹ 1,00,000	₹1,80,000
Total Variable Costs	₹ 6,00,000	₹ 7,40,000	₹.13,0500
Fixed Costs 20,000 x 6	₹ 1,20,000	₹ 1,20,000	₹ 1,20,000
Total Costs [Variable Cost + Fixed Cost]	₹ 7,20,000	₹ 8,16,000	₹ 14,25000
Profit/Loss [Sales – Total Costs]	₹ 80,000	₹ 1,20,000	₹ 2,85,000

Problem 2 :

Vani manufacturing company is currently working at 50% capacity and produces 10,000 units at a cost of ₹ 200 per unit as per the following details.

Materials :	₹ 100
Labour :	₹ 50
Factory Overheads :	₹ 30 [40% fixed]
Administrative Overheads :	₹ 20 [50% fixed]
Total Cost Per Unit :	₹ 200

The selling price per unit at present is ₹ 250. At 60% working, material cost per unit increases by 2% and selling price per unit falls by 2%. At 80% working, material cost per unit increases by 5% and selling price per unit falls by 5%.

Prepare a Flexible Budget to show the profits/losses at 50%, 60% and 80% capacity utilization.

Solution :

Flexible Budget

	Particulars	Capacity Utilization	Capacity Utilization	Capacity Utilization
		50%	60%	80%
A]	Number of Units	10,000	12,000	16,000
B]	Selling Price Per Unit	₹ 250	₹ 245	₹ 237.50
C]	Variable Cost Per Unit			
	• Direct Material	₹ 100	₹ 102	₹ 105
	• Direct Labour	₹ 50	₹ 50	₹ 50
	• Factory Overheads [60%]	₹ 18	₹ 18	₹ 18
	• Administrative Overheads [50%]	₹ 10	₹ 10	₹ 10
D]	Total Variable Cost Per Unit	₹ 178	₹ 180	₹ 183
E]	Total Variable Cost [A × D]	₹ 17,80,000	₹ 21,60,000	₹ 29,28,000
F]	Fixed Costs [₹12 + ₹10 = ₹22 per unit at existing level of 10, 000 units.]	₹ 2,20,000	₹ 2,20,000	₹ 2,20,000
G]	Total Cost [E + F]	₹ 18,00,000	₹ 21,40,000	₹ 28,28,000
H]	Sales Revenue [A × B]	₹ 20,00,000	₹ 23,52,000	₹ 30,40,000
I]	Profits/Losses [H – G]	₹ 2,00,000	₹ 2,12,000	₹ 2,12,000

Problem 3 :

The following data are available from KGR Company for the year ended.

Particulars	₹ in Lakhs
FIXED EXPENSES	
Wages and Salaries	15
Rent, Rates and Taxes	5
Depreciation	6
Sundry Administrative Expenses	8
SEMI VARIABLE EXPENSES	
Maintenance and Repairs	4
Indirect Labour	8
Sales Department's Salaries	4
Sundry Administrative Expenses	3
VARIABLE EXPENSES [AT 50% CAPACITY]	
Materials	30
Labour	10
Other Expenses	7
Total	100

Assume that the fixed expenses remain constant at all levels of production. Semi variable expenses remain constant between 45% and 65% capacity, increasing by 10% between 65% and 80% capacity and by 20% between 80% and 100% capacity. The variable expenses at 60% capacity increased by 20% and at 90% increased by 80%.

Sales at various levels are,

At 50% ₹ 150 lakhs

At 60% ₹ 170 lakhs

At 75% ₹ 200 lakhs

At 90% ₹ 220 lakhs

At 100% ₹ 250 lakhs

Prepare a flexible budget for the year at 60% and 90% capacity utilizations and calculate the profits or loss at this level.

Solution :

Flexible Budget

₹ in Lakhs

Particulars	Capacity Utilization 50%	Capacity Utilization 60%	Capacity Utilization 90%
A] Sales	150.00	170.00	220.00
B] Variable Costs			
Materials	30	36	54
Labour	10	12	18
Other Expenses	7	8.4	12.6
C] Total Variable Costs	47	56.4	84.6
D] Semi Variable Costs			
Maintenance and Repairs	4	4	4.80
Indirect Labour	8	8	9.60
Sales Dept. Salaries	4	4	4.80
Sundry Admn. Expenses	3	3	3.60
E] Total Semi Variable Costs	19.0	19	22.80
F] Fixed Costs			
Wages and Salaries	15	15	15
Rent, Rates and Taxes	5	5	5
Depreciation	6	6	6
Sundry Administrative Expenses	8	8	8
G] Total Fixed Costs	34	34	34
H] Total Costs [C + E + F]	100	109.40	141.40
I] Profit/Loss [A - H]	50	60.60	78.6

Problem 4 :

The monthly budget for manufacturing overheads of a manufacturing company is given below.

Particulars	Capacity 60%	Capacity 100%
Budgeted Production	1000 units	1,200 units
Wages	₹ 1,500	₹ 2,500
Consumable Stores	1,200	2,000
Maintenance	1,500	1,700
Power and Fuel	1,800	2,000
Depreciation	5,000	5,000
Insurance	2,000	2,000
Total	13,000	15,700

You are required to indicate which of the items are fixed, variable and semi variable and prepare a budget for 80% capacity. Show the total cost, both fixed and variable per unit of output at 60%, 80% and 100% capacity levels.

Solution : Flexible Budget at 60%, 80% and 100% Capacity

Particulars	Capacity	Capacity	Capacity
	60%	80%	100%
A] Budgeted Production - Units	1000	1333	1667
B] Variable Costs:	₹	₹	₹
Wages	1,500	1,999.50	2,500.50
Consumable Stores	1200	1,599.6	2,000.40
C] Total Variable Costs	2,700	3,599.10	4,500.90
D] Semi Variable Costs	1,500	1,833	2,167
Maintenance [W.N.1]	1,800	2,133	2, 467
Power and Fuel [W.N.2]			
E] Total Semi Variable Costs	3,300	3,966	4,634
F] Fixed Costs			
Depreciation	5,000	5,000	5,000
Insurance	2,000	2,000	2,000
G] Total Fixed Costs	7,000	7,000	7,000
H] Total Costs [C + E + F]	13,000	14,565.10	12,000
I] Variable Cost per Unit [C / A]	2.70	2.7	2.7
J] Fixed Cost per Unit	7	5.25	4.20

Notes :

From the data given in the problem, it is clear that depreciation and insurance are fixed expenses, as they have remained constant at all levels of capacity utilization. Wages and Consumable Stores are variable as they have increased in the same proportion of production. Maintenance and Power and Fuel are semi variable expenses because they have not increased in the same proportion of the production.

Working Note No. 1 : Maintenance

60% level = ₹ 1,500

100% level= ₹ 1,700

Difference= ₹ 200 for a difference of 200 units Variable element is thus : ₹ 200/200 units = Re. 1

The amount at different levels of capacity is calculated

Particulars	60% Capacity	80% Capacity	100% Capacity
	1000 units	1333 units	1667 units
Variable Element [Re 1 per unit]	₹ 1000	₹ 1333	₹ 1667
Fixed Element	₹. 500	₹ 500	₹ 500
Total Amount as given in the problem	₹ 1,500	₹ 1,833	₹ 2,167

Working Note No. 2 : Power and Fuel

60% level = ₹ 1,800

100% level = ₹ 2,000

Difference = ₹ 200 for a difference of 200 units

Variable element is thus ₹ 200/200 units = Re. 1

Thus the amount at different levels of capacity utilization is computed as shown below.

Particulars	60% Capacity	80% Capacity	100% Capacity
	1000 units	1333 units	1667 units
Variable Element [Re.1 per unit]	₹ 1000	₹ 1333	₹ 1667
Fixed Element	₹ 800	₹ 800	₹ 800
Total Amount as given in the Problem	₹ 1800	₹ 2133	₹ 2467

These amounts are worked out by computing variable element at Re.1 per unit and the balance as fixed element.

Problem 5 :

XYZ Ltd. manufactures a single product for which market demand exists for additional quantity. Present sales of Rs.60, 000 per month utilize only 60% capacity of the plant. Sales Manager assures that with a reduction of 10% in the price, he would be in a position to increase the sales by about 25% to 30%. The following data are available.

Selling price:	₹ 10 per unit
Variable cost:	₹ 3 per unit
Semi variable cost:	₹ 6, 000 fixed plus Rs.0.50 per unit
Fixed cost:	₹ 20, 000 at present level estimated to be ₹ 24, 000 at 80% output. You are required to

- Prepare a statement showing the operating profit at 60%, 70% and 80% levels of capacity utilization at current selling price and at proposed selling price.
- The percentage increase in the present output which will be required to maintain the present profit margin at the proposed selling price.

Solution :

A] Comparative Statement of Operating Profit at Current Selling Price

	Particulars	60% Capacity	70% Capacity	80% Capacity
I]	Output - Units	6,000	7,000	8,000
II]	Selling Price Per Unit ₹	10	10	10
III]	Sales Value [I x II] ₹	60,000	70,000	80,000
IV]	Variable Cost Rs.3 per unit × Number of units	18,000	21,000	24,000
V]	Semi Variable Cost ₹ 6, 000 fixed + ₹ 0.50 per unit	9,000	9,500	10,000
VI]	Fixed Cost	20,000	20,000	24,000
VII]	Total Cost [IV + V + VI]	47,000	50,500	58,000
VIII]	Profit/Loss [III - VII]	13,000	19,500	22,000

B] Comparative Statement of Operating Profit at Proposed Selling Price

	Particulars	60% Capacity	70% Capacity	80% Capacity
I]	Output - Units	6,000	7,000	8,000
II]	Selling Price Per Unit ₹	9	9	9
III]	Sales Value [I x II] ₹	54,000	63,000	72,000
IV]	Total Cost [Same as shown in Statement A]	47,000	50,500	58,000
V]	Profit/Loss III - IV	7,000	12,500	14,000

C] Percentage Increase in the Present Output Required to maintain the Present Profit Margin at the Proposed Selling Price:

Proposed Selling Price:	₹ 9.00
Variable Cost :	₹ 3.50
Contribution:	₹ 5.50
Present Profit:	₹ 13, 000
Fixed Cost	₹ 26, 000 [₹ 20, 000 + ₹ 6, 000]
Required Contribution:	₹ 39, 000 [Profit + Fixed Cost]

Required output : Required Contribution/Contribution per Unit = 39, 000/5.5 = 7091 units % Increase in output required = 1091/6000 X 100 = 18.18%

Problem 6 :

The following budget of Rithvik Ltd, a manufacturing organization, has been prepared for the year 2012-2013.

Particulars	% of SalesValue
Raw Materials	40
Direct Wages	25
Factory Overheads - Variable	10
Factory Overheads - Fixed	5
Administration and Selling and Distribution Overheads -Variable	6
Administration and Selling and Distribution Overheads - Fixed	12
Profit	2
Sales Value	100

After considering the quarterly performance, it is felt that the budgeted volume of sales would not be achieved. But the company expects to achieve 80% of the budgeted sales [equivalent to sales value of ₹ 160,00,000] at this stage; the company has received an export order for its usual line of products. The estimated prime cost and special export expenses for fulfilling the export order are ₹ 13,00,000 and ₹ 40,000 respectively.

You are required to

1) Present the original budget and the revised budget based on 80% achievement of the target sales, showing the quantum of profit/loss

2) Prepare a statement of budgeted costs for working out the overhead recovery rates in percentages

3) Work out the lowest quotation for the export order.

[ICWAI Intermediate]

Solution :

1) Statement showing the original Budget and the Revised Budget and Profit/Loss

Particulars	% of Sales Value	Original Budget	% of Sales Value	Revised Budget
		₹ in 00, 000		₹ in 00, 000
A] Sales	100	200.00*	80	160.00
B] Variable Costs				
• Raw Materials	40	80.00		64.00
• Direct Wages	25	50.00		40.00
• Factory Overheads	10	20.00		16.00
• Adm. and S. & D. Overheads	6	12.00		9.60
C] Total Variable Costs	81	162.00		129.60
D] Fixed Costs				
• Factory Overheads	5	10.00		10.00
• Adm. and S. & D. Overheads	12	24.00		24.00
E] Total Fixed Costs	17	34.00		34.00
F] Total Costs [C + E]	98	196.00		163.60
G] Profit/Loss [A – F]	2	4		3.60

* Sales at 80% level are Rs. 160, hence sales at 100% level= (160/80) × 100 = Rs.200

2. Statement Showing Overhead Recovery Rates Based On Original Budget

- Variable Factory Overheads = (20,00,000/ 50,00,000) x 100 = 40% of Direct Wages.

- Fixed Factory Overheads = (10, 00, 000/50, 00, 000) x 100 = 20% of Direct Wages.
- Variable Administrative and Selling & Distribution Overheads
  (12, 00, 000/160, 00,000) x 100 = 7.5% of Works Cost
- Fixed Administrative and Selling & Distribution Overheads
  (24, 00, 000/160, 00,000) x 100 = 15% of Works Cost

Note : Factory overheads, fixed and variable are based on direct wages while administrative and selling and distribution overheads are based on works cost.

Statement showing Quotation for Export Order

Particulars	*Amount ₹*
Raw Materials ₹ 13, 00, 000 x (40/65)	8,00,000
Direct Wages ₹13, 00, 000 x (25/65)	5,00,000
Prime Cost [Raw Materials + Direct Wages]	13,00,000
Variable Factory Overheads [40% of Direct Wages]	2,00,000
Works Cost [Prime Cost + Variable Factory Overheads]	15,00,000
Variable Administration and Selling and Distribution Overheads [7.5% of Works Cost]	1,12,500
Special Export Expenses	40,000
Total Cost of Export Order	16,52,500

Note : Export order can be priced at any price above ₹ 16,52,500

Works Cost = Total Variable Cost – Variable Administration and Selling & Distribution Overheads + Fixed Factory Overheads

Prime Cost is given as ₹ 13, 00,000 [Export Order]. Prime Cost is 65% of total sales and material content is 40%. Accordingly amount of material is computed

Similarly the amount of direct wages is computed.

Problem 7 :

The following information relates to the production activities of RK Ltd for 3 months ending on 31st December, 2012.

Particulars	Amount in ₹
Fixed Expenses:	
Management Salaries	2,10,000
Rent and Taxes	1,40,000
Depreciation of Machinery	1,75,000
Sundry Office Expenses	2,22,000
Total Fixed Expenses	7,47,000
Semi Variable Expenses at 50% capacity:	
Plant Maintenance	62,500
Labour	2,47,000
Salesmen's salaries	72,500
Sundry Expenses	65,000
Total Semi Variable Expenses	4,47,000
Variable Expenses:	
Materials	6,00,000
Labour	6,40,000
Salesmen's commission	95,000
Total Variable Expenses	13,35,000

It is further noted that semi-variable expenses remain constant between 40% and 70% capacity, increase by 10% of the above figures between 70% and 85% capacity and increase by 15% of the above figures between 85% and 100% capacity. Fixed expenses remain constant whatever the level of activity may be. Sales at 60% capacity are ₹ 25,50,000, at 80% capacity ₹ 34,00,000 and at 100% capacity ₹ 42,50,000. Assuming that all items of produced are sold, prepare a Flexible Budget at 60%, 80% and 100% productive capacity.

Flexible Budget for Three Months Ending 31st December 2012

Particulars	60% Capacity Level Amount ₹	80% Capacity Level Amount ₹	100% Capacity Level Amount ₹
Sales	25,50,000	34,00,000	42,50,000
A] Variable Expenses:			
Material	7,20, 000	9,60, 000	12,00,000
Labour	7,68, 000	10,24, 000	12,80,000
Salesmen's Commission	1,14, 000	1,52, 000	1,90, 000
Total [A]	16,02, 000	21,36, 000	26,70, 000
B] Semi-variable Expenses:			
Plant Maintenance	62, 500	68, 750	71,875
Indirect Labour	2,47, 500	2,72, 250	2,84, 625
Salesmen's salaries	72, 500	79, 750	83, 375
Sundry Expenses	65, 000	71, 500	74, 750
Total [B]	20,49,500	26,28,250	31,84,625
C] Fixed Expenses:			
Management Salaries	2,10, 000	2,10, 000	2,10, 000
Rent and Taxes	1,40, 000	1,40, 000	1,40, 000
Depreciation on Machinery	1,75, 000	1,75, 000	1,75, 000
Sundry Office Expenses	2,22, 500	2,22, 500	2,22, 500
Total [C]	7,47, 500	7,47, 500	7,47, 500
Total Costs [A+B+C]	27,97, 000	33,75, 750	39,32, 125
Profit/Loss	[-] 2, 47, 000	24,250	3,17, 875

Problem 8 :

S.M. Ltd. produces two products, A and B. The budget for these products [at 60% level of activity] for the year 2012-13 is given as follows:

Particulars	Product A	Product B
Raw Material Per Unit	₹ 7.50	₹ 3.50
Direct Labour Per Unit	₹ 4.00	₹ 3.00
Variable Overheads Per Unit	₹ 2.00	₹ 1.50
Fixed Overheads Per Unit	₹ 6.00	₹ 4.50
Selling Price Per Unit	₹ 20.00	₹ 15.00
Production and Sales [Units]	4,000	6,000

The Managing Director is not satisfied with the projected results presented above is the budget to the Marketing Director for his observations regarding performance improvement. The Marketing Director suggested that the sales in quantity of both the products A and B could be increased by 50% provided the selling price were reduced by 5% and 10% for the products A and B respectively. The price reduction should be made applicable to the entire sales in quantity of both the products A and B.

You are required to prepare a statement of overall profitability on the basis of original budget and the revised budget.

Solution :

I] Statement showing the Overall Profitability

Particulars	Product A 4000 Units ₹	Product B 6000 Units ₹	Total ₹
A] Selling Price Per Unit	20.00	15.00	
B] Sales Value [A X Number of Units]	80,000	90,000	
C] Variable Costs			
• Raw Materials	30,000	21,000	
• Direct Labour	16,000	18,000	
• Variable Overheads	8,000	9,000	
D] Total Variable Costs	54,000	48,000	
E] Fixed Overheads	24,000	27,000	
F] Total Costs [D + E]	78,000	75,000	
G] Profit [B- F]	2,000	15,000	17,000

II] Statement showing the Overall Profitability with Revised Budget

Particulars	Product A 6000 Units ₹	Product B 9000 Units ₹	Total ₹
A] Selling Price Per Unit	19.00	13.50	
B] Sales Value [A × Number of Units]	1,14,000	1,21,500	
C] Variable Costs			
• Raw Materials	45,000	31,500	
• Direct Labour	24,000	27,000	
• Variable Overheads	12,000	13,500	
D] Total Variable Costs	81,000	72,000	
E] Fixed Overheads	24,000	27,000	
F] Total Costs [D + E]	1,05,000	99,000	
G] Profit [B- F]	9,000	22,500	31,500

Raw Material per unit for Product A is Rs. 7.50 and for Product B Rs. 3.50

Direct Labour per unit for Product A Rs. 4.00 and for B Rs. 3.00

Variable Overheads for Product A Rs. 2.00 and for B Rs. 1.50 per unit

Fixed Overheads at present level for A and B Rs. 6.00 and Rs. 4.50 per unit

Sales Budget

A Sales Budget is an estimate of expected sales during a budget period. A sales budget is known as a head of the enterprise. The degree of accuracy with which sales are estimated will determine the practicability of operating budgets. A sales budget is the starting point for preparing budgets. It lays down potential sales figures in value as well as in quantity and comprehensive plan for sales department. The sales manager is made responsible for preparing sales budget. He uses all possible information available from internal and external sources. The possible factors to be taken into account while preparing a sales budget are discussed as follows:

1. **Past Sales Figures :** The sales forecasts are based on past sales figures. The sale figures of a number of years enable in the determination of trends of sales. The upward and downward sales trends will be of great use in fixing future sales. The actual past sales figures will be the most reliable criterion for preparing current sales budget. The expected seasonal fluctuations, potential demand and position of trade cycles will also be helpful in preparing sales budget.

2. **Assessment and Reports by Salesman :** The salesmen are the most appropriate persons for estimating future demand. They are in touch with the market and the customers. Their experience will enable them to forecast sales figures more realistically. The sales manager should cautiously scrutinize the figures of salesmen so as to eliminate their bias. The attitude and personal thinking of the salesmen may tempt them to underestimate or overestimate sales estimates. The sale manager gets an idea about the market situation from salesmen's estimates. He should wisely use these figures for incorporating them in sales budget.

3. **Availability of Raw Materials :** The availability of raw materials is an important factor in preparing a sales budget. In some cases, raw material is a key factor. The quantum of raw materials available to the enterprise will enable the sales manager to anticipate sales figures. Moreover, the smooth supply of materials is necessary for achieving sales targets.

4. **Seasonal Fluctuations :** The effect of seasonal fluctuations should also be considered while preparing a sales budget. The demand for goods may be more in some periods while they may be in less demand at other times. An effort should be made to reduce the seasonal effect by giving discounts or other concessions during off seasons.

5. **Availability of Finances :** The availability of finances sometimes becomes a limiting factor. The finances will be required for purchasing various inputs. The

sales budget is prepared along with the financial budget. The expansion of sales effort will need additional capital outlay. Financial aspect should be taken into consideration while preparing a sales budget.

6. **Plant Capacity :** The goods will be sold only when they are produced. The capacity for producing goods should be taken into account. On the other hand, sales effort must ensure fill utilization of plant capacity.

A business firm can use any of the above methods to prepare sales forecast and incorporate the same in the sales budget.

Problem I :

Lalitha Company manufactures two products, A and B. Its sales department has three area divisions, North, East and South. Preliminary sales budgets for the year ending 31st March 2012, based on the assessment of the divisional managers were as follows.

Product A : North 3,00,000 units, South 6,00,000 units and East 2,00,000 units

Product B : North 3,00,000 units, South 5,00,000 units and East Nil

Sale Price : A Rs. 5 and B Rs. 4 in all areas.

Arrangements are made for the extensive advertising of Products A and B and it is estimated that the North division sales will increase by 1,00,000 units. Arrangements are also made to advertise and distribute product in Eastern area in the second half of the year 2012-13 when sales are expected to be 4,00,000 units in 'B'.

Solution :

Product A				Product B			
Division	Quantity	Price ₹	Value ₹	Division	Quantity	Price ₹	Value ₹
North	4,00,000	5	20,00,000	Norh	4,00,000	4	16,00,000
South	6,00,000	5	30,00,000	South	5,00,000	4	20,00,000
East	2,00,000	5	10,00,000	East	4,00,000	4	16,00,000
Total	12,00,000		60,00,000	Total	9,00,000		36,00,000

Problem II :

Koti Ltd. manufactures two products, A and B and sells them through two divisions, north and south. For the purpose of submission of Sales Budget to the budget committee the following information is available.

Budgeted Sales for the current year were,

Product A : North 4,000 units @ ₹ 9 each, south 6,000 units @ ₹ 9 each

Product B : North 3,000 units @ ₹ 21 each, south 5,000 @ ₹ 21 each. Actual sales for the current year were,

Particulars	North	South
Product A	5,000 units @ ₹ 9 each	7,000 units @ ₹ 9 each
Product B	2,000 units @ ₹ 21 each	4,000 units @ ₹ 21 each

Adequate market studies reveal that Product A is popular but under priced. It is observed that if the price of A is increased by ₹ 1 it will still find a ready market. On the other hand, B is overpriced to customers and the market could absorb more if sales price of B is reduced by ₹ 1. The management has agreed to give effect to the above price changes.

From the information based on these price changes and reports from salesmen, the following estimates have been prepared by divisional managers.

Percentage increase in sales over current budget is,

Particulars	North	South
Product A	+ 10%	+ 5%
Product B	+ 20%	+ 10%

With the help of an intensive advertisement campaign, the following additional sales over the estimated sales of divisional managers are possible.

Additional sales above the estimated sales of divisional managers

Particulars	North	South
Product A	600	700
Product B	400	500

You are required to prepare a budget for sales incorporating the above estimates and also show the budgeted sales and actual sales for the current year.

Solution :

Sales Budget Koti Ltd

Division	Product	Budgeted For Future Period	Budgeted For Current Period	Actual Sales For Current Period
North	Product A	5,000 units @ ₹ 10	4000 units @ ₹ 9	5000 units @ ₹9
		= ₹ 50000	= ₹ 36000	= ₹ 45000
	Product B	4,000 units @ ₹ 20	3000 units @ ₹ 21	2000 units @ ₹21
		= Rs .80000	= ₹ 63000	= ₹ 42000
Total	Quantity	9000 units	7,000 units	7000 units
	Amount	₹ 1,30,000	₹ 99000	₹ 87000
South	Product A	7000 units @ ₹ 10	6,000 units @ ₹ 9	7000 units @ ₹ 9
		= ₹ 70000	= ₹54000	= ₹ 63000
	Product B	6,000 units @₹ 20	5000 units @ ₹ 21	4,000 units @ ₹ 21
		= Rs .1,20,000	=₹ 1,05,000	= ₹ 84000
Total	Quantity	13,000 units	11000 units	11000 units
		₹ 1,0,000	₹ 1,59,000	₹ 1, 47,000
Total	Product A	12000 units @₹10	10000 units @ ₹ 9	12000 units @₹ 9
		₹ 1, 20,000	= ₹ 90000	= ₹ 1, 08,000
	Product B	10000 units @₹ 20	8000 units@21 ₹ 21	6000 units @₹ 21
		= ₹ 2, 00,000	= ₹ 1,68,000	= ₹ 1, 26,000
Total		22000 units	18000 units	18000 units
		₹ 3,20,000	₹ 2,58,000	₹ 2,34,000

Problem :

Kalyan manufactures two types of toys kittu and bittu and sells them in Agra and Bombay markets. The following information is made available for the current year:

Market	Types	Budgeted Sales	Actual Sales
Hyd	kittu	500 at ₹ 10 each	500 at ₹ 10 each
	Bittu	400 at ₹ 20 each	300 at ₹ 20 each
Delhi	Kittu	700 at ₹ 10 each	800 at ₹ 10 each
	Bittu	600 at ₹ 20 each	500 at ₹ 20 each

Market studies reveal that toy kittu is popular as it is under priced. It is observed that if its price is increased by Re. 1 it will find a ready made market. On the other hand, Bittu is over-priced and market could absorb more sales if its selling price is reduced to Rs. 19. The management has agreed to give effect to the above price changes.

On the above basis, the following estimates have been prepared by sales manager:

Product	% increase in Sales	Over current budget
	Hyd	Delhi
Raja	10%	5%
Rani	20%	10%

With the help of an intensive advertisement compaign, the following additional sales above the estimated sales of sales manager are possible:

Product	Hyd	Bombay
Raja	100 units	90 units
Rani	50 units	70 units

You are required to prepare a budget for sales incorporating the above estimates.

Solution :

Area	Product	Budget for the Current Year			Actual Sales			Budget for the Future Period		
		Units	Price ₹	Value ₹	Units	Price ₹	Value ₹	Units	Price ₹	Value ₹
Hyd	Kittu	500	10	5,000	550	10	5,500	550	11	6,050
	Bittu	400	20	8,000	300	20	6,000	530	19	10,070
	Total	900		13,000	850		11,500	1080		16,120
Delhi	Kittu	700	10	7,000	800	10	8,000	825	11	9,075
	Bittu	600	20	12,000	500	20	10,000	730	19	13,870
	Total	1300		19,000	1300		18,000	1,555		22,945
Total	Kittu	1200		12,000	1350		13,500	1,375		15,125
	Bittu	1000		20,000	800		16,000	1,260		23,940
Total Sales		2,200		32,000	2150		29,500	2,635		39,065

Working :

Budgeted Sales for Agra	**Raja Units**	**Rani Units**
Budgeted	500	300
Add: Increase	(10%) 50	(20%) 60
	450	480
	100	50
Increase due to Advertisement	500	530

Budgeted Sales for Bombay	Raja Units	Rani Units
Budgeted	700	600
Add : Increase	(5%) 35	(10%) 60
	735	660
Increase due to Advertisement	90	70
Total	825	730

Production Budget :

The Production budget is prepared in relation to the sales budget. Whatever is to be sold should be produced in time so that it delivered to the customer. It is a forecast of the production for the budget period. Production budget is prepared for the number of units to be produced and also for the cost to be incurred on materials, labour and factory overheads. Two important considerations are involved in preparation of production budget:

(a) What is to be produced?

(b) When is it to be produced?

Production units = Sales unit – Opening stock units + Closing stock units.

The preparation of production budget involves the following stages:

1. **Consideration of plant capacity** : The number of units of different products to be produced should be determined and the capacity which the plant will be able to work throughout the budget period should be decided. One should not fix the capacity either too high or too low. A normal plant capacity which will be a realistic estimate should be budgeted.

2. **Consideration sales budget :** The production budget is fixed with reference to sales budget. The sales budget will provide a guideline for production planning. If both the budgets do not coordinate then there may arise problems of either selling the whole stock or of producing it. In case the sales are not undertaken as per schedule then production should be reduced or *vice versa*. A production budget may be prepared as given under.

3. **Production planning** : A proper production planning schedule is essential for preparing production budget. The number of physical units to be produced is determined. The utilization of optimum plant capacity and avoidance of bottlenecks due to shortage of materials and labour, etc., is considered while preparing a production plan. Production planning will ensure a smooth production schedule.

4. **Stock quantity to be held** : The quantity of finished goods to be carried forward should be decided. This quantity will depend upon a number of factors like sales potential, storage facilities available and cost of the stock. While fixing production target, the required closing stock figures will be added to the

estimated sales figures and opening stock figures will be deducted from it. The work in progress will also be taken into account while fixing a production target.

Production Budget for the period ending 31st Dec, 2012

Month	Units required for sale	*Add* closing Stock of finished goods	Total units required	*Less* opening stock of finished goods	Units to be produced
January					
February					
March					
April					
May					
June					
July					
August					
September					
October					
November					
December					
Total					

4. From the following data, prepare a Production Budget for Rani Ltd for a period of 6 months ending 30th June.

Product	Opening Stock 1st January 2011 Units	Closing Stock 30th June 2011 Units	Sales Forecast Units	Normal Loss in Production [%]
X	10,000	15,000	70,000	5
Y	12,000	10,000	60,000	4
Z	15,000	15,000	100,000	7

Solution :

Particulars	X	Y	Z	Total Units
I] Sales Forecast	70,000	60,000	100,000	2,30,000
II] Estimated Closing Stock	15,000	10,000	15,000	40,000
III] Gross Requirements [I + II]	85,000	70,000	1,15,000	2,70,000
IV] Opening Stock	10,000	12,000	15,000	37,000
V] Required Good Units [III - IV]	75,000	58,000	1,00,000	2,33,000
VI] Loss in Production	3947	2417	11,111	17,475
VII] Units to be Produced	78,947	60,417	1,11,111	2,50,475

Problem :

Prepare Production Budget from the following details for Kiran Ltd.

Product	Estimated Inventory 1st April 2008	Estimated Inventory 31st March 2009	Sales Forecast as per Sales Budget
X	4,000 units	5,000 units	25,000 units
Y	5,000 units	6,000 units	30,000 units

Solution :

Production Budget XYZ Ltd. Year 2008-09

Particulars	Product A - Units	Product B - Units
Sales Forecast	25000	30000
Add: Estimated Closing Stock	5000	6000
Total Requirements	30,000	36000
Less: Opening Stock	4000	5000
Net Requirement	26,000	31000

Cost of Production Budget :

The production budget determines the number of units to be produced. When these units are converted into monetary terms, it becomes a cost of production budget. The cost of production budget is the total to be spent on producing the units stipulated in production budget. The physical units are broken into elements, i.e., material, quantity, labour, time and manufacturing overheads. The materials cost, labour cost and overheads required for manufacturing units to make it a cost of production budget. A specimen of the cost of production budget is given below:

Product	Department	Items of Materials Required	Total Material Cost	Total Labour Cost	Cost per Unit
1 2					

Problem :

Prepare a production budget for each month and a summarized production cost budget for the six months period ending 31st December, 2011 from the following data of product 'X'.

(i) The units to be sold for different months are as follows.

July, 2011		2000
August		2000
September		3000
October		3500
November		4000
December		3500
January 2012		3000

(ii) There will be no work in progress at the end of any month.

(iii) Finished units equal to half the sales for the next month will be in stock at the end of each month (including June, 2011)

(iv) Budgeted production and production cost for the year ending 31st December, 2011 are as follows:

Production (Units) Direct materials (per unit) Direct Wages (per unit)		25,000 ₹ 15 ₹ 5

Total Factory Overheads apportioned to products Rs. 1,00,000.

Solution :

Production = (sales + closing stock) – opening stock

(i) Production Budget (for each month from July, 2011 to December, 2011)

Month 2011	Opening Stock (units)	Sales (Units)	Closing Stock (Units)	Production (units)
July	1000	2000	1000	2000
August	1000	2000	1500	2500
September	1500	3000	1750	3250
October	1750	3500	2000	3750
November	2000	4000	1750	3750
December	1750	3500	1500	3250
			Total	18,500 Units

(II) Production Cost Budgetfor six months ending 31st Dec. 2011

	Rate per Unit (₹)	(Production Units 11,050,) Amount (₹)
Direct Materials	15.00	2,77,500
Direct Wages	5.00	92,500
Factory Overheads	4.00	74,000
1,00,000 ÷ 25,000		
	Total	₹ 4,44,000

Problem :

A Kittu Company manufactures two products P and Q and the budgeted data for the year are follows.

	Product P (₹)	Product Q (₹)
Sales price per Unit	100	75
Direct Materials per unit	18	15
Direct wages per units	7	5
Total works Overhead	12,000	10,000
Total Marketing Overhead	1500	1500
The sales manager forecasts the sales in unit as follows:		
January	30	16
February	30	18
March	25	20
April	20	16
May	15	14
June	15	30
July to December, each month	20	18

It is assumed that (i) there will be no work in progress at the end of any month and (ii) finished units equal to half the sales for the following month will be kept in stock.

Prepare a production budget for each month and production cost budget.

Solution :

Production Budget (Units)

	P				Q			
Month	Sales	*Add* Closing Stock	*Less* Opening Stock	Production (P)	Sales	*Add* Closing Stock	*Less* Opening Stock	Production (Q)
January	30	15	15	30	16	9	8	17
February	30	13	15	28	18	10	9	19
March	26	10	13	23	20	8	10	18
April	20	9	10	19	16	7	8	15
May	18	9	9	18	14	15	7	22
June	18	10	9	19	30	9	15	24
July	20	10	10	20	18	9	9	18
August	20	10	10	20	18	9	9	18
September	20	10	10	20	18	9	9	18
October	20	10	10	20	18	9	9	18
November	20	10	10	20	18	9	9	18
December	20	10	10	20	18	9	9	18
Total	262			257	222			223

Note : Opening stock is half of the budgeted sales for the same month because closing stock of finished goods is equal to half the sales in the next month.

Summarized Production Cost budget

Particulars		Product P 257 units	Product Q 223 units	Total
		₹	₹	₹
Direct material	X : @ ₹ 20 } Y : @ ₹ 10 }	4,626	3,345	7,971
Direct labor	X : @ ₹ 5 } Y : @ ₹ 4 }	1,645	1,155	2,800
Works Overheads		12,000	10,000	22,000
Total Production Cost		18,271	14,500	32,771
Cost per Unit		71.09	65.02	

Materials Budget :

The material budget is concerned with determining the quantity of raw materials required for production. The programme for purchasing raw materials is adjusted according to the production budget. The materials are purchased as per the requirements of production department. The requirements of materials are determined product wise. The rates of consumption of raw materials are also determined. The number of units to be produced multiplied by the rate of consumption will give the figure of materials required for production. The opening stock of materials is deducted from material purchased during the year and closing stock and the requirement of materials in units will be determined. The units of materials required multiplied by the rate per unit of raw material will give us material cost. The raw materials budget will serve the following purposes:

1. The Purchase Department will be able to plan the purchase of raw materials at different times.
2. It will enable the fixation of minimum stock level, maximum stock level and re-ordering level.
3. The raw materials purchase budget will be determined
4. The budgeted cost of raw materials will be determined.

Material Purchase Budget : This budget shows the quantity of materials to be purchased during the coming year. For the preparation of this budget, production budget is the starting point if it is the key factor. If the raw material availability is the key factor, it becomes the starting point. The desired closing inventory of the raw materials is added to the requirement as per the production budget and the opening inventory is subtracted from the gross requirements. This budget is prepared in quantity as well as in the monetary terms and helps immensely in planning of the purchases of raw materials. Availability of storage space, financial resources, various levels of materials like maximum, minimum, re-order and economic order quantity are taken into consideration while preparing the budget. A separate material utilization budget may also be prepared as a preparation of material purchase budget.

Problem :

R Ltd. manufactures three products, X, Y and Z. You are required to prepare for the month of January 2012, the following budgets from the information given below.

i. Sales Budget in quantity and value
ii. Production Budget
iii. Material Utilization Budget
iv. Purchase Budget in quantity and value Sales Forecast

Product	Quantity	Price Per Unit
X	2000	₹ 150
Y	3000	₹ 170
Z	2500	₹ 190

Materials Used in Company's Products are,

Material M1 ₹ 5 per unit

Material M2 ₹ 7 per unit

Material M2 ₹ 10 per unit

Quantities used in Product

Product	M1	M2	M3
X	5	3	-
Y	4	4	3
Z	3	2	2

Finished Stocks :

Product	X	Y	Z
Opening Inventory- units	2000	2500	1500
Closing Inventory- units	2100	2600	1600

Material Stocks :

Particulars	M1	M2	M3
Opening Stock [Units]	25000	15000	10000
Closing Stock [Units]	30000	18000	12000

Solution :

Sales Budget

Particulars	Product X	Product Y	Product Z	Total
Units	2000	3000	2500	
Selling Price Per Unit [₹]	150	170	190	
Sales Value [₹]	3, 00,000	5, 10,000	4, 75,000	12,85,000

Production Budget - in Units

Particulars	Product X	Product Y	Product Z
Sales Forecast	2000	3000	2500
Add: Expected Closing Stock	2100	2600	1600
Gross Requirement	4100	5600	4100
Less: Opening Stock	2000	2500	1500
Net Production Requirement	2100	3100	2600

Material Utilization Budget

Budgeted	M1	M2	M3
X : 2100	2100 x 5 = 10,500	2100 x 3 = 6,300	
Y: 3100	3100 x 4 = 12,400	3100 x 4 = 12,400	3100 x 3 = 9300
Z: 2600	2600 x 3 = 7,800	2600 x 2 = 5,200	2600 x 2 = 5,200
Total	30,700	23,900	14,500

Material Purchase Budget

Particulars	M1	M2	M3	Total
Requirement as per Material Utilization Budget [units]	30,700	23,900	14,500	
Add: Closing Stock [units]	30,000	18,000	12,000	
Total Requirements	60,700	41,900	26,500	
Less: Opening Stock [units]	25,000	15,000	10,000	
Required Purchases [units]	35,700	26,900	16,500	
Unit Cost [₹]	5	7	10	
Purchase Cost [₹]	1,78,500	1,88,300	16,5000	5,31,800

Problem :

The sales director of a manufacturing company reports that next year he expects to sell 40,000 units of a particular product. The production department gives the following figures.

Two kinds of raw material A and B are required for manufacturing the product. Each product requires 3 units of material A and 2 units of material B. the estimated opening balances next year will be:

Finished product - 10,000 units, material A – 12,000 units, material B – 15,000 Units.

The desirable closing balances at the end of the year are :

Finished product – 16,000 units, material A – 14,000 units, material B – 15,000 units.

Draw up a materials purchase budget.

Solution :

Materals Purchase Budget (Quantitative)

	Material A (Units)	Material B (Units)
Materials required to produce 46,000 units		
Material A @ 3 units for 46,000 units	1,38,000	
Materials B @ 2 units for 46,000 units		92,000
Desired closing balance of materials at the end of year	14,000	15,000
	1,52,000	1,07,000
Less: Opening balances of materials at the beginning of the year	12,000	15,000
Materials required to be purchased during the year	1,40,000	92,000

Working Notes :

(1) Production during the year is calculated as :

Estimated sales units + desired closing stock of finished goods – opening stock of finished goods. (40,000 + 16,000 – 10,000 = 46,000 units)

Problem :

From the following figures prepare Raw Materials Purchase Budget for Jan. 2012

	Materials (Units)					
	A	B	C	D	E	F
Estimated Stock on January 1	1,600	600	2,400	200	1,400	2,800
Estimated stock on January 31	2,000	800	2,800	400	1,600	3,200
Estimated Consumption	12,000	4,400	13,200	3,600	8,800	17,200
Standard Price per unit (₹)	2	3	2		3	5

Solution :

Raw Materials Purchase Budgetfor January, 2005

	A	B	C	D	E	F
Estimate Consumption (units)	1,20,00	4,400	13,200	3,600	8,800	17,200
Add: Estimated Stock on Jan. 31 (units)	2,000	800	2,800	400	1,600	3,200
	14,000	5,200	16,000	4,000	10,400	20,400
Less: Estimated Stock on Jan 1 units	1,600	600	2,400	200	1,400	2,800
Estimated Purchase (Units)	12,400	4,600	13,600	3,800	9,000	17,600
Rate per unit (₹)	2	3	2	4	3	5
Estimated Purchase (₹)	24,800	13,800	27,200	15,200	27,000	88,000

Direct Labour Budget :

The labour may be classified into direct and indirect labour. The labour required for manufacturing the product is knows as direct labour. The labour which cannot be specified with production is called indirect labour. Though two budgets may be prepared, direct and indirect labour, but from costing point of view only direct labour budget is prepared because indirect labour is made a part of manufacturing overheads.

The labour content of each item is determined in terms of workers required as per production budget. The labour time needed for each job, process and operation is determined with the help of time and motion study. The rates of pay including all allowances are multiplied by labour time for calculating labour cost. If labour incentive schemes are in operation then labour rates should be suitably increased. If a piece rate system for paying wages is in operation then labour cost will be calculated by multiplying budget units by the labour rate per unit.

Labour budget is useful for anticipating labour time required for production. The personnel department is also able to make arrangements for recruitment of workers, etc.

Problem :

The direct labour hour requirements of three of the products manufactured in a factory, each involving more than one labour operation, are estimated as follows:

Direct labour hours per units (in minutes)

	Products		
	1	2	3
Operation 1	18	42	30
Operation 2	-	12	24
Operation 3	9	6	-

The factory worked 8 hours per day, 6 days in a week. The budget quarter is taken as 13 weeks and during a quarter, lost hours due to leave and holidays and other causes are estimated to be 124 hours.The budget hourly rates for the workers manning the operation 1,2, and 3 are Rs. 2,00 ; ₹ 2.50 and ₹ 3.00 respectively. The budgeted sales for the product during the quarter are:

Product 1	9,000 Units
Product 2	15,000 Units
Product 3	12,000 Units

There is a carryover of 5,000 units of product 2 and 4,000 units of product 3 and it is proposed to build up a stock at the end of the budget quarter as follows:

Product 1	1,000 Units
Product 3	2,000 Units

Prepare a man - power budget for the quarter showing for each operation (i) direct labour hours(ii) direct labour cost and (iii) the number of workers.

Solution :

Quarterly Man - Power Budget

		Product 1		Product 2		Product 3		Total		
Operations	Hourly Rate	Direct Labour Hrs	Cost ₹	Direct Labour Hrs	Cost ₹	Direct Labour Hrs	Cost ₹	Direct Labour Hrs	Cost ₹	No of Workers
1	2.00	3,000	6,000	7,000	14,000	5,000	10,000	15,000	30,000	30
2	2.50	-	-	2,000	5,000	4,000	10,000	6,000	15,000	12
3	3.00	1,500	4,500	1,000	3,000	-	--	2,500	7,500	5

Working Notes :

1. Production budget

	Production units		
	1	2	3
Sales	9,000	15,000	12,000
Add: Closing Stock	1,000	-	2,000
	10,000	15,000	14,000
Less : Opening Stock	-	5,000	4,000
	10,000	10,000	10,000

2. Total Hours Available (per man in a quarter)

Total hours	8 x 6 x 13 = 624
Less: Hours lost due to leave etc.	124
Total hours available per man	500

3. Direct labour Hours

Product 1

Operation 1 $\frac{18 \times 10{,}000}{60} = 3{,}000$

Operation 3 $\frac{9 \times 10{,}000}{60} = 1{,}500$

Product 2

Operation 1 $\frac{42 \times 10,000}{60} = 7,000$

Operation 2 $\frac{12 \times 10,000}{60} = 2,000$

Operation 3 $\frac{6 \times 10,000}{60} = 1,000$

Product 3

Operation 1 $\frac{30 \times 10,000}{60} = 5,000$

Operation 2 $\frac{24 \times 10,000}{60} = 4,000$

4. Direct Labour Cost

Product 1

Operation 1 = 3,000 hours x ₹ 2 = ₹. 6,000

Operation 2 = 1,500 hours x ₹ 3 = ₹ 4,500

Product 2

Operation 1 = 7,000 hours x ₹ 2 = ₹ 14,000

Operation 2 = 2,000 hours x ₹ 2.50 = ₹ 5,000

Operation 3 = 1,000 hours x ₹ 3.00 = ₹ 3,000

Product 3

Operation 1 = 5,000 hours x ₹ 2.00 = ₹ 10,000

Operation 2 = 4,000 hours x ₹ 2.50 = ₹ 10,000

5. Number of Men Required

Number of Men Required = $\frac{\text{Direct labour hours required}}{\text{Total available hours per man}}$

Operation 1 = $\frac{15,000}{500} = 30$ men

Operation 2 = $\frac{6,000}{500} = 12$ men

Operation 3 = $\frac{2,500}{500} = 5$ men

Manufacturing Overheads Cost Budget :

The manufacturing cost is divided direct and indirect cost. The indirect cost of overheads cost is the part of works cost which arises from indirect labour. Indirect materials, overheads and other factory expenses, manufacturing cost is excluded from direct material and direct labour. Manufacturing overheads cost may be classified into fixed cost, variable cost and semi variable cost.

The fixed works overheads cost remains constant irrespective of output and it is estimated one of past experience. The variable works overhead cost is determined per unit of cost and it is calculated by multiplying the rate per unit. The semi variable cost increases with the increase in output but the rate per unit decreases with the increase in output. While budgeting manufacturing overheads, cost, management must consider the level of activity to be attained in future so that the expenses are estimated accurately.

Problem :

From the information given below, prepare a manufacturing overheads budget for the quarter ending December 31, 2014:

Budget output during the quarter	6,000 units
Fixed overheads	₹ 32,000
Variable Overheads (Varying at the rate of Rs. 5 per unit)	₹ 30,000
Semi Variable Overheads (40 % fixed and 60 % varying @ Rs. 3 per unit)	18,000

Solution :

Manufacturing Overheads Budget for the quarter ending Dec. 31, 2014

		₹
Fixed Overheads		32,000
Variable Overheads (5,000 x 5)		30,000
Semi - Variable Overheads	10,800	
Fixed (40 %)	7,200	18,000
Total		80,000

Selling and Distribution Overheads Budget :

This budget included all expenses relating to selling, advertising and distribution of goods, these expenses may be analyzed according to products, territories, salesmen, etc., the fixed expenses under this category may be estimated on the past experience and anticipated changes. Variable selling and distribution overheads will vary with the anticipated sales figures. The responsibility for preparing this budget lies with the executives of sales departments. The volume of these expenses should be in direct proportion to expected sales figures. The future expectations, estimated by the management, advertising policies, research programmes and nature of these expenses will influence the selling and distribution overhead budget.

Problem :

You are required to prepare a sales overheads budget from the estimates given below.

Advertisement	3000
Salaries of the sales department	5,500
Expenses of sales department	2000
Counter salesmen's salaries and dearness allowance	7,000

The travelling salesmen commission at 10% on their sales, expenses at 5% on their sales and counter salesman commission 1% on counter sales.

Sales during the period were estimated as follows:

Counter Sales	Travelling Salesmen's
₹	₹
100,000	15,000
1,50,000	20,000
2,00,000	25,000

Solution :

Sales Overheads Budget

	Estimated Sales		
	₹	₹	₹
Fixed Overheads			
Advertisement	3000	3000	3000
Salaries of Sales department	5,000	5,000	5,000
Expense of sales department	2,000	2,000	2,000
Counter salesman's Salaries & D.A	7,000	7,000	7,000
	17,500	17,500	17,500
Variable Overheads			
Counter Salesman's Commission @ 1% on Sales	1000	1,500	2000
Travelling Salesmens's Commission @ 10 %	1,500	2,000	2,500
Expenses @ 5 %	750	1000	1,250
Total Sales Overheads	3250	4500	5750
	20,750	22,000	23,250

Cash budget :

A cash budget is the combination of cash receipts and payments of a particular period. It proceeds various other budgets like materials budget and research and development budget. "The cash budget is an analysis of flow of cash in a business over a future, short or long period of time. It is a forecast of expected cash intake and outlay"

The cash receipts from various sources are anticipated. The estimated cash collections for sales, debts, bills receivables, interests, dividends and other incomes will be taken into account. The amounts to be spent on purchase of materials, payment to creditors and meeting various other revenue and capital expenditure needs should be considered. Cash forecasts will include all possible sources from which cash will be received and the channels in which payments are to be made so that a consolidated cash position is determined.

Problem :

XYZ Co. wished to arrange overdraft facilities with its bankers during the period April 2011 to June 2011 when it will be manufacturing mostly for the stock. Prepare a Cash Budget for the above period from the following data, indicating the extent of the bank facilities the company will require at the end of each month.

Particulars	Sales	Purchases	Wages
February 2011	₹ 1,80,000	₹ 1,24,800	₹ 12,000
March	1,92,000	1,44,000	14,000
April	1,08,000	2,43,000	11,000
May	1,74,000	2,46,000	10,000
June	1,26,000	2,68,000	15,000

Additional Information :

Working Notes :

Collection from debtors :

April :

50% of sales of February ₹ 90, 000} Total ₹ 1, 86,000

50% of sales of March ₹ 96, 000}

May

50% of sales of March ₹ 96, 000} Total ₹ 1, 50,000

50% of sales of April ₹ 54, 000}

June

50% of sales of April ₹ 54, 000} Total ₹ 1, 41,000

50% of sales of May ₹ 87, 000}

Solution :

Cash Budget April – June 2011

Particulars	April ₹	May ₹	June ₹
A] Opening Balance [Overdraft]	25, 000	56, 000	[47, 000]
B] Expected Receipts Collections from debtors	1, 86,000	1, 50,000	1, 41,000
C] Total Cash Available [A + B]	2, 11,000	2, 06,000	94,000
D] Expected Payments			
i. Payment to creditors	1, 44,000	2, 43,000	2, 46,000
ii. Wages	11,000	10,000	15,000
E] Total Payments	1, 55,000	2, 53,000	2, 61,000
F] Closing Balance [C – E]	56,000	[47,000]	[1, 67,000]

Problem :

A company is expecting to have ₹ 32,000 cash in hand on 1st April 2011 and it requests you to prepare cash budget for the three months. April to June 2011. The following information is supplied to you:

Month	Sales (₹)	Purchases (₹)	Wages (₹)	Expenses (₹)
February	70,000	44,000	6,000	5,000
March	80,000	56,000	9,000	6,000
April	96,000	60,000	9,000	7,000
May	1,00,000	68,000	11,000	9,000
June	1,20,000	62,000	14,000	9,000

Other information :

(a) Period of credit allowed by suppliers is two months.

(b) 25% of sales are for cash and the period of credit allowed to customers for credit sales is one month.

(c) Delay in payment of wages and expenses one month.

(d) Income tax ₹ 28,000 is to be paid in June 2011.

Solution :

Cash Budget for the months from April to June 2011

	April ₹	May ₹	June ₹
Receipts:			
Opening balance of cash in hand	32,000	57,000	82,000
Receipts from cash sales (25 %)	24,000	25,000	30,000
Cash realised from debtors (75 % of previous months sales)	60,000	72,000	75,000
Total (a)	1,16,000	1,54,000	1,87,000
Payments			
Creditors for purchase (Feb. paid April and so on)			
Wages	44,000	56,000	60,000
Expenses	9,000	9,000	11,000
Income Tax	6,000	7,000	9,000
Total (b)	-	-	30,000
Closing Balance of Cash (a – b)	59,000	72,000	1,10,000
	57,000	82,000	77,000

Problem :

Bharathi Ltd wishes to arrange overdraft facilities with bankers during the period April to June of a particular year, when it will be manufacturing mostly for stock. Prepared a cash budget for the above period from the following data, indicating the extent of the bank facilities, the company will require at the end of each month:

Month	Sales (₹)	Purchases (₹)	Wages (₹)
February	1,80,000	1,24,800	12,000
March	1,92,000	1,44,000	14,000
April	1,08,000	2,43,000	11,000
May	1,74,000	2,46,000	10,000
June	1,26,000	2,68,000	15,000

(b) 50 % of the credit sale are realized in the month following the sales and the remaining sales in second month following.

(c) Creditors are paid in the following month of purchase.

(d) Cash at bank on 1st April ₹ 25,000.

Solution :

Cash Budgetfor the months from April to June 2011

	April ₹	May ₹	June ₹
Receipts :			
Opening balance of cash at Bank / Overdraft	25,000	56,000	-47,000
Realised from Debtors	1,86,000	1,50,000	1,41,000
Total (a)	2,11,000	2,06,000	94,000
Payments :			
Creditors for prchases	1,44,000	2,43,000	2,46,000
Wages	11,000	10,000	15,000
Total (b)	1,55,000	2,53,000	2,61,000
Closing Balance of Cash at Bank / Overdraft	56,000	-47,000	1,67,000

1. Figures in brackets indicate bank overdreaft.
2. Calculation of Receipts from debtors:

April : 50 % of sales for February + 50 % of Sales for March

= ₹ 90,000 + 96,000 = ₹ 1, 86,000

May : 50 % of Sales for March + 50 % of Sales for April

= ₹ 96,000 + 54,000 = ₹ 1, 50,000

June : 50 % of Sales for April + 50 % of Sales for May

= ₹ 54,000 + 87,000 = ₹ 1, 41,000

Problem :

A newly started company wishes to prepare Cash Budget from January 2011. Prepare a Cash Budget for the first six months from the following estimated receipts and expenditures.

Month	Total Sales ₹	Materials ₹	Wages ₹	Production Overheads ₹	Selling & Distribution Overheads ₹
January	20,000	20,000	4,000	3,200	800
February	22,000	14,000	4,400	3,300	900
March	24,000	14,000	4,600	3,300	800
April	26,000	12,000	4,600	3,400	900
May	28,000	12,000	4,800	3,500	900
June	30,000	16,000	4,800	3,600	1,000

Cash balance on 1st January was ₹10, 000. A new machine is to be installed at ₹ 30, 000 on credit to be repaid by two equal installments in March and April. Sales commission @ 5% on total sales is to be paid within the month following actual sales. ₹ 10, 000 being the amount of 2nd call on shares may be received in March. Share premium amounting to ₹ 2, 000 is also receivable with 2nd call.

Credit allowed by suppliers is 2 months, credit allowed to customers is 1 month, delay in payment of overheads is 1 month, and delay in payment in wages is ½ month.

Assume cash sales to be 50% of total sales.

Cash Budget (January – June 2011 ₹)

Particulars	Jan.	Feb	March	April	May	June
A] Opening Balance	10,000	18,000	29,800	20,000	6,100	8,800
B] Expected Receipts						
I] Cash Sales [50% of total sales]	10,000	11,000	12,000	13,000	14,000	15,000
II] Collections from Debtors [1 month credit]		10,000	11,000	12,000	13,000	14,000
III] Share 2nd Call			10,000			
IV] Share Premium			2,000			
C] Total Expected Receipts [I + II + III + IV]	10,000	21,000	35,000	25,000	27,000	29,000
D] Total Cash Available [A + C]	20,000	39,000	64,800	45,000	33,100	37,800
E] Expected Payments						
I] Payment for Purchases [2 months credit]			20,000	14,000	14,000	12,000
II] Production overheads [1 month delay]		3,200	3,300	3,300	3,400	3,500
IV] S & D overheads 1 month delay]		800	900	800	900	900
V] Wages*	2,000	4,200	4,500	4,600	4,700	4,800
VI] Sales Commission		1,000	1,100	1,200	1,300	1,400
VII] Machine Purchase			15,000	15,000		
F] Total Payments	2,000	9,200	44,800	38,900	24,300	22,600
G] Cl. Balance [D – F]	18,000	29,800	20,000	6,100	8,800	15,200

* There is a delay in payment of wages by ½ month; hence 50% of current month and 50% of previous month is paid in the current month. The payment made in each month is show below.

Particulars	January	February	March	April	May	June
Wages	2,000	2,000 Jan 2,200 Feb	2,200 Feb 2,300 Mar	2,300 M 2,300 A	2,300 A 2,400 M	2,400 M 2,400 J
Total	2,000	4,200	4,500	4,600	4,700	4,800

Problem :

Summarized below are the Income and Expenditure forecasts for the month March to August 2011.

Month	Credit Sales ₹	Credit Purchases ₹	Wages ₹	Mfg. Expenses ₹	Office Expenses ₹	Selling Expenses ₹
March	60,000	36,000	9,000	4,000	2,000	4,000
April	62,000	38,000	8,000	3,000	1,500	5,000
May	64,000	33,000	10,000	4,500	2,500	4,500
June	58,000	35,000	8,500	3,500	2,000	3,500
July	56,000	39,000	9,000	4,000	1,000	4,500
August	60,000	34,000	8,000	3,000	1,500	4,500

You are given the following further information.

Plant costing ₹ 16, 000 due for delivery in June. 10% on delivery and balance after three months. ~ Advance tax ₹ 8, 000 is payable in March and June

Period of credit allowed, Suppliers 2 months and customers 1 month

Lag in payment of manufacturing expenses half month

Lag in payment of all other expenses one month

Cash balance on 1st May 2011 is ₹ 8, 000

Prepare Cash Budget for three months starting from 1st May 2011

Solution :

Cash Budget

May – August 2011 (₹)

Particulars	May	June	July
I] Opening Cash Balance	8,000	15,750	12,750
II] Expected Cash Receipts:			
A] Collections from Debtors [Credit 1 month]	62,000	64,000	58,000
III] Total Expected Receipts	62,000	64,000	58,000
IV] Total Cash Available [I + III]	70,000	79,750	70,750
V] Expected Payments			
A] Purchases [2 months credit]	36,000	38,000	33,000
B] Manufacturing Expenses [Half month credit] *	3,750	4,000	3,750
C] Wages [Half month credit] *	8,000	10,000	8,500
D] Office Expenses [one month credit]	1,500	2,500	2,000
E] Selling Expenses [one month credit]	5,000	4,500	3,500
F] Purchase of Machine			1,600
G] Advance Tax		8,000	
VI] Total Payments [A + B + C + D + E + F + G]	54,250	67,000	52,350
VII] Closing Balance [IV – VI]	15,750	12,750	18,400

* There is a delay of half a month for payment of Manufacturing Expenses and wages and hence current month's 50% and previous month's 50% are paid in the current month.

Problem :

Prepare a Cash Budget from the following information for XYZ Ltd.

Particulars	1st Quarter [₹]	IInd Quarter [₹]	III rd Quarter [₹]	IVth Quarter [₹]
Opening Cash	10,000			
Collections from customers	1,25,000	1,50,000	1,60,000	2,21,000
Payments:				
Purchase of Materials	20,000	35,000	35,000	54,200
Other expenses	25,000	20,000	20,000	17,000
Salaries and wages	90,000	95,000	95,000	1,09,000
Income tax		5, 000		
Machinery Purchase				20,000

The company desires to maintain a cash balance of ₹ 15,000 at the end of each quarter. Cash can be borrowed or repaid in multiples of ₹ 500 at an interest rate of 10% p.a. Management does not want to borrow cash more than what is necessary and wants to repay as early as possible. In any event, loans cannot be extended beyond a quarter. Interest is computed and paid when principal is repaid. Assume that borrowing takes place at the beginning and repayments are made at the end of the quarter.

[ICWAI Intermediate]

Solution :

XYZ Ltd.

Cash Budget Period I – IV Quarter

Particulars	Quarter I [₹]	Quarter II [₹]	Quarter III[₹]	Quarter IV [₹]
A] Opening Cash Balance	10,000	15, 000	15, 000	15, 325
B] Cash Receipts From Debtors	1,25,000	1,50,000	1,60,000	2,21,000
C] Total Cash Available [A + B]	1,35,000	1,65,000	1,75, 000	2,36,325
D] Expected Payments				
Materials	20,000	35,000	35,000	54,200
Other Expenses	25,000	20,000	20,000	17,000

Salaries and Wages	90,000	95,000	95,000	1,09,200
Income Tax•	5,000	–	–	–
Machinery Purchase	–	–	–	20,000
E] Total Payments	1,40, 000	1,50,000	1,50,000	2,00,400
F] Minimum Cash Balance Required	15,000	15,000	15,000	15,000
G] Total Cash Required [E + F]	1,55,000	1,65,000	1,65,000	2,15,400
H] Excess/Deficit[C – G]	20,000	–	10,000	20,925
I] Borrowing		20, 000	–	–
J] Repayment			9, 000	11,000
K] Interest			675 *	1,100
L] Total Effect of Financing	20, 000	–	9, 675	12,100
M] Closing Cash Balance [C + L – E]	15, 000	15, 000	15, 325	23, 825

* Interest is calculated as follows.

10% p.a. on ₹ 9, 000 = ₹ 900. Since the amount is repaid in the third quarter, interest is calculated for 9 months, i.e. for 12 months ₹ 900, for 9 months = ₹ 675.

Similarly, in the last quarter interest is calculated @ 10% on ₹ 11,000 = ₹ 1,100

Capital Expenditure Budget :

The budget lays down the amount of estimated expenditure to be incurred on fixed assets during the budget period. As the amount involved in capital expenditure is usually high this requires careful attention of the top management. The budget is based upon the annual forecasts of capital expenditure of various divisions or departments. Each division or department of an organization sends the annual forecast of capital expenditure of its own department to capital expenditure sanction committee. The committee after considering the profitabilities of the capital expenditure sanctions the expenditure and then the amount is incorporated in the budget.

Master Budget :

The master budget is the summary of various functional budgets. It is prepared by integrating various budgets into one consolidated budget so as to represent the budgeted profit and loss account and the budgeted balance sheet as at the end of the budget period. In the words of Rowland and William H Harr, the master budget is "a summary of the budget schedules in capsule from made for the purpose of presenting in one report the highlights of the budget forecast. "The institute of Management Account, London defines it as "the summary budget, incorporating its component functional budgets and which is finally approved, adopted and employed.

The master budget is prepared by the budget officer and requires the approval of the Budget Committee before it is put into operation. This budget is used to coordinate the activities of various functional departments and also to serve as a control device.

The various steps involved in the preparation of this budget include the construction of (i) Sales budget, as the starting point; (ii) Production budget; (iii) Cost of production budget; (iv) Cash budget and (v) The projected income statement and the balance sheet.

Problem

A Glass Manufacturing Company requires you to calculate and present the budget for the next year from the following information.

Sales:		
Throughened Glass		₹ 5,00,000
Bent Toughened Glass		₹ 4,00,000
Direct material Cost	60% of Sales	
Direct Wages	20 workers @ ₹ 200 per month.	
Factory Overheads		
Indirect Labour		
Foreman Salary ₹ 200 per Month		
Stores & Spares	2 % on Sales	Rs
Depreciation on Machinery		13,500
Light and Power		6,000
Repairs and maintenance		10,000
Other sundries	10 % on direct wages	
Administration, selling and distribution expenses	₹20,000 per year	

Solution :

Master Budget

for the period..............

I. Sales Budget		₹
Throughened Glass		5,00,000
Bent Throughened Glass		4,00,000
		9,00,000
II. Production Cost Budget		
Direct Materials, 60 % of sales		5,40,000
Direct Wages		48,000
Prime Cost		4,92,000
Factory Overheads:		

	₹	
Variable: Stores and Spares		
(2½) on sales	18,000	
Light and power	6,000	
Repairs and Maintenance	10,000	34,000
		4,58,000
Fixed : Indirect Labour:		
Works Manager		
Foreman	6,000	
Depreciation	2,400	
Sundries	13,500	
	4,800	26,700
III. Gross Profit (I - II)		4,31,300
IV. Administration, Selling and Distribution Cost		20,000
V. Expected Net Profit (III- IV)		4,11,300

Problem :

PYE Ltd. produces and markets a very popular product called P. the company is interested in presenting its budget for the second quarter of 2011

The following information's are made available for this purpose:

(a) It expects to sell 50,000 bags of P during the second quarter of 2005 at the selling price of ₹ 9 per bag.

(b) Each bag of P requires 2.5 kgs of a raw material called Q and 7.5 kgs of raw material called R.

(c) Stock levels are planned as follows:

	Beginning of Quarter	End of Quarter
Finished bags of P (Nos)	15,000	11,000
Raw Material Q (Kgs)	32,000	26,000
Raw material R (kg)	57,000	47,000
Empty bag (Nos)	37,000	28,000

(d) Q costs ₹ 1.20 per kg. R costs 20 per kg. and empty bag costs 80 paise each.

(e) It requires 9 minutes of direct labour time to produce and fill one bag of P. Labour cost is ₹ 5 per hour.

(f) Variable ₹ 0.45 per bag. Fixed manufacturing costs ₹ 30,000 per quarter

(g) Variable selling and administration expenses are 5 % of sales and fixed administration and selling expenses are ₹ 25,000 per quarter.

You are required to :

(1) Prepare a production budget for the said quarter

(2) Prepare a raw materials purchase budget for Q, R and empty bags for the said quarter in quantity as well as in rupees.

(3) Compute the budgeted variable cost to produce one bag of P

(4) Prepare a statement of budgeted net income for the said quarter and show both per unit and total cost.

Solution :

(i) Production Budget for Product P for Second Quarter of 2011

			Bags (Nos)
Budgeted Sales			50,000
Add : Planned Level of Closing Stock			11,000
Total Requirements			61,000
Less: Planned Level of Opening Stock			15,000
Production Requirements for the Quarter			46,000

(ii) Raw Material Purchase Budget

	Q (kgs)	R (kgs)	Empty Bags (Nos)
Requirements per bag of P	2.5	7.5	1
Requirements for 46,000 bags of P	1,15,000	3,45,000	46,000
Add: Planned Level of Closing / stock	26,000	47,000	28,000
Total Requirements	1,41,000	3,92,000	74,000
Less: Planned Level of Opening Stock	32,000	57,000	37,000
Quantity of Raw Material to be purchased	1,09,000	3,35,000	37,000
cost of Raw Material per kg / bag	₹1.20	₹ 0.20	₹ 0.80
Cost of Raw material to be purchased for the Quarter	₹1,30,800	₹ 67,000	₹ 29,600

(iii) Computation of Budgeted Variable Cost to produce one Bag of P

Raw Material	Qty	Rate (₹)	Total ₹
Q	2.5 (kg)	1.20	3.00
R	7.5 (kg)	0.20	1.5
Empty Bag	1 (No)	0.80	0.80
Direct Labour Cost	9	5	0.75
Variable Manufacturing Cost	(Minutes)	(Per hour)	0.45
Total			6.50

(iv) Statement of Budgeted Net Incomefor the second Quarter of 2011

	₹	Total	Per Unit ₹
Sales Revenue (50,000 x 9)		4,50,000	9.00
Less: Variable Cost:			
Manufacturing Cost (50,000 x 6.50)	3,25,000		
Selling and Administrative Expenses (5 % of Sales)	22,500	3,47,500	6.95
Less: Fixed Cost		1,02,500	2.05
Fixed Manufacturing Cost	30,000		
Fixed Administration and Selling Cost	25,000	55,000	
Budgeted Net Income		47,500	

Performance Budgeting :

Performance budget has been defined as a "budget based on functions, activities and projects" performance budgeting may be described as the budgeting system in which input costs are related to the performance, i.e., end results. It is a system of budgeting which provides for appraisal of performance as well as follow-up measures

Under conventional system of budgeting, a budget represents a statement of various amounts provided for different kinds of expenditures to be incurred. It takes the form of what is called as "List of appropriations" and so long as expenses incurred by the concerned department do not exceed the budget amount, there is no apparent irregularity. Thus, the conventional budgeting lays emphasis only on the amount of expenses to be incurred. The performance budgeting, on the other hand, lays emphasis on the results achieved or the performance rather then the expenditure incurred. The performance budget as defined in the Report of the Estimates Committee on Budgetary Reforms reads as follows:

The performance budget is a budget based on functions, activities and projects which focus attention on the accomplishment, the general and relative importance of the work to be done and the service to be rendered rather than upon the means of accomplishments such as personnel, service, supplies, equipment, etc. Under this system, the functions of various organizational units would be split into programmes of activities, sub-programmes and component schemes, etc., and estimates would be presented for each"

Performance budgeting seeks to establish relationship between inputs (costs) and their direct outputs. According to National Institute of Bank Management, performance budgeting is " the process of analyzing identifying, simplifying and crystalising specific performance objectives of a job to be achieved over a period, in the framework of the organizational objectives, the purpose and objectives of the job. The technique is characterized by its specific direction towards the business objectives of the organisation".

Performance budgeting involves (i) development of performance criteria of various programmes; (ii) assessment of performance of each programme and by each responsibility unit (iii) comparision of the actual performance with the budget; and (iv) undertaking periodic review of the programme with a view to make modifications as required

Problem :

The following data relate to a company which had a profit plan approved for selling 5000 units per month at an average selling price of ₹ 10 per unit. The budgeted variable cost of production was ₹ 4 per unit and fixed costs were budgeted at ₹ 20,000, planned income being ₹ 10,000 per month Because of shortage of raw materials the plant could produce only 4000 units and the cost or production was increased by 0.50 per unit. Consequently the selling price was raised by Re. 1.00 per unit. To modify production processes in order to meet material shortage, the company incurred an expenditure of ₹ 1000 in Research and Development. Set out a performance budget and a summary report.

	Performance Budget for the month of					
	Budget			Actual		
	Units	Amount per unit (₹)	Total Amount (₹)	Units	Amount per unit (₹)	Total Amount (₹)
Sales	5000	10,00	50,000	4,000	11.00	44,000
Less: Variable Cost	5,000	4.00	20,000	4000	4.50	18,000
Contribution		6.00	30,000		6.50	26,000
Less: Fixed Cost			20,000			21,000
Profit			10,000			5,000

Traditional Budgeting Vs Zero Base Budgeting

1.	Emphasis	It is more accounting - oriented than decision - oriented. Depends upon past data and lays emphasis on 'how much'	It is decision - oriented. Lays emphasis on 'why'
2.	Approach	Its approach is monitoring toward expenditures.	Its approach is towards achievement of objectives
3.	Focus	Its focus is on increase or decrease in expenditures over the past.	Its focus is on cost benefit analysis.
4.	Communication	In traditional budgeting, communication is usually vertical	It encourages communication both vertically and horizontally
5.	Method	The method preparation of traditional budget is based upon extrapolation.	Its preparation is based upon selection of decision package in view of cost - benefit analysis.

Zero-based Budgeting :

Zero-based Budgeting is method of budgeting whereby, all activities are revaluated each time budget is formulated and every item of expenditure in the budget is fully justified. Thus the Zero-based Budgeting involves from scratch or zero.

Zero-based budgeting [also known as priority based budgeting], actually emerged in the late 1960s as an attempt to overcome the limitations of incremental budgeting. This approach requires that all activities are justified and prioritized before decisions are taken relating to the amount of resources allocated to each activity. In incremental budgeting or traditional budgeting, previous year's figures are taken as base and based on the same the budgeted figures for the next year are worked out. Thus, the previous year is taken as the base for preparation of the budget. However, the main limitation of this system of budgeting is that an activity is continued in the future only because it is being continued in the past. Hence in Zero-based Budgeting, the beginning is made from scratch and each activity and function is reviewed thoroughly before sanctioning the same and all expenditures are analyzed and sanctioned only if they are justified.

Besides adopting a 'Zero-based' approach, the Zero-based Budgeting also focuses on programs or activities instead of functional departments based on line items, which is a feature of traditional budgeting. It is an extension of program budgeting. In program budgeting, programs are identified and goals are developed for the organization for the particular program. By inserting decision packages in the system and ranking the packages, the analysis is strengthened and priorities are determined.

Applications of Zero-based Budgeting :

The following stages/steps are involved in the application of Zero-Based Budgeting.

- Each separate activity of the organization is identified and is called as a decision package. Decision package is actually nothing but a document that identifies and describes an activity in such a manner that it can be evaluated by the management and rank against other activities competing for limited resources and decide whether to sanction the same or not.

- It should be ensured that each decision package is justified in the sense it should be ascertained whether the package is consistent with the goal of the organization or not.
- If the package is consistent with the overall objectives of the organization, the cost of minimum efforts required to sustain the decision should be determined.
- Based on the cost and benefit analysis a particular decision packages/ should be selected and resources are allocated to the selected package.

Benefits from Zero-based Budgeting :

ZBB was first introduced by Peter A. Pyhrr, a staff control manager at Texas Instruments Corporation, U.S.A. He developed this technique and implemented it for the first time during the year 1969-70 in Texas in the private sector and popularized its wider use. He wrote an article on ZBB in *Harvard Business Review* and later, wrote a book on the same. The ZBB concept was first applied in the State of Georgia, U.S.A. when Mr. Jimmy Carter was the Governor of the State. Later after becoming the President of U.S.A. Mr. Carter introduced and implemented the ZBB in the country in the year 1987. ZBB has a wide application not only in the Government Departments but also in the private sector in a variety of business. In India, the ZBB was applied in the State of Maharashtra in 80s and early 90s. Benefits from ZBB can be summarized in the following manner.

Limitations of Zero-based Budgeting :

The following are the limitations of Zero-based Budgeting.

1. It is a very detailed procedure and naturally time consuming and lot of paper work is involved in the same.
2. Cost involved in preparation and implementation of this system is very high.
3. Morale of staff may be very low as they might feel threatened if a particular activity is discontinued.
4. Ranking of activities and decision making may become subjective at times.
5. It may not be advisable to apply this method when there are non financial considerations, such as ethical and social responsibility because this will dictate rejecting a budget claim on low ranking projects.

Problems :

A company manufactures two products, X and Y. A forecast of units to be sold in the first four months of the year is given below.

Particulars	Product X [units]	Product Y [units]
January	1, 000	2, 800
February	1, 200	2, 800
March	1, 600	2, 400
April	2, 000	2, 000
May	2, 400	1, 600

Other information is given below.

Particulars	Product X ₹ Per Unit	Product Y ₹ Per Unit
Direct material	12.50	19.00
Direct labour	4.50	7.00
Factory overheads per unit	3.00	4.00

There will be no opening and closing work in progress [WIP] at the end of any month and finished product [in units] equal to half of the budgeted sale of the next month should be in stock at the end of each month. [including previous year December]

You are required to prepare,

A] Production budget for January to April and

B] Summarized production cost budget *[ICWAI- Inter December 2006]*

Solution :

Production Budget – [Units] Product X January – April

	Particulars	January	February	March	April	Total
A]	Sales Forecast	1, 000	1, 200	1, 600	2, 000	
B]	Expected Closing Stock [50% of budgeted sales of next month]	600	800	1, 000	1, 200	
C]	Total Requirements [A + B]	1, 600	2, 000	2, 600	3, 200	
D]	Opening Stock	500	600	800	1, 000	
E]	Net Requirements [C – D]	1, 100	1, 400	1, 800	2, 200	6,500

Production Budget – [Units] Product Y January - April

	Particulars	January	February	March	April	Total
A]	Sales Forecast	2, 800	2,800	2,400	2, 000	
B]	Expected Closing Stock [50% of budgeted sales of next month]	1, 400	1,200	1,000	800	
C]	Total Requirements [A + B]	4, 200	4,000	3,400	2, 800	
D]	Opening Stock	1, 400	1,400	1,200	1, 000	
E]	Net Requirements [C – D]	2, 800	2,600	2,200	1, 800	9,400

Production Cost Budget

January – April

Particulars	Product X – 6,500 units		Product Y- 9400 units	
	Per Unit [₹]	Total Amt [₹]	Per Unit [₹]	Total Amt. [₹]
Direct Material	12.50	81, 250	19.00	1,78,600
Direct Labour	4.50	29,250	7.00	65,800
Factory Overheads	3.00	19,500	4.00	37,600
Total	20.00	1, 30, 000	30.00	2,82,000

Problem :

Zenith Ltd. has prepared the following Sales Budget for the first five months of 2008

Month	Sales Budget [units]
January	10,800
February	15,600
March	12,200
April	10,400
May	9,800

Inventory of finished goods at the end of every month is to be equal to 25% of sales estimate for the next month. On 1st January 2008, there were 2,700 units of product on hand. There is no work in progress at the end of any month.

Every unit of product requires two types of materials in the following quantities.

Material A : 4 kg

Material B : 5 kg

Materials equal to one half of the requirements of the next month's production are to be in hand at the end of every month. This requirement was met on 1st January 2008.

Prepare the following budgets for the quarter ending on 31st March 2008

I] Production Budget – Quantity Wise

II] Materials Purchase Budget – Quantity Wise.

Solution :

Zenith Ltd. Production Budget [In Units] January – March 2008

Particulars	January	February	March
I] Sales	10,800	15,600	12,200
II] Estimated Closing Stock	3,900	3,050	2,600
III] Gross Requirements [I + II]	14,700	18,650	14,800
IV] Opening Stock	2,700	3,900	3,050
V] Net Requirements [III – IV]	12,000	14,750	11,750

Materials Requirement Budget [Quantitative]

Material A – January – March 2008

Particulars	January	February	March
Production [As per Production Budget – units]	12,000	14,750	11,750
Requirements for Production: 4 kg per Unit	48,000	59,000	47,000
Add: Desired Closing Stock	29,500	23,500	20,500
Gross Requirements	77,500	82,500	67,500
Less: Opening Stock	24,000	29,500	23,500
Net Requirements	53,500	53,000	44,000

Materials Requirement Budget [Quantitative]

Material B – January – March 2008

Particulars	January	February	March
Production [As per Production Budget – units]	12,000	14,750	11,750
Requirements for Production: 5 kg per unit	60,000	73,750	58,750
Add: Desired Closing Stock	36,875	29,375	25,625
Gross Requirements	96,875	1,03,125	84,375
Less: Opening Stock	30,000	36,875	29,375
Net Requirements	66,875	66,250	55,000

Working Notes :

1. Production for April: Sales 10,400 [units] + Closing Stock 2,450 [units] = 12,850 [units] – Opening Stock 2600 [units] = 10,250 units.
2. Material required for Production in April :

   A : 10,250 x 4 = 41,000 kg

   B : 10,250 x 5 = 51,250 kg
3. A Ltd. manufactures a single product P with a single grade of labour. The sales budget and finished goods stock budget for the 1st Quarter ending on 30th June 2008 are as follows.

Problem :

Sales : 1,400 units, Opening finished units: 100 units and Closing finished units: 140 units

The goods are imported only when production work is complete and it is budgeted that 10% of finished work will be scrapped.

The standard direct labour content of the product P is 3 hours. The budgeted productivity ratio for direct labour is 80% only.

The company employs 36 direct operatives who are expected to average 144 working hours each in the 1st quarter.

You are required to prepare production Budget.

A Ltd. Production Budget April – June 2012

Particulars	Number of Units
I] Sales Forecast	1,400
II] Estimated Closing Stock	140
III] Gross Requirements [I + II]	1,540
IV] Opening Stock	100
V] Net Production Requirements [III –IV] Good Production	1,440
VI] Wastage [10% of total production – assumed]	160
VII] Total Production Requirement [V + VI]	1,600

Practice Questions

1. What do you mean by a budget?
2. What are the essentials of a budget?
3. What are the difference between budgets and forecasts?
4. What do you understand by budgetary control? Explain briefly the characteristics of a good budget.

5. What are the objectives of budgetary control?
6. What are the scope and techniques of standard costing and budgetary control?
7. Describe essential requisites for effective budgetary control?
8. What do you understand by organization for budgetary control?
9. Write short notes on :
   (a) Budget Centre, (b) Budget Officer (c) Budget Committee (d) Budget Manual (e) Budget Period, (f) Key Factor (g) Performance of Budgeting.
10. What are the advantages of budgetary control?
11. What are the limitations of budgetary control?
12. Briefly explain the different types of budgets.
13. What you understand by control ratios?
14. What is sales budget? What are the factors considered in developing the sales budget?
15. Write short notes on :
    (a) Production Budget (b) Cost of Production Budget, (c) Materials Budget.
16. What do you understand by cash budget? Discuss the procedure for preparing the cost budget.
17. What do you understand by master budget?
18. What do you understand by fixed budget and flexible budget? What are the advantages of flexible budget?
19. What are the difference between fixed budget and flexible budget?
20. Describe the different methods of preparing flexible budget.

Multiple Answer Questions

1. Sales Budget and Production Budget fall into the category of
   A. Operating Budgets
   B. Investments Budgets
   C. Financing Budgets
   D. None of the above
2. Budgetary Control is a system of controlling
   A. Revenue
   B. Costs
   C. Profits
   D. Investments

3. Categorization of Costs into variable and fixed is desirable for the preparation of –
   A. Cash Budget
   B. Capital Budget
   C. Flexible Budget
   D. Fixed Budget
4. Budgets prepared for a single level of activity are referred to as.
   A. Flexible Budgets
   B. Zero-based Budgets
   C. Functional Budgets
   D. Fixed Budgets
5. For the purpose of preparing Flexible Budgets, it is necessary to study carefully and classify the expense into.
   A. Past, Present and Future Expenses
   B. Production, Administrative, and Selling and Distribution Expenses
   C. Revenue and Capital Expenditure
   D. Variable, Semi Variable and Fixed Expenses
6. A Budget of indirect material costs, indirect labour costs and other indirect expenses is widely known as ,
   A. Operating Expenses Budget
   B. Overhead Budget
   C. Cash Budget
   D. Rolling Budget
7. Master Budget incorporates results of all Functional Budgets' is it true?
   A. Yes
   B. No
   C. Cannot Say
   D. None of the above
8. Cash Budget is widely used as a tool of _______ Financial Planning
   A. Long-term
   B. Short-term
   C. Capital
   D. None of the above

9. While preparing the Flexible Budgets, any increase in the level of activity normally necessitate the increase in

   A. Total Variable Cost

   B. Unit Variable Cost

   C. Total Cost

   D. Both (A) and (C)

10. For majority of the organizations, ____ is the Key Budget.

    A. Production Budget

    B. Cash Budget

    C. Purchase Budget

    D. Sales Budget

11. The scarce factor of production is known as— —-

    A. Key factor

    B. Linking factor

    C. Critical factor

    D. Production factor.

PRACTICAL PROBLEMS

1. ABC Ltd. was prepared the budget for the production of a lakh units of the only commodity manufacture by them for a costing period as under :

Raw Material	2.52 per unit
Direct Labour	0.75 Per unit
Direct Expenses	0.10 Per Unit
Works overheads (60 % Fixed)	2.50 per unit
Administration overhead (80 % Fixed)	0.40 per unit
Selling Overheads (50 % Fixed)	0.20 Per Unit

The actual production during the period was only 60,000 units. Calculate the revised budget cost per unit.

[**Ans:** Cost of sales Rs 4,65,000; Per Unit @ ₹ 7.75]

2. The expenses budget for production of 10,000 units in a factory are furnished below:

	Per unit
Material	70
Labour	25

Variable Overheads	20
Fixed Overheads (₹ 1,00,000)	10
Variable expenses (direct)	5
Selling expenses (10% fixed)	13
Distribution expenses (20% fixed)	7
Administration expenses (₹ 50,000)	5
Total cost of sales per unit (to make and sell)	155

Prepare a budget for the product of (A) 8,000 units, and (b) 6,000 units

Assume that administration expenses are rigid for all levels of production.

[**Ans:** Total Cost ₹ 12,75,400 for 8,000 units; ₹ 10,00,800 for 6,000 units]

3. The income and expenditure forecasts for months of March to August, 2003 are given as follows:

Months	Sales (Credit)	Purchases (Credit)	Wages	Manufacturing Expenses	Office Expenses	Selling Expenses
March	60,000	36,000	9,000	3,500	2,000	4,000
April	62,000	38,000	8,000	3,750	1,500	5,000
May	64,000	33,000	10,000	4,000	2,500	4,500
June	58,000	35,000	8,500	3,750	2,000	3,500
July	56,000	39,000	9,500	5,000	1,000	3,500
August	60,000	34,000	8,000	5,200	1,500	4,500

Additional Information

You are given the following further information:

(a) Plant costing ₹ 16,000 is due for delivery in July payable 10% on delivery and the balance after 3 months

(b) Advance tax of ₹ 8,000 is payable in March and June each.

(c) Credito₹ allow 2 months credit and debto₹ are paying one month late. Opening balance of cash ₹ 8,000 lag or one month in expenses.

[**Ans:** Balance: May ₹ 15,750; June ₹ 12,750; July ₹ 18,400]

4. From the following average figures of previous quarters, prepare a manufacturing overhead budgeted for the quarter ending on March 31, 2003. The budget output during this quarter is 6,000 units:

Fixed Overheads ₹ 60,000

Variable Overheads ₹ 30,000 (Varying @ ₹ 5 per unit)

Sem Variable Overheads 30,000 (40% Fixed and 60% Varying @ ₹ 3 per unit)

[Ans : 1,68,000]

5. Calculate, (a) Efficiency Ratio; (b) Activity Ratio, And (c) Capacity Ratio from the following figures

Budgeted Production	176 units
Actual Production	150 Units
Standard hour per unit	20
Actual working hours	1,200

[Ans : (a) Efficiency Ratio = 125%; (b) Activity Ratio = 85.23%; (c) Capacity Ratio = 68.18%]

6. A department of Tan India Company attains sale of Rs 6,00,000 at 80% on its normal Capacity and its expenses are give below :

Particulars	₹
Adminstration Costs:	
Office Salaries	90,000
General expenses	2% on Sales
Depreciation	₹ 7,500
Rate and Taxes	₹ 8,750
Distribution Costs:	
Wages	₹ 15,000
Rent	1% of Sales
Other expenses	4% of Sales
Selling Cost:	
Salaries	8% of Sales
Travelling expenses	2% of Sales
Sales office	1% of Sales
General expenses	1% of Sales

Draw up flexible administration, selling and distribution costs budget, operating at 90 per cent, 100 per cent and 110 per cent of normal capacity.

7. The following express relate to a cost center operating at 80% of normal capacity (Sales are in 12,00,000). Draw up flexible administration, selling and distribution costs budget operating at 90% 100% and 110% of normal capacity.

Administrative Costs	₹
Office Salaries	30,000
General Expenses	1.5 % of Sales
Depreciation	15,000
Rate and Taxes	17,500
Selling Costs	₹
Salaries	4% of Sales
Traveling Expenses	1.5% of Sales
Sales Office	1% of Sales
General Expenses	1% of Sales
Distribution Costs	₹
Wages	30,000
Rent	5% of sales
Other expenses	2% of sales

[**Ans :** Total costs : 80% of Capacity ₹ 6,000; 90 % of Capacity ₹ 67,500; 100% of capacity ₹ 75,000; 110 % of capacity ₹ 82,500]

8. PQR Company Ltd has given the following particulars, you are required to prepare a cash budget for three months ending 1st Dec. 2003.

Months	Sales	Materials	Wages	Overheads
August	20,000	10,200	3,800	1,900
September	21,000	10,000	3,800	210
October	23,000	9,800	4,000	2,300
November	25,000	10,000	4,200	2,400
December	30,000	10,800	4,500	2,500

(i) Credit Terms are:

Sales/ Debtors – 10% sales are on cash bais : 50% of the credit sales are collected next month and the balance in the following month:

Creditors - materials 2 months

- Wages 1/5 month

- Overheads ½ month

(ii) Cash balance on 1st October 2003 in expected to be ₹ 8,000

(iii) A machinery will be miscalled in August, 2003 at a cost of ₹ 1,00,000 the monthly installment of ₹ 5,000 payable from October onwards.

(iv) Dividend at 10% on preference there capital of ₹ 3,00,000 will be paid on 1st December 2003.

(v) Advance to be received for sales of vehicle ₹ 20,000 in December.

(vi) Income tax (advance) to be paid December ₹ 5,000

[**Ans** : October closing balance ₹ 7,390 ; November closing balance ₹ 8,180 ; December bank overdraft ₹ 3,190].

9. From the following data for a 60% capacity, prepare a budget for production at 80% and 100 % activity.

- Production at 60% activity 600 units materials ₹ 100 per unit (100 % Variable)
- Materials ₹ 40 per unit (100% Variable)
- Labou₹ ₹ 40 per unit (100 % Variable)
- Direct Expense ₹ 10 per unit (₹ 6 per unit fixed)
- Factory Expenses ₹ 40,000 (40% Fixed)
- Administrative expenses ₹ 30,000 (60 5 Fixed)

[**Ans** : Total costs : 60% capacity ₹ 1,60,000, 80% capacity ₹ 2,00,800, 100% Capacity ₹ 2,41,600]

10. A factory is currently to 50% capacity and produces 10,000 units estimate the profits of the company when it works at 60% and 80% capacity and offer your critical comments.

At 60% working raw materials cost increases by 2% and selling price falls by 2% at the 80% working raw material cost increases by 5% and selling price falls by 5%. At 50% capacity working the product costs ₹ 180 per unit and is sold at ₹ 200 per unit. The unit cost of ₹ 180 is made up as follows;

Materials	₹ 180
Labour	₹ 30
Factory Overhead	₹ 30 (40% fixed)
Administrative overhead	₹ 20 (50% fixed)

[**Ans** : ₹ 2,00,000 ; ₹ 2,12,000; ₹ 2,12,000]

11. PQR Ltd manufactures two products X and Y. product X takes 6 hours to make while product Y takes 12 hours. In a month of 25 days of 8 hours each, 1,200 units of X and 750 units of Y were produced. The firm employs 75 men in the department responsible for producing these two products. The budget hours are 1, 86,000 per annum. You are required to calculate a Activity Ratio, Capacity Ratio and Efficiency ratio.

[**Ans** : Activity ratio 104.5% ; Capacity Ratio 96.8%; Efficiency Ratio 108%]

12. Glass manufacturing company requires you to calculate and present the budget for the next year from the following information:

Sales :

Toughened glass ₹ 3,00,000

Bent toughened glass: ₹ 5,00,000

Direct Material cost 60% of sales

Direct wages 20 worke₹ @ ₹ 150 P.M

Factory Overheads

Indirect Labour – Works Manager ₹ 500 per month, Foreman ₹ 400 per month

Stores and spares 2 ½ % on sales

Depreciation machinery ₹ 12,600

Light and power ₹ 5,000

Repairs etc ₹ 8,000

Other sundries 10% on Daily Wages

Administration selling and distribution expenses ₹ 14,000 per annum

[**Ans** : Sales budget – Sales Revenues ₹ 7,86,000 ; production cost budget ₹ 5,76,000; expected profit as budgeted ₹ 2,10,000]

13. Modern Manufactures Ltd. Make an automobile component using a special kind of alloy steel as raw material. Each component requires 3lb of raw material costing ₹. 90 per lb and 8 ounces of paint at ₹. 3.50 per ounce. It takes half an hour for fabrication and assembly, and quarter of an hour to paint the unit. Fabrication and assembly labour is paid at ₹. 6 per hour while painters are paid ₹. 3.20 per hour. The variable overheads per component work out to ₹. 5.50 while the fixed Overheads assuming a normal annual production of 17,500 Components, amount to ₹. 3,50,000. The manager – materials management is worried about the procurement of the special kind of alloy steel which is in scare supply. Considering this aspect, the management envisages a maximum production of 15,000 components only for next year.

    a. In the first instance, you are required to work out the total budget costs for next year, based on the present working.

    b. Even to make 15,000 components, the manager – materials management feels that only two thirds of the requirement of raw material could be procured locally, that too at a 10% price increase; for the balance requirement, imports have to be made in the form of semi finished components at a cost of ₹ 380 per piece. As the components would have been painted, there would be no painting operations. Besides the fabrication and assembly time would be reduced by half and the variable overheads would be only ₹ 4 per component. You are required to take note of this eventually also and prepare the total budget cost for next year on this basis also. ICWA (final), June 1982]

[**Ans.** (a) ₹ 49, 59,500, (b) ₹ 53, 40,500]

14. Chemicals Ltd, Manufacture two products AB and CD by mixing the following raw material in the proportion shown.

Raw Material	Product AB	Product CD
A	80%	
B	20%	

C	50%
D	50%

The finished weight of products AB and CD are equal to the weight of their ingredients. During the month of June, it is expected that 60 tons of AB and 200 tons of CD will be sold. Actual and budgeted inventories for the month of June are as follows.

Material	Actual Inventory (1st June)	Budgeted Inventory (30 June)
		Quantity (tons)
A	15	20
B	10	40
C	200	300
D	250	200
Product AB	10	5
Product CD	50	60

The purchase price of material for June is expected to be as follows.

Material	A	B	C	D
Cost per ton :	₹ 500	400	100	200

All materials will be purchased on 3rd of June.

Prepare :

a. Production budget for the month of June.

b. The material requirement budget for June.

c. The material purchase budget indicating the expenditure for materials for the month of June.

[ICWA (Final), June 1986]

Answer : Budgeted Production (tons): 55 (AB) and 210 (CD), Material to be purchased (tons) : 49 (A), 41 (B), 205 (C) and 55 (D) and Total Purchase Bill: ₹ 24,500 (A), ₹ 16,400 (B) ₹ 20,500 (C) and ₹ 11,000 (D)

15. The projected sales and anticipated purchases of ABC Limited for the months of July to November 1983 are

Month	Sales	Purchases
1983 July	6,20,000	3,80,000
August	6,40,000	3,33,000
September	5,80,000	3,50,000
October	5,60,000	3,90,000
November	6,00,000	3,40,000

The wages are expected to be ₹ 1,00,000 per month, the management is expected to pay two months wages as bonus during October 1983. The company is expected to pay an advance tax for income tax ₹ 90,000 before September 1983. The company has ordered in June 1983 for a machine costing ₹ 16 lakh which is expected to be delivered in January 1984. The company pays 5 % as advance on June 30, 1983 and another 10 % advance after 3 months. The balance on the delivery of the machine. The company extends two months. Credit for the customers and the company enjoys one month credit from the supplie₹ The general expense for the company is ₹ 60,000 per month payable at the end of each month. The company anticipates receiving interim dividend of 10 % for the investment of 90,000 shares of Rs 10 each during October 1983. The company anticipates to have an overdraft of ₹ 40,000 on 1st September 1983 (limit sanctioned is ₹ 55,000) Draw a cash budget for September to November 1983 for approaching your bankers for a short term further credit.

[Company Secretary]

Ans : Month–end Cash balance: September – ₹ 3,000, October ₹ 1, 43,000 and November ₹ 1, 13,000

16. Vinayak Ltd. A company engaged in the manufacture of electrical appliances, has set the following budget for 1984.

Particulars	Immersion Heaters	Table Lamps	Bread Toasters	Room Heaters
Production (Units)	40,000	10,000	50,000	30,000
Selling Price per Unit (₹)	30.00	50.00	60.00	80.00
Cost per unit :				
Direct Materials	6.00	13.50	10.50	24.00
Direct Labour	7.50	10.00	18.00	24.00
Variable Overheads	4.50	10.00	12.00	13.00
Fixed Overheads	7.50	10.00	18.00	24.00
Profit / Loss	4.50	6.50	1.50	-5.00

When the budget was placed before the budget Committee, the Marketing Manger put up a proposal to increase the sales by 20,000 additional units for which capacity existed. The additional 20,000 units could be one product or any combination of products. The proposal was accepted by the committee. The committee also decided that the production capacity for the next year 1985 could be set in such way that there would be a further increase in the output by 50,000 units would be of table lamps only for which a new plant would be acquired. The additional fixed expenses of the new plant were estimated at ₹ 70,000 per annum. During 1985, raw material and labour costs were expected to increase by 10% but the other costs and selling expenses would remain the same.

Required : (a) Set a budget for 1984 in such a way that the additional capacity of 20,000 units is utilized to maximize the profits.

(b) Set a budget for 1985.

(c) Assuming That the increased output may not fully materialize, calculate the number of units of Table Lamps required to be sold in 1985 at the given price inorder to ensure that profitability, at least at 1984 level, is maintained.

[ICWA (Final), December 1983]

Answer : (a) Since the Bread Toaster is the most profitable product. Among the four, the additional capacity of 20,000 units shall be utilized to produce an additional 20,000 units of Bread Toaster, Profit for 1984 = ₹ 5,60,000 (b) Profit = ₹ 7,76,500 (c) 34,700 units

17. For the year ended 31st December (Year 1), the actual costs, output and sales of a company manufacturing a range of products are as under.

Product	A	B	C	D
Per unit Selling price	20	40	50	30
Variable Costs: Direct Material	4	9	10	3
Direct Wages	3	5	10	4
Units Manufactured and Sold	7,500	5,000	3,000	6,000

Variable Overheads are incurred at a rate of 200 % of direct wages. Fixed overheads are ₹ 2, 00,000 for the year. The company's summarized budgeted results for the year 1 ended December 31st is:

Sales	7,00,000
Variable Cost of Sales	4,55,000
Contribution	2,45,000
Fixed overheads	1,90,000
Budgeted Profit	55,000

In preparing its budget for the year 2 ending December 31st, the company has made the following allowances for inflation over the actual figures for year 1:

a. An increase of 10 % in all the selling prices; these increase are not expected to alter the quantities of each product sold as compared with year 1:

b. An increase in unit product cost of :

Direct material	10%
Direct Wages	20%
Variable overheads	10%

c. An increase of 2% in fixed overheads.

In addition to these allowances for inflation, the company proposes the following changes in its cost, sales volume, and selling price structure.

Product A : Increase the price by 10 % yielding a reduction of 5 % in the volume sold.

Product B : Use different materials which will reduce direct material cost by ₹ 2 per unit and reduce volume sold by 4 %

Product C: (a) Incur advertising cost of ₹ 10,000 for the year which is expected to increase sales by 20 % (b) Buy a machine costing ₹ 8,000

Product D : Reduce the selling price by 10 % giving a 15 % increase in the sales volume.

Increase the stocks held by an average of ₹ 40,000 over the whole year, this would be financed by bank overdraft at an interest rate of 12 % per annum.

Increase the size of the delivery van fleet at an outlay of ₹ 9,000 and an increase in annual fixed costs of ₹ 2,000 (Excluding depreciation)

The company calculates its depreciation on a straight line basis with a standard life of five years of production equipment and three years for non - production equipments

You are required.

a. To show, in a format helpful to management, a summary statement of the budgeted and actual results for the year 1 ended December 31st with an analysis of the difference between the two profits.

b. To compile a budgeted profit and loss account for the company for the year 2 ending December 31st after taking account of allowance for inflation and the traditional changes proposed.

[ICWA (Final), December 1989)

Answer : (a) profit for year - 1 = ₹ 52,500 ; variances, Sales Revenue ₹ 20,000 (a) ; Contribution ₹ 7,500 (F) Fixed Overheads ₹ 10,000 (A) Profit ₹ 2,500 (A);

(b) Budgeted profit for year - 2 Rs 59,000 (for this purpose, compute the material cost . Direct wages, variable overheads, selling price per unit; Budgeted sales volume. Total Fixed overheads etc. in the light of the anticipated changes. This facilitates the preparation of Budgeted income statement for year - 2)

18. Prepare a Cash Budget in respect of six months from July to December from the following information.

Month	Sales ₹000	Mat. ₹000	Wages ₹000	Production O/H ₹000	Admn O/H ₹	Selling O/H ₹	Dist. O/H ₹	R & D O/H ₹
April	100	40	10.0	4.4	3,000	1,600	800	1,000
May	120	60	11.2	4.8	2,900	1,700	900	1,000
June	80	40	8.0	5.0	3,040	1,500	700	1,200
July	100	60	8.4	4.6	2,960	1,700	900	1,200
Aug.	120	70	9.2	5.2	3,020	1,900	1,100	1,400
Sept	140	80	10.0	5.4	3,080	2,000	1,200	1,400
Oct	160	90	10.4	5.8	3,120	2,050	1,250	1,600
Nov	180	100	10.8	6.0	3,140	2,150	1,350	1,600
Dec	200	110	11.6	6.4	3,200	2,300	1,500	1,600

The cash balance as on 1st July was expected ₹1, 50,000, Plant and Machinery to be installed in August to a cost of ₹40, 000 will be payable on September 1st. The extension to the Research and Development Department amounting to ₹10, 000 will be completed on August 1st, payable ₹2, 000 per month from the date of completion. Under a hire purchase agreement ₹4, 000 is to be paid each month.

The Cash Sales of ₹2, 000 per month are expected. No commission is payable. However a commission of 5% on credit sales is to be paid within the month following the sale.

Period of credit allowed by suppliers 3 months, credit allowed to customers 2 months, delay in payment of overheads 1 month, delay in payment of wages 1st week of the following month.

An income tax of ₹1, 00, 000 is due to be paid on October 1st. A preference share dividend of 10% on ₹2, 00, 000 is payable on November 1st. 10% calls on the ordinary share capital of ₹4, 00, 000 is due on July 1st and September 1st. The dividend from investments amounting to ₹30, 000 is expected on November 1st.

19. Amicable Relations Ltd, is facing a trade union demand for an increase of 15% on the hourly wage rates. In response to a management offer to 5%. The management is reluctant to agree to such a demand but is willing to consider an increase offer provided it is linked with productivity the suggestion is to offer 5% on basis hourly rates plus ₹ 0.15 for every standard hour of output produced. If this is agreed to, then it is expected that production would increase by 10 % within the budgeted hours (normal factory capacity). One Standard hour is required to produce one unit. In output. In order to sell the increased output, it would become necessary to effect a reduction of 2.5 % in the selling price. The draft budget for the forthcoming year, excluding the wages and sales increase, is as follows. (₹ in lakhs)

Sales (15,00,000 units)		60
Direct Material	12	
Direct Wages	18	
Variable production overheads	3	
Fixed production overheads	10	
Variable Sales overheads (5% of turnover)	3	
Fixed Sales overheads	6	
Variable distribution overheads	1	
Fixed distribution overheads	1	
Fixed administration overheads	2	56
Profit		4

You are required to work out alterations in the budget based on the following;

a. If the trade union demand is accepted by management

b. If the management's proposal of wage increase linked to productivity in accepted by the trade union.

[CA(Final), November 1988)

Answer : (a) if the union's demand is accepted, revised budgeted profit = ₹ 1, 30,000;
(b) If management proposal is implemented; revised budgeted profit = ₹ 3, 15,170.

❖ ❖ ❖

Chapter - 7

Standard Costing

Introduction

Two important functions of the management of any organization are planning and controlling. The planning helps the management to make systematic efforts to achieve the well defined objectives, control enables them to review the actual performance and locate the difference between the planned performance and actual performance. Thus for evaluating performance, it is necessary to compare the actual performance with some predetermined targets. One of the important parameters of performance is the cost of production. According to M. Porter, for achieving sustainable competitive advantage it is necessary to establish cost leadership. For achieving this, it is of vital importance that the various costs are monitored closely and there is a constant comparison of the actual costs with some pre-determined targets. Standard Costing is a tool in the hands of management for improving the management control by providing standards for comparison of actual with these standards.

Meaning of Standard

The word standard means a yardstick. The standard cost is a predetermined cost which determines in advance what each product or service should cost under given circumstances.

Definition

Backer and Jacobsen, defined "Standard cost is the amount the firm thinks a product or the operation of the process for a period of time should cost, based upon certain assumed conditions of efficiency, economic conditions and other factors."

The CIMA, London has defined standard cost as "a predetermined cost which is calculated from management's standards of efficient operations and the relevant necessary expenditure." CIMA – UK 1) Standard Costing is defined as, 'preparation and use of standard costs, their comparison with actual costs and analysis of variances into their causes and points of incidences". They are the predetermined costs on technical estimate of material labour and overhead for a selected period of time and for a prescribed set of working conditions. In other words, a standard cost is a planned cost for a unit of product or service rendered.

The technique of using standard costs for the purposes of cost control is known as standard costing. It is a system of cost accounting which is designed to find out how much should be the cost of a product under the existing conditions. The actual cost can be ascertained only when production is undertaken. The predetermined cost is compared to the actual cost and a variance between the two enables the management to take necessary corrective measures.

Standard Cost Accounting

In modern cost accounting, the concept of recording historical costs was taken further, by allocating the company's fixed costs over a given period of time to the items produced during that period and recording the result as the total cost of production. This allowed the full cost of products that were not sold in the period they were produced to be recorded in inventory using a variety of complex accounting methods, which was consistent with the principles of GAAP (Generally Accepted Accounting Principles). It also essentially enabled managers to ignore the fixed costs and look at the results of each period in relation to the "standard cost" for any given product. This method tended to slightly distort the resulting unit cost, but in mass-production industries that made one product line and where the fixed costs were relatively low, the distortion was very minor.

An important part of standard cost accounting is a variance analysis, which breaks down the variation between actual cost and standard costs into various components like volume variation, material cost variation, labour cost variation, etc., so managers can understand why costs were different from what was planned and take appropriate action to correct the situation.

Features of Standard Cost

1. Standard cost is a predetermined cost. This means that the standard cost is determined even before the commencement of production. For example, if a firm is planning to launch a product in the year 2013, the standard cost of the same will be determined in the year 2012.

2. Standard cost is not an estimated cost. There is a difference between saying what would be the cost and what should be the cost. Standard cost is a planned cost and it is a cost that should be the actual cost of production.

3. It is calculated after taking into consideration the management's standard of efficient operation. Thus, standard cost fixed on the assumption of 80% efficiency will be different from what it will be if the assumption is of 90% efficiency.

4. Standard cost can be used as a basis for price fixation as well as for exercising control over the cost.

5. Standard costing involves setting of standards for various elements of cost. Thus, standards are set for material costs, labour costs and overhead costs. Setting of standard is the heart of standard costing.

6. Standard costing ensures that there is a constant comparison between the standards and accruals. The difference is known as 'variance'.

7. The variances are analyzing them to find out the reasons for the variances and taking corrective action in order to ensure that the variances are not repeated.

Setting of Standards

The heart of the standard costing is setting of standards. It should be done carefully to ensure that the standards are realistic and neither too high nor too low. If very high standards are set, it will be impossible to attain the same and there will be always an adverse variance and it results in lowering the morale of the employees. On the other hand, if standards are set too low, they will be attained very easily and the favourable variances will create satisfaction amongst the employees. For the above reasons, standards should be set very carefully. The following aspects should be taken into consideration before setting the standards.

Types of Standards : The important aspect is that what should be the level of standard from the point of attainment? Whether it should be very difficult to achieve or too easy to achieve? In other words whether the standards set should be too high or too low? Thus, from the standard of attainment, there can be the following types of standards.

Current Standards : A current standard is a standard which is established for use over a short period of time and is related to current condition. It reflects the performance that should be attained during the current period. The period for current standard is normally one year. It is presumed that conditions of production will remain unchanged. In case there is any change in price or manufacturing condition, the standards are also revised. Current standard may be ideal standard and expected standard.

Ideal Standards : It is the standard which represents a high level of efficiency. It is fixed on the assumption that favourable conditions will prevail and management will be at its best. The price paid for materials will be lowest and wastes, etc., will be minimum possible. The labour time for making the production will be minimum and rates of wages will also be low. The overheads expenses are also set with maximum efficiency in mind. All the conditions, internal and external, should be favourable and then only ideal standard will be achieved. This standard is not practicable and may not be achieved even then an effort is made. The deviation between targets and actual performance is ignorable. In practice, ideal standard has an adverse effect on the employees. They do not reach the standard because the standards are not considered realistic.

Basic Standards : A basic standard may be defined as a standard which is established for use for an indefinite period which may a long period. It is established for a long period and is not adjusted to the specific conations. The same standard remains in force for a long period. These standards are revised only on the changes in specification of material and technology productions. It is indeed just like a number against which subsequent process changes can be measured. Basic standard enables the measurement of changes in costs. For example, if the basic cost for material is Rs. 30 per unit and the current price is Rs. 35 per unit, it will show an increase of 16.67% in the cost of materials. The changes in manufacturing costs can be measured by taking basic standard, as a base standard cannot serve as a tool for cost control purpose because the standard is not revised for a long time. The deviation between standard cost and actual cost cannot be used as a yardstick for measuring efficiency.

Normal Standards : It has been defined as a standard which, it is anticipated, can be attained over a future period of time and preferably long enough to cover one trade cycle. This standard is based on the conditions which will cover a future period of five years and concerning one trade cycle. If a normal cycle of ups and downs in sales and production is 10 years, then standard will be set on average sales and production which will cover all the years. The standard attempts to cover variance in the production from one time to another time. An average is taken from the periods of recession and depression. The normal standard concept is theoretical and cannot be used for cost control purpose. Normal standard can be properly applied for absorption of overhead cost over a long period of time.

Expected Standard : It is anticipated and can be attained during a future specified standard period. It is quite attainable consistent and fulfils the purposes of a good standard. It provides incentive to improve performance and get the better of the adverse conditions. These standards are formulated after making allowance for the cost of normal spoilage, cost of idle time due to machine breakdowns and the cost of other events, which are unavoidable in normal efficient operations. Thus, all the normal losses are taken into consideration. Hence, it is accurate and useful to the management in product costing and inventory valuations.

Historical Standard : This is the average standard based on past results achieved. It tends to be a movable standard because there is a possibility that the average past performance may include inefficiencies. Hence, the utility of these standards is that past performance can be used as a basis for setting of standard in future.

Length of the Period of Use : The management has to take another vital decision about the length of the period for which the standard will remain suitable. In other words, it will have to be decided whether the standards should be revised frequently or after a long time. But the basic standards remain unchanged for a long period of time while the current standards and expected standards are revised more frequently. Hence, it will be decided that what should be the frequency of revision.

Attainment Level : The management has to ascertain the level of attainment as regards to the output. While fixing the level, due considerations should be given to the constraints on the production, level of efficiency, availability of skilled manpower and sales potential.

Setting of Standard Costs

The setting of standard costs is elements of cost like material, labour and overheads calculation and analysis of variances. It should be remembered that setting of standard costs is not the job of cost accounting department, it is a task which is to be completed with the cooperation of departments like production, sales, manpower planning, personnel, works study engineer and the cost accounting department. Without the cooperation and active participation of all the departments, setting of standard cost will be impossible and hence, it is said that techniques like standard costing and budgeting promotes coordination and team work in an organization. The setting of standard costs is discussed in the following steps.

Direct Material Cost Standard : Direct material is an important element of cost and in several industries; the direct material cost is 50% - 60% of the total cost. In case of industry like sugar, the material cost is nearly 60 –70 % of the total cost. In view of this, there is a need to observe the cost of material closely and take steps to control and reduce the same. Standard for direct material cost is set with this particular objective. The standard direct material cost indicates as to how much the material cost should have been and then it is compared with the actual cost to find out the difference between the two. The establishment of standard cost for direct materials involves the resolve of standard quantity of standard raw materials and standard price of raw material consumed. The standard quantity of materials is determined with the help of production department for fixing the standards; normal losses are taken into consideration. The cost accounting department in co-operation with the purchase department determines standard price of material consumed. The prices are considered with recent prices, past prices and the trend of prices in the future are taken into consideration while fixing the standard prices. Similarly stock on hand, purchase orders placed and fluctuations in the price should be taken into consideration while fixing the material price standards.

Direct Labour : The standard labour cost indicates the labour cost that should be incurred based on two factors. The standard labour cost first one is the standard time and the second one is the standard rate. For setting the standard time, it should conduct time and motion study with the help of work study engineer. the motion study is conducted to identify unnecessary motions and then to eliminate them. After elimination of unnecessary motions, standard time is allotted to the motions that are required to be performed for producing the product. While determining the standard time, allowance is made for normal idle time to cover mental and physical tiredness. The standard wage rate is fixed after considering the level of rates in the market, the degree of skill required for performing the job, the availability of manpower and the wage structure in the concerned industry. Concept of 'Standard Hour' is really important in setting the standards for labour. It is a hypothetical hour, which represents the amount of work and performed in one hour under standard conditions.

Setting Standards of Overheads : The purpose of setting standard for overheads is to minimize the total cost. Standard overhead rates are computed by dividing overhead expenses by direct labour hours or units produced. The standard overhead cost is obtained by multiplying standard overhead rate by the labour hours spent or number of units produced. The determination of overhead rate involves three things:

A. Determination of overheads

B. Determination of labour hours or units manufactured

C. Calculating overheads rate by dividing A by B

The overheads are classified into fixed overheads, variable overheads and semi-variable overheads. The fixed overheads remain the same irrespective of level of production, while variable overheads change in the proportion of production. The expenses increase or decrease with the increase or decrease in output. Semi variable overheads are neither fixed nor variable. These overheads increase with the increase in production but the rate of increase will be less than the rate of increase in production. The division of overheads into fixed, variable and semi variable categories will help in determining overheads.

Setting Price and Quantity Standards : It requires the combined expertise of all persons who have responsibility over input prices and over effective use of inputs. In a manufacturing firm include accountants, purchasing managers, engineers, production supervisors, line mangers and production workers. Earlier period records of purchase prices and input usage can help in setting standards. However, the standards should be designed to encourage efficient future operations, not a repetition of past inefficient operations.

Ideal vs Practical Standards

Ideal Standards : Ideal standards are those that can be attained only under the best circumstances. They allow for no machine breakdowns or other work interruptions and they call for a level of effort that can be attained only by the most skilled and efficient employees working at peak effort 100% of the time. Some managers feel that such standards have a motivational value these managers argue that even though employees know that they will rarely meet the standards, it is a constant reminder of the need for ever increasing efficiency and effort. Few firms use ideal standards and most managers' feel that ideal standards tend to discourage even the most diligent workers. Moreover, variances from ideal standards are difficult to interpret. Large variances from the ideal are normal and it is difficult to manage by exceptions.

Practical Standards : Practical standards are those standards that are tight but attainable and serve multiple purposes. They allow for normal machine downtime and employee rest period. They can be attained through reasonable, though highly efficient, efforts by the average worker. Variances from such standards represent deviations that fall outside of normal operating conditions and signal a need for management attention. In addition to signaling abnormal conditions, they can also be used in forecasting cash flows and in planning inventory. By contrast, ideal standards cannot be used in forecasting and planning; they do not allow for normal inefficiencies and thus, they result in unrealistic planning and forecasting figures.

Comparison of Budgets and Standards

The budget is a method of securing reliable and prompt information concerning the operation and control of an enterprise. When manufacturing budgets are based on standards for materials, labour, and factory overheads a strong team for possible control and reduction of costs is created.

Standards are almost indispensable in establishing a budget. Because both standard and budgets aim at the same objective managerial control, it is felt that the two are the same and cannot function independently. This opinion is supported by the fact that both use predetermined costs for the coming period. Both budgets and standard costs make it possible to prepare reports which compare actual costs and predetermined costs for management.

Building budgets without the use of standard cost figures can never lead to a real budgetary control system. The principle difference between budgets and standard costs lies in their scope. The budget is a statement of expected costs and acts as a guidepost which keeps the business on a charted course. Standards, on other hand, do not tell what costs are expected to be, but rather what they will be if certain performances are achieved. A budget emphasizes the volume of business and the cost level which should be maintained.

Importance of Standard Costing

Standard cost systems aid in planning operations and gaining insights into the probable impact of managerial decisions on cost levels and profits. Standard costs are used for:

1. Establishing budgets.
2. Controlling costs, directing and motivating employees and measuring efficiencies.
3. Promoting possible cost reduction.
4. Simplifying costing procedures and expediting cost reports.
5. Assigning costs to materials, work in process and finished goods inventories.
6. Forming the basis for establishing bids, contracts and for setting sales prices.

Advantages of Standard Costing

The following are the advantages of standard costing:

1. It is useful for production planning and policy formulation.
2. The comparison of actual costs with standard costs enables the management to evaluate performance of various cost centers.
3. The performance variances are determined by comparing actual costs with standard costs. Management is able to spot out the place of inefficiencies.
4. It can fix responsibility for deviation in performance and to take corrective measures at the earliest.
5. The targets of different individuals are fixed if the performance is according to predetermined standards.
6. The attention of the management is drawn only when actual performance is less than the budgeted performance.
7. Management by exception means that everybody is given a target to be achieved and management need not supervise each and everything.
8. It enables and provides useful information to the management in taking vital decisions. For example, the problem created by inflation, rising prices. It can also be used to provide incentive plans for employees, etc.

Disadvantages of Standard Costing:

The following are the disadvantages of standard costing:

1. It takes more time and is a costly affair for small organizations.
2. It cannot be used in those organizations where non-standard products are produced.
3. If the production is undertaken according to the customer specifications, then each job will involve different amount of expenditures.
4. The process of setting standard is a difficult task because it requires technical skills.
5. The time and motion study is required to be undertaken for this purpose. These studies require a lot of time and money.

6. The conditions under which standards are fixed do not remain static. With the change in circumstances, if the standards are not revised the same become impracticable.
7. The fixing of responsibility is not an easy task.
8. The variances are to be classified into controllable and uncontrollable variances. It is applicable only for controllable variances.
9. A frequent revision of standards will become costly.
10. The industry changes the technology then the system will not be suitable.

Revision of Standards

Standard costing technique is used for effectively it requires to revise the standards which can be better control. The standards are also subjected to change like the method production, environment, raw materials, and technology used. The standard cost will no longer be accurate. Standards are out of date will not act as effective control tools. They will not help us to predict the inputs required nor help us to evaluate the efficiency of a particular department. If standards are continually not being achieved and large deviations or variances from the standard are reported, they should be carefully reviewed. The changes in the physical productive capacity of the organization or in material prices and wage rates may indicate that standards need to be revised. In practice, changing standards frequently is an expensive operation and can cause confusion. For this reason, standard cost revisions are usually made only once a year. At the times of rapid price inflation, many managers have felt that the high level of inflation forced them to change price and wage rate standards continually. However, it leads to reduction in value of the standard as a yardstick and the other extreme is the adoption of basic standard which will remain unchanged for many years. They provide a constant base for comparison but this is only just satisfactory when there is technological change in working procedures and conditions.

Difference between Estimated and Standard Cost

Estimated costs should not be confused with standard costs. Though both of them are future costs and there is a fundamental difference between the two. Estimated costs are developed on the basis of projections based on past performance as well as expected future trends. Standard costs are predetermined in a scientific manner through technical analysis regarding the material consumption and time and motion study for determining labour requirements. Estimated costs may not help management in decision making as they are not scientifically predetermined costs but standard costs are decided after a comprehensive study and analysis of all relevant factors. Hence it provides reliable measures for product costing, product pricing, planning, coordination and cost control as well as reduction purposes. Under estimated costing, the cost is estimated in advance based on the assumption that costs are more or less free to move and that what is made is the best estimate of the cost. Under standard costing, a cost is established which is based on the assumption that cost will not be allowed to move freely but will be controlled as far as possible. So that the actual cost will be close to the standard cost as far as possible and any variation between the standard and actual cost will be capable of reasonable explanation.

Computation of Variances

After setting the standards and standard costs for various elements of cost, the next important step is to compute variances for each element of cost. Variance is the difference between the standard cost and the actual cost.

I. MATERIAL VARIANCES

In material variances, the main objective is to find out the difference between the standard cost of material used for actual production and actual cost of material used. The material variances are divided into material cost, material price and material quantity variances.

1. **Material Cost Variance :** The variance shows the difference between the standard cost of material consumed for actual production and the actual cost of production for material. The following formula is used for calculation of variance.

   Material Cost Variance :

   Standard Cost of Material Consumed – Actual Cost of Material Consumed

   OR $(SQ \times SP) - (AQ \times AP)$

   Where, SQ = Standard Quantity

   SP = Standard Price

   AQ = Actual Quantity

   AP = Actual Price

   If the actual cost of material consumed is less than the standard cost of material consumed, the variance is 'favourable', otherwise it is adverse.

2. **Material Price Variance :** It measures the difference between the standard price and actual price with reference to the actual quantity consumed. The computation is as shown below:

   Material Price Variance : Actual Quantity [Standard Price – Actual Price]

3. **Material Quantity or Volume or Usage Variance**

   The difference between the standard quantity of material consumed for actual production and the actual quantity consumed and the same is multiplied by standard price. The calculation of this variance is as follows.

   Material Quantity [Usage] Variance :

   Standard Price [Standard Quantity – Actual Quantity]

   Verfication :

   Material Cost Variance = Material Price Variance + Material Quantity Variance

SOLVED PROBLEMS

Problem 1

From the following particulars furnished by M/s. Starlight Co. Ltd. find out (i) Material cost variance; (ii) Material usage variance and (iii) Material price variance.

Value of Material purchased	..	9,000
Quantity of Material purchased	..	3,000 units
Standard quantity of materials required per tonne of finished product	..	25 units
Standard rate of material	..	2 per unit
Opening Stock		Nil
Closing Stock of material	..	500 units
Finished production during the period	..	80 tonnes.

ICWA June 2012

Solution :

Standard quantity of materials required = 80 × 25 = 2000 units

Standard Price = 2 per Unit

Actual Price = $\frac{9000}{3000}$ = 3 per unit

Actual quantity of materials used = (3,000 – 500) units = 2,500 units

Materials Cost Variance

= Total Standard cost – Total Actual cost.

= (Std Price × Std Qty) – (Actual price × Actual quantity)

= (₹ 2 × 2000) – (₹ 3 × 2500)

= 4000 – 7500

= 3500 (Adv)

Materials Usage Variance

= Std price × (Std Qty – Actual Qty)

= 2 × (2000 – 2500)

= 2 × (500) = 1000 (Adv)

Materials Price Variance

= Actual Qty × (Std Price – Actual Price)

= 2500 × (2 – 3)

= 2500 (Adv)

Problem 2

Calculate Material Variances from the following details:

Standard quantity of materials for producing one unit of finished product 'X' is 10 kg. The standard price is ₹ 10 per kg and actual price is ₹ 12 per kg . During a particular period, 500 units of 'X' were produced. Actual material consumed was 5400 kg at a cost of ₹ 64,800.

Solution :

1. Material Cost Variance

   = Standard Cost of Materials – Actual Cost of Materials

   = (SQ × SP) – (AQ × AP)

   = (5000 units × 10 kg) - (5400 units × ₹12)

   = ₹ 50,000 – ₹ 64, 800 = ₹ 14,800 [A]

2. Material Price Variance = Actual Quantity [Standard Price – Actual Price]

   5,400 [₹10 – ₹12] = ₹ 10,800 [A]

3. Material Quantity Variance = Standard Price [Std. Qty – Actual Qty]

   ₹10 [5,000 – 5,400] = ₹4, 000 [A]

Reconciliation

Material Cost Variance = Material Price Variance + Material Quantity Variance.

= ₹ 14,800[A] = ₹ 10,800 [A] + ₹ 4,000 [A]

Material Usage Variance is subclassified into two, i.e., Material Mix Variance and Material Yield Variance.

Material Mix Variance :

Two or more types of raw materials are used to produce the final product. This standard proportion of mixture is decided in advance. For example, we manufacture one unit of product 'X', material P and Q may have to be mixed in a standard proportion of 5:3. This is called as a standard mix. However, when the actual production begins, the actual proportion of mix may have to be changed due to several reasons like non-availability of a particular material, etc. In such cases material mix variance arises. The mix variance is computed in the following formula.

Material Mix Variance = Standard Cost of Standard Mix – Standard Cost of Actual Mix

Material Yield Variance :

The manufacturing process, some unavoidable loss always takes place. If the input is 100, output may be 99 units, one unit being normal or unavoidable loss. The normal loss is always anticipated and taken into consideration while determining the standard quantity.

Yield variance arises when the actual loss is more or less than the normal loss. The calculation of yield variance is as follows:

Material Yield Variance = SYR [Actual Yield – Standard Yield]

SYR = Standard Yield Rate, i.e. 1) standard cost per unit of standard output.

Verification : Quantity Variance = Mix Variance + Yield variance.

Problem 2 :

The standard material cost to produce ten units of product Z is given below:

200 kg of material P @ ₹20 per kg 300 kg of material Q @ ₹10 per kg 400 kg of material R @ ₹12per kg

During a particular period, 1000 units of mixture Z was produced from the usage of

25,000 kgs of material P @ ₹18 per kg

32,000 kgs of material Q @ ₹12 per kg

43,000 kgs of material R @ ₹14 per kg

Calculate material cost, price, usage and mix variances.

Solution :

Calculation of material variances

Material	Standard Quantity 10 Units Kg	Standard Rate ₹	Standard Cost ₹	Actual Quantity 1000 units Kg	Actual Rate ₹	Actual Amount ₹
P	200	20	4000	25, 000	18	4, 50, 000
Q	300	10	3000	32, 000	12	3,84, 000
R	400	12	4800	43, 000	14	6,02, 000
Total	900		11800	1, 00, 000		14,36, 000

1. Material Cost Variance :

   Standard Cost for actual production – Actual Cost

   ₹ 11,80,000 – ₹ 14,36,000 = ₹ 2,56,000 [A]

   Standard cost of materials for actual production = 11,800 x 100 = 11, 80,000

   For 10 units of production, the standard cost is ₹ 11,800, so for 1000 units, the standard cost is ₹ 11,80, 000.

2. Material Price Variance: Actual Quantity [Std. Price – Actual Price]

   Material P = 35, 000 [₹20 – ₹18] = ₹50, 000 [F]

   Material Q = 32, 000 [₹10 – ₹12] = ₹64, 000 [A]

Material R = 43, 000 [₹12 – ₹14] = ₹86, 000 [A]

Total Material Price Variance = ₹1,00, 000 [A]

3. Material Quantity Variance = Standard Price [Std. Quantity – Actual Quantity]

Material P = ₹20 [20, 000 – 25, 000] = ₹1,00, 000 [A]

Material Q = ₹10 [30, 000 – 32,000] = ₹20, 000 [A]

Material R = ₹12 [40, 000 – 43, 000] = ₹36, 000 [A]

Total Material Quantity Variance = ₹1,56,, 000 [A]

4. Material Mix Variance

= Std Cost of Std Mix – Std Cost of Actual Mix

= ₹13,11, 110 – Rs 13,36,000 = ₹ 24,890 [A]

Calculation of Standard Cost of Standard Mix

If Actual mix would have been in the standard proportion, the quantities of material P, Q and R would have been,

- P: (200/900)x 1,00,000 = 22, 222 x ₹20 = ₹4, 44, 444
- Q: (300/900) x 1,00,000 = 33, 333.33 x ₹10 = ₹3, 33, 333
- R: (400/900) x 1,00, 000 = 44, 444 x ₹12 = ₹5, 33, 333
- Total standard cost of standard mix = ₹13,11, 110

Note : Calculation of Standard cost of actual mix

Formula = Actual Quantity X Standard Cost

P : 2500 x 20	= 5,00,000
Q : 32000 x 10	= 3,20,000
R : 43000 x 12	= 5,16,000
Total	= 13, 36,000

Problem 3

The standard cost of a certain chemical mixture is as follows:

40% of Material A @ ₹200 per ton

60% of Material B @ ₹300 per ton

A standard loss of 10% is expected in the production. During a particular period materials used are, 90 tons Material A @ ₹180 per ton. 110 tons Material B @ ₹340 per ton. Actual production produced was 182 tons of the finished goods and actual loss is 18 tons. Calculate Material Price Variance, Material Usage Variance and Material Yield Variance.

Standards			Actuals	
Material A 40 tons @ ₹200 =		₹8,000	90 tons @ ₹180 per ton =	₹16,200
Material B 60 tons @ ₹300 =		₹18,000	110 tons @ ₹340 per ton =	₹37,400
Total 100 tons =		₹26,000	200 tons =	₹53,600
Less: 10% Std. Loss	10 tons		*Less:* Actual loss	18 tons
Standard Production	90 tons =	₹26,000		182 tons = ₹53, 600

I] Material Price Variance = AQ [SP – AP]

Material A = 90[200-180]= ₹1,800 [F]

Material B =110[300-340]= ₹4,400[A]

Total Price Variance = ₹2,600 [A]

II] Material Usage Variance SP [SQ – AQ]

Material A = 200[81-90]= ₹1,800[A]

Material B = 300[121-110]= ₹3,3 00[F]

Total Usage Variance = 1,500 [F]

III] Material Yield Variance = Std. Yield Rate[Actual Yield – Standard yield]

26, 000/90[182-180] = ₹577.77[F]

Standard Yield Rate = Standard cost per unit of standard production

Problem 4 :

Calculate Material Price and Mix variance from the following

Standard	Actual
Material P – 20 kg @ ₹5	20 kg @ ₹6
Material Q – 30 kg @ ₹4	20 kg @ ₹3
Material R – 50 kg @ ₹6	60 kg @ ₹5
Total – 100 kg	Total – 100 kg

Solution :

Material Price Variance = AQ [SP – AP]

Material P = 20[₹5 - ₹6] = ₹20[A]

Material Q = 20[₹4 - ₹3] = ₹20[F]

Material R = 60[₹6 - ₹5] = ₹60[F]

Total Material Price Variance =₹60[F]

Material Mix Variance

= Standard Cost of Standard Mix – Standard Cost of Actual Mix

= ₹520 – ₹540 = ₹20 [A]

Standard Cost of Standard Mix = (20x 5) + (30 x 4) + (50 x 6) = 520

Standard Cost of Actual Mix = (20 x 5) + (20 x 4) + (60 x 6) = 540

Problem 5 :

X,Y,Z producing a standard mix using 60 kg of chemical X and 40 kg of chemical Y. The standard loss of production is 30%. The standard price of X is Rs.5 per kg and of Y is Rs.10 per kg. The actual mixture and yield were as follows:

X – 80 kg @ ₹4.50 per kg

Y – 70 kg @ ₹8.00 per kg Actual yield 115 kg.

Calculate all Material Variances

Solution :

The following statement will have to be prepared for calculation of variances.

Standard	Actual
Material X – 60 kg @ ₹5 = ₹300	80 kg @ ₹4.50 = ₹360
Material Y – 40 kg @ ₹10= ₹400	70 kg @ ₹8 = ₹560
Std. Loss – 30%	Actual Loss = 35 kg
Std. Production – 70 kg = ₹700	Actual Production – 115 kg

I] Material Cost Variance = SQx SP – AQ x AP

X= (90 x 5) – (80 x 4.5) = ₹450 - 360= 90 [F]

Y = (60 x 10) – (70 x 8) = ₹600 - 560= 40 [F]

Total Material Cost Variance = 130[F]

Calculation of Standard Quantity for Actual output:

Material X= (60/100) x 150 = 90kg

Material Y= (40/100) x 150 = 60kg

II] Material Price Variance – AQ [SP – AP] :

X = 80 [₹5 - ₹4.50] = ₹40[F]

Y = 70 [₹10 - ₹8] = ₹140[F]

Total Price Variance = ₹180[F]

III] Material Quantity Variance = SP [SQ – AQ]

X = ₹5[90 – 80]=₹50[F]

Y = ₹10 [60 - 70] = ₹100[A]

Total Quantity Variance = ₹50 [A]

Verification :

Material Cost Variance = Material Price Variance + Material Quantity Variance

= 130[F] = ₹180[F] + ₹50 [A]

IV] Material Mix Variance = Std Cost of Std Mix – Std Cost of Actual Mix

= ₹1,050 – ₹1,100 = ₹50 [A]

Calculation of standard cost of standard mix: SQ for Actual output x SP

X = 90 x 5 = 450

Y = 60x 10 = 600

Standard Cost of Standard Mix 1050

Calculation of standard cost of actual mix: AQ x SP

X = 80 x 5 = 400

Y = 70x 10 = 700

Standard Cost of Actual Mix 1100

V] Material Yield Variance = Std Yield Rate [Actual Yield – Standard Yield]

= ₹10 [115 - 105] = ₹100 [F]

Problem 6 :

S.V. Ltd. manufactures a single product, the standard mix of which are as follows: Material A 60% at ₹20 per kg

Material B 40% at ₹10 per kg

Normal loss in the production is 20% of input. Due to shortage of material A, the standard mix was changed and the actual mix was as follows:

Material A 105 kg at ₹20 per kg

Material B 95 kg at ₹9 per kg

Actual loss was 35 kg, while the actual output was 165 kg Calculate all material variances.

Solution :

Calculation of Variances

Material	Standard Quantity kg	Standard Price ₹	Standard Cost ₹	Actual Quantity kg	Actual Price ₹	Actual Cost ₹
A	60	20	1200	105	20	2100
B	40	10	400	95	9	855
Total	100		1600	200		2955
Normal Loss	20			35		
Standard Output	80		1600	165 Actual Output		2955

I] **Material Cost Variance :** Standard Cost for Actual Production – Actual Cost

₹3,300 – ₹2,955 = ₹ 345 [F]

Note: Calculation of standard cost for actual production:

For 80 kg, the standard cost is ₹1, 600, so for actual production of 165 kg, the standard cost is (165/80) x1600 = ₹3, 300

II] **Material Price Variance :** Actual Quantity [Standard Price – Actual Price]

Material A = 105 [₹20 – ₹20] = Nil

Material B = 95 [₹10 – ₹9] = ₹95 [F]

Total Material Price Variance = ₹95 [F]

III] **Material Quantity Variance :** Standard Price [Std. Quantity – Actual Quantity]

Material A = ₹20 [124 – 105] = ₹380 [F]

Material B = ₹10 [83 – 95] = ₹120 [A]

Total Material Quantity Variance = ₹260 [F]

Note : Calculation of standard quantity for actual production: Material A = 165/80 X 60 = 123.75 or 124

Material B = 165/80 X 40 = 82.5 or 83

IV] **Material Mix Variance :** Standard Cost of Standard Mix – Std. Cost of Actual Mix

₹ 3, 200 – ₹3, 050 =₹150 [F]

Note : Calculation of standard cost of standard mix:

Material A: 60% of 200 [Actual Input] = 120 X ₹20 =	₹ 2400
Material B: 40% of 200 [Actual Input] = 80 X ₹10 =	₹ 800
Total Cost =	₹3200

Calculation of standard cost of actual mix:

Material A = 105x 20 =	2,100
Material B = 95 x 10 =	950
	3,050

V] **Material Yield Variance :** Standard Yield Rate [Actual Yield – Standard Yield]

= ₹20 [165 –160] = ₹100 [F]

Note : Standard yield is in relation to the actual input of 200 kg and hence the standard yield is 200 less 20% normal loss i.e.40 kg and the standard yield is 160 kg.

Calculation of standard yield rate = Standard cost/ Standard yield = 1600/80= ₹ 20

Calculation of standard yield for input of 200kg

Normal loss is 20%

Hence = 200 – [200(20/100)] = 200-40 = 160 Units

Standard Yield = 160 units

Problem 7 :

ABC Ltd. produces an article by blending two basic raw materials. It operates a standard costing system and the following standards have been set for raw materials.

Material	Standard Mix	Standard Price
A	40%	₹4.00
B	60%	₹3.00

The standard loss in processing is 15%. During September 2012, the company produced 1, 700 kg of finished output.

The position of stock and purchases for the month of September 2012 is as under,

Material	Quantity as on 1/9/2012 Kg	Quantity as on 30/9/2012 -Kg	Purchases Kg	Cost ₹
A	35	5	800	3, 400
B	40	50	1, 200	3, 000

Calculate Material Cost Variance, Price Variance, Quantity Variance, Mix Variance and Yield Variance. Assume that First in First Out method is followed for material issues.

ICWA

Solution :

The following table is prepared for the computation of the variances.

Standard	Actual
Material A: 40 kg X ₹4 = ₹160	Material A: Total Quantity Used = Opening Stock + Purchases – Closing Stock i.e. 35 + 800 – 5 = 830 kg Actual Cost of Actual Quantity Opening Stock 35 kg @ ₹4 = ₹140.00 Actual Price = (3400/ 800) = 4.25 Purchases: 795 kg @ ₹4.25 = ₹ 3,378.25 Total = ₹ 3,518.25
Material B: 60 kg X ₹3 = ₹180	Material B: Total Quantity Used = Opening Stock + Purchases – Closing Stock 40 + 1200 – 50 = 1190 kg

	Actual Cost Of Actual Quantity From Opening Stock: 40 kg @ ₹3 = ₹120 From Purchases: 1150 kg @ ₹2.5 = ₹2875 Total Cost = ₹2995
Total 100 kg = ₹ 340	Total Actual Cost ₹6513.25 [₹3518.25 + ₹2995]
Less: Normal Loss 15% = 15 kg	Actual Loss = 320 kg
Normal Output = 85 kg	Actual Output = 1700 kg

Computation of Variances

1. **Material Cost Variance :** Standard Cost for Actual Production – Actual Cost

   ₹6800 – ₹6513.25 = ₹2,86.75 [F]

   Calculation of standard:

   For 85 kg output, standard cost is ₹340

   For actual output of 1700 kg, the standard cost is ₹6800

   (1700/85) x 340 = ₹ 6800

2. Material Price Variance: Actual Quantity [Standard Price – Actual Price]

   Material A (Opening) = 35[₹4 - ₹4] = Nil

   Remaining Purchases = 795[₹4 - ₹4.25] = ₹198.75 [A]

   Material B (Opening) = 40[₹3 – ₹3] = Nil

   Remaining Purchases = 1150[₹3 – ₹2.5] = ₹575 [F]

   Total Material Price Variance = ₹376.25 [F]

3. Material Quantity Variance: Standard Price [Standard Quantity – Actual Quantity]

   Material A = ₹4 [800 –830] = ₹120 [A]

   Material B = ₹3 [1200 – 1190] = ₹30 [F]

   Total Material Quantity Variance = ₹90 [A]

   Calculation of standard quantity for A and B:

   A : (1700/85) X 40 = 800 kg

   B : (1700/85) X 60 = 1200 kg

4. Material Mix Variance: Standard Cost of Standard Mix – Standard Cost of Actual Mix

   ₹6,868 – ₹6,890 = ₹22 [A]

   Calculation of standard Cost of Standard Mix and Actual cost of actual mix:

   Actual quantity of A and B consumed together = 830 + 1190 = 2020 kg

If this quantity were mixed in standard proportion, quantity of A would be 808 kg and B 1212 kg. Standard cost of this mix then would be,

A: 808 kg × ₹4 per kg = ₹3,232

B: 1212 kg × ₹3 per kg = ₹3,636

Total standard cost of standard mix = ₹6,868

Standard cost of actual mix :

A : Actual quantity 830 X ₹4 = ₹3,320

B : Actual quantity 1190 X ₹3 = ₹3,570

Total standard cost for actual mix = ₹6,890

5. Material Yield Variance: Standard Yield Rate [Actual Yield – Standard Yield] ₹340/85 kg [1700 – 1717] = ₹68 [A]

Calculation of standard yield:

Actual input is A 830 + B 1190 = 2020 kg

Standard loss is 15% of the input, thus standard loss for actual input is 303 kg Standard yield from actual input is 2020 kg – 303 kg = 1717 kg.

Problem 8 :

In a manufacturing process, the following standards apply,

Standard prices: Raw Material X ₹20 per kg,

Raw Material Y ₹100 per kg

Standard mix: 75% X and 25% Y [by weight]

Standard output90% [weight of product as a percentage of weight of raw material]

In a particular period actual cost, usages and output were as follows:

4400 kg of A costing ₹ 93,000

1600 kg of B costing ₹ 1,57,000

Output 5670 kg of product

The budgeted output for the period was 7200 kg

Calculate Material cost variances

Solution :

Computation of material variances

Standard	Actual
Material X (8000x75/100) = 6000 kg x ₹ 20 = ₹1,20, 000	Material X 4400 kg = ₹93,000
Material Y 2000 x ₹100 = ₹2,00,000	Material Y 1600 kg = ₹1,57,000
Total 8000 : (8000x90/100) ₹3,20,000	Total 6000 kg = ₹2,50,000
Less: Normal Loss 10%	*Less:* Actual Loss 330 kg
Normal Output 7200 kg at a standard cost ₹3,20,000	Actual Output = 5670 kg at actual cost of ₹ 2,50,000

1. **Material Cost Variance :**

   Standard Cost of Materials for Actual Production - Actual Cost.

   = ₹2, 52,000 - ₹2, 50, 000 = ₹2, 000 [F]

   Calculation of standard cost of materials for actual production:

   For 7200 kg the standard cost is ₹ 3,20,000 so for 5670 kg, the standard cost is

   5670/7200 X 3,20,000= ₹2, 52, 000

1. **Material Price Variance :** Actual Quantity [Standard Price - Actual Price]

   Material A = 4400 [₹20 - ₹93,000 /4400] = ₹5,016 [A]

   Material B = 1600 [₹100 - ₹1,57,000/1600] = ₹3008 [F]

   Total Material Price Variance: ₹2008 [A]

3. **Material Quantity Variance :** Standard Price [Standard Quantity - Actual Quantity]

   Material A = ₹20 [4725 - 4400] = ₹6,500 [F]

   Material B = ₹100 [1575 - 1600] = ₹2,500 [A]

   Total Material Quantity Variance = ₹4,000 [F]

4. **Material Mix Variance :**

   Standard Cost of Standard Mix - Standard Cost of Actual Mix

   ₹ 2,40,000 - ₹2,48,000 = ₹ 8,000 [A]

   Calculation of Standard Cost of Standard Mix:

   Actual total input is 6000 kg, if it is mixed in standard proportion; quantity of X would have been 4500 kg [75% of 6000] and that of Y 1500 kg [25% of 6000]. The standard cost of this mix would be, X: 4500 kg X ₹20 per kg = ₹90, 000

Y: 1500 kg X₹100 per kg = ₹1,50, 000

Total = ₹2, 40, 000

Standard cost of actual mix is computed by multiplying the actual quantity of X and Y by the standard price per kg

X: 4400 kg X ₹20 per kg = ₹88, 000

Y: 1600 kg X₹100 per kg = ₹1,60, 000

Total = ₹2, 48, 000

5. Material Yield Variance: Standard Yield Rate [Actual Yield – Standard Yield]

₹ 3,20,000/7200 [5670 – 5400] = ₹12,000 [F]

Calculation of Standard yield:

Input 8000 – – 7200 Output

Input 6000 – – ?

(6000/8000) x7200 = 5400 Units

Verification : MQV = MMV + MYV

4000[F] = 8000[A] + 12,000[F]

Problem 9 :

The standard material inputs required for 1,000 kg of a finished output are given below.

Material in kg	Quantity [₹]	Standard Rate Per Kg – ₹
P	450	20
Q	400	40
R	250	60
Total Input	1100	
Less: Standard Loss	100	
Standard Output	1000	

Actual production in a period was 20, 000 kg of the finished product for which the actual quantities of materials used and the prices paid thereof are as under.

Material	Quantity Used - Kg	Purchased Price Per Unit [Rs]
P	10,000	19
Q	8,500	42
R	4,500	65

Calculate Material Cost, Price, Quantity, Mix and Yield Variances. Prepare reconciliation among the variances

ICWA

Solution :

Table showing Standards and Actual Details

Material	Standard	Actual
P	450 kg @ ₹20 = ₹9,000	10, 000 kg @ ₹19 = ₹1,90,000
Q	400 kg @ ₹40 = ₹16,000	8, 500 kg @ ₹42 = ₹3,57,000
R	250 kg @ ₹60 = ₹15,000	4, 500 kg @ ₹65 = ₹2,92,500
Total Input	1, 100 kg = ₹40,000	23, 000 kg = ₹8,39,500
Less: Standard Loss	100 kg	3,000 kg [Actual Loss]
Standard Output	1, 000 kg = ₹40,000	20,000 [Actual Production]

1. **Material Cost Variance:** Standard Material Cost [for Actual Production] – Actual Cost ₹8,00,000 – ₹8,39,500 = ₹39,500 [A]

   Note: Standard Material Cost for actual production is computed as shown below.

   For 1000 kg [standard production], the standard cost is ₹40,000, so for actual production of 20,000 kg, the standard cost is (20,000/1000) x 40,000 = ₹8,00,000

2. **Material Price Variance:** Actual Quantity [Standard Price – Actual Price]

   Material P = 10,000 [₹20 – ₹19] = ₹10,000 [F]

   Material Q = 8,500 [₹40 – ₹42] = ₹17,000 [A]

   Material R = 4,500 [₹60 – ₹65] = ₹22,500 [A]

   Total Material Price Variance = ₹29,500 [A]

3. **Material Quantity Variance:** Standard Price [Standard Quantity – Actual Quantity]

   Material P = ₹20 [9,000 – 10,000]= ₹20,000 [A]

   Material Q = ₹40 [8,000 – 8,500] = ₹20,000 [A]

   Material R = ₹60 [5,000 – 4,500] = ₹30,000 [F]

   Total Material Quantity Variance = ₹10,000 [A]

   Calculation of standard quantity of materials:

   Material P = 20,000/1000 X 450 = 9,000 kg

   Material Q = 20,000/1000 X 400 = 8,000 kg

   Material R = 20,000/1000 X 250 = 5,000 kg

4. **Material Mix Variance :**

Standard Cost of Standard Mix – Standard Cost of Actual Mix

₹ 8,36,360 – ₹ 8,10,000 = ₹26,360 [F]

Calculation of standard cost of standard mix:

If the actual input of 23,000 would have been mixed in standard proportion, the quantities along with cost of P, Q and R would have been,

P : 23,000 /1100 × 450 = 9409 × ₹20 = ₹1,88,180

Q : 23,000/1100 × 400 = 8364 × ₹40 = ₹3,34,560

R : 23,000/1100 × 250 = 5227 × ₹60 = ₹3,13,620

Total Cost = ₹8, 36, 360

5. **Material Yield Variance :** Standard Yield Rate [Actual Yield – Standard Yield]

₹40,000/1000 [20,000 – 20,909] = ₹36,360 [A]

Note : Standard yield is computed as under

Standard loss is 1/11th of input, hence normal loss for actual input is, 23,000 /11 = 2,091 Therefore standard production for actual input is 23,000 – 2091 = 20,909 kg

II. LABOUR VARIANCES

Labour variances arise due to the difference between the standard labour cost for actual production and the actual labour cost. The following are the types of labour variances.

1. **Labour Cost Variance :** This variance arises due to the difference between the standard labour cost for actual production and the actual labour cost. The following formula is used for Labour Cost Variance :

Labour Cost Variance

= Standard Labour Cost for Actual Production – Actual Labour Cost

OR

LCV = (SH x SR) – (AH x AR)

SH = Standard Hours

SR = Standard Hourly Rate

AH = Actual Hours worked

AR = Actual Rate

This variance will be favourable if the actual labour cost is less than the standard labour cost and adverse if the actual labour cost is more than the standard labour cost.

2. **Labour Rate Variance :** Labour rate variance is the difference between the standard rate of wages and actual wages rate. The labour rate variance indicates the difference between the standard labour rate and the actual labour rate paid. The formula for calculation is as under.

Labour Rate Variance: Actual Hours Paid [Standard Rate – Actual Rate]

This variance will be favourable if the actual rate paid is less than the standard rate. The labour rate variance is that portion of direct labour cost variance, which is due to the difference between the labour rates.

3. **Labour Efficiency Variance :** It is of most importance for measuring efficiency of labour. In this the actual time taken by the workers should be compared with the standard time allowed for the job. The standard time allowed for a particular job is decided with the help of time and motion study. The efficiency variance is calculated with the help of the following formula.

Labour Efficiency Variance

= Standard Rate [Standard Hours for Actual Output – Actual Hours worked]

This variance will be favourable if the actual time taken is less than the standard time, otherwise it is adverse

5. **Labour Mix Variance or Gang Composition Variance :** This variance is similar to the material mix variance and is computed in the same manner. In doing a particular job, there may be a particular combination of labour force, which may consist of skilled, semi skilled and unskilled workers. However due to some practical difficulties, this composition may have to be changed. How much is the loss caused due to this change or how much is the gain due to this change is indicated by this variance. The computation is done with the help of the following formula. The variance will be favourable if the actual output achieved is more than the standard output otherwise it is adverse. The computation is done in the following manner.

When standard and actual times of the labour mix are same :

= Standard Cost of Standard Labour mix – Standard cost of actual labour mix.

When standard and actual times of the labour mix are different :

$$\frac{\text{Total Time of Actual Labour Mix}}{\text{Total Time standard Labour Mix}} \times \text{Standard Cost of Standard Labour Mix} - \text{Standard Cost of Actual Labour Mix}$$

If labour composition is revised because of non- availability of one grade of labour then revised standard mix will be used instead of standard mix and the formula will become.

$$\frac{\text{Total Time of Actual Labour Mix}}{\text{Total Time Reised Labour Mix}} \times \text{Standard Cost of Revised Standard Labour Mix} - \text{Standard Cost of Actual Labour Mix}$$

6. **Labour Yield or Sub Efficiency Variance :** The labour yield variance or the labour sub efficiency variance arises due to the standard output specified and the actual output obtained. This variance is calculated as follows.

Labour Yield/Sub Efficiency Variance

= Standard Labour Cost per unit of output

(Actual Yield – Standard Yield for Actual Time)

7. **Idle Time Variance :** This variance indicates the loss caused due to abnormal idle time. While fixing the standard time, normal idle time is taken into consideration. However if the actual idle time is more than the standard/normal idle time, it is called as abnormal idle time. This variance always adverse and computed as shown below.

Idle Time Variance = Abnormal Idle Time × Standard Rate.

Problem 9A :

Calculate labour variances from the following data

Particulars	**Standard**	**Actual**
Output Units	3,000	3,500
Number of workers employed	75	85
Number of working days in a month	23	25
Average wage per man per month	345	400

Solution :

Calculation of standard and actual wage rate per day:

$$\text{Standard wage rate per day} = \frac{345}{23} = ₹\ 15$$

$$\text{Actual wage rate per day} = \frac{400}{25} = ₹\ 16$$

Standard man days for an output of 3,000 units = 75 x 23 = 1725

Actual output is more than the standard output, standard time will be adjusted.

$$\text{Standard man days for actual output} = \frac{1{,}725}{3{,}000} \times 3{,}500 = 2013$$

1. **Labour Rate Variance** = Actual Time [Standard Rate – Actual Rate]

= 2125 [15- 16] = 2125 [A]

2. **Labour Efficiency Variance** = Standard Rate [Standard Time – Actual Time]

= 15 [2013 - 2125] = 15 [-112] = 1680 [A]

3. **Labour Cost Variance** = Labour Rate Variance + Labour Efficiency Variance

= 2125 [A] + 1680 [A] = 3805 [A]

OR

[Standard Time for Actual Output x SR] – [Actual Time x Actual Rate]

= (2013 x 15) – (2125 x 16) = 30195 – 34,000 = 3805 [A]

Verification : Labour Cost Variance = Labour Rate Variance + Labour efficiency variance

3805 [A] = 2125 [A] + 1680 [A]

Problem 10 :

Standard hours for manufacturing two products M and N are 15 hours per unit and 20 hours per unit respectively. Both products require identical kind of labour and the standard wage rate per hour is ₹5. In a particular year, 10,000 units of M and 15,000 units of N were produced. The total labour hours worked were 4,50,000 and the actual wage bill came to ₹23,00,000. This includes 12,000 hours paid for @ ₹7 per hour and 9400 hours paid for @ ₹7.50 per hour, the balance having been paid at ₹5 per hour. You are required to calculate labour variances.

[ICWAI Inter]

Solution :

1. **Labour Cost Variance :**

Standard Labour Cost for Actual Production – Actual Labour Cost

₹22, 50, 000 – ₹23, 00, 000 = ₹50, 000 [A]

Note : Standard Labour Cost for Actual Production is computed as under,

Product M : 10, 000 units x 15 hrs per unit x ₹5 per hour = ₹7,50,000

Product N: 15, 000 units x 20 hrs per unit x ₹5 per hour = ₹15,00,000

Total standard labour cost for actual production = ₹22,50,000

2. **Labour Rate Variance :** Actual Hours [Standard Rate – Actual Rate]

- 12, 000 [₹5 – ₹7] = ₹24,000 [A]
- 9, 400 [₹5 – ₹7.50] = ₹23,500 [A]
- 4, 29, 100 [₹5 – ₹5] = Nil

Total Labour Rate Variance = ₹47,500 [A]

3. **Labour Efficiency Variance** = Standard Rate [Standard Time – Actual Time]

= ₹5 [4,50,000 – 4,50,500] = ₹2,500 [A]

Verification :

Labour Cost Variance = Labour Rate Variance + Labour Efficiency

Variance ₹50,000 [A] = ₹47,500 [A] + ₹2,500 [A]

Problem 11 :

The standard output of production B is 50 units per hour in a manufacturing department of a company employing 200 workers. The standard wage rate per labour hour is ₹10.

In a 42 hours week, the department produced 2050 units of the product despite 10% of the time paid were lost due to an abnormal reason. The hourly wage rate actually paid were ₹12, ₹10 and ₹9 respectively to 20, 60 and 120 of the workers.

Compute various relevant labour variances.

Solution :

Calculation of labour variances.

Standard	Actual Hours	Actual Rate ₹	Actual Cost ₹
Standard output 50 units per hour for	42 hrs × 20 workers = 840 hrs	₹12	10,080
200 employees Hence standard man hours per unit = 200 workers/50 units per hr = 4	42 hrs × 60 workers = 2520 hrs	₹10	25,200
	42 hrs × 120 workers = 5040	₹9	45,360
Actual output = 2050 units	Total: 8400 hrs		80,640
Standard hrs for 2050 units = 2050 × 4= 8200	Idle Time 10% of 8400 = 840 hrs		
Standard cost for actual output = 8200 hrs × ₹10 per hr = ₹82,000	Actual Hrs Worked 8400 – 840 = 7560 hrs		

1. **Labour Cost Variance :**

   Standard Cost for Actual Production – Actual Cost

   ₹82,000 – ₹80,640 = ₹1,360 [F]

2. **Labour Rate Variance :** Actual Hours [Standard Rate – Actual Rate]

   840 [₹10 – ₹12] = ₹1,680 [A]

   2,520 [₹10 – ₹10] = Nil

   5,040 [₹10 – ₹9] = ₹5,040 [F]

   Total Labour Rate Variance = ₹3,360 [F]

3. **Labour Efficiency Variance :**

   = Standard Rate [Standard Time –Actual Time Worked]

   = ₹10 [8,200 – 7,560] = ₹6,400 [F]

4. **Labour Idle Time Variance :** Abnormal Idle Time X Standard Rate

   840 hrs X ₹10 = ₹8400 [A]

Problem 12 :

Calculate labour variances from the following information.

Budgeted Labour Force

100 skilled worker @ ₹ 300 per month.

150 semi skilled worker @ ₹ 250 per month

Actual Labour Force:

130 skilled workers @ Rs 325 per month

120 Semi skilled workers @ Rs 275 per month

Due to shortage of skilled workers it was decided to reduce skilled workers by 20% and increase semi- skilled workers by 10%

Solution :

Calculation of Revised standard:

$$\text{Skilled} = 100 - 20 \left[100 \times \frac{20}{100}\right] = \quad 80$$

$$\text{Semi-skilled} = 150 + 15 \left[150 \times \frac{10}{100}\right] = \quad 165$$

$$245$$

There is difference between revised standard labour mix and actual labour mix hence the following is the formula.

$$\left[\frac{\text{Total Time of Actual Labour mix}}{\text{Std. Time of Rev. Std. Labour mix}} \times \text{Std. Cost of Rev. Std. Labour mix}\right] - (\text{Std. Cost of Actual labour mix})$$

$$= \frac{330}{245} \times (80 \times 300 + 165 \times 250) - (130 \times 300 + 200 \times 250)$$

$$= (24000 + 41{,}250) - (39{,}000 + 50{,}000)$$

$$= (65{,}250) - (89{,}000)$$

$$= 87{,}888 - 89{,}000 = 1112\ [\text{A}]$$

Problem 13 :

The following was the composition of a gang of workers in a KGR Company during a particular month, in one of the production departments. The standard composition of workers and wage rates per hour were as follows.

Skilled: Four workers at a standard rate of ₹10 per hour each

Semi-Skilled: Eight workers at a standard rate of ₹6 per hour each

Unskilled: Eight workers at a standard rate of ₹4 per hour each.

The standard output of the gang was four units per hour of the product. During the month in question, however the actual composition of the gang and hourly rates paid were as under

Skilled: 4 workers @ ₹10 per hour

Semi-Skilled: 6 workers @ ₹07 per hour

Un-skilled: 10 workers @ ₹5 per hour

The gang was engaged for 100 hours during the month, which included 6 hours when no production was possible due to the machine breakdown. 400 units of the product was recorded as output of the gang during the month. Calculate various labour variances.

Solution :

Calculation of labour variances

Category of Workers	Standard Composition of Gang	Standard Rate ₹	Standard Cost ₹	Actual Composition of Gang and number of hrs	Actual Rate ₹	Actual Cost ₹
Skilled	4	10	40	4 × 100 = 400	10	4, 000
Semi-skilled	8	6	48	6 × 100 = 600	7	4, 200
Unskilled	8	4	32	10 × 100 = 1000	5	5, 000
Total		20	120	20 × 100 = 2000		13, 200

I] **Labour Cost Variance :** Standard Cost for Actual Production – Actual Cost]

₹.12,000 – ₹13,200 = ₹1,200 [A]

Note: Standard labour cost for actual production: For 1 man-hour the standard cost is ₹120 as shown in the table. In one hour 4 units are produced and so the standard labour cost per unit is ₹120/4 units = ₹30 per unit. Thus standard labour cost for actual production will be 400 units X ₹30 = ₹12,000.

II] **Labour Rate Variance :** Actual Hours [Standard Rate – Actual Rate]

Skilled: 400 [₹10 – ₹10] = Nil

Semi-skilled: 600 [Rs 6 – ₹7] = ₹600 [A]

Unskilled: 1000 [₹4 – ₹5] = ₹1,000 [A]

Total Labour Rate Variance = ₹1,600 [A]

III] **Labour Efficiency Variance :** Standard Rate [Standard Time – Actual Time]

Skilled: ₹10 [(₹4 x 100) – 400] = Nil

Semi-skilled: Rs 6 [(₹8 x 100) – 600] = 1200 F

Un-skilled: ₹4 [(₹8 x 100) – 1000] = 800 A

Total Labour Efficiency Variance = 400 favourable

Verification :

Labour Cost Variance = Labour RateVariance + Labour Efficiency Variance

= 1200 [A] = 1600 [A] + 400 [F].

Problem 14 :

From the following particulars of a manufacturing company, compute material and labour variances.

An input of 100 kg of material yields to standard output of 10,000 units.

Standard price per kg of material ₹20

Actual quantity of material issued and used by production department 10,000 kg

Actual price per kg of material ₹21 per kg Actual output 9,00,000 units

Number of employees 200

Standard wage rate per employee per day = ₹ 40

Standard daily output per employee = 100 units

Total number of days worked = 50 days

[Idle time paid for and included in the above half day for each employee]

Actual wage rate per day = ₹ 45

ICWAI

Solution :

A] Material Variances :

1. Material Cost Variance:

Standard Cost of Materials for actual production – Actual Cost

9,000 kg × ₹20 – 10,000 X ₹21

= ₹1,80,000 – ₹2,10,000 = ₹30,000 [A]

Note : For 10,000 units of finished product, 100 kg of materials are required, hence for actual output of 9,00,000 units, standard quantity of materials is 9,000 kg.

2. Material Price Variance : Actual Quantity [Standard Price – Actual Price

10,000 [₹20 – ₹21] = ₹10,000 [A]

3. Material Quantity Variance :

Standard Price [Standard Quantity – Actual Quantity]

₹20 [9,000 – 10,000] = ₹20,000 [A]

B] Labour Variances :

1. **Labour Cost Variance :**

   Standard Cost of Labour for actual production – Actual Labour Cost

   (9,000 units x ₹40) – (50 days x 200 employees x ₹45)

   ₹3, 60, 000 – ₹4, 50, 000 = ₹90, 000 [A]

   Calculation of standard rate per unit:

   = ₹40 [daily wages per employee]/100 [number of employees] = ₹40

2. **Labour Rate Variance :** Actual Time Paid For [Standard Rate – Actual Rate]

   50 days × 200 number of employees [₹40 – ₹45]

   10,000 × ₹5 = ₹ 50,000 [A]

3. **Efficiency Variance**

   Standard Rate [Standard Time for Actual Production – Actual Time]

   = ₹40 [9,000 – 5,000] = ₹1,60,000 [F]

   Note : Standard output per employee per day is 100 and so for 9,00,000 units of actual production, 9,000 days are required. Idle time is half day for each employee and hence idle time is 200 employees x 25 days = 5,000. Therefore the time taken is 10,000 man days less idle time of 5,000 man days i.e. 5,000 man days.

4. **Idle Time Variance :** Abnormal Idle Time x Standard Rate

   5,000 man days x ₹40 = ₹2,00,000 [A]

Problem 15 :

The following standards have been set to manufacture a product Direct Materials:

2 units of A @ ₹4 per unit: ₹8

3 units of B @ ₹3 per unit: ₹9.

15 units of C @ Re.1 per unit: ₹15

Direct Labour 3 hrs @ ₹8 per hour: ₹24

Standard Prime Cost: ₹56

The company manufactured and sold 6000 units of the product during the year. Direct Material cost was as follows:

12, 500 units of A @ ₹4.40 per unit

18, 000 units of B @ ₹2.80 per unit

88, 500 units of C @ ₹1.20 per unit

The company worked for 17, 500 direct labour hours during the year. For 2500 of these hours the company paid ₹12 per hour while for the remaining the wages were paid at the standard rate. Calculate material price and usage variances and labour rate and efficiency variances.

Solution :

Calculation of Standards and Actual Cost

Material	Standards		Actual	
A	12,000	@ ₹4 = ₹48,000	12,500	@ ₹4.40 = ₹55,000
B	18,000	@ ₹3 = ₹54,000	18,000	@ ₹2.80 = ₹50,400
C	90,000	@ Re.1 = ₹90,000		88,500 @ ₹1.20 = ₹1,06,200
Total		1,20,000 = ₹1, 92,000		1,19,000 = ₹2,11,600

I. Material Variances:

1. **Material Price Variance :** Actual Quantity [Standard Price – Actual Price]

Material A = 12,500 [₹4 – ₹4.40] = ₹5,000 [A]

Material B = 18,500 [₹3 – ₹2.80] = ₹3,600 [F]

Material C = 88,500 [Re.1 – ₹1.20] = ₹17,700 [A]

Total Material Price Variance = ₹19,100 [A]

2. **Material Usage [Quantity] Variance:**

Standard Price [Standard Quantity – Actual Quantity]

Material A = ₹4 [12,000 – ₹12, 500] = ₹2,000 [A]

Material B = ₹3 [18,000 – 18,000] = Nil

Material C = Re.1 [90,000 – 88,500] = ₹1,500 [F]

Total Material Usage [Quantity] Variance = ₹500 [A]

II] Labour Variances :

1. **Labour Rate Variance :** Actual Hours [Standard Rate – Actual Rate

- For 2, 500 hours: 2,500 [₹8 – ₹12] = ₹10,000 [A]
- For 15, 000 hours: 15,000 [₹8 – ₹8] = Nil

2. **Labour Efficiency Variance :**

Standard Rate [Standard Time For Actual Output] – Actual Time]

₹8 [18,000 – 17,500] = ₹ 4,000 [F]

Calculation of standard time for actual output : 3 labour hours per unit is the standard and so for producing 6,000 units, the number of hours required are 6,000 × 3 = 18,000.

III] Overhead Variances : It indicates the difference between the standard overhead cost and the actual overhead cost. In case of direct material and direct labour variances, there is no question of dividing them into fixed and variable as the direct material and direct labour costs are variable. However, in case of overheads, it is necessary to divide them into fixed and variable for computation of variances.

A] **Fixed Overhead Variances :** The fixed overhead variances are subdivided into the following ways.

1. **Fixed Overhead Cost Variance :** It indicates the difference between the standard fixed overheads for actual production and the actual fixed overheads incurred. This variance may be under/over absorbed of fixed overheads. If the actual overheads incurred are more than the standard fixed overheads, it indicates the under absorption of fixed overheads otherwise it is over absorption of fixed overheads.

   Fixed Overhead Cost Variance : Standard Fixed Overheads for Actual Production – Actual Fixed Overheads.

2. **Fixed Overhead Expenditure/Budget Variance :** This variance indicates the difference between the budgeted fixed overheads and the actual fixed overhead expenses. If the actual fixed overheads are more than the budgeted fixed overheads, it is an adverse variance as it means overspending as compared to the budgeted amount. On the other hand, if the actual fixed overheads are less than the budgeted fixed overheads, it is a favourable variance.

   Fixed Overhead Expenditure Variance : Budgeted Fixed Overheads – Actual Fixed Overheads

3. **Fixed Overheads Volume Variance :** This variance indicates the under/over absorption of fixed overheads due to the difference in the budgeted quantity of production and actual quantity of production. If the actual quantity produced is more than the budgeted one, this variance will be favourable but it will indicate over absorption of fixed overheads. On the other hand, if the actual quantity produced is less than the budgeted one, it indicates adverse variance and there will be under absorption of overheads. The formula for computation of this variance is as shown below:

   Fixed Overhead Volume Variance : Standard Rate [Budgeted Quantity – Actual Quantity] Verification: Fixed Overhead Cost Variance = Expenditure Variance + Volume Variance

4. **Fixed Overhead Efficiency Variance :** The volume variance arises due to the difference between the output actually achieved and the output which should have been achieved in the actual hours worked. This variance will be favourable if the actual production is more than the standard production in actual hours.
   Fixed Overhead Efficiency Variance = Standard Rate [Standard Production – Actual Production]

5. **Fixed Overhead Capacity Variance :** It arises due to the difference between, the capacity actually utilized and the budgeted capacity. If the capacity utilization is more than the budgeted capacity, the variance is favourable, otherwise it will be adverse. The formula is as follows:

   Fixed Overheads Capacity Variance = Standard Rate [Standard Quantity – Budgeted Quantity] Verification: Volume Variance = Efficiency Variance + Capacity Variance

6. **Fixed Overhead Revised Capacity Variance :** This variance indicates the difference in capacity utilization due to working for more or less number of days than the budgeted one. The computation of this variance is done by using the following formula.

   Fixed Overhead Revised Capacity Variance = Standard Rate [Standard Quantity – Revised Budgeted Quantity]

7. **Fixed Overheads Calendar Variance :** This variance indicates the difference between the budgeted quantity of production and actual quantity of production achieved arising due to the difference in the number of days worked and budgeted.

   Fixed Overheads Calendar Variance = Standard Rate [Budgeted Quantity – Revised Budgeted Quantity]

B] **Variable Overhead Variances :** It indicates the difference between the standard variable overhead for actual output and the actual variable overheads.

1. **Variable Overhead Cost Variance :** It is the difference between the standard variable overheads for actual prodution and the actual overheads. The difference between the two arises due to the variation between the budgeted and actual quantity.

   Variable Overhead Cost Variance = Standard Variable Overhead for Actual Production – Actual Variable Overhead. Or

   (Actual Hours x Standard Variable Overhead Rate) – (Actual Variable Overhead)

2. **Variable Overhead Expenditure Variance**

   It is the difference between the budgeted variable overheads and the actual variable expenses. Variable Overhead Expenditure Variance

   = Standard Variable Overheads for Standard Production – Actual Variable Overheads.

   (OR)

   Actual Hours (Standard Variable Overheads Rate – Actual Variable Overheads Rate)

3. **Variable Overheads Efficiency Variance :** It indicates the efficiency by comparing between the output actually achieved and the output that should have been achieved in the actual hours worked. It variance will be favourable if the actual output achieved is more than the standard output.

   Variable Overheads Efficiency Variance = Standard Variable Overheads Rate [Standard Quantity – Actual Quantity]

Problem 16 :

From the following information extracted from the books of a Navabharat company, calculate Fixed and Variable Overheads Variances.

Particulars	Budgeted	Actual
Production - Units	25,000	28,000
Fixed Overheads	₹ 50,000	₹ 58,000
Variable Overheads	₹37, 500	₹47,750
Number of Days	24	25
Number of man hours	30,000	32,000

Fixed Overhead Variances :

I] Fixed Overhead Cost Variance

Standard Fixed Overheads for Actual Production - Actual Fixed Overheads

= ₹56,000 - ₹50,000 = ₹2,000 [A]

Note : Standard fixed overheads for actual production = Actual Production 28,000 × standard rate ₹2 [₹50,000 budgeted fixed overheads / 25,000 budgeted production = ₹2]

28,000Units x 2 = 56,000

II] Fixed Overhead Expenditure Variance

Budgeted Fixed Overheads - Actual Fixed Overheads

= ₹50,000 - ₹58,000 = ₹8,000 [A]

III] Fixed Overhead Volume Variance

Standard Rate [Budgeted Quantity - Actual Quantity]

= ₹2 [25,000 - 28,000] = ₹6,000 [F]

The variance is favourable as the actual quantity produced is more than the budgeted quantity.

Verification

Cost Variance = Expenditure Variance + Volume Variance

₹2,000 [A] = ₹8,000 [A] + ₹6,000 [F]

IV] Fixed Overhead Efficiency Variance

Standard Rate [Standard Quantity - Actual Quantity]

= ₹2 [26,667 - 28,000] = ₹2,666 [F]

Note : Standard quantity of production is in reference to actual number of hours. If 25,000 units are produced in 30,000 hrs [standard hours], in actual 32,000 hours, 26,667 units should have been produced. When number of days and number of hours, both are given, the standard quantity is always to be computed in relation to the actual hours. However, if only number of days is given, the standard quantity will have to be computed in relation to number of days.

V] Fixed Overhead Capacity Variance:

Standard Rate [Standard Quantity – Budgeted Quantity]

= ₹2 [26,667 – 25,000] = ₹3,334 [F]

Verification : Volume Variance = Efficiency Variance + Capacity Variance

₹6,000 [F] = ₹2,666 [F] + 3,334 [F]

VI] Fixed Overhead Revised Capacity Variance :

= Standard Rate [Standard Quantity – Revised Budgeted Quantity]

= ₹2 [26,667 – 26,042] = ₹2 × 625 = ₹1250 [F]

Note : Standard quantity is computed as shown in the Efficiency Variance. Revised Budget Quantity is computed as: in 24 days, the production is 25,000 so in 25 days the revised quantity is 26,042 units.

Fixed Overhead Calendar Variance

Standard Rate [Revised Budgeted Quantity – Budgeted Quantity]

= ₹2 [26,042 – 25,000] = ₹2 x 1,042 = ₹2,084 [F]

B] Variable Overheads Variance:

I] Variable Overhead Cost Variance :

Standard Variable Overheads for Actual Production – Actual Variable Overheads: ₹42,000 – ₹47,750 = ₹5,750 [A]

Standard Variable Overheads for Actual Production = Standard Rate Per Unit x Actual Production Units = ₹1.5 [Budgeted variable overheads ₹37,500 / Budgeted production units 25,000 = ₹1.5] x 28,000 units = ₹42,000

II] Variable Overhead Expenditure Variance

Standard Variable Overheads for Standard Production – Actual Variable Overheads: (₹1.5 x 26,667) – ₹47,750 = ₹40,000 – 47,750 = 7,750 [A]

III] Variable Overhead Efficiency Variance

Standard Rate [Standard Quantity – Actual Quantity]

₹1.5 [26,667 – 28,000] = ₹2,000 [F]

Problem 17 :

The following information is available from the records of a manufacturing company using standard costing system.

Particulars	Standard	Actual
Production	5,000 units	4,500 units
Working days	25	26
Fixed overhead	₹50,000	₹47,250
Variable overheads	₹15,000	₹15,000

Calculate the following overhead variances

I] Variable overhead variance

II] Fixed overhead cost variance

III] Fixed overhead expenditure variance

IV] Fixed overhead volume variance

V] Fixed overhead efficiency variance

VI] Fixed overhead calendar variance

Solution :

Standard variable overhead rate per unit = Budgeted variable overheads/ budgeted number of units = ₹15,000/ 5,000 units = ₹3

Standard production per day = 5,000 units/25 days = 200 units

Standard fixed overhead per day = 200 x ₹10 = ₹2,000

Computation of Variances:

I] **Variable overhead cost variance:**

Actual variable overheads – Recoverable variable overheads

= ₹15,000 – [4,500 units × ₹3] = 15,000 – 13,500 = 1,500[A]

II] **Fixed overhead variance:**

Standard fixed overheads for actual production – Actual fixed overheads

= [4,500 units ₹10] – ₹47,250 = ₹2,250 [A]

III] **Fixed overhead expenditure variance:**

Budgeted fixed overheads – Actual fixed overheads

= ₹50, 000 – ₹47,250 = ₹2,750 [F]

IV] **Fixed overhead volume variance:**

Recoverable overheads – Budgeted overheads

= (₹ 4,500 x 10) – ₹50,000 = ₹5,000 [A]

V] **Fixed overhead efficiency variance:**

Standard fixed overhead rate per day [Actual time – standard time for actual output]

= ₹2,000 [26 – 22.5] = 2,000 x 3.5 = ₹7,000 [F]

VI] **Fixed overhead calendar variance:**

Standard fixed overhead rate per day [Actual days – Budgeted days]

= ₹2,000 [26 – 25] = ₹2,000 [F]

Problem 18 :

The following data are available in respect of a manufacturing company

Particulars	Budget	Actual
Production - units	400	360
Total Man-hours to production	8,000	7,000
Total Variable overheads	₹10,000	₹9,150

The standard time to produce one unit of the product is 20 hours. Calculate variable overhead variances.

Solution :

Calculation of standard variable overhead per unit and per hour:

1. Standard variable overhead per unit = ₹10,000/400 units = ₹25 per unit
2. Standard variable overhead per hour = ₹10,000/8,000 hrs = ₹1.25 per hour
3. Recovered variable overhead

   = Actual output × Standard variable overhead per hour

   = 360 units × ₹25 = ₹9,000
4. Budgeted variable overheads

   = Actual hours worked × Standard variable overhead per hour

   = 7,000 hrs × ₹1.25 = ₹8,750
5. Standard hours for actual output = Actual output × Standard hours per unit

   = 360 units × 20 hours = 7,200 hours

Computation of Variable overhead variances:

- Variable overhead cost variance

  = Recoverable variable overhead – Actual variable overhead

  = ₹9,000 – ₹9,150 = ₹150 [A]

- Variable overhead budget or expenditure variance

  = Budgeted variable overheads – Actual variable overhead

  = ₹8,750 – ₹9,150 = ₹400 [A]

- Variable overhead efficiency variance

  = Standard variable overhead per hour [Standard hours for actual output – Actual hours]

  = ₹1.25(7,200 - 7,000) = ₹250[F]

Problem 19 :

The following information was obtained from the records of a manufacturing unit using standard costing system.

Particulars	Standard	Actual
Production	4,000	3,800
Working Days	20	21
Fixed Overheads	₹40,000	₹39,000
Variable Overheads	₹12,000	₹12,000

Calculate,

1. Variable Overhead Variance
2. Fixed Overhead Expenditure Variance
3. Fixed Overhead Volume Variance
4. Fixed Overhead Efficiency Variance
5. Fixed Overhead Calendar Variance
6. Also prepare a reconciliation statement for the standard fixed expenses worked out at standard fixed overhead rate and the actual fixed overhead.

ICWAI

Solution :

Calculation of Standard Variable Overhead Rate per Unit = ₹12, 000/4,000 units = ₹3 per unit Standard production per day = 4, 000 units/20 days = 200 units

Standard fixed overheads per day = 200 x ₹10 = ₹2,000

Standard fixed overheads per unit = ₹40,000/4,000 = ₹10

Computation of Variances:

1) Variable Overhead Variance:

Standard Variable Overheads for Actual Production – Actual Variable Overheads:

₹3 x 3,800 units – ₹12,000 = ₹600 [A]

2) **Fixed Overhead Variance:**

Standard Fixed Overheads for Actual Production – Actual Fixed Overheads:

₹10 x 3,800 – ₹39,000 = ₹1,000 [A]

3) **Fixed Overhead Expenditure Variance:**

Budgeted Fixed Overheads – Actual Fixed Overheads

= ₹40,000 – ₹39,000 = ₹1,000 [F]

4) **Fixed Overhead Volume Variance:**

Standard Rate [Budgeted Quantity – Actual Quantity]

= ₹10 [4,000 – 3,800] = ₹2,000 [A]

5) **Fixed Overhead Efficiency Variance:**

Standard Rate [Standard Quantity * – Actual Quantity]

= ₹10 [4,200 – 3,800] = ₹4,000 [A

6) **Fixed Overhead Calendar Variance:**

Standard Rate [Revised Budgeted Quantity ** – Budgeted Quantity]

= ₹10 [4,200 – 4,000] = ₹2,000 [F]

* Standard quantity: in 20 days, 4000 units are produced and hence in 21 days, the standard quantity will be (21/20) x 4000 = 4,200 units

** Revised budgeted quantity is calculated in the similar manner as mentioned above. In this example, number of working hours is not given and hence the standard quantity and the revised budgeted quantity is one and the same. When working hours are given, standard quantity is always computed in relation to the working hours while the revised budgeted quantity is computed in terms of number of days.

- Reconciliation Statement: Fixed Overheads

Particulars	₹	₹
Standard Fixed Overheads: 3, 800 units × ₹10		38,000
Less: Fixed Overhead Expenditure Variance	1,000 [F]	
Less: Fixed Overhead Calendar Variance	2,000 [F]	3,000 [F]
		35,000
Add: Fixed Overhead Efficiency Variance		4,000 [A]
Actual Fixed Overheads		39,000

Problem 20 :

The following data has been collected from the cost records of a unit for computing various fixed overhead variances for a particular period.

Particular	Details
Number of budgeted working days	25
Budgeted man-hours per day	6,000
Output [budgeted] per man hours	1 unit
Fixed overhead cost as budgeted	₹1,50,000
Actual number of working days	27
Actual man hour per day	6,300
Actual output per man hour	0.9 units
Actual fixed overheads	₹1,56,000

Calculate the following Fixed Overhead Variances

1. Expenditure variance
2. Calendar variance
3. Capacity variance
4. Efficiency variance
5. Volume Variance
6. Cost Variance

ICWAI

Solution :

Fixed Overhead Variances

1. Fixed Overhead Expenditure Variance:

   Budgeted Fixed Overheads – Actual Fixed Overheads

   = ₹1,50,000 – ₹1,56,000 = ₹6,000 [A]

2. Fixed Overhead Calendar Variance:

   Standard Rate [Revised Budgeted Quantity – Budgeted Quantity]

   = Re.1 [1,62,000 – 1,50,000] = ₹12,000 [F]

   Note: Standard Rate = 25 days × 6000 man hours per day × 1 unit per man hour = 1, 50, 000 units is the budgeted production, fixed overheads budgeted are ₹1, 50, 000 and hence standard rate is ₹1,50,000/1,50,000 units = Re1

   Revised Budgeted Quantity = in 25 days, 1,50,000 units, therefore in 27 days, the revised quantity will be (27/25) x 1,50,000 = 1,62,000 units

3. **Fixed Overhead Capacity Variance:**

Standard Rate [Standard Quantity – Budgeted Quantity]

Re.1 [1,70,100 – 1,50,000] = ₹20,100 [F]

Note: Standard Rate is as per the computation in the Note to the Calendar variance. Standard quantity is computed as shown below.

Actual number of hours worked are, 27 days × 6300 man hrs per day = 1,70,100

As per the standard, 1 unit per man hour is the output and so in 1,70,100 man hours, 1,70,100 units are supposed to be produced which is the standard quantity in actual hours. The variance is favourable as the standard quantity is more than the budgeted one that indicates more number of working hours than budgeted.

4. **Fixed Overhead Efficiency Variance:**

Standard Rate [Standard Quantity – Actual Quantity]

Re.1 [1,70,100 – 1,53,090] = ₹17,010 [F]

5. **Fixed Overhead Volume Variance:**

Standard Rate [Budgeted Quantity – Actual Quantity]

Re.1 [1,50,000 – 1,53,090] = ₹3,090 [F]

6. **Fixed Overhead Cost Variance:**

Standard Fixed Overheads for Actual Production – Actual Fixed Overheads

= (₹1 x 1,53,090) – ₹1,56,000 = ₹2,910 [A]

Problem 21 :

A company manufacturing two products uses standard costing system. The following data relating to August 2012 have been furnished to you:

Particulars	Product A	Product B
Standard Cost Per Unit -Direct Materials	₹2	₹4
Direct Wages	₹8	₹6
Fixed Overheads	₹16	₹12
Total	₹26	₹22
Units processed/in process		
Beginning of the month, all materials applied and 50% complete in respect of labour and overheads	4,000	12,000
End of the month, all materials applied and 80% complete in respect of labour and overheads	8,000	12,000
Units completed and transferred to warehouse during the month	16,000	20,000

You may use average cost method to analyze

The following were the actual costs recorded during the month.

Direct materials purchased at standard price amount to ₹2,00,000 and actual cost of which is ₹2,20,000. Direct materials used for consumption at standard price amount to ₹1,75,000. Direct wages for actual hours worked at standard wages rates were ₹4,20,000 and at actual wages rate were ₹4,12,000. Fixed overheads budgeted were ₹8,25,000 and actual fixed overheads incurred were ₹8,50,000.

Required,

1. Direct material price variance at the point of consumption and at the point of purchase.
2. Direct material usage variance.
3. Direct wage rate and efficiency variance.
4. Fixed overheads volume and expenditure variance Standard cost of WIP at the end of the month.

ICWAI

Solution :

I] Statement Showing Equivalent Production Units - Materials, Labour & Overheads

Particulars	Units	M. % of Completion	Number of Units	L & O %	Units
Units completed -A	16,000	100%	16,000	100%	16,000
Closing WIP	8,000	100%	8,000	80%	6,400
Total	24,000		24,000		22,400
Units completed -B	20,000	100%	20,000	100%	20,000
Closing WIP	12,000	100%	12,000	80%	9,600
Total	32,000		32,000		29,600

II] Direct Materials:

Particulars	Product A	Product B	Total
Equivalent Units [1]	24,000	32,000	
Standard Cost per unit [II]	₹2	₹4	
Std. Cost of std. requirement of materials [1 × 2]	₹48,000	₹1,28,000	
Std. Cost of actual quantity of material used			₹1,75,000
Actual Cost of actual quantity of materials (₹2,20,000/2,00,000) × 1,75,000			₹1,92,500

III] Direct Labour :

Particulars	Product A	Product B	Total
Equivalent Units [1]	22, 400	29,600	
Standard direct wages per unit [2]	₹8	₹6	
Standard direct wages at standard rates [1 × 2]	₹1,79,200	₹1,77,600	₹3,56,800
Direct wages for actual hours at standard rates			₹4,20,000
Actual direct wages [actual rates]			₹4,12,000

IV] Fixed Overheads :

Particulars	Product A	Product B	Total
Equivalent Units [1]	22,400	29,600	
Fixed overheads per unit [2]	₹16	₹12	
Fixed overheads charged to production [1 × 2]	₹3,58,400	₹3,55,200	₹7,13,600
Budgeted fixed overheads			₹8,25,000
Actual Fixed Overheads			₹8,50,000

Computation of Variances :

- Direct Material Price Variance [At the point of consumption]: Standard Cost of Actual quantity – Actual Cost of Actual Quantity: ₹1,75,000 – ₹1,92,500 = ₹17,500 [A] [Note 2]
- Direct Material Price Variance [At the point of purchase]: Standard Price of material purchased – Actual Cost of material purchased:
  ₹2,00,000 – ₹2,20,000 = ₹20,000 [A
- Direct Material Usage Variance: Standard Cost of Standard Quantity of Materials – Standard Cost of Actual Quantity used:
  ₹1,76,000 – ₹1,75,000 = ₹1,000 [F] [Note 2]
- Direct Wage Rate Variance: Direct Wages at Standard Rate – Actual Direct Wages at Actual Rate = ₹4,20,000 – ₹4,12,000 = ₹8,000 [F]
  [Note 3]
- Labour Efficiency Variance: Standard Direct Wages at Standard Rate – Direct Wages for Actual Hours at Standard Rate = ₹3,56,800 – ₹4,20,000
  = ₹63,200 [A] [Note 3]

- Fixed Overhead Volume Variance: Fixed Overheads Charged to Production – Budgeted Fixed Overheads: ₹7,13,600 – ₹8,25,000 = ₹1,11,400 [A]

  [Note 4]

- Fixed Overhead Expenditure Variance: Budgeted Fixed Overheads – Actual Fixed Overheads: ₹8,25,000 – ₹8,50,000 = ₹25,000 [A]

  [Note 4]

Valuation of Closing Work in Progress :

Particulars	Material	Labour and Overheads	Total
Product A Equivalent Units	8,000	6,400	
Standard Cost Per Unit	₹2	₹24	
Value of WIP	₹16,000	₹1,53,600	₹1,69,600
Product B Equivalent Units	12,000	9, 600	
Standard Cost Per Unit	₹4	₹18	
Value of WIP	₹48,000	₹1,72,800	₹2,20,800

Cause of Variances

A large number of factors may give rise to cost variances. The measurement of variances is useless unless these are analyzed and interpreted. Analysis of variance highlights the areas of strengths and weaknesses in the operation of a firm. but in itself, it does not indicate what corrective action, if any, should be taken. Thus, it is very important to identify and report quickly the cause of variances to the management so that remedial measures may be taken. The following are some of the possible causes for different cost variance indicating the persons responsible for the same. The cause of one variance may be wholly or partly dependent upon the cause of another variance.

Variance	Possible Cause	Person Responsibilities
1. Material Price Variance	(a) Change in market price	Uncontrollable
	(b) Loss of discount	Accounts officer
	(c) Changes in taxes & duties	Uncontrollable
	(d) Emergency purchases	Production or Sales manager
	(e) Inefficient purchasing	Purchase officer
	(f) Uneconomic size of order	Purchase officer
	(g) Lack of funds resulting in failure to take advantage of seasonal purchases.	Finance manager

2. Material Usage Variance	(a) Poor quality of material	Purchase officer
	(b) Changes in mix	Production manager
	(c) Changes in production method	Production manager
	(d) Excessive wastage	Foreman
	(e) Careless handling	Storekeeper
	(f) Pilferage of material	Storekeeper/ Security officer
	(g) Non-availability of standard material	Uncontrollable
	(h) Labour inefficiency	Foreman
3. Direct Labour Rate of Pay Variance	(a) General rise in wage rates	Uncontrollable
	(b) Poor supervision	Foreman
	(c) Defective grade of employees	Foreman
	(d) Overtime working for urgent orders	Uncontrollable or production/ Sales Manager
4. Labour Efficiency Variance	(a) Poor working conditions	Personnel manager
	(b) Poor planning & Scheduling	Planning officer
	(c) Poor maintenance of machines	Maintenance officer
	(d) Poor quality of materials	Purchase officer
	(e) Power failures	Maintenance
	(f) Increase in labour turnover	Uncontrollable
5. Overhead Expenditure Variance	(a) Price fluctuations	Uncontrollable
	(b) Improper use of facilities	Concerned departmental manager officer
6. Overhead Capacity Variance	(a) Change in production schedule or method	Production manager
	(b) Machine/Power break-down	Maintenance officer
	(c) Industrial unrest	Uncontrollable
	(d) Shortage of material	Purchase officer ;
7. Overhead Efficiency Variance	Same as causes for labour efficiency variance	Uncontrollable

Source: Guptha & Sharma, Management Accounting, Kalyani Publishers pp 12,49

Sales Variances :

First we discussed the cost variances strike materials, labour and overheads, which are related to cost of production. Lastly, we discuss the sales variances because it is also important to study the profit variances. Sales variances are subclassified into four variances.

1. Sales Value Variance
2. Sales Price Variance
3. Sales Volume Variance
4. Sales Mix Variance

1. **Sales Value Variance:** It reveals the difference between actual sales and budgeted sales. If actual sales are more than the budgeted sales the variance will be favourable, otherwise it will be adverse.

   Sales value variance = Actual value of sales - Budgeted value of sales.

2. **Sales Price Variance:** It is the part of sales value variance which arises due to the difference between the standard price and the actual selling price.

   Sales price variance = Actual quantity (Actual price - Standard price)

3. **Sales Volume Variance:** This is also part of sales value variance which is due to the difference between actual quantity of sales and budgeted quantity of sales.

   Sales volume variance = Standard price (Actual quantity of sales - Standard quantity of sales)

4. **Sales Mix Variance:** It is part of sales volume variance. The proportion in which different quantities were budgeted may be different from the proportion of actual quantities sold. It is the difference of standard value of revised mix and standard value of actual mix.

Profit Method of Sales Variance

Sales variance is calculated based on profit, which is more important to a businessman. Business organizations main aim is to achieve the more profits in future as well as current period also. The variance is categorized into the following manner.

1. Total Sales Margin Variance
2. Sales Margin Variance due to selling price.
3. Sales Margin Variance due to volume.

1. **Total Sales Margin Variance :** It is the difference between budgeted profit and actual profit

   Total sales margin variance = Actual profit - Budgeted profit

   Actual profit = Actual Quantity sold x Actual profit per unit.

   Budgeted profit = Budgeted quantity of sales x Budgeted profit per unit.

2. **Sales Margin Variance due to Selling Price :** It arises due to the difference between actual selling price and standard selling price.

Sales Margin Variance = Actual quantity (Actual price – Standard price)

3. **Sales Margin Variance due to Volume :** It arises due to the difference between actual quantity of sales and budgeted quantity of sales

Standard profit per unit (Actual quantity of sales – Standard quantity of sales)

Problem 22 :

Compute the following variances from the data given below.

I. Total sales margin variance

II. Sales margin volume variance

III. Sales margin price variance

Sales margin quantity [sub volume] variance

Product	Budgeted Quantity Units	Actual Quantity Units	Budgeted Sales Price Per Unit	Actual Sale Price Per Unit	Standard Cost Per Unit
A	300	350	₹100	₹90	₹60
B	200	250	50	40	30

Solution :

Product	Budgeted Sale Price Per Unit	Standard Cost Per Unit	Standard Sales Margin	Budgeted Qty.	Budget Profit	Actual Sales Price	Actual Sales Margin	Actual Sales Qty	Actual Profit
	₹	₹	₹		₹	₹	₹		₹
X	100	60	40	300	12,000	90	30	350	10,500
Y	50	30	20	200	4,000	40	10	250	2,500
Total					16,000				13,000

Computation of Variances :

1. **Total Sales Margin Variance :**

Actual Profit – Budgeted Profit

₹13,000 – ₹16,000 = ₹3,000 [A]

2. **Sales Margin Volume Variance :**

Budgeted Margin per Unit × [Actual Quantity – Budgeted Quantity]

Product A = ₹40 [350 – 300] = ₹2,000 [F]

Product B = ₹20 [250 –200] = ₹1,000 [F]

Total Variance = ₹3,000 [F]

3. Sales Margin Price Variance :

Actual Quantity [Actual price Per Unit - Budgeted price Per Unit]

Product A = 350 [₹90 – ₹100] = ₹3,500 [A]

Product B = 250 [₹40 – ₹50] = ₹2,500 [A]

Total Variance = ₹6,000 [A]

4. Sales Margin Quantity [Sub Volume] Variance:

Budgeted Margin Per Unit of Budgeted Mix [Actual quantity – Budgeted quantity]

= 1600/500 [600 – 500] = ₹3200 [F]

Problem 23

From the following information, calculate the following sales variances

I. Total Sales Variance

II. Sales Price Variance

III. Sales Volume Variance

IV. Sales Mix Variance

V. Sales Quantity Variance.

Product	Number of Units	Standard Rate Per Unit ₹	Amount ₹	Actual Number of Units	Actual Rate Per Unit ₹	Amount ₹
A	5000	5	25, 000	6000	6	36, 000
B	4000	6	24, 000	5000	5	25, 000
C	3000	7	21, 000	4000	8	32, 000

Solution :

I] Total Sales Variance = Actual Sales – Standard Sales

₹93,000 – ₹70,000 = ₹23, 000 [F]

II] Sales Price Variance = Actual Quantity [Actual Price – Standard Price]

Product A = 6,000 [₹6 – ₹5] = ₹6,000 [F] Product B = 5,000 [₹5 – ₹6] = ₹5,000 [A]
Product C = 4,000 [₹8 –₹7] = ₹4,000 [F]

Total Sales Price Variance = ₹5000 [F]

III] Sales Volume Variance = Standard Price [Actual Quantity – Standard Quantity]

Product A = ₹5 [6,000 – 5,000] = ₹5,000 [F]

Product B = ₹6 [5,000 – 4,000] = ₹6,000 [F]

Product C = ₹7 [4000 – 3000] = ₹7,000 [F]

Total Sales Volume Variance = ₹18,000 [F]

IV] Sales Mix Variance = [Actual mix – Revised sales mix] Standard price per unit

₹88, 000 – ₹87, 500 = ₹500 [F] [Note 1]

V] Sales Quantity Variance = Standard Unit Sales Price [Actual quantity – Std. quantity]

70,000/12 [15,000 – 12,000] = ₹17,500 [F]

Note 1

Product	Revised Mix	Amount ₹	Actual Mix	Amount ₹ per unit	Amount ₹
A	(15000/12000) × 5000 = 6250 @ ₹5	31,250	6000	5	30,000
B	(15000/12000) × 4000 = 5000 @ ₹6	30,000	5000	6	30,000
C	(15000/12000) × 3000 = 3750 @ ₹7	26,250	4000	7	28,000
Total	15, 000	87,500	15,000		88,000

Problem 24

KGM Ltd has given the following budgeted and actual sales information.

Products	Budgeted		Actual	
	Quantity	Selling Price	Quantity	Selling Price
X	200	70	300	80
Y	300	60	250	50

The cost per unit of product x and y was ₹ 60 and 40 respectively. Calculated the sales variance based profit method.

Solution :

1. Total Sales Margin Variance = Actual profit – Budgeted profit

(Actual Quantity x Actual profit per unit) – (Budgeted quantity x Budgeted profit per unit)

Actual profit per unit = Actual Selling price – Actual Cost

Product X = ₹ 80 – Rs 60 = ₹ 20

Product Y = ₹ 50 – Rs 4. = ₹ 10

Budgeted profit per unit = Budgeted selling price – Actual cost

Product X = ₹ 70 – ₹ 60 = ₹ 10

Product Y = ₹ 60 – ₹ 40 = ₹ 20

Actual Profit

Product X = 300 x 20 = ₹	6,000
Product Y = 250 x 10 = ₹	2500
Budgeted Profit: ₹	8,500
Product X = 200 x 10 = ₹	2,000
Product Y = 300 x 20 = ₹	6,000
	₹ 8,000

Total Sales Margin Variance = 8,500 – 8000 = ₹ 500

2. Sales Margin Variance due to Selling Price

   = Actual Quantity (Actual price – Standard price)

   Product X = 300 (80 – 70) = 300 x 10 = ₹ 3,000 (F)

   Product Y = 250 (50 – 60) = 250 x (-10) = ₹ 2500 (A)

3. Sales Margin Variance due to Volume

   = Standard profit per unit (Actual quantity – Standard Quantity)

   Product X = 10 (300 – 200) = 10 (100) = ₹ 1000 (F)

   Product Y = 20 (50 – 60) = 250 x (-10) = ₹ 2500 (A)

   Sales Margin variance due to selling price = 500 (F)

4. Sales Margin Variance due to Volume

   = Standard profit per unit (Actual Quantity – Standard Quantity)

   Product X = 10 (300 – 200) = 10 (100) = ₹ 1000 (F)

   Product Y = 20 (250 – 300) = 20 (50) = ₹ 1000 (A)

   Sales Margin Variance due to volume = NIL

A] Essay Type Questions

1. Define 'Standard Cost' and 'Standard Costing'. In which type of industries can standard costing be employed?
2. What is the difference between 'budgetary control' and 'standard costing'?
3. Discuss the benefits and limitations of standard costing.
4. Explain the various types of standards.

5. Discuss briefly the procedure of establishment of standard costs regarding material, labour and overheads.
6. Describe and compare the different methods of accounting for standard costs.
7. Define and explain briefly the following terms:

   Material price variance

   Material usage variance

   Material mixture variance

   Material yield variance
8. Define and explain briefly the following terms:

   Wage rate variance

   Labour efficiency variance

   Variable overhead efficiency variance
9. Define and explain the following terms:

   Fixed overhead cost variance

   Fixed overhead volume variance

   Fixed overhead capacity variance

   Fixed overhead calendar variance

   Fixed overhead efficiency variance.
10. Define and explain the sales variances based on a] profits and b] turnover.
11. Write short notes on investigation of variances and management by exception in connection with standard costing.
12. Recently there have been significant developments in budgetary control and standard costing systems. You are required to discuss, a] five factors which should be kept in mind in deciding whether or not to investigate a variance and b] the importance of recognizing the behavioral aspects in effective system.
13. Explain the meaning, causes and disposal of labour variances.
14. What do you understand by 'learning curve'? State the uses of learning curve in cost and management accounting.
15. What are the behavioral aspects which should be borne in mind by those who are designing and operating standard costing and budgetary control system?

B] State whether the following statements are True or False

1. Standard costing works on the principle of exception.
2. Standard costs and estimated costs differ from each other.

3. Difference between the standard cost and actual cost is called as variance.
4. All variances should be investigated.
5. A variance may be either favourable or adverse.
6. There is no difference between standard costing and budgeting.
7. Standard costing cannot be followed in process costing.
8. Material yield variance arises due to the difference between the normal loss and actual loss in the production process.
9. Overhead standards are based on budgeted overhead costs and budgeted production.
10. Standards are arrived at on the basis of past performance.

C] **State the correct answer in each of the following.**

1. Cost variance is the difference between

A] standard cost and actual cost B] standard cost and the budgeted cost

C] standard cost and the actual cost.

2. Standard cost is used

A] as a basis for price fixation and cost control through variance analysis.

B] to ascertain the break-even-point

C] to establish cost-volume-profit relationship

3. A standard cost system may be used in

A] either job order costing or process costing

B] job order costing but not in process costing

C] process costing but not in the job order processing

D] neither process costing nor job order costing.

4. An unfavourable material price variance occurs because of

A] price increase in raw material B] price decrease in raw material

C] less than anticipated normal wastage in the manufacturing process

D] more than anticipated normal wastage in the manufacturing process.

5. Which of the following is a purpose of standard costing?

A] Determine a break-even production level

B] Control costs C] Allocate cost with more accuracy

D] Eliminate the need for subjective decisions by management.

6. Material mix variance arises due to

   A] increase or decrease in the cost of material consumed

   B] increase or decrease in the normal loss

   C] change in the standard proportion of mix

   D] none of these.

7. Material usage variance is normally chargeable to

   A] production department B] purchase department

   C] finished goods D] materials stores.

8. If actual hours worked exceed the standard hours allowed, the variance, which will occur is called as

   A] favourable labour efficiency variance

   B] favourable labour rate variance

   C] unfavourable labour efficiency variance

   D] unfavourable labour rate variance.

9. Standard costs are

   A] estimated costs B] budgeted costs

   C] expected costs D] scientifically pre-determined costs.

10. Standards are fixed for

    A] costs only B] costs and Profits

    C] costs, profits and sales D] only for profits

Practical Questions

1. From the following, you are required to calculate (a) Material Price Variance (b) Material Usage Variance, and (C) Material Cost Variance

   Quantity of Material purchased: 3,000 units

   Value of material purchased: ₹ 9,000

   Standard quantity of material required for one tone of finished product: 25 units

   Standard rate of material: Rs 2 per unit

   Opening Stock of material: nil

   Closing Stock of material: 500 units

   Finished Production during the period: 80 tonnes. *[ICWA (inter)]*

   Answer : (a) MPV = ₹ 2,500 (A), (b) MUV = ₹ 1,000 (A), (C) MCV = ₹ 3,500 (A)

2. Naresh Ltd. Manufacturers of Product P, uses a standard cost system. Standard Product and cost specifications for 1,000 Kgs of product P are as follows:

Ingredients	Quantity (Kgs)	Price per kg (₹)	Cost (₹)	
A	800	2.5	2,000	
B	200	4.00	800	
C	200	1.00	200	
Input	1,200		3,000	(₹ 2.50 per kg)
Output	1,000		3,000	(₹ 3.00 per kg)

Material records indicate: Consumption in January:

A= 1, 57,000 kgs @ ₹ 2.40

B = 38,000 kgs @ ₹ 4.20

C = 36,000 kgs @ ₹ 1.10

Actual finished production for the month of January is 2,00,000 Kgs.

Calculate (a) Material Price Variance, (b) Material Usage Variance, (c) Material Mix variance, and (d) Material Yield Variance. [ICWA (inter), December 1979]

Answer : (a) MPV = Rs, 4,500 (F), (b) MUV = ₹ 19,500 (F), (c) MMV = ₹ 3,000 (A), (d) MYV = Rs 22,500 (F)

3. Basha Ltd. produces an article by blending two basic raw materials. It operates a standard costing system and the following standards have been set for raw materials.

Material	Standard Mix	Standard price/kg
A	40%	₹ 4
B	60%	₹ 3

The standard loss in processing is 15 %

During April 1980, the company produced 1,700 kgs of finished output.

The position of stocks and purchases for the month of April 1980 is as under:

Material	Stock on	Stock on	Purchased during	Cost
	1-4-80 (kgs)	30-4 - 80 (kgs)	April 1980 (kgs)	₹
A	35	5	800	3,400
B	40	50	1,200	3,000

Calculate the following variances : (a) Material Price Variance, (b) Material Usage Variance (c) Material Mix Variance, (d) Material Yield Variance (e) Total Material Cost Variance. [CA (inter), May 1980]

Answer : (a) MPV = ₹ 376.25 (F), (b) MUV = ₹ 90 (A), (c) MMV = ₹ 22 (A), (d) MYV = ₹ 68 (A), (e), MCV = ₹ 286.25 (F)

4. A company is manufacturing a chemical product making use of four different types of raw materials. The following information is available regarding the standards and actual.

Material	Share of total input Standard - %	Raw material cost Standard Rs/kg	Quantity consumed Actual	Raw material cost – Actual ₹/kg
A	40	50	42, 000	48
B	30	80	31, 000	80
C	20	90	18, 000	92
D	10	100	9, 000	110

There is an inevitable normal loss of 10% during the processing and actual output 92,000 kg. Calculate Material Cost, Price, Quantity, Mix and Yield variances.

5. KGR Ltd. Is engaged in producing a standard mix using 60 Kgs of chemical M and 40 kgs of Chemical N. the standard loss of production is 30 %. The standard price of M is ₹. 5 per kg and of N is ₹. 10 per kg. The actual mixture and yield were as follows.

M : 80 kgs ₹ 4.80 per kg

N : 70 kgs ₹. 8.00 per kg

Actual yield 115 kgs

Calculate Material Variances (Price, Usage, Yield, Mix) [ICWA (inter)]

Answer : MPV = ₹ 180 (F), MUV = ₹ 50 (F), MMV = ₹. 50 (A), MYV = ₹. 100 (F)

7. A standard set of material consumption was 100 kgs @ ₹ 2.25 per kg

In a cost period: Opening Stock was 100 kgs @ 2.25 per kg

Purchase made : 500 kgs @ ₹ 2.15 per kg

Consumption 110 kgs

(1) Calculate :

a. Usage Variance.

b. Price Variance when variance is accumulated at point of purchase.

c. Price Variance when variance is accumulated at point of issue on FIFO basis.

d. Price Variance when variance is accumulated at point of issue on LIFO basis.

(2) What is the effect on closing stock valuation when materials are charged out to cost o bases (C) and (d) above ?

(3) Value of Closing stock will be lower by ₹ 49, under FIFO, and by ₹ 39 under LIFO. [ICWA (inter), June 1975]

Answer : (1) (a) MUV = ₹ 22.50 (A), (b) MPV = ₹ 50 (F), (C) MPV = ₹ 1 (F), (d) MPV = ₹ 11 (F)

9. The standard labour component and the actual labour component engaged in a week for a week are as under.

	Skilled Workers	Semi - Skilled workers	Unskilled workers
a. Standard number of workers in a gang.	32	12	6
b. Standard wage rate per hour	3	2	1
c. Actual number of workers employed in a gang during the week	28	18	4
d. Actual wage rate per hour (Rs)	4	3	2

During the 40 hours working week, the gang produced 1,800 standard labour hours of work calculate: (a) Labour Efficiency Variance (b) Labour Mix Variance, (C) Rate of Wages variance, and (d) Total Labour Cost Variance.

[CA (inter), November 1980]

Answer : (a) LEV = ₹ 504 (A), (b) LMV = ₹ 80(F) ,
(c) LRV = ₹ 2,000 (A), (d) LCV = ₹ 2,024(A)

10. Following details are available from the records of XYZ Ltd, engaged in manufacturing article ₹ A for the week ended 28th September. The Standard labour hour and rates of payment per article 'A' were as follows.

	Hours	Rate per hour	Total
Skilled Labour	10	3.00	30
Semi Skilled labour	8	1.50	12
Un skilled labour	16	1.00	16
			58

The actual production was 1,000 articles of 'A' for which the actual hours worked and rates are given below.

	Hours	Rate per hour	Total
Skilled labour	9,000	4.00	36,000
Semi skilled labour	8,400	1.50	12,600
Unskilled labour	20,000	0.90	18,000
			66,600

From the Above set of data, you are asked to calculate (a) Labour Cost variance, (b) Labour Rate Variance, (c) Labour Efficiency Variance, and (d) Labour Mix Variance.

[ICWA (inter), December 1985]

Answer : (a) LCV = Rs 8,600 (A), (b) LRV = ₹ 7,000 (A),
(c) LEV = ₹ 1,600 (A), (d) LMV = ₹ 4,200 (F)

11. A gang of workers normally consists of 30 men, 15 women and 10 boys. They are paid at standard hourly rates as under.

Men	₹ 0.8
Women	₹ 0.6
Boys	₹ 0.4

In a normal working week of 40 hours, the gang is expected to produce 2,000 units of output. During the week ended 31st December 1977, the gang consisted of 40 men, 10 women and 5 boys. The actual wages paid were @ ₹ 0.70 ₹ 0.65 and ₹ 0.30 respectively. 4 hours were lost due to abnormal idle time and 1,600 units were produced. Calculate (i) Wage Variance, (ii) Wage Rate Variance, (iii) Labour Efficiency Variance (iv) Gang Composition variance (ie Labour Mix Variance), and (v) Labour Time Variance. [CA (Final), May 1978]

Answer : LCV = ₹ 256 (A), LRV = ₹ 160 (F), LEV = ₹ 268 (A), ITV = ₹ 148 (A), LMV = ₹ 120(A)

13. A Company's annual expenditure budget for 1977 was set at ₹ 4,80,000. Monthly budget accordingly was taken at ₹ 40,000. Standard output for the year, on a 300 - working day basis was 3,00,000 units and on this, standard overhead recovery rate was fixed.

In February 1977, there were 24 working days (28 days less 4 Sundays). During this month production achieved was 23,000 units. Actual expenses in February 1977 totalled to ₹ 41,000. Calculate Total Overhead Variance, Efficiency Variance, and Calendar Variance. [ICWA (inter), December 1977]

Answer : FOCV = ₹ 4200 (A), FOEfv = ₹ 1,600 (A), FOCIV = ₹ 1,600 (A)

16. A Company operates on standard costing and budgetary control systems. The budget for April 1981 and the actual for the same month are indicated below.

Product	Budgeted			Actual		
	Sales Kgs	Price ₹/kg	Amount (₹)	Sales Kgs	Price ₹/kg	Amount (₹)
TA	50,000	10.50	5,25,000	52,000	11.00	5,72,000
MB	20,000	12.00	2,40,000	16,000	11.75	1,88,000
CC	6,000	15.00	90,000	5,000	15.00	75,000
OC	4,000	16.00	64,000	5,000	16.00	80,000
Total	80,000		9,19,000	78,000		9,15,000

Calculate Sales Variance. [ICWA (Final), December 1981]

Answer : SRV = ₹. 4,000 (A) , SPV = ₹ 22,000 (F), SVV = ₹ 26,000 (A), SQV = ₹ 22975 (A), SMV = ₹ 3025.

17. Budgeted and actual sales for the month of December 1984 of two products A and B of Messers XY Ltd were as follows.

Product	Budgeted		Actual	
	Units	Price / Unit	Units	Price/ Unit
A	6,000	5.00	5,000	5.00
			1,500	4.75
B	10,000	2.00	7,500	2.00
			1,750	1.90

Budgeted Costs for products A and B were ₹ 4.00 and ₹ 1.50 per unit respectively. Work out from the above data the following variances:

(a) Sales value Variance

(b) Sales Volume Variance

(b) Sales Price Variance

(d) Sales Mixture Variance

(e) Sales Quantity Variance.

[ICWA (inter), June 1985]

Answer : SRV = ₹ 450 (F), (b) SVV = ₹ 1,000 (f), (c) SPV = ₹ 550 (A), (d) SMV = ₹ 1,781 (F), (e) SQV = ₹ 781 (A)

17. From the Following Information, Calculate:

(a) Material Cost Variance

(b) Material Price Variance

(c) Material Usage Variance

Quantity of Materials Purchased 3,000 units

Value of material purchased ₹ 9,000

Standard quantity of material required per (tone of finished product = 25 units)

Standard rate of materials = ₹ 2 per unit.

Opening Stock of materials = Nil

Closing Stock of materials = 500 Units

Finished production during the year = 800 tons

[**Ans :** Material Cost Variance ₹ 3,500 (A) Material Price Variance ₹ 2,500 (A) Material Usage Variance ₹ 1,000 (A)]

18. From the following details calculate (a) Material Cost Variance (b) Material Price Variance (c) Material Usage Variance (d) Material Mix Variance and (e) Material Yield Variance.

Materials	Standard		Actual	
	Qty	Rate	Qty	Rate
A	8,000	1.05	7,500	1.20
B	3,000	2.15	3,300	2.30
C	2,000	3.30	2,400	3.50

[Ans : (a) ₹ 3,540 (A) ; b ₹ 2,100 (A) ; (c) ₹ 1,440 (A)
(d) ₹ 1,110 (A) ; (e) Cannot be Calculated]

18A. Calculate labour Variances from the following information standard hours for manufacturing a product.

X – 7,800 hours:

Actual Hours worked = ₹. 8,050 hours

Actual Wages paid during the period = ₹. 16,100

Standard Wages = ₹. 15,600

[**Ans :** (a) Labour cost Variance = ₹ 500 (A); (b) Labour Rate Variance = Nil;
(c) Labour Efficiency = ₹ 500 (A)]

19. From the following data, calculate labour variances:

The budgeted labour force for producing product A is :

200 Semi – skilled workers @ ₹ 0.75 per hour for 50 hours

10 Skilled workers @ ₹ 1.25 per hour for 50 hours

The actual labour force employed for producing A is :

22 Semi skilled workers @ ₹ 0.80 per hour for 50 hours

8 skilled workers @ ₹ 1.20 per hour for 50 hours

[Ans : (a) Labour Cost Variance = ₹ 15 (F)
(a) Labour Rate Variance = ₹ 35 (A)
(b) Labour Efficiency Variance ₹ 50 (F)
(c) Labour Mix Variance = ₹ (F)]

20. From the following data, calculate overhead Variance:

	Budgeted	Actual
Output 15,000 Units	16,000 Units	
Number of Working days	25	27
Fixed Overheads	₹ 30,000	₹ 30,500
Variable Overheads	₹ 45,000	₹ 47,000

There was in increase of 5% in Capacity.

[**Ans :** (1) Total Overhead Cost Variance ₹ 2,500 (F)

(2) Variable Overhead Expenditure Variance ₹ 1,000 (f)

(3) Fixed Overhead Variance ₹ 1,500 (F)

(4) Expenditure Variance ₹ 500 (A)

(5) Volume Variance ₹ 2,000 (F)

(6) Capacity Variance ₹ 1,620 (F)

(7) Calendar Variance ₹ 2,400 (F)

(8) Efficiency Variance ₹ 2,020 (A)]

21. From the following information, Calculate: (1) Overhead Budget Variance (2) Volume Variance (3) Efficiency Variance (4) Capacity Variance (5) Total Overhead Cost Variance:

Normal Overhead Rate ₹ 3

Actual hours worked 20,000

Allowed Overheads for budgeled hours ₹ 70,000

Actual Overheads ₹ 72,000

[**Ans :** (1) Overhead Budget Variance ₹ 2,000 (A)

(2) Volume Variance ₹ 7,000 (A)

(3) Efficiency Variance ₹ 3,000 (F)

(4) Capacity Variance ₹ 10,000 (A)

(5) Total Overhead Cost Variance ₹ 9,000 (A)

22. From the following informations Calculate: (a) Calendar Variance (b) Capacity Variance (c) Efficiency Variance and (d) Volume Variance :

Actual Overheads ₹ 1,800

Budgeted Overheads ₹ 2,000

Budgeted period 4,000 labour hours

Standard hours per unit 10 labour hours

Budgeted number of days 20

Standard overhead per hour ₹ 0.50

Actual number of days 22

Actual hours 4,300

Actual production 425 units.

[Ans : (a) Calendar Variance ₹ 200 (F) ; (b) Capacity Variance ₹ 150 (F)

(c) Efficiency Variance ₹ 25 (A); (d) Volume Variance ₹ 125 (F)]

23. The Budgeted and actual sales of a concern manufacturing a single product are given below :

Sales as budgeted : 10,000 units at ₹ 3 per unit ₹ 30,000 ; Actual Sales.

5,000 units at ₹ 3 per unit ₹ 15,000

8,000 units at ₹ 2.50 per unit ₹ 20,000

Ascertain Sales price variance and sales volume Variance

[Ans : Sales Value Variance ₹ 5,000 (f) Sales Price Variance ₹ 4,000 (A) Sales Volume Variance ₹ 9,000 (F)]

24. From the following information relating to the month of Jan 2013 you are required to compute sales Margin Variances:

Product	Budgeted Sales			Actual Sales		
	Qty	Price	Value	Qty	Price	Value
X	2,500	4	10,000	2,000	4	8,000
				600	3.75	2,250
Y	3,000	2	6,000	2,500	2	5,000
				350	1.8	630
	5,500		16,000	4,500		15,880
				950		

Budgeted Costs:

X : ₹ 3 per unit

Y : ₹ 1.50 Per Unit

Calculate Sales Margin Variance:

[Ans. (1) Total Sales Margin Variance x ₹ 50 (A) : Y ₹ 145 (A)
(2) Sales Margin Price Variance x ₹ 150 (A) ; Y ₹ 70 (A)
(3) Sales Margin Volume Variance x ₹ 100 (F) ; Y ₹ 75 (A)
(4) Sales Margin Quantity Variance x ₹ 15.63 (F) ; Y ₹ 9.37 (F)
(5) Sales Margin Mix Variance x ₹ 84.37 (F) ; Y ₹ 84.37 (A)]

25. From the following information, calculate Labour Variance of TPL Ltd.

	Department X	Department Y
Actual Gross Wages	₹ 2,000	₹ 1,800
Standard Hours Produced	8,000	6,000
Standard Rate per hour	80 Paise	35 paise
Actual Hours Worked	8,200	5,800

[**Ans.** Labour Cost Variance X ₹ 400 (F) ; Y ₹ 300; (F) Labour Rate Variance X ₹ 460 ; (f) Y ₹ 230 (F) Labour Efficiency Variance X ₹ 60 (A); Y ₹ 70 (F)

26. The standard materials required to produce 100 units is 120 kgs. A standard price of 0.50 paise per kg is fixed and 2,40,000 units were produced during the period. Actual materials purchased were 3,00,000 kgs at a cost of ₹ 1,65,000. Calculate material variance.

[Ans. Material cost variance ₹ 21,000 unfavourable: material price variance ₹ 15,000 unfavourable; materials usage variance ₹ 6,000 unfavourable]

27. The standard cost of a certain chemical mixtures of Pharmacy Drug Ltd is;

Material P – 40% at ₹ 20 per tone

Material Q – 60% at ₹ 30 per tone

A standard loss of 10% as expected in production. During a period there is used:

90 tonnes material P at the cost of ₹ 18 per tonne; 110 tonnes material Q at the cost of ₹ 354 per tonne.

The weight produced is 182 tonnes of good production, Calculate : (a) material cost variance (b) material price variance (c) material mix variance and (d) material yield variance.

[**Ans:** material cost variance ₹ 102.22 Adverse. Material price variance ₹ 260 Adverse. Material usage variance ₹ 157.78 Favourable. Material mix variance ₹ 100 Favourable. Material yield variance ₹ 57.78 Favourable]

28. The following figures have been extracted from the cost books of Sonu Ltd for the month of January 2013;

	Standard ₹	Actual ₹
Number of units produced	30,000	32,000
Capacity	100%	100%
Number of days worked	25	26
Variable overheads	60,000	63,000
Fixed overheads	90,000	93,000

Analyze the total overhead variance in to :

(a) Expenditure

(b) Capacity

(c) Calendar

(d) Efficiency Variance

[**Ans :** Expenditure variance ₹ 300 (A). Efficiency Variance ₹ 800 (F). Total Variable overhead variance ₹ 500 (F). Fixed Overhead Variance ₹ 1,500 (f). Fixed expenditure variance ₹ 1,500 (A) Fixed Volume Variance ₹ 3,000 (f) Capacity Variance ₹ 1,800 (F). Efficiency Variance ₹ 1,200 (F). Calender Variance ₹ 1,800 (F)]

29. KPR Co Ltd manufacture a simple product the standard mix of which is ;

Material X 60% at ₹ 20 per kg

Material X 40% at ₹ 10 per kg

Normal loss is production is 20% of input. Due to shortage of material X, the standard mix was changed.

Actual results for March 2012 were:

Materials X 105 kg at	20 per kg
Materials Y 95 kg at	3 per kg
Input	200 kg
Loss	35 kg
Output	165 kg

Calculate :

(1) Material price variance

(2) Material usage variance

(3) Material mix variance, and

(4) Material yield variance.

[**Ans.** Material price variance X Nil ; Y ₹ 95 (F). Material usage variance X ₹ 375 (F); Y ₹ 125 (F) Material mix Variance X ₹ 300 (F) ; Y ₹ 150 (A). Material yield Variance ₹ 100 (f)]

30. A gang of workers normally consists of 30 men, 15 women and 10 boys. They are paid at standard hours rates as under:

Men	₹ 0.80
Women	₹ 0.60
Boys	₹ 0.40

In a normal week of 40 hours, the gang is expected to produce 2000 units of output. During the weekend 31st December 2003, the gang consisted of 40 men, 10 women and 5 boys. The actual wages paid were @ Re 0.70 Re 0.65 and re 0.30 respectively. 4 hours were lost due to abnormal idle time and 1600 units were produced. Calculate (1) Wage Variance (2) Wage rate variance (3) Labour efficiency variance (4) Gang composition variance (ie Labour mix variance) and (5) Labour idle time variance.

[Ans: Labour cost variance ₹ 256 (A)

Labour rate Variance ₹ 160 (F)

Labour efficiency variance ₹ 416 (A)

Labour mix variance ₹ 108 (A)

Labour idle time Variance ₹ 160]

❖ ❖ ❖

Chapter - 8
Responsibility Accounting

Introduction

Responsibility accounting is the accounting system of control through which the responsibilities are assigning towards the control of costs. Planning and control are essential for achieving good results in any business. First, a budget is prepared and then actual results are compared with budgeted ones. Any difference is made the responsibility of the key individuals who were involved in setting standards, given necessary resources and powers to use them. It is an underlying concept of accounting performance measurement systems. The basic idea is that large diversified organizations are difficult, if not impossible to manage as a single segment hence they must be decentralized into manageable segments. These segments are referred to as responsibility centres, i.e., revenue centres, cost centres, profit centres and investment centres. This method allows responsibility to be assigned to the segment managers that have the greatest amount of influence over the key elements to be managed.

These elements includes revenue centre, a segment that mainly generates revenue with relatively little costs. The cost centre is a segment that generates costs but no revenue. Profit centre is a segment that generates both revenue and costs and return on investment for an investment centre. In Investment centre, the manager controls the acquisition and utilization of assets as well as revenue and costs. An organization has one or more mangers; they decide the goals of the organization and communicate the same to the members of the organization. A manager can supervise only a limited number of subordinates. A manager should take responsibility on behalf of subordinates. Financial performance of the organization can be measured by the whole organization taken as one unit or by every division taken as one unit. For measuring the performance of the organization as a whole, financial accounting will suffice. Standard costing, budgetary control, marginal costing and responsibility accounting are useful to the management for controlling the costs.

Responsibility accounting, the emphasis is on men rather than on machines. It is a system of control where responsibility is assigned for the control of costs. The persons are made responsible for the control of costs. The responsibility of the persons at the responsibility centers is to find out the reasons for variance between the budgeted and the actual performance.

Meaning

The term 'Responsibility Accounting' means an accounting process which reports as to how well managers of responsibility centres have fulfilled their responsibility. It is closely related to the goal of controllability. Those elements in a certain area of activity which are controllable are identified and a person is given the responsibility for managing such elements. Thus, individuals in an organization are made responsible for only those elements which can be controlled by them.

Process

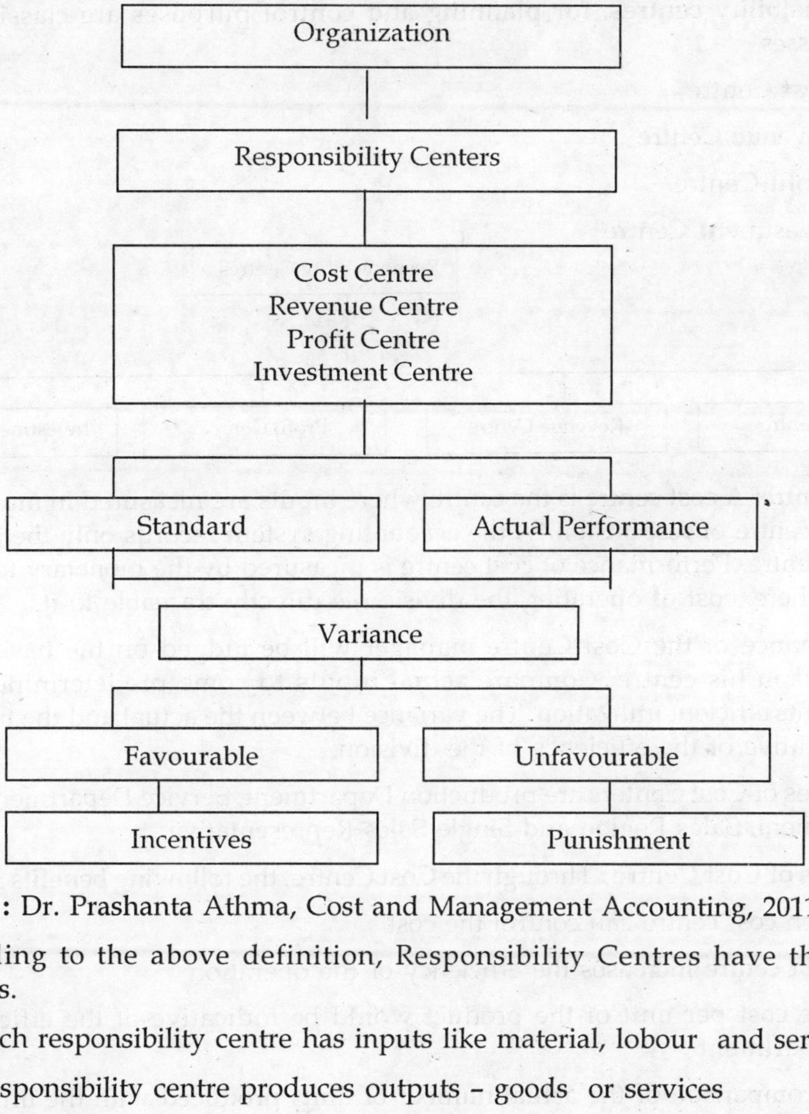

Source : Dr. Prashanta Athma, Cost and Management Accounting, 2011.

According to the above definition, Responsibility Centres have the following characteristics.

(a) Each responsibility centre has inputs like material, lobour and services

(b) Responsibility centre produces outputs – goods or services

(c) Responsibility centres require working capital and fixed assets

(d) Goods produced in one responsibility centre are transferred to another responsibility centre within the company or to the outside customers.

Responsibility accounting is used to measure both inputs and outputs: inputs of responsibility centre are measure as costs any input of the center can be expressed in monetary terms. Outputs i.e. goods and services are measured as revenues by responsibility centres. It is easy to measure the value of revenue when goods or services are sold to the outsiders. But it is difficult to measure when outputs are used within the organization. A number of approaches can be followed for this purpose. Usually, the methods suggested are (a) market price (b) cost based price (c) Full cost price.

Responsibility centres, for planning and control purposes are classified into the following classes.

1. Cost Centre
2. Revenue Centre
3. Profit Centre
4. Investment Centre

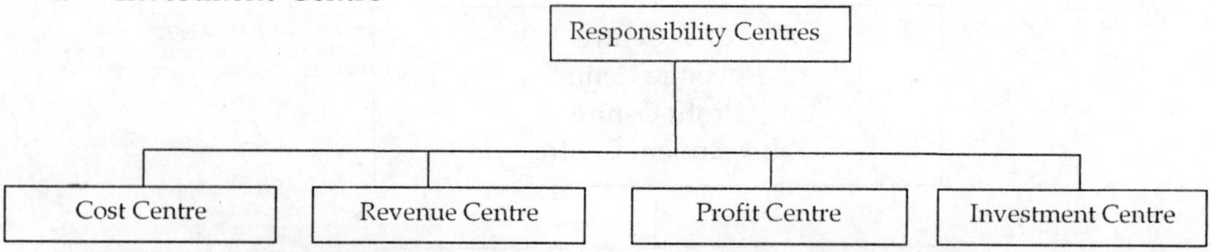

1. **Cost centre:** A cost centre is the centre where inputs are measured in monetary terms. In cost centre of responsibility, the accounting system records only the cost incurred in the centre. Performance of cost centre is measured by the monetary terms of input only, where, cost of operating the division is directly traceable to it.

   Performance of the Cost Centre manager will be judged on the basis of the cost incurred in his centre. Compare actual inputs to come predetermined level that represents efficient utilization. The variance between the actual and the budget would be indicative of the efficiency of the division.

   Examples of Cost Centers are production Department, Service Department, Marketing Department, Sales Region and Single Sales Representative.

   Benefits of Cost Centre : Through the Cost Centre, the following benefits are available:

   - Each cost centre can control the cost
   - Cost centre increases the efficiency of the operation
   - The cost per unit of the product would be indicative of the efficiency of the department
   - A comparison of the actual number of units produced with the units produced in previous period leads to improvement in the performance.

   Limitations of Cost Centre : The following are the limitations of the cost centre:

   - It ignores output measured in financial terms.
   - Cost Centre manager is not responsible for common costs, which is common in the organization.
   - The efficiency and effective of the Responsibility Centre cannot be measured, if elements in Cost Centre are not measured in monetary terms.

In this, the areas of responsibility are defined for which managers are held responsible. They are charged with only those items. Here, the managers should actively participate in establishing the goals or budgets which are attainable with efficient and effective performance against which their performance are measured. Responsibility centre managers should try to accomplish the budgets established for their areas of responsibility a control reports should contain significant information related to each area of responsibility.

Definition

AICWAI defined it as "a system of manager accounting under which accountability is established according to the responsibility delegated to various levels of management and a management information and reporting system instituted to give adequate feedback in terms of the delegated responsibility. Under this system, divisions or units of an organization specified to authority in a person are developed as responsibility centres and evaluated individually for their performance"

Charles, T. Horngreen defined as "Responsibility accounting is a system of accounting that recognizes various responsibility centres throughout the organization and reflects the plans and actions of each of these centers by assigning particular revenues and cost to the one having the pertinent responsibility. It is also called profitability accounting and activity accounting"

According to **Anthony and Reece**. "Responsibility accounting is that type of Management accounting, that collects and reports both planned and actual accounting information in terms of responsibility centres."

According to **David Fanning**. It is a system or mechanism for controlling the wider freedom of action that executive's decision centers managers in other words are given by senior management and for holding those executives responsible for the consequences of their decisions.

Characteristics of the Responsibility Accounting

1. The organization is divided into various responsibility centres
2. The objectives of responsibilities for each centre are set.
3. The cost centres are put under certain persons and adequate authority is delegated to them.
4. The actual performance is recorded.
5. The variance between budgeted and actual figures is ascertained and the concerned executives are held responsible for controlling the costs of their centres.
6. The performance is constantly compared to the standards set and this process is very useful in exercising cost controls.

Steps in Responsibility Accounting

Responsibility Accounting is used as a control device. Responsibility Accounting helps the management in achieving organizational objectives. The following steps are involved in this system.

1. The organization is divided into various responsibility centres. Each responsibility centre is put under the charge of responsibility manager. These managers are responsible for the performance of their divisions.
2. The objectives are set in consultation with the managers of the responsibility centre is put under the charge of information from the managers about their departments. The goals of the organization must be properly communicated to their subordinates, so that they will help in achieving the goals.
3. The actual performance of each responsibility centre is measure and recorded. It helps in future for comparison with the standards.
4. The actual performance is compared with the objectives set for responsibility centres. It helps in assessing the work of these centres.
5. The variance is ascertained by comparing the actual performance with the standards set. Variance means the difference between standard performance and actual performance. This variance may be favourable or unfavourable. If actual performance is less than the standard performance, it is unfavourable. In case, actual performance is more than the standard performance, it is a favourable performance.
6. Timely action is taken and necessary corrective measures are initiated on the basis of the variance so that the work does not suffer in future.

Responsibility Centres

A small firm may possible to manage by a small group of people. But the activities of a large firm are difficult to be supervised by an individual or by a small group of people. For effective control of its activities, a large firm is divided into some segments like divisions or departments. Each segment has certain activities to perform; its manager is assigned specific authority and responsibility to carry-out those activities and is held responsible for his actions and decisions affecting those activities. The units of an organization for the purpose of control are called Responsibility Centres. A Responsibility Centres is a unit of an organization under the supervision of a manager, who has the responsibility for the activities of that unit.

According to Anthony and Reece, "A Responsibility Centre is like an engine in that it has inputs, which are physical quantities of material, hours of various types of labour and a variety of services; it works with these resources usually; working capital and fixed assets area also required. As a result of this work, it produces outputs, which are classified either as goods, if they are tangible or as services, if they are intangible. These goods or services go either to other Responsibility centres within the company or to customer in the outside world."

Problem 1

The following information is available relating to the cost of production of Z limited:

Cost Item		Amount (₹)
Direct Material		1,00,000
Direct Labour		60,000
Overheads		
Supervision	17,000	
Indirect Labour	28,000	
Supplies	6,000	
Other Overheads	10,000	
		61,000
		2,21,000

It may be assumed that Z Ltd. has four departments – two productions (P and Q) and service (R and S). Assume that the overheads are absorbed by 2:2:3:3 ratio. The company's estimated cost for these departments are ₹ 1,10,000, 80,000, 20,000 and 20,000 respectively. Production Departments share the material and labour in the ratio of 6:4 and Measure the performance of departments of Z limited.

Solution :

Responsibility Centre

		Production Departments		Service Departments	
Particulars	Total ₹	P ₹	Q ₹	R ₹	S ₹
Direct Material (6:4)	100,000	60,000	40,000	--	--
Direct Labour (6.4)	60,000	36,000	24,000	--	--
Prime Cost (A)	1,60,000	96,000	64,000		

Responsibility Accounting

		Production Departments		Service Departments	
Particulars	Total ₹	P ₹	Q ₹	R ₹	S ₹
Factory Overheads					
Supervision (2:2:3:3)	17000	3400	3400	5100	5100
Indirect Labour (2 : 2 : 3 : 3)	28,000	5,600	5600	8400	8400
Supplies (2:2:3:3)	6000	1200	1,200	1800	1800
Other Overheads (2 : 2 : 3 : 3)	10,000	2000	2000	3000	3000
Total Overheads (B)	61,000	12,200	12,200	18,300	18,300
Total Cost (A + B)	**2,21,000**	**108200**	**76,200**	**18,300**	**18,300**
Eliminated Cost	**2,30,000**	**1,10,000**	**80,000**	**20,000**	**20,000**
Variance	**9,000 F**	**1200 F**	**3800 F**	**1700 F**	**1700 F**

(2) **Revenue Centre :** It is a segment of the organization which is primarily responsible for generating sales revenue. A Revenue Centre manager does not have control over the cost or the investment in assets, but generally has control over some of the expenses of the marketing department. This Centre's performance is measured by comparing the actual revenue with budgeted revenue and the actual marketing expenses with that of the budgeted marketing expenses. Examples of Revenue Centre are Marketing Manager of a product line or an individual sales representative.

(3) **Profit Centre :** Responsibility Centers may have both inputs and outputs. The inputs are taken as costs and outputs are taken as revenues. Managers of profit centers have control over both the costs and the revenues because profit is the difference between the revenues and the costs. The main purpose of a profit centre is to earn profit. Management decided to make a responsibility centre as a profit centre when it thinks that the outputs are capable of beings measured in monetary terms and that it would be beneficial to do so.

A division of the company which produces and markets the products may be called a profit centre.

Benefits of Profit Centre : A profit centre provides more effective assessment of the manger's performance

1. A profit centre manager is motivated to make decisions about inputs and outputs
2. There is accountability for the transfer of goods to another department or selling to the outsiders.

Problem 2

Vimal Limited employs a Budgetary Control System and measure its performance on segmented basis of its product line Division X and Y. the budgeted and actual sales figures for the month of March are as follows:

Division	Budgeted		Actual	
	Units	Amount ₹	Units	Amount ₹
X	30,000	3,00,000	32,000	3,20,000
Y	50,000	3,00,000	60,000	4,20,000

The standard unit controllable variable costs are ₹ 4 and 3 for the products X and Y respectively. But actual variable manufacturing costs during March were ₹ 1,00,000 and ₹ 1,55,000 for the products X and Y, whereas, the actual amounted to ₹ 28,000 for product X and ₹ 25,000 for product Y. and budgeted Controllable cost amount to ₹ 30,000 each product

The attributable budgeted segment costs are ₹ 50,000 and ₹ 60,000 for the products X and Y respectively but actual costs incurred were ₹ 60,000 and ₹ 70,000 for X and Y respectively. The common costs are assumed to be ₹ 70,000 to be apportioned on the basis of segment sales revenue for budgeted & Actual.

From the above information, prepare a performance Evaluation Report, if the Vimal Ltd. Employs Profit Centre basis of Divisional Performance Measurement.

Solution :

Performance Evaluation Report

Particulars	Product A			Product B			Total		
	Budget ₹	Actual ₹	Variance ₹	Budget ₹	Actual ₹	Variance ₹	Budget ₹	Actual ₹	Variance ₹
Sales Revenue	300	320	20F	300	420	120F	600	740	140F
Less Controllable Variable Cost	120	100	20 F	150	155	5A	270	255	15F
Controllable Contribution Margin	180	220	40F	150	265	115F	330	485	155F
Less Controllable Fixed Cost	30	28	2F	30	25	5F	60	53	7F
Controllable Segment Margin	150	192	42F	120	240	120F	270	432	162F
Less Attribute Segment Cost	50	60	10A	60	70	10A	110	130	20A
Segment profit Contribution	100	132	32F	60	170	110F	160	302	142F
Less Common Costs (250:300 – Sales Ratio)	35	35		35	35		70	70	
Net Income	65	97	32F	25	135	110F	90	232	142F

(4) **Investment Centre :** It is a division of an organization wherein its performance is assessed by considering not only its costs and revenues but also by establishing a relationship between the profit (difference between revenues and costs), capital invested or employed and revenue. It is responsible for both profits and investments. When only top management takes the decision regarding the capital expenditure decision i.e., capital budgeting decision, there will be only one investment Centre covering the entire organization. Whereas, when such decision making is delegated

to the divisional heads, there will be more number of investment centers. Thus, the number of investment centers will be fewer compared to profit or cost centres. Therefore, all the investments centres are normally profit centers and cost centres but not all profit centres are investment centres. The performance of a division is measured by establishing a relationship between its net income and total capital employed in that division.

Problem 3 :

Division R and S are both considering an outlay on new investment projects.

Particular	Division R	Division S
Investment Accordingly (₹)	3,50,000	3,50,000
Net return on the new investment (₹)	65,000	65,000
Current ROI	20%	15%

The company's cost of capital is 14%. Should the projected be accepted or rejected?

Solution :

$$\text{ROI on New Investment} = \frac{\text{New Return}}{\text{New Investment}} \times 100$$

$$\text{Division R} = \frac{65,000}{3,00,000} \times 100 = 18.57\%$$

$$\text{Division S} = \frac{65,000}{3,00,000} \times 100 = 18.57\%$$

Division R should reject the new investment as its ROI is 18.57%, though more than the cost of capital, it is less than the current ROI of 20%.

Division S can accept the new investment as its ROI of is 18.57%, which is more than the current ROI of 15%

Objectives of Responsibility Performance Reporting

Responsibility Performance Reporting is the reporting phase of Responsibility Accounting. The main objectives of Responsibility Reporting are

1. To determine the degree of performance in the are of responsibility for which the concerned Responsibility Centre's manager is directly responsible and
2. To formulate measures to improve the performance of the Responsibility Centre's manager after ascertaining the deviation of the actual performance from the budgeted performance.

Reports : The reports can be Responsibility Reporting for Cost Centers and Profit Canters. Responsibility Report contains items and information which are required by the concerned Responsibility Centre Manager and which are within his responsibility area.

Responsibility Reporting goes on aggregating information as the reports are prepared for higher level managers in the organizational hierarchy. The amount of detail decreases as reports reach higher and higher levels of management. If the information is too detailed and voluminous, the managers cannot make effective use of information as the time at their disposal is very limited. In case, detailed information is required, they can get it and might seek it, if they are concerned about some particular elements of cost.

Responsibility Accounting Reports for profit centers are normally in the form of income statements. Here, the principle of controllability is applied. The managers at the lower level are responsible for the product lines and they are subordinate to the manages of the geographical areas, who in turn are responsible to the managing director of the organization.

Problem 4

Dhanush manufactures ready–made garments by a simple process of cutting the clothes in various shapes and sewing the pieces to form the finished dress.The sewing Department and the cutting Department report to the Production Manager who along with Engineering Manager reports to the Director – Manufacturing. The Sales Manager, Publicity Manager and Credit Manager report to the Marketing Director of the Company.

The Accounts Department reports the following for the month of March 2012

Particulars	Budget ₹	Actual ₹
Cloth Utilized	40,000	45,000
Advertising	5,000	5,000
Bad depts losses	7,000	5,000
Audit Fee	5,000	5,000
Credit reports	1,500	1,350
Sales Reprsentatives Travelling Expenses	7,000	8,200
Sales commission	6,000	6,000
Thread	650	600
Sewing labour	19,600	21,000
Cutting labour	7,400	8,000
Credit department salaries	10,000	10,000
Rewing utilities	1,900	1,950
Cutting utilities	1,800	1,700
Marketing manager Salaries and Administrative expenses	25,000	26,400
Production Engineering expenses	15,000	14,200
Publicity Management office Expenses	18,000	17,700
Production Management office Expenses	19,000	18,000
Directors Manufacturing Salaries and Administrative expenses	31,000	30,100

Using the above data, prepare Responsibility Accounting Reports for the Director – Manufacturing, the Director – Marketing and the Production Manager.

(ICWA, Inter, June, 2001)

Solution :

Particulars	Budget ₹	Actual ₹	Variance ₹
For the Production Manager			
Cutting Department			
Cloth	40,000	45,000	5,000 A
Cutting Labour	7,400	8,000	600 A
Cutting Utilities	1,800	1,700	100 F
Total (A)	**49,200**	**54,700**	**5,500 A**
Sewing Department			
Thread	650	600	50 F
Sewing Labour	19,600	21,000	1,400 A
Sewing utilities	1,900	1,950	50 A
Total (B)	**22,150**	**23,550**	**1,400 A**
Total (A + B)	**71,350**	**78,250**	**6,900 A**
Direct Manufacturing			
Product Department	71,350	78,250	6900 A
Production Engineering expenses	15,000	14,200	800 F
production Manager – Office	19,000	18,000	1,000 F
Total	**105,350**	**110,450**	**5,100 A**
For the Director - Marketing			
Sales Manager			
Travelling expenses	7,000	8,200	1,200 A
Sales commission	6,000	6,000	-
Total (A)	**13,000**	**14,200**	**1,200 A**
Publicity Manager			
Office expenses	18,000	17,700	300 F
Advertising	5,000	5,000	-
Total (B)	**23,000**	**22,700**	**300 F**
Total (A + B) (c)	**36,000**	**36,900**	**900 A**
Credit Manager			
Salaries	10,000	10,000	-
Credit reports	1,500	1,350	150 F
Bad debt losses	7,000	5,000	2,000 F
Total (D)	**18,500**	**16,350**	**2,150 F**
Gross Total (C + D)	**5 4,500**	**53,250**	**1,250**

Note : Audit fees, salaries and administration expenses are ignored as marketing manager and director, manufacturing are not reporting to anyone.

Problem 5 :

Hindustan Fuels Limited has three production departments Machine shop, Fabrication and Assembly, which are the responsibility of the shop superintendent who along with materials manager, planning superintendent and maintenance engineer, reports to the works manager at the factory. The office administration, sales and publicity come under the sales manager who, along with the works manager, reports to the managing director of the company. The following data relating to a month's performance is extracted from the books of the company:

Particulars	Budgeted ₹	Actual ₹
Raw Material:		
Machine shop	1,900	1,920
Assembly	960	1,000
Fabrication	500	510
Sales Commission	1,000	1,050
Publicity expenses	2,100	2,200
Printing and Stationery	4,200	4,000
Travelling expenses	5,000	5,200
Wages:		
machine Shop	700	690
Fabrication	800	820
Assembly	920	930
Utilities:		
Machine shop	540	550
Fabrication	670	610
Assembly	570	540
Maintenance	600	620
Stores	410	370
Planning	280	300
Shop Superintendent Office:		
Sales and Expenses	2,200	2,178
Depreciation : Factory	5,880	6,920
works Manager's Office:		
General Office:		
Salaries and Administrative expenses	4,270	4,300
Managing Directors Office Salaries and Administrative expenses	2,800	2,780

(i) Treating the machine shop, fabrication and assembly as Cost Centres, Prepare cost sheets for each centre with the help of the following additional information:

The shop superintendent devotes his time amongst machine shop, fabrication and assembly in the ratio of 4:3:4. Other factors overheads are absorbed on the basis of direct labour in each Cost Centre. Office, administration, selling and distribution overheads are borne equally by the Cost Centres.

(ii) Treating the machine shop, fabrication and assembly as responsibility centres, prepare a responsibility accounting report for the shop superintendent.

Particulars	Machine shop		Fabrication		Assembly	
	Budget ₹	Actual ₹	Budget ₹	Actual ₹	Budget ₹	Actual ₹
Raw materials	1,900	1,920	500	510	960	1000
Wages	700	690	800	820	920	930
Utilities	540	550	670	610	570	540
Prime Cost (A)	3,140	3,160	1,970	1,940	2,450	2,470
Factory Overheads						
Salaries and Expenses *	800	792	600	594	800	792
Other Factory Overheads*	2,073	2,322	2,370	2,759	2,727	3,129
Factory cost(Prime cost+ Factory Overheads) (B)	**6,013**	**6,274**	**4,940**	**5,293**	**5,977**	**6,391**
Administrative Overheads	3,757	3,693	3,757	3,693	3,756	3,694
Administrative Expenses***						
Cost of Production (Factory Cost+Admin. Overheads) (c)	**9,770**	**9,967**	**8,697**	**8,986**	**9,733**	**10,085**
Selling and Distribution Overheads	2,700	2,816	2,700	2,816	2,700	2,817
Selling and Distribution Expenses ****						
Total Cost (C + Selling OH)	**12,470**	**12,783**	**11,397**	**11,802**	**12,433**	**12,902**

Working Notes

- Shop superintendent office salaries and expenses
- Shop superintendent devotes his time amongst Machine shop, Fabrication and Assembly in ratio of 4 : 3 : 4

	Budget		Actual	
Machine shop	2,200 X 4/11	800	2,178 X 4/11	792
Fabrication	2,200 X 3/11	600	2,178 x 3/11	594
Assembly	2,200 x 4/11	800	2,178 x 4/11	792

****Other Factory Overheads**

Particulars	Budget ₹	Actual ₹
Stores	410	370
Planning	280	300
Depreciation	5,880	6,920
	600	620
Total	7,170	8,210

These are absorbed on the basis of direct labour i.e., 700 : 800 : 920 : and 690 : 820 : 930 budgeted and actual respectively.

***** Administration Overheads**

Particulars	Budget ₹	Actual ₹
Printing and Stationery	4,200	4,000
General Office and Adm. Expenses	4,270	4,300
MD's Salary	2,800	2,780
Total	11,270	11,080

Administrative Overheads is absorbed by all respective centres equally

***** Selling and Administrative Overheads**

Particulars	Budget ₹	Actual ₹
Sales Commission	1,000	1,050
Publicity expenses	2,100	2,200
Traveling expenses	5,000	5,200
Total	8,100	8,450

Selling and Distribution expenditure is absorbed by all Responsibility Centres equally.

Particulars	Budget ₹	Actual ₹	Variance ₹
For the shop superintendent			
Machine shop			
Material	1,900	1,920	20 A
Labour	700	690	10 F
Utilities	540	550	10. A
Total	3,140	3,160	20 A
Fabrication			
Material	500	510	10. A
Labour	800	820	20 A
Utilities	670	610	60 F
Total	1,970	1,940	30 F
Assembly			
Material	960	1,000	40 A
Labour	920	930	10. A
Utilities	570	540	30 F
Total	2,450	2,470	20 A
Grand Total	7,560	7,570	10.A

Problem 6 :

BHEL manufacturing company has five plans A, B, C,D and E Each plant has a forming cleaning and packing Department.

Each Level of Management has the Responsibility over costs incurred at its level.

The budget for the current year has been set up as follows:

Plant	Budget Cost
A	1,35,000
B	1,22,500
C	1,08,400
D	1,35,000
E	1,35,000

Budget Information for Plant C is as Follows	
Plant Manager's Office	2,350
Forming Department	30,000
Cleaning Department	55,450
Packing Department	20,600
Direct Material	8,167
Direct Labour	15,000
Factory Overheads	6,833
The Following additional budgeted data are available	
President Office	16,250
Vice-President, Marketing	20,000
Vice-President, Manufacturing Office	4,168
The following actual costs are incurred during the year:	
Plant A	1,27,650
B	1,24,300
C	1,08,476
D	1,31,100
E	1,36,800
Vice President, Manufacturing Office	4,990
The actual costs for the plant C were as follows:	
Direct Material	8,000
Direct Labour	13,000
Factory Overheads	7,000
Actual Costs for plant C (plant manager) were:	
Plant Manager's Office	2,476
Cleaning Department	57,500
Packing Department	22,500
Forming Department	26,000
Actual cost for the presidents level were :	
President office	16,376
Vice president, marketing	29,800
Vice president , manufacturing	6,33,316

Prepare a Responsibility Report for the year showing the details of the budgeted, actual and variance amounts for the following areas:

Level 1 , Forming Department, Plant C

Level 2, Plant Manager, Plant C

Level 3, Vice President, Manufacturing

Level 4, President

Solution :

Responsibility Report

Particulars	Budgeted ₹	Actual ₹	Variance ₹
Forming Department, Plant C (Level 1)			
Direct Material	8,167	8,000	167F
Direct Labour	15,000	13,000	2,000 F
Factory Overheads	6,833	7,000	167 A
Total Controllable Costs	**30,000**	**28,000**	**2,000 F**
Plant Manager, Plant C (Level 2)			
Plant Manager's Office	2,350	2,476	126A
Forming Department	30,000	26,000	4,000 F
Clearing Department	55,450	57,500	2,050 F
Packing Department	20,600	22,500	1,900 A
Total Controllable Costs	**1,08,400**	**1,08,476**	**76 A**

Particulars	**Budget** ₹	**Actual** ₹	**Variance** ₹
Vice president, Manufacturing (Level 3)			
Vice President, Manufacturing Office	4,168	4,990	822 A
Plant A	135,000	127,650	7350 F
Plant B	122,500	124,300	1800 A
Plant C	108,400	108,486	76 A
Plant D	135,000	131,100	3900 F
Plant E	135,000	136,800	1800 A
Total Controllable Costs	6,40,068	6,33,316	6,752 F
President (level 4)			
President Office	16,250	16,376	126 A
Vice President, Marketing	20,000	29,800	9,800 A
Vice President, Manufacturing	640,068	633,316	6752 F
Total Controllable Costs	676,318	679,492	3,174 A

Problem 7 :

Shiva Home Needs Limited deals in three products chairs. Tables and iron stands and these are sold directly through salesmen in three zones namely Southern, Northern and Western. The responsibility for sales promotion rests with the headquarters and so does the overall control of distribution and sales. Cost of sales as percent of sales are: chairs ₹ 85. Tables ₹ 80 and iron stands ₹ 75 Details of sales and selling and distribution expenses for the year are as follows:

Zones	Product	Sales ₹	Selling and Distribution expenses allocated direct ₹
Southern	Chairs	11,00,000	83,000
	Tables	11,00,000	94,500
	Iron Stands	6,50,000	56,000
		28,50,000	**2,33,500**
Northern	Chairs	875,000	47,000
	Tables	650,000	50,000
	Iron Stands	425,000	25,000
		1,950,000	**122,000**
Western	Chairs	425,000	19,000
	Tables	380,000	20,000
	Iron Stands	695,000	80,000
		1,500,000	119,000

Selling and distribution expenses at headquarters area as follows:

	₹
Office expenses	1,50,000
Advertisement	1,76,500
Other expenses	1,83,000

Advertisement costs are allocated to zones and products on the basis of sales. Office expenses and other expenses are apportioned equally to the zones or the products, while computing the profit or loss for the zones or the products as the case may be.

Prepare a Comparative profit and Loss Statement, presenting Zonal Performance as distinct from Product Performance.

Solution :

Comparative Profit and Loss Statement (evaluating Zonal Performance)

Particulars	Southern ₹	Northern ₹	Western ₹	Total ₹
Sales Revenue (A)	28,50,000	19,50,000	15,00,000	63,00,000
Less: Cost of Sales:				
Chairs (85 %)	9,35,000	7,43,750	3,61,250	20,40,000
Tables (80 %)	8,80,000	5,20,000	3,04,000	17,04,000
Iron Stands (75 %)	4,87,5000	3,18,750	5,21,250	13,27,500
Total (B)	23,02,500	15,82,500	11,86,500	50,71,500
Gross profit (A – B) (c)	5,47,500	3,67,500	3,13,500	12,28,500
Less: Selling and Distribution Expenses				
Direct Cost (allocated)	2,33,500	1,22,000	1,19,000	4,74,500
Advertisement (apportioned in Sales Ratio: 285:195:150)	79,845	54,631	42,024	1,76,500
Office Expenses (Equally)	50,000	50,000	50,000	1,50,000
Other Expenses (Equally)	61,000	61,000	61,000	1,83,000
Total Selling and Distribution Expenses (D)	4,24,345	2,87,631	2,72,024	9,84,000
Net Profit (C- D) E	1,23,155	79,869	41,476	2,44,500

Divisional Performance: An organization consists of many units of parallel authority. Which are created into several divisions for the purpose of decentralization and diversification. These units reflect autonomous Responsibility Centres, authorized by the divisional heads to carry out the tasks and achieved the goal confined to the respective division. Generally, divisions refer to profit centers in the organization.

The purpose of divisionalisation is to crate accountability for generation of profit by those divisions which reflect separate product/services, area, processes, etc., it also enables inter-division comparison relating to profit performance of different divisions and also their impact on the overall profitability of the organization. Divisional performance helps in strategy formulation and operational planning. It poses a challenge to divisional managers by generating an inter-competitive spirit amongst them.

For the success of divisionalisation, it is necessary to verify if the boundary lines between different divisions area specific and clear. Each division has is own link of expenses and revenue authority.

The divisional operations should be carried out in such a way that one division does not affect the profitability of the other. There should be a proper division. i.e, a proper system for the recording and pricing of inter division transfer.

A Divisional Manager has autonomy and is authorized to take production and marketing decisions, which make him accountable to the top management for the profitability of his division.

The following is the organizational chart that reflects divisionalisation in the organization.

Division 'A'	Division 'B'	Division 'C'	Division 'D'
Profit Target Personnel	Profit Target Finance	Profit Target Administration	Profit Target Marketing

Evaluation of Divisional Performance

Divisional Performance can be evaluated using the following methods.

(1) The Contribution Margin Approach/Net Profit/Operational Profit Approach

(2) Return on Investment Approach

(3) Residual Income Approach

The Net Profit/Operational Profit/Contribution Margin Approach

For the purpose of assessing the profitability of a Division in absolute figures. Profit can take the form of net profit either before or after tax. The only disadvantage arising is that , he net profit may be more or less, due to certain non - operating incomes or expenses of higher amounts like profit on sale of capital assets or loss on it.

The other basis can be the figures of Operating Profit. The profit arising from the main business for which a company was incorporated is termed as operating profit. Thus, greater the value of absolute net profit/ operating profit , better is the performance.

The contribution approach statement can be as follows which include cost controllability and cost allocation relating to the net profit earned by the Division.

Statement :

Sales	****
Less: Variable costs	****
Less: Controllable Divisional Overheads	****
Controllable Profit	****
Less: Fixed Non Controllable Divisional Overheads	****
Contribution Margin	****
Less : Allocation for Fixed Expenses	****
Net Profit before Tax	****
Less: Tax	****
Net Profit after Tax	****

Problem 8

From the following particular prepare X Ltd Divisional Performance.

Particulars	Division A ₹	Division B ₹	Division C ₹
Sales	2,00,000	5,00,000	800,000
Variable Cost	60,000	2,50,000	4,20,000
Fixed Cost controllable	30,000	90,000	1,40,000

Note : Company's Common fixed cost is 2,00,000

Solution :

Particulars	Total ₹	Unalloca-ted ₹	Division X ₹	Division Y ₹	Division Z ₹
Revenue	15,00,000		2,00,000	5,00,000	8,00,000
Less: Variable Cost	7,00,000		60,000	2,50,000	4,20,000
Contribution	8,00,000		1,40,000	2,50,000	3,80,000
Less: Separate Fixed Cost	2,60,000		30,000	90,000	1,40,000
Division Profit	5,40,000		1,10,000	1,60,000	2,40,000
Less: Common Fixed Cost	2,00,000				
Net Profit	3,40,000				

Criteria for Measurement of Divisional Profit: There are three criteria against which Divisional Profit Measurement must be judged before they are considered acceptable.

(1) Divisional Profit should not be increased by any action that reduces the total company's profit.

(2) Each Division's Profit should be as independent as possible of performance efficiency and managerial decisions elsewhere in the company.

(3) Each Divisions Profit should reflect all items that are subject to any substantial degree of control by the Division Manager of his subordinates.

II. **Return on Investment Method :** The most common form of performance evaluation in a divisionalisation company is Return on Investment (ROI) Method. Return on Investment is calculated as a ratio of net divisional profit i.e before tax, to the net assets employed in the division. This is calculated with the help of the following formula.

ROI = (Profit Margin × 100) / Invested Capital

Or

$$\text{ROI} = \frac{\text{Sale Revenue}}{\text{Investment Capital}} \times \frac{\text{Profit Margin}}{\text{Sale Revenue}}$$

$$= \text{Return on Capital} \times \text{Margin on Sales}$$

Note :

(1) Net Divisional Profit means divisional profit before tax

(2) Net Assets should always be taken at book values.

Advantages of ROI : The advantages of this method are:

(1) It relates to level of investment

(2) The ROI can be analyzed into other ratios which are useful for analytical purposes

(3) It can be used for inter firm comparison, provided, the firms whose result are being compared, are of comparable size and of the same industry.

Disadvantages of ROI : The disadvantages of ROI Method are :

(1) Usually, Capital employed will be valued at net book value, and the fixed assets are indexed to provide at current cost profit which is usually calculated before deducting tax and after charging controllable allocated head office expenses.

(2) The ROI may influence a divisional manager to select only those investments with high rates of return. But other investments which could increase the value of the business may be rejected.

These types of decisions are sub-optional and result in under investing in order to maintain ROI.

III. Residual Income Method : As an alternative to ROI, the performance of a division can be measure by means of Residual Income Method. This Method deducts a charge for the use of assets from divisional profits, and bases this charge on Company's cost of capital. It is an operating profit or income of Division. Less the imputed interest on the assets used by the Division.

In other words, interest on the capital invested in the Division is treated as cost and any surplus after deducting this cost is the residual income.

Residual income is the excess of net earnings over the cost of capital. This criterion is relevant when manages of divisions are autonomous and accountable for their performance and makes their own decision on capital investment.

Divisional Residual Income Statement

Particulars	Rs
Revenue	***
Less: Variable Cost	***
Contribution	***
Less : Controllable Fixed Cost	***
Controllable Profit	***
Less : Interest on Controllable Investment	***
Controllable Residual Income	***
Less : Uncontrollable Cost Collected (Head office charges)	***
Less : Interest on Uncontrollable Investment	***
Net Residual Income	***

Advantages of Residual Income Method (RI) :

(1) Unlike the ROI, the RI approach is not concerned with preserving a relative measure. It strives to maximize the absolute figure, and thus, increase the shareholders wealth.

(2) The cost of capital charge on divisional investments ensures that manages are aware of the opportunity cost of funds.

(3) If each Division is charged with a common group cost of capital, the interest taken at Division level will be compatible with the interest of the organization as a whole.

Disadvantages of RI : The following are the disadvantages of RI Method.

(1) There may be difficulties in defining the net operating income and the value of the divisional investments

(2) Identifying controllable and uncontrollable factors at divisional level may be difficult. There can be problems in calculating a accurate cost of capital.

It can be understood from the statement below (with the assumed figures) that the Residual Income will be arrived at after charging a notional amount for the target return that should be made on capital investment.

Particulars	Organization as a whole (₹)	Division X (₹)	Division Y (₹)	Division Z (₹)
Investment	20,85,000	4,00,000	6,25,000	8,50,000
Residual Income				
Operating Profit	2,10,000	40,000	90,000	1,60,000
Required Return (10% on Investment)	2,08,500	40,000	62,500	85,000
Residual Income	1,500	---	27,500	75,000

Problem 9 :

The following data has been collected relating to W division of the MACRO group.

Data for W Division		
		₹
Sales Revenue	External Customers	6,00,000
	Internal transfers	3,50,000
Variable operating Costs	Labour	95,000
	Materials	1,60,000
	Overheads	42,500
Fixed Operating costs	Controllable by divisions	78,000
	Controllable Centrally	41,000
Divisional Management Cost	Controllable Centrally	26,500
Fixed Assets (at Cost)	Divisional purchases	4,50,000
	Central Purchases	2,50,000

Total central administration and management cost.(these are apportioned on the basis of sales revenue which was ₹ 52 lakhs for the group as a whole)

The group's weighted average cost of capital is estimated at 15% and it is the group policy to calculate depreciation on a straight line basis at 25 % and to impute interest on a gross investment basis.

Prepare from the above data, a divisional performance statement on

(i) Profit Centre approach

(ii) Investment Centre approach *(ICWA, Final, Dec. 2005)*

Solution :

Divisional Performance Statement

Divisional Revenue	9,50,000	
(*Less*) Variable Cost:		
Labour	95,000	
Materials	1,60,000	
Overheads	42,500	(2,97,500)
Divisional Contribution		6,52,500
		78,000
(*Less*) Controllable depreciation [4,50,000 × 25 %]		
Controllable Profit		₹ 4,62,000

(a) Profit Centre Approach

Controllable Profit as worked above	4,62,000
(*Less*) Non- controllable fixed operating costs	
41,000 + 26,500 = 67,500	
Non-Controllable depreciation = 62,500	1,30,000
(*Less*) Apportioned Central Charges	
(6,84,210 / 52,00,000) × 9,50,000	1,25,000
Net Profit before tax	₹ 2,07,000

(b) Investment Centre Approach

Net profit before tax (same as in Profit Centre Approach)		₹ 2,07,000
(Less) 15% Cost of Capital		
(Being imputed interest on gross investment in fixed assets:		
Controllable	67,500	
Non- Controllable	37,500 =	(1,05,000)
Net Residual Income Before tax		₹ 1,02,000

Problem 10 :

Sujatha Comforts Ltd. Deals in three products. Ace, Nice and Grace and these are sold directly through salesmen in three zones, Prime, Extension and Outreach. The responsibility for sales promotion rests with the headquarters and so does the overall control of distribution and sales. Costs of sales are:

ACE	75	per cent of sales
Nice	70	
Grace	60	

Details of sales and selling and distribution expenses for the year are as follows :

		Sales	Selling and Distribution Expenses Allocated Direct (₹)
Prime	Ace	1,000,000	70,000
	Nice	1000000	80,000
	Grace	500000	48,000
		2,500,000	198,000
Extension Zone	Ace	700,000	50,000
	Nice	500,000	50,000
	Grace	300,000	30,000
		15,00,000	1,30,000
Outreach Zone	Ace	300,000	25,000
	Nice	200,000	20,000
	Grace	500,000	70,000
		1,000,000	115,000

Selling and distribution expenses at headquarters are as follows:

	₹
Office expenses	10,000
Advertisement	1, 40,000
Other expenses	1, 30,000

Advertisement costs are allocated to zones and products on the basis of sales, office expenses and other expenses are apportioned equally to the zones or the products, while computing the profit or loss for the zones or the products, as the case may be.

Prepare a comparative profit and loss statement, presenting zonal performance as distinct from product performance.

Comparative Profit And Loss Statement

	Particulars	Prime Zone (₹)	Extension Zone (₹)	Outreach Zone (₹)	Total (₹)
(a)	Sales	25,00,000	15,00,000	10,00,000	50,00,000
(b)	Cost of Sales				
	Ace (85 per cent of sales)	7,50,000	5,25,000	2,25,000	15,00,000
	Nice (80 per cent of sales)	7,00,000	3,50,000	1,40,000	11,90,000
	Grace (75 per cent of sales)	3,00,000	1,80,000	3,00,000	7,80,000
(c)	Total Cost of sales (b)	17,50,000	10,55,000	6,65,000	34,70,000
	Gross Margin (a – b)	7,50,000	4,45,000	3,35,000	15,30,000

Problem 11 :

Suresh Ltd. Is having production shops which are cost Centres. Each Shop charges other shops for materials supplied and services rendered.

The shops are motivated through goal congruence, autonomy and management efforts. Suresh Ltd. Is having a welding shop and painting shop. The welding shop annually 7, 50,000 purchased items with other 15,00,000 shop made parts into 1,20,000 assemblies.

The assemblies are having variable cost of ₹ 19 each and are sold in the market at ₹ 24 per assembly. Out of the total production, 80 % is diverted to painting shop at same price ruling in the market. Welding shop incurs a fixed cost of ₹ 5,00,000 per annum.

The painting shop is having a fixed cost of ₹ 6,00,000 and its cost of painting including transfer price from welding shop comes to ₹ 40 per unit. The painting shop sells all units transfer to it by welding shop at ₹ 50 per assembly.

Requirements :

(i) Find out profit of individual cost Centres and Overall profitability of the company.

(ii) Recommend Course of action, if painting shop wishes to purchases its full requirement either from open market (@ ₹ 20 per assembly) or from welding shop at ₹ 20 per assembly. Give reasons for your recommendations.

(ICWA, Inter, June 2007)

Solution :

Suresh Ltd.

(i) Present Profitability of Individual Shops and Overall Profitability

Particulars	Welding shop			Painting Shop		
	Qty. Unit	Rate (₹)	Value (₹)	Qty. Unit	Rate (₹)	Value (₹)
Sale in Open Market	24,000	24.00	5,76,000	96,000	50.00	48,00,000
Transfer to Painting Shop	96,000	24.00	23,04,000			
Total Sales (A)	1,20,000		28,80,000	96,000		48,00,000
Less: Variable Cost (B) (120000 x 19)			22,80,000	(96,000 × 40)		38,40,000
Contribution (A – B)			6,00,000			96,0000
Less: Fixed Cost			5,00,000			60,0000
Profit			1,00,000			3,60,000

Overall profit for the company = Rs. 460000

(100000 + 360000)

(ii) (a) When painting shop purchases all its requirement from open market at a price of ₹ 20 per unit.

Particulars	Welding shop			Painting Shop		
	Qty. Unit	Rate (₹)	Value (₹)	Qty. Unit	Rate (₹)	Value (₹)
Sale	24,000	24.00	5,76,000	96,000	50.00	48,00,000
Less: Variable cost	24,000	19.00	4,56,000	96,000	36.00	34,56,000
Contribution			1,20,000			13,44,000
Fixed Cost			5,00,000			6,00,000
Profit (Loss)			3,80,000			7,44,000

- Overall profit for the company = ₹ 364000

  (744000 – 380000)

- Total Variable Cost of the unit of Painting Shop :

  (Purchase Price from the market + own Variable Cost)

  = ₹ 20 + (40 – Transfer Price from welding shop) = 20 + (40 – 24) = ₹ 36.00

(ii) (b) When all the requirements of painting shop is met

By transfer from welding shop at a transfer price of ₹ 20 per unit.

Particulars	Welding shop			Painting Shop		
	Qty. Unit	Rate (₹)	Value (₹)	Qty. Unit	Rate (₹)	Value (₹)
Sale in the Open Market	24,000	24.00	5,76,000	96000	50.00	48,00,000
Transfer to Painting Shop	9,600	24.00	19,20,000			
Total Sales	1,20,000		24,96,000	96000		48,00,000
Less: Variable Cost	(1,20,000 x 19)		22,80,000	(96000 x 36)		34,56,000
Contribution			2,16,000			13,44,000
Less: Fixed Cost			5,00,000			6,00,000
Profit / (Loss)			2,84,000			7,44,000

- Overall profit for the company = ₹ 364000
  (744000 – 380000)
- Total Variable Cost of the unit of Painting Shop :
  (Purchase Price from the market + own variable Cost)
  = ₹ 20 + (40 – Transfer price from welding shop) = 20 + (40 – 24) = ₹ 36.00

(ii) (b) When all the requirements of painting shop is met

By transfer from welding shop at a transfer price of ₹ 20 per unit

Particulars	Welding shop			Painting Shop		
	Qty. Unit	Rate (₹)	Value (₹)	Qty. Unit	Rate (₹)	Value (₹)
Sale in the Open Market	24,000	24.00	5,76,000	96,000	50.00	48,00,000
Transfer to Painting Shop	9,600	24.00	19,20,000			
Total Sales	1,20,000		24,96,000	96,000		48,00,000
Less: Variable Cost	(1,20,000 x 19)		22,80,000	(96,000 x 36)		34,56,000
Contribution			2,16,000			13,44,000
Less: Fixed Cost			5,00,000			6,00,000
Profit / (Loss)			2,84,000			7,44,000

Overall profit of the company = ₹ 4,60,000

(7,44,000 – 2,84,000)

The results of the three alternatives are summarized below :

	Welding Shop	Painting Shop
Profit under alternative (i)	1,00,000	3,60,000
Profit / (Loss) under alternative (ii) (a)	3,80,000	7,44,000
Profit / (Loss) under alternative (ii) (b)	2,84,000	7,44,000

	₹
Overall Profit of the company under alternative (i)	4,60,000
Under alternative (ii) (a)	3,64,000
Under alternative (ii) (b)	4,60,000

Recommendation :

After analyzing of the summarized results of three alternatives pertaining to individual shops and Overall Company, we may recommend to accept the alternative (ii) (b) (requirements of painting shop to be met by transfer from Welding Shop at a T.P. of ₹ 20 per unit) due to the following reasons:

(A) It gives a maximum overall profit of ₹ 4,60,000. The discussion is confined to either alternative (ii) (a) or (ii) (b)

(B) Each shop is treated as a separate Cost Centre and not a Profit Centre.

(C) The policy of overall goal congruence of the company is followed.

Glossary

- **Responsibility Accounting** is that type of Management Accounting that collects and reports both planned and actual accounting information in terms of Responsibility Centres
- **Cost Centre** is the Centre where inputs are measured in monetary terms. In Cost Center Responsibility, the accounting system records only the cost incurred in the center. Performance of cost centre is measured by the monetary terms of input only, where cost of operating the division is directly traceable to it.
- **Revenue Centre** is a segment of the organization which is primarily responsible for generating sales revenue. This Centre's performance is measure by comparing the actual revenue with the budgeted revenue and the actual marketing expenses with that of the budgeted marketing expenses.
- **Profit Centre** is a division of the company which produces and markets the products. Managers of profit centres have control over both the costs and the revenues because profit is the difference between the revenues and the costs.

- **Investment Centre** is a division of an organization wherein its performance is assessed by considering not only its costs and revenues but also by establishing the relationship between profit (difference - between revenues and costs) capital invested or employed and revenue. It is responsible for both profit and investments.
- **Responsible Performance Reporting** is the reporting phase of Responsibility Accounting.
- **Operating Profit** is the profit arising from the main business for which a company was incorporated.
- **Return on Investment** is calculated as a ratio of net divisional profit i.e profit before tax to the net assets employed in the Division.
- **Residual income** is an operating profit or income of a Division less the imputed interest on the assets used by the division.

Objective Type Questions

1. A good responsibility accounting and reporting system is dependent upon
   (a) the correct allocation of controllable fixed costs.
   (b) the correct allocation of controllable variable costs.
   (c) identification of the management level at which all costs are controllable
   (d) the proper delegation of responsibility and authority.
2. Input is concerned with
   (a) cost centre
   (b) investments
   (c) profit Centre
   (d) none of these
3. Profit centre is responsible for maximizing the
   (a) profit of the organization
   (b) profit of the centre
   (c) profit of the industry
   (d) none of the above
4. Classification of cost centre is not concerned with the
   (a) productive, unproductive and mixed cost centre following
   (b) personal and impersonal cost centre.
   (c) selling and distribution cost centre.
   (d) operation and Process cost centre.

5. Responsibility accounting is a part of
   (a) global responsibility system.
   (b) external reporting system
   (c) internal reporting system
   (d) corporate reporting system

Ans : 1. (d), 2. (a), 3. (b), 4. (c), 5. (c)

SHORT ANSWER QUESTIONS

1. What is responsibility accounting?
2. What is responsibility centres?
3. Name of the various types of responsibility centres.
4. What is a profit centre?
5. What is the function of cost centre?
6. What is investment centere?

LONG ANSWER QUESTIONS

1. Explain the meaning and different types of ' Responsibility Centres, ' what steps need to be taken to set up a system of responsibility accounting in an organization ?
2. Discuss various steps involved in responsibility accounting.
3. What are the objectives of responsibility accounting ?
4. What is meant by responsibility centres ? How far are these centres helpful to the management ?
5. Responsibility accounting is an important device for control. Explain.

❖ ❖ ❖

Chapter - 9
Transfer Pricing

Introduction

In managerial accounting, different divisions of a multi-entity company are responsible for their own profit and returns on invested capital. Hence, divisions are required to transact with each other, a transfer price is used to decide costs. It tends not much difference from the price in the market because they will either be buying for more than the prevailing market price or selling below the market price and this will affect their performance. Transfer pricing, deals with the technique where parent companies sell goods and services to subsidiary entities at an inflated price to deliberately reduce profits and tax liability.

We will restrict attention to transfers that involve a tangible product and refer to the two corporate entities engaged in the transfer as divisions. Hence, the transfer price is the price that the "selling" division charges the "buying" division for the product. Because objects that float usually flow downstream hence, the selling division is called the **upstream division** and the buying division is called the **downstream division**.

Transferred product can be classified along two criteria. The first criterion is whether there is a readily available external market price for the product. The second criterion is whether the downstream division will sell the product as is or whether the transferred product becomes an input in the downstream division's own production process. When the transferred product becomes an input in the downstream division's production process, it is referred to as an **intermediate product**.

Definition

A transfer price is what one part of a company charges another part of the same company for goods or services. Transactions may include the trade of supplies or labour between departments. Transfer prices are used when individual entities of a larger multi-entity firm are treated and measured as separately run entities and is also known as "transfer cost".

Need of Transfer pricing

When product is transferred between profit centers or investment centers within a decentralized firm, transfer prices are necessary to calculate divisional profits, which can affect divisional performance evaluation. When divisional managers have the authority to decide whether to buy or sell internally or on the external market. The transfer price can determine whether managers' incentives align with the incentives of the overall company and its owners. The objective is to achieve **goal congruence** in which divisional managers will want to transfer products. Hence, maximizes consolidated corporate profits and at least one manager will refuse the transfer because transferring product is not the profit-maximizing strategy of the company.

When multinational firms transfer products across international borders, transfer prices are relevant in the calculation of income taxes and are sometimes relevant in connection with other international trade and regulatory issues. The transfer generates journal entries on the books of both divisions but usually no money changes hands. The transfer price becomes an expense for the downstream division and revenue for the upstream division.

Transfer Pricing Methods

The following are the important methods for establishing transfer prices.

1. **Market-based Transfer Prices:** Microeconomic theory shows that when divisional managers strive to maximize divisional profits, a market-based transfer price aligns their incentives with owners' incentives of maximizing overall corporate profits. The transfer will occur when it is in the best interests of shareholders and the transfer will be refused by at least one divisional manager when shareholders would prefer for the transfer not to occur. The upstream division is generally indifferent between receiving the market price from an external customer and receiving the same price from an internal customer. Consequently, the determining factor is whether the downstream division is willing to pay the market price. If the downstream division is willing to do hence, the implication of downstream division can generate incremental profits for the company by purchasing the product from the upstream division and either reselling it or using the product in its own production process. On the other hand, if the downstream division is unwilling to pay the market price the implication is that corporate profits are maximized when the upstream division sells the product on the external market, even if this leaves the downstream division idle. Sometimes there are cost savings on internal transfers compared with external sales. These savings might arise for example, the upstream division can avoid a customer credit check and collection efforts and the downstream division might avoid inspection procedures in the receiving department. Market-based transfer pricing continues to align managerial incentives with corporate goals even in the presence of these cost savings. In this case does appropriate adjustments to the transfer price, i.e., the market-based transfer price is reduced by these cost savings.

   However, many intermediate products do not have readily available market prices. Examples, a pharmaceutical company with a drug under patent protection (an effective monopoly); and an appliance company that makes component parts in the Parts Division, transfers those parts to its assembly divisions. Obviously, if there is no market price, a market-based transfer price cannot be used.

   Advantages : Actual costs are fluctuating and hence, difficult to ascertain. On the other hands market prices can be easily ascertained.

   (i) Profits resulting from market price based transfer prices are good parameters for performance evaluation of selling and buying divisions.

   (ii) It represents the basis of purchasing/selling from outside and thus, supplying division gets a fair reward.

Limitations of Market-based Pricing : Buying division generally results market price. They may question buying from the selling division if in any way they have to pay the market price?

(i) Market price is a rather vague term as such prices may be ex-factory prices, wholesale prices, retail prices etc.

(ii) Market prices may not be available for intermediate products, as these products may not have any market.

(iii) It is difficult to operate if the intermediate product is for captive consumption.

(iv) The prices for some commodities can fluctuate widely and quickly. Companies sometimes attempt to protect divisional managers from these large unpredictable price changes.

2. **Cost-based Transfer Prices:** It can also align managerial incentives with corporate goals, if various factors are properly considered. This includes the outside market opportunities for both the divisions and possible capacity constraints of the upstream division.

First, consider the case in which the upstream division sells the intermediate product to external customers as well as to the downstream division. In this situation, capacity constraints are crucial. If the upstream division has excess capacity a cost-based transfer price using the variable cost of production will align incentives. Because the upstream division is indifferent about the transfer and the downstream division will fully incorporate the company's incremental cost of making the intermediate product in its production and marketing decisions. However, senior management might want to allow the upstream division to mark-up the transfer price a little above variable cost. If the upstream division has a capacity constraint, transfers to the downstream division displace external sales. In this case, to align incentives based on the opportunity cost of these lost sales must be passed on to the downstream division, which is accomplished by setting the transfer price equal to the upstream division's external market sales price.

Next, consider the case in which there is no external market for the upstream division. If the upstream division is to be treated as a profit center, it must be allowed the opportunity to recover its full cost of production plus a reasonable profit. If the downstream division is charged the full cost of production, incentives are aligned because the downstream division will refuse the transfer under only two circumstances.

If the downstream division can source the intermediate product for a lower cost elsewhere; and second, if the downstream division cannot generate a reasonable profit on the sale of the final product when it pays the upstream division's full cost of production for the intermediate product.

If the downstream division can source the intermediate product for a lower cost elsewhere, to the extent the upstream division's full cost of production reflects its future long run average cost, the company should consider eliminating the upstream division. If the downstream division cannot generate a reasonable profit on the sale of the final product when it pays the upstream division's full cost of production for the intermediate product, the optimal corporate decision might be to close the upstream division and stop production and sale of the final product. However, if either the upstream division or the downstream division manufactures and markets multiple products, the analysis becomes more complex. Also, if the downstream division can source the intermediate product from an external supplier for a price greater than the upstream division's full cost, but less than full cost plus a reasonable profit margin for the upstream division, suboptimal decisions could result.

3. **Marginal Cost Pricing:** When the internal price is too high compared to the market price and purchasing department is free to acquire the goods from the market. If we use there will be a heavy loss to the company as the company's own production cannot be disposed off. But it will be in the interest of the company to utilize the goods produced internally to the maximum extent. Under such situation goods should be invoiced at marginal cost only excluding the fixed cost.

4. **Opportunity Cost Pricing:** It recognizes the minimum price that the selling division is ready to accept and the maximum price that the buying division is ready to pay. The final transfer price may be based on these minimum expectations of both the divisions. The most ideal situation will be when the minimum price expected by the selling division is less that the maximum price accepted by the buying division. However, it may happen very rarely and there is possibility of conflicts over the opportunity cost. It is also important to note that the fixation of transfer prices is a very delicate decision. There might be clash of interests between the selling and buying division. Hence when fixing the transfer price, overall interest of the organization should be taken into consideration. However, goal congruence should be given highest importance rather than interests of the selling or buying division alone.

   Advantages :

   1. It is based on minimum expectations of divisions concerned.
   2. It helps in providing a minimum base for pricing decisions.

   Limitations :

   1. It is illusory in nature.
   2. It is affected by conflict of interest of parties concerned.

5. **Negotiated Transfer Prices:** This method has the advantage of emulating a free market in which divisional managers buy and sell from each other in a manner that simulates arm's length transactions. However, there is no reason to assume that the outcome of these transfer price negotiations will serve the best interests of the company or shareholders. The transfer price could depend on which divisional manager is the better poker player, rather than whether the transfer results in profit-maximizing production and sourcing decisions. If divisional managers fail to reach an agreement on price, even though the transfer is in the best interests of the company, senior

management might decide to impose a transfer price. However, senior management's imposition of a transfer price defeats the motivation for using a negotiated transfer price in the first place.

Advantages :

(i) It is governed by mutuality of the part concerned.

(ii) It helps in getting a competitive price for supplies.

Limitations :

(i) A lot of time is spent by both the negotiating parties in fixation of negotiated prices.

(ii) Negotiating skills are required for the managers for arriving at a mutually acceptable price; otherwise, there is a possibility of conflicts between the divisions.

6. **Dual Transfer Price (Two Sets of Prices):** This method of transfer pricing motivates both the buying and transferring division to demand and supply of the optimal quantity of the product. The selling division is credited with one price but the buying division is charged at a different price. The difference between these two prices is made to the main account of the company and discarded when the centres' statements are consolidated.

Under a dual transfer pricing scheme, the selling price received by the upstream division differs from the purchase price paid by the downstream division. Usually, the motivation for using dual transfer pricing is to allow the selling price to exceed the purchase price, resulting in a corporate-level subsidy that encourages the divisions to participate in the transfer. In the following example, the Basle Water Company charges from a negotiated transfer price of ₹ 180 per case to a dual transfer price in which the upstream division receives the local market price of ₹ 190 per case and the downstream division pays ₹170 per case.

Advantages :

1. This method of pricing helps to avoid conflicts between the buying and selling divisions, which occurred because there was one transfer priced and the contribution of profit received varied.

2. This method helps in better assessment of the exchange value of the transferred product and performance evaluation.

Disadvantages :

1. The profits of the various centres would vary from that of the whole company.

2. This method involves additional book-keeping and where the company's main account is debited.

3. This method is misleading because it shows the different centres as making more profit than that of the whole company.

4. Outside sales may be neglected or not given that much attention, because the focus is more on internal transfers.
5. When conflict between centres are resolved by the dual method, problems that could have been due to the organizational structure overlooked by the top management.

International Transfer Pricing

There are certain business organizations engaged internationally. They have their subsidiaries or divisions in foreign countries. Most of the multinational companies generally do business with the help of their subsidiaries. These subsidiaries develop their production base in those countries where they can get their goods and services produced at minimum possible costs. Thus, to facilitate their marketing effectiveness international intra-group transfer pricing of goods moved from one country to another. MNC's are giving special consideration to transfer pricing system.

Transfer price may be set for two subsidiaries of a corporate body so as to minimize the implication of tax on their overall profits. For example, if tax rate on profit in country A is lower than in country B, the subsidiary will go down by this process. So tax on its profit will be less, whilst the profit of the latter subsidiary will be inflated and thereby it will bear a lower tax burden.

A subsidiary in a country with high import duty may try to get the goods from a sister subsidiary situated in a different country at an unduly reduced price so as to reduce the ad valorem import duty on the goods transferred. In some countries, there may be restriction on repatriation of income and dividend. Goods may be transferred to subsidiaries in these countries at more than the price otherwise settled at arm's length. If a country that hosts a subsidiary has a high rate of inflation, early repatriation of funds is done by overcharging good exported to it so that money may not be tied up in a currency that depreciates.

Transfer pricing has been assigned to play its role in international scenario. However, regulatory system of the host country should also be considered at the time of formulating transfer pricing system.

Objectives of International Intra-group Transfer Pricing : Objectives to be considered for international intra-group transfer pricing are as follows;

1. The goal congruence is the basic objective; the divisional managers must settle the transfer price between themselves.
2. The transfer price to be fixed should *prima facie* be fair to the authorities concerned. It must comply with government regulations.
3. Impact of import duty on transferred goods and direct and indirect taxes on the goods produced and sold may be sought to be reduced by fixing suitable transfer price but care should be taken not to attract rage and penalty of the government that may face from such unfair fixation of transfer price.

4. In some countries there may be restrictions in repatriation of profit. In such cases, a price may be that fixed that will be advantageous to both the home and foreign countries while not violating the relevant regulations.
5. In case of transfers between two foreign subsidiaries, they must deal with each other at arm's length to the extent possible, as the minority parties have a legal right to a fair share of their corporation's profit.
6. If the subsidiary is in a very competitive market, transfer price may be so fixed that the subsidiary can market the end product at a competitive price.
7. Joint ventures create additional complications in transfer pricing. The transfer price must satisfy both the home and foreign ventures.

Factors Affecting Multinational Prices :

1. Transfer price is a tool to solve tax implications and to be set between two subsidiaries of a holding company or two units of a corporate body in such a way to minimize the taxes, duties and tariffs on their overall profit.
2. Financial restrictions on profit repatriations are imposed by the government. Transfer price is set among two subsidiaries by over invoicing its imports. In some countries there may be restriction on repatriation of income and dividends/ profits. Goods are sought to be transferred to subsidiaries in these countries at more than the price otherwise settled at arm's length.
3. Transfer price is set among the units in such a way that general coordination between units and the implementation of appropriate procedures to ensure, as far as possible, uniformity in the classification and application of costs and divisional conflicts are reduced.
4. Overall goal congruence is the profit/income and customer satisfaction. So, Transfer price is set in such a way that overall goal congruence is achieved.
5. If a country hosting a subsidiary, has a high rate of inflation, early repatriation of fund is done by overcharging goods exported to it. However, the tax and fiscal authorities of the host countries are vigilant. They impose penalty for manipulated evasion of taxation or import duties. To safeguard the position, the taxpayer may enter into an advanced pricing agreement with the related tax authorities.

Advantages of transfer pricing :

It provides market price for goal congruence and managerial effort in competitive market under profit center concept.

1. It facilitates variable cost which is ideal when excess capacity exists for selling division.
2. It is based on the total cost. Selling division is not required to bear any loss. Fixed costs are also recovered.

Disadvantages of Transfer pricing :

1. Market prices are not always available.
2. It fails to encourage selling division for supply and does not reflect the efficiency of buying unit as material is obtained at less than market price.
3. It fails to measure the performance of selling division and difficult to understand the efficiency of buying unit as material is obtained at less than market price.

Transfer Pricing and Multinational Income Taxes

When divisions transfer product across tax jurisdictions, transfer prices play a role in the calculation of the company's income tax liability. In this situation, the company's transfer pricing policy can become a tax planning tool. The United States has agreements with most other nations that determine how multinational companies are taxed. These agreements are called bilateral tax treaties. It establishes rules for apportioning multinational corporate income among the nations in which the companies conduct business. These rules attempt to tax all multinational corporate income once and only once (excluding the double-taxation that occurs at the Federal and state levels). In other words, the tax treaties attempt to avoid the double-taxation that would occur if two nations taxed the same income. Since transfer prices represent revenue to the upstream division and an expense to the downstream division, the transfer price affects the calculation of divisional profits that represent taxable income in the nations where the divisions are based.

For example, if a U.K based pharmaceutical company manufactures a drug in a factory that it operates in India and transfers the drug to the U.K. for sale a high transfer price increases divisional income to the Indian division of the company and hence, increases the company's tax liability in India. At the same time, the high transfer price increases the cost of product to the U.K. marketing division, lowers U.K. income and lowers U.K. taxes. The company's incentives with regard to the transfer price depend on whether the marginal tax rate is higher in the U.K. or in India. If the marginal tax rate is higher in the U.K., the company prefers a high transfer price, whereas if the marginal tax rate is higher in India, the company prefers a low transfer price. The situation reverses if the drug is manufactured in the U.K. and sold in India. The general rule is that the company wants to shift income from the high tax jurisdiction to the low tax jurisdiction.

There are limits to the extent to which companies can shift income in this manner. When a market price is available for the goods transferred, the taxing authorities will usually impose the market-based transfer price. When a market-based transfer price is not feasible, U.S. tax law specifies detailed and complicated rules that limit the extent to which companies can shift income out of the United States.

Other Regulatory Issues

Transfer pricing sometimes becomes relevant in the context of other regulatory issues. It includes international trade disputes for example, when tariffs are based on the value of goods imported, the transfer price of goods shipped from a manufacturing division in one country to a marketing division in another country can form the basis for the tariff. As another example, in order to increase investment in their economies, developing nations sometimes restrict the extent to which multinational companies can repatriate profits. However, when product is transferred from manufacturing divisions located elsewhere into the developing nation for sale, the local marketing division can export funds to pay for the merchandise received. As a final example, when nations accuse foreign companies of dumping product onto their markets, transfer pricing is often involved. Dumping refers to selling product below cost and it generally violates international trade laws. Foreign companies frequently transfer products from manufacturing divisions in their home countries to marketing affiliates elsewhere, so that the determination of whether the company has dumped products depends on comparing the transfer price charged to the marketing affiliate with the upstream division's cost of production.

Solved Problems

Problem 1 :

A company is organized into two divisions. Division A produces a component which is sold to division B. Division A has no external buyer for its components. Division B assembles the component into a product to sell the same to external customers. The demand for the product is elastic to selling price. The estimate of the number of units which division B proposed to sell at different prices during the next year is as under:

No of Units of sales	Selling price per unit (Rs)
1,000	250
2,000	200
3,000	180
4,000	150
6,000	120
8,000	100

Division A has quoted a price of ₹ 80 per unit of the component on the basis of the following cost sheet:

	(Figures in ₹)
Direct Material	10
Direct Labour	20
Factory Overheads	30
Factory Cost	60
Profit	20
Transfer Price	80

The factory overhead costs are fixed. Division B incurs a variable cost of ₹ 20 on assembly of the product into finished item.

Required:

(i) Prepare a statement for each division and the company as a whole to show the profitability at each level of output.

(ii) Determine the profit of the company as a whole at the output level at which (a) Division A's profit is maximum; (b) Division B's profit is maximum.

(iii) What transfer price will ensure overall optimality of the company as a whole? Show your calculations. **(I.C.W.A. Final, Dec. 2003)**

Solution :

Statement showing profitability of Division A

Output	Sales @ Rs. 80 transfer price	Variable cost @ Rs. 30	Contribution
Units	Rs.	Rs.	Rs.
1,000	80,000	30,000	50,000
2,000	160,000	60,000	1,00,000
3,000	240,000	90,000	1,50,000
4,000	320,000	120,000	2,00,000
6,000	480,000	180,000	3,00,000
8,000	640,000	240,000	4,00,000

Statement showing Profitability of Division B

Output	Selling Price	Total Sales	Division B Variable Cost @ ₹ 20	Transfer Value from Department A @ ₹ 80	Total Variable Cost of Division B	Contribution
Units	₹	₹	₹	₹	₹	
1,000	250	2,50,000	20,000	80,000	1,00,000	1,50,000
2,000	200	4,00,000	40,000	1,60,000	2,00,000	2,00,000
3,000	180	5,40,000	60,000	2,40,000	3,00,000	2,40,000
4,000	150	6,00,000	80,000	3,20,000	4,00,000	2,00,000
6,000	120	7,20,000	1,20,000	4,80,000	6,00,000	1,20,000
8,000	100	8,00,000	1,60,000	6,40,000	8,00,000	Nil

Statement Showing Profitability of the Company as a Whole

Output	Selling Price	Total Sales	Division A Variable Cost @ ₹ 30	Transfer Value from Department B @ ₹ 20	Total Variable Cost	Contribution
Units	₹	₹	₹	₹	₹	
1,000	250	2,50,000	30,000	20,000	50,000	2,00,000
2,000	200	4,00,000	60,000	40,000	1,00,000	3,00,000
3,000	180	5,40,000	90,000	60,000	1,50,000	3,90,000
4,000	150	6,00,000	1,20,000	80,000	2,00,000	4,00,000
6,000	120	7,20,000	1,80,000	1,20,000	3,00,000	4,20,000
8,000	100	8,00,000	2,40,000	1,60,000	4,00,000	4,00,000

(i) From the Tables given above, it can be concluded that Division A's profit is maximum at 8,000 units at which level company's profit as a whole is ₹ 4,00,000.

(ii) Division B's profit is maximum at 3,000 units at which level company's profit as a whole is Rs 3, 90,000.

(iii) Transfer price at variable cost will ensure overall optimality of the company as a whole. When transfer price for transfer of a component from division A to division B is at ₹ 30 (i.e. variable cost), optimum profit of the company will be ₹ 4,20,000 at output of 6,000 units as is visible from Table (iii).

Problem 2 :

Department X of Universal Ltd manufactures a single product which it sells to other departments of Universal Ltd at Rs 50 per unit and to outside buyers at Rs 60 per unit. Cost of sales for products manufactures for inter-departmental sales is Rs 42 per unit and for sales outside the company Rs 50 per unit. The fixed costs of Department X are Rs 4, 00,000 per annum and these are allocated at the rate of Rs 10 per unit over normal production of 40,000 units

Department Y normally purchases 10,000 units annually from department X. However, during the current year, an outside supplier has offered to sell similar products to department Y at Rs 40 per unit. The manager of this department has an inclination to purchase from outside to save costs. However, the manager of Department X argues that if his department loses the order of 10,000 units from Department Y, he will be able to sell only 2,000 units of these units outside at current prices and the remaining 8,000 units will be unmarketable resulting in a loss. Department Y replies by saying that his Department will save Rs 10 per unit on 10,000 units by purchasing outside. You are required to prepare a report advising the management of Universal Limited on the following questions.

1. Should Department Y be permitted to buy from the outside supplier?
2. If Department X sold 10,000 units to Department Y at ₹ 40 per unit, what would be the net effect of this change on (a) Department X; (b) Department Y; and (c) Universal Ltd?

3. If it is possible for Department X to effect some saving in its fixed costs of ₹ 4,00,000 per annum as a result of fall in production, would this affect your advice under (1)? **[M.Com, June 1984]**

Solution :

1. Contribution from Department X – A Comparative Statement

Particulars	If Department Y is not permitted to buy from Outside Supplier (₹)			If Y is Permitted to but from Outsider (₹)
	Sales Y	Sales in open Market	Total	
Sales Revenue (10,000 Units at ₹ 50;30,000 units at ₹ 60 and 32,000 units at ₹ 60	5,00,000	18,00,000	23,00,000	19,20,000
Less: Variable Cost (at ₹ 32 and ₹ 40)	3,20,000	12,00,000	15,20,000	12,80,000
Contribution	1,80,000	6,00,000	7,80,000	6,40,000
Less : Fixed Cost		4,00,000	4,00,000	
Profit			3,80,000	2,40,000

Assumed that the unit cost figures given in the problem include fixed cost of Rs 10 per unit.

1. If department Y is allowed to obtain its requirement from the outside supplier at ₹ 40 per unit and if department X is able to sell an additional 2,000 units (totaling 32,000 units) at ₹ 60 per unit to outside buyers, it will have the following effects.
   a. Contribution from Department X to the Company (i.e, Universal Ltd) reduces by ₹ 1.40,000 resulting in the reduction in the profit of the Company by ₹ 1,40,000;
   b. Department Y is able to contribute ₹ 1,00,000 more (ie equivalent to saying in the purchase = 10,000 units × ₹ 10) and it, therefore, increases the profit of the company by ₹ 1,00,000 and
   c. Consequent to the above, the company reports ₹ 40,000 lower profit that what it otherwise would have reported.
   d. In the light of the above, it is advisable not to permit Department Y to buy from outside supplier.

Problem 3 :

A company has two divisions, A and B. Division A manufactures a component which is used by Divison B to produce a finished product. For the next period, output and costs have been budgeted as follows

	Division A	Division B
Component Units	50,000	-
Finished Units	-	50,000
Total Variable Costs	2,50,000	6,00,000
Fixed Costs	1,50,000	2,00,000

The fixed costs are separable for each division. You are required to advise on the transfer price to be fixed for Davison A's component under the following circumstances:

1. Division A can sell the component in a competitive market for ₹ 10 per unit Division B can also purchase the component from the open market at that price.
2. As per the situation described in (1) above, and further assuming that Division B currently buys the component from an external supplier at the market price of ₹ 10 and there is reciprocal agreement between the external supplier and another Division C, with the group, Under this agreement, the external supplier agrees to buy one product unit from Division C, at a profit of ₹ 4 per unit to that division, for every component which Division B buys from the supplier.

Solution :

1. Transfer Price = Incremental(marginal) cost + opportunity costs of the company

   Due to not being able to use the components in the next most profitable way.

   = ₹5 + ₹ 5 (Contribution foregone by transferring internally as opposed to selling in the open market)

The transfer price of ₹ 10 is equal to the market price of the component which is also ₹ 10.

2. Transfer Price = Marginal Cost + Contribution + Profit foregone by Division Case Division B will acquire its units from Divison A in place of External supplier.

   = ₹ 5 + ₹ 5 + 4

   = ₹ 5 + ₹ 9 (₹ 9 is the opportunity cost to the whole company)

   = ₹ 14.

The transfer price of ₹ 14 should result in the manager of Division B continuing to buy from the external supplier at the market price of ₹ 10. However, the transfer price of ₹ 14 is appropriate from the viewpoint of the organization as a whole, since if the component is transferred internally, not only will Division A forego and external profit of ₹ 5, but Division C will also foregon an external profit of ₹ 4. It is assumed that Division C Could not achieve the same profit by selling elsewhere.

Problem 4 :

A company has two divisions, A and B. The division A is currently operating at full capacity. It has been asked to supply its product to divisions B. Division A sells its product to its regular customers for ₹ 30 each. Division B (Currently operating at 50 % capacity) is willing to pay ₹ 20 each for the component produced by division A(this represents the full absorption cost per component at division A)

The component will be used by Division B in supplementing its main product to conform to the need of special order.

As per the contract terms of sales, the buyer calls for reimbursement of full cost to Division B plus 10 %

Division A has a variable cost of ₹ 17 per component. The cost per unit of division B subsequent to the buying part from Division A is estimated as follows.

Purchased Parts - Outside Vendors	₹ 90
Purchased Parts - Division A	₹ 20
Other Variable Costs	₹ 50
Fixed Overheads and Administration	₹ 40
	₹ 200

The company uses return on investment in the measurement of division and the division manager's performance.

(a) As manager of Division A, would you recommend sales of your output of Division B at the stipulated price of ₹ 20?

(b) Would it be in the overall interest of the company for division A to sell its output to Divison B?

(c) Suggest an alternative transfer price and show how could it lead to goal congruence?

Solution :

(a) As manager of Division A, sales or ₹ 20 per unit to Division B should not be recommended. The division is already operating at its full capacity and the market is presumably absorbing all its output at ₹ 30 per unit. The internal transfer made to Division B, hence, would reduce its profits (by ₹ 10 per unit) as well as the ROI.

(b) Decision analysis (whether to transfer part from Division A to Division B at ₹ 20 per unit or not)

Particulars	Sold Externally (₹)	Transferred to Division B (₹)
Sale Price (Division A)	30.0	220.0
Sale price (Division B) (₹ 200 +10%)		
Less: relevant on incremental cost:		
For part of Division A	17.0	17.0
Purchased parts from outside	-	90.0
Other valuable costs	-	50.0
Profit per unit	13.0	63.0

It will be in the overall interest of the company that the transfer takes place as it would increase the firm's profit by ₹ 50 per unit.

(c) Dual price basis of effecting transfer is the most appropriate. In this case, the relevant transfer price will be ₹ 30 (sale) so far as Division A is concerned and ₹ 20 (purchase) so far as Division B is concerned. It will keep the profits of Division A unaffected and will facilitate the utilization of idle capacity of Division B and also increases its profit.

Sale price (₹ 210 + 10%)	₹ 231
Less: Costs (₹ 90 + 50)	₹ 140
	91

Problem 5 :

A company has two divisions, A and B. Division A manufactures a component which is used by Division B to produce a finished product. For the next period, output and costs have been budgeted as follows.

Particulars	Division A	Division B
Component units	50,000	---
Finished Units	---	50,000
Total Variable Costs - Rupees	2,50,000	6,00,000
Fixed Costs Rupees	1,50,000	2,00,000

The fixed costs are separable for each division. You are required to advise on the transfer price to be fixed for Division A's component under the following circumstances.

A. Division A can sell the component in a competitive market for ₹ 10 per unit. Division B can also purchase the component from the open market at that price.

B. As per the situation mentioned in (A) above, and further assume that division B currently buys the component from an external supplier at the market price of

₹ 10 and there is reciprocal agreement between the external supplier and another Division C, within the same group. Under this agreement, the external supplier agrees to buy one product unit from Division C at a profit of ₹ 4 per unit to that division, for every component which Division B buys from the Sup

(ICWA, Final, Dec, 2005)

Solution :

Transfer price decisions can be taken o the following basis.

A. Transfer Price: Marginal Cost + Opportunity Cost i.e., ₹ 5 + ₹ 5 = ₹ 10

Note : Marginal Cost = Rs 2,5000/50,000 units = ₹ 5

Opportunity Cost ₹ 5 is computed on the basis that the Division A will sacrifice ₹ 5 if they sell the product to Division B.

B. In this situation, the transfer price will be worked out as under,

Transfer Price = Marginal Cost + Contribution + Profit foregone by Division C ₹ 5 + ₹ 5 + ₹ 4 = ₹ 14

In situation (b), if Division B purchases from Division A, it will not purchase from external supplier. Hence, the supplier will stop purchasing from Division C, which will result in a loss of profit to Division C @ ₹ 4 per unit, and therefore this amount will be recovered from the transfer price.

Problem 6 :

A company fixes the inter-divisional transfer prices for its products on the basis of cost plus an estimated return on investment in its division. The relevant portion of the budget for the Division A for the year 2010 -11 is given below :

Fixed Assets	₹ 5,00,000
Current Assets (Other than debtors)	3,00,000
Debtors	2,00,000
Annual fixed cost of the division	2,00,000
Variable cost per unit of product	8,00,000
Budgeted volume of production per year (units)	10
Desired return on investment	4,00,000
You are required to determine the transfer price for the Division A	28%

You are required to determine the transfer price for the Division A.

(ICWA, Inter, June 2006)

Solution :

Statement showing the Transfer Price for the Division A

Fixed Assets		₹ 5,00,000
Working Capital - Current Assets	₹ 3,00,000	
Debtors	₹ 2,00,000	5,00,000
Total Investment		10,00,000
Desired rate of return		28%
Total return (ie, profit) ₹ 10,00,000 x 28 % =		2,80,000
Budgeted production p.a. (units)		4,00,000
Return per unit		Re. 0.70
Variable cost per unit		10.00
Fixed cost per unit (₹ 8,00,000/4,00,000)		2.00
Transfer price for Division A		12.70

- As the transfer price is based on cost plus estimated return in investment, it is necessary to first determine the investment in fixed assets and working capital.

Problem 7 :

When goods are passed between divisions of an organisation, central transfer price policy is needed so that no sub optimal or dysfunctional results ensure one way to attain this.

Objective is to aim at the same contribution margin ratio (P/V ratio) on the goods subject to internal transfer for both the transferor division and the transferee division "

The Managing Director of Fairdeal Limited has just attended a lecture on Transfer Pricing in a seminar organized by ICWAI. The above is a quote from the said lecture.

Fairdeal has two divisons. Wholesale (W), and Retail ®. As per the existing rule, W sells its products @ ₹ 150 per tone in the external market but supplies identical product @ ₹ 90 per tone to R, R uses the transferred material as captive consumption and produces finished goods in the ratio of 1 tonne input: 100 pieces of output. R sells all its output in the external environment. W insists that R be charged at market price, to which R does not agree.

The MD of Fairdeal Ltd. Requests you to find the transfer price of the goods that his wholesale divison supplies to the Retail division, conforming to the principle laid out in the above quote.

For your information the Accountant of Fairdeal Ltd. Furnishes you with an estimated Profit statement of the company as under:

Estimated Profit Statemetn of Fairdeal Ltd. For the current quarter (July – Sept '10)

	Wholesale division ₹ 000	Retail division ₹ 000	Company ₹ 000
External sale 1,200t @ ₹ 150	180	-	180
1,20,000 pcs @ ₹ 2.67	-	320	320
internal transfer 1,200 t. @ ₹ 90	108	108	
Variable cost 2,400t @ ₹ 58.33	140	-	140
1,20,000 pcs @ Re. 0.50	-	60	60
Fixed Costs	100	40	140
Profit	48	112	160

Note : Your answer should (i) highlight the need for a change in the ruling transfer price and (ii) show that the suggested transfer price meets the MD's requirement.

(ICWA, Final June 2006)

Solution :

As per the projected profit statement for the quarter ended 30 Sept '06 the contribution margin (P/V) ratios are :

	Wholesale division	Retail division	Company
	₹ 000	₹ 000	₹ 000
External sales	180	320	500
Variable cost of external sales			
At W	70	70	140
At R	-	60	60
Contribution	110	190	300
P/V or Contribution margin ratio	61.10%	59.40%	60%

Comments : The difference in P/V ratio between W and R has to be borne as the products are different with different market prices. Obviously, the divisional managers admit this fact. The bone of contention is then the ruling transfer price which is 60 % of current market price. So, the MD wants to fix the transfer price on a reasonable basis. He wants that the P/V ratios on internal transferred material are same for both W and R.

(i) Let the value of transferred material for the quarter ended 30 Sep'06 be ₹ T ('000). Then, for W the P/V ratio is { (T-70)/T x 100 % and for R the P/V ratio is { 320 – T- 60)/320 } x 100 %. These two ratios should be equal.

i.e., $(T - 70)/T = (320 - T - 60) / 320$

or $T^2 + 60T - 22{,}400 = 0$

Where, T = 122.6 or – 182.6 (using the quadratic equation):

T = {- b± v (b^2 - 4ac)} / 2a}]

Since T = (transferred value) cannot be negative.

T = ₹ 1, 22,600

To required transfer price is ₹ 1,22,600 / 1,200 t = ₹ 102.17 per tone.

P/V Ratio on internal transfer :

With projected transfer price (₹ In ₹ 000) with suggested (required) transfer price of

Rs 90 per tone				₹ 102.17 per tone			
Sales	-	320	320	Sales	-	320	320
Transfer	108	108	-	Transfer	122.6	122.6	-
Var. cost	70	60	130	Var.Cost	70	60	130
Contbn.	38	152	190	Contbn.	52.6	137.4	190
P/V %	35.20%	47.50%	59.40%	P/V %	42.90%	42.90%	59.40%

It is seen that the difference in P/V ratios between W and R is gone with the introduction of the suggested (as required by MD) transfer price. This change will do away wit the grievance of the divisional managers but will not affect the overall PV ratio of the company.

Problem 8 :

Metflow Division is a part of the AKG Group, requires units of the product available from Metflow as input to a product which will be sold outside the group. Akali Division's requirements are equal to 40 % of Metflow Division's Production capacity.

Akali division has a potential source of supply from outside the AKG Group. This outside supplier can supply 75 % of Akali Divison's requirements. The outside Source may wish to quote a higher price if Akali Divison only intends to take up part of its product availability.

Required :

Discuss the aspects of transfer pricing principles and information availability which will affect the likely achievement of group profit maximization from the sourcing decision made by Akali Division in the above Situation.

(ICWA, Final, Dec. 2006)

Solution :

The Metflow Division - AKG Division situation may be studied from a number of View points :

(i) Where Metflow Division has an external market for its product (80 % of its capacity), the transfer price (tp) should be set at market price in order to comply with the general rule;

Tp = marginal cost + opportunity cost to the supply division

In this way, an external supply available to Akali Division at less than the market price of Metflow Division's product will increase group profit.

(ii) Inter-divisional transfers may be effected with less packing costs and less delivery costs (say, using group vehicles). In this case the opportunity foregone by the group must be adjusted by the external costs that have been avoided. In this way, Metflow Division will earn the same profit as from external sales and Akali division will reject supplier quotes which are in excess of the adjusted market price quoted by Metflow Division.

(iii) For the 20 % spare capacity, it appears Metflow Division has no external market. So, the opportunity cost is zero. Metflow division can offer the product to Akali Division must be rejected in this case.

(iv) The question states that the external supplier can supply 75% of Akali Division's requirement. This is equivalent to 30 % of the capacity of the Metflow. Since Metflow divisions spare capacity is only 20 %, the balance 10 % must be outsource, by Akali division. The price of this balance quantity should not exceed the market price of Metflow Division's external sales.

It will be useful for Metflow Division to indicate the quantities which it is willing supply at different prices. *viz.*, 20% capacity at marginal cost and 10% capacity at adjusted market price. In this way Akali Divisions can evaluate this offer from the external source taking into account the probability the external source may require a higher price for a part order.

Problem 9 :

Novelty Ltd. has two divisions - division DA and division DB. Division DA is currently operating at full capacity. It has been asked to supply its product to division DB. Division DA sells its Product to its regular customer for ₹ 60 each. Division DB. Currently operating at 50 per cent capacity, is willing to pay ₹ 40 each for the component produced by Division DA (this represents the full absorption cost per component at division DA). The components will be used by division DB in supplementing its main product to conform to the need of special order. As per the Contract terms of sale. The buyer calls for reimbursement of full cost to division DB, plus 10 %

Division DA has a variable cost of ₹ 34 per component. The cost per unit of division DB subsequent to the buying part fro division DA is estimated as follows:

Purchased parts - outside vendors	180
Purchased component from division DA	40
Other variable costs	100
Fixed overheads including administration	80
	400

The company uses the return on investment (ROI) in the measurement of divisional and Division manager's performance.

Required :

(i) As manager of division DA would you recommend sales of your product to division DB at the stipulated of ₹ 40 ?

(ii) Would it be in the overall interest of the company for division DA to sell its product to division DB.

(iii) Suggest an alternative transfer price and show how could lead to goal congruence.

(ICWA, Inter, June 2005)

Solution :

(i) A Manager of Division DA. I would not recommend sales at ₹ 40 per unit to Division DB. Division – DA is already operating at its full capacity and the market is presumably absorbing all its products (output) at ₹ 60 per unit. The internal transfer made in Division DB, hence, would reduce its profit (by ₹ 60 – Rs 40 = 20 per unit) as well as the Return on Investment (ROI).

(ii) Decision Analysis:

Whether to transfer component from DA to DB at ₹ 40 per unit or not.

Particulars	Sold Externally	Transferred to divisions DB
Sale price (Division - DA)	60.00	
Sale price (Division - DB)		440.00
(Rs. 400 + 10%)		
Less: Relevant/ Incremental cost		
For component of Division DA	34.00	34.00
Purchased parts from		180.00
Other variable cost		100.00
Profit per unit	26.00	126.00

Decision :

Yes, it will be in the overall interest of the Company that the transfer takes place, as it would augment the company's profit by ₹ 100 per unit.

(iii) Dual price basis of effecting transfer is the most appropriate. This will enhance co – operation between divisions, prevent sub-optimization by Managers, encourage the transferring Division to maximize income and provide the purchasing Division with cost information

In this case, the relevant transfer price will be ₹ 60.00 (sale) so far as Division – DA is concerned and ₹ 40 (purchase) so far as Division DB is concerned. It will keep the profits of division unaffected and will facilitate the utilization of the idle capacity of Division – DB as also increase profit.

	₹
Sale Price (₹ 420 + 10 percent)	462.00
Less: Cost (₹ 180 + ₹ 60 + ₹ 100)	340.00
	122.00

Problem 10 :

A companies has two divisions, Division A and Division B. Division A has a budget of selling 20,000 number of a particular component X to fetch a return of 20 % on the average assets employed. The following particulars of Division A are also known.

Particulars	Amount in Rupees
Fixed cost	5,00,000
Variable Cost	Rs. 1 per unit
Average Assets – Debtors	2,00,000
Inventories	5,00,000
Plant	5,00,000

However there is a constraint in marketing and only 1,50,000 units of the component X can be directly sold to the market at the proposed price.

It has been gathered that Division B can take up the balance 50,000 units of component X. A wants a price of ₹ 4 per unit but B is prepared to pay ₹ 2 per unit of X.

Division A has another option on hand, which is to produce only 1, 50,000 units of component X. A wants a price of ₹ 4 per unit but B is prepared to pay ₹ 2 per unit of X

Division A has another option on hand, which is to produce only 1, 50,000 units of component X. this will reduce the holding of assets by ₹ 2,00,000 and fixed overheads by ₹ 25,000

You are required to advise the most profitable division.

(ICWA, Final, Dec 2004)

Solution :

For arriving at the solution, we will have to find out the amount of desired profit and the sales value of product X along with the selling price per unit. The following working notes are required for this.

Working Note "I – Amount of desired profit = 20 % of average assets employed

Average Assets Employed = Debtors + investories + plan and Equipments

= Rs 2, 00,000 + 5, 00,000 + 5, 00,000 = ₹ 12, 00,000

Desired Profit – 20 % of average assets ie of ₹ 12, 00,000 = ₹ 2, 40,000

Working Note – II

Particulars	Amount in Rupees
Fixed cost	5,00,000
Variable Cost	2,00,000 [2,00,000 units @ Re. 1 per unit]
Profit (As per working Note No. 1)	2,40,000
Total Sales	9,40,000

Selling price Per Unit = ₹ 9, 40,000 / 2, 00,000 units = ₹ 4.70 per unit

Now, we will evaluate the two options available to division A. the first option to sell 1,50,000 units of the product @ ₹ 4.70 to outsiders and 50,000 units to Division B @ ₹ 2 the second option is to produce and sell only 1,50,000 units to Division B@ ₹ 2. The Second option is to produce and sell only 1, 50,000 units to outsiders @ ₹ 4.70 per unit. The statement of evaluation is prepared is given below.

Particulars	Option I - Amount in Rupees	Option II - Amount in Rupees
Sales - 1,50,000 units @ ₹ 4.70 per unit	7,05,000	7,05,000
Transfer to Division B 50,000 units @ ₹ 2 per unit	1,00,000	
Total Sales	5,05,000	7,05,000
Variable Overheads	2,00,000	1,50,000
Contribution Margin [Sales - variables overheads]		
Less: Fixed Cost	5,00,000	4,75,000
Profit	1,05,000	80,000
Capital Employed	12,00,000	10,00,000
Retun on Capital Employed	1,05,000 / 12,00,000 x 100 = 8.75%	80,000 / 10,00,000 x 100 = 8%

Observation – From the above calculation it is clear that the Option I results into 8.75% rate of return while option II results into 8 % return on Capital Employed. Hence, Option I is recommended.

Problem 11 :

XYZ Ltd which has a system of assessment of Divisional Performance on the basis of residual income has two Divisions, Alfa and Beta. Alfa has annual capacity to manufacture 15,00,000 numbers of a special component that it sells to outside customers, but has idle capacity. The budgeted residual income of Beta is ₹ 120,00,000 while that of Alfa is ₹ 100,00,000. Other relevant details extracted from the budget of Alfa for the current years were as follows.

Particulars	Details
Sale(Outside customers)	12,00,000 units @ ₹ 180 per unit
Variable cost per unit	₹ 160
Divisional fixed cost	₹ 80,00,000
Capital employed	₹ 750,00,000
Cost of Capital	12%

Beta has just received a special order for which it requires components similar to the ones made by – Alfa. Fully aware of the idle capacity of Alfa, Beta has asked Alfa to quote for manufacture and supply of 3, 00,000 numbers of the components with a slight modification during final processing. Alfa and Beta agree that this will involve an extra variable cost of ₹ 5 per unit.

You are required to calculate,

I. Calculate the transfer price which Alia should quote to Beta to achieve its budgeted residual income.

II. Also indicate the circumstances in which the proposed transfer price may result in a sub optimal decision for the company as a whole.

(ICWA, Final, June, 2003)

Solution :

We will have to prepare a statement showing details of cost and income desired as shown below.

Division - Alfa

Particulars	Amount in Rupees
Fixed Cost	80,00,000
Return on Capital Employed	12% of 750,00,000 = 90,00,000
Residual income desired	100,00,000
Total	270,00,000

Contribution per unit = ₹ 180 [Selling Price per unit] – ₹ 160 [Variable cost]

= ₹ 20

Total desired contribution = 12,00,000 units X ₹ 20 per unit = ₹ 240,00,000

Minimum contribution to be earned from additional 3,00,000 units

= ₹ 270 lakhs - ₹ 240

Lakhs = ₹ 30 lakhs.

Contribution per unit Rs: 30,00,000/3,00,000 = ₹ 10 per unit

Additional variable cost for modification = ₹ 5 per unit.

Hence, the minimum transfer price per unit = ₹ 160 + ₹ 10 + ₹ 5 = ₹ 175 per unit.

If Beta can buy from outside at less than the variable cost of manufacture. Ie ₹ 165 then only the decision to transfer at a price of ₹ 175 will be suboptimal for the group as a whole.

Problem 12 :

Transfer Ltd. have two processes – preparing and finishing. The normal output per week is 7,500 units [completed] at a capacity of 75 %

Transferee Ltd. had production problems in preparing and require 2,000 units per week of prepared material for their finishing process.

The existing cost structure of one prepared unit of Transferor Ltd. at the existing capacity is as follows.

Material: ₹ 2.00 [Variable 100 %]

Labour: ₹ 2.00 [Variable 50 %]

Overheads: ₹ 4.00 [variable 25 %]

The sale price of a completed unit of Transferor Ltd. is ₹ 16 with a profit of ₹ 4 per unit.

Contrast the effect on the profits of Transferor Ltd. for 6 montsh [25 weeks] of supplying units to Transferor Ltd. with the following alternatives transfer prices per unit.

I] Marginal Cost II] Marginal Cost + 25 % III] Marginal Cost + 15 % return on capital employed. [Assume capital employed ₹ 20 lakhs] IV] Existing Cost V] Existing cost + a portion of profit on the basis of preparing cost/ total cost X unit profit. VI] At an agreed market price of ₹ 8.50

Assume no increase in the fixed costs. **(ICWA, Final, Dec. 2004)**

Solution :

The existing normal output of Transferor Ltd. is 7,500 units per week or 1,87,500 units for 6 month [25 weeks] the rate of profit is ₹ 4 per unit. Thus the total profit for 6 months will be ₹ 4 × 1,87,500 units = ₹ 7,50,000. The impact on profit under various alternatives is as follows.

(i) Marginal cost ₹ 4 per unit [material ₹ 2 + Labour Re. 1 + Overhead Re. 1] if output is transferred at ₹ 4, there will be no change in the profits.

(ii) Marginal Cost + 25% = ₹ 4 + Re. 1 = ₹ 5 Extra profit = ₹ 5 – ₹ 4 = ₹ 1 per unit. Number of units required by Transferee Ltd. = 2,000 units per week or 50,000 units in 25 weeks, Extra profit earned = 50,000 x Re. 1 = ₹ 50,000

(iii) Marginal Cost + 15% return on capital = ₹ 4.J.15 % p.a. of ₹ 20 lakhs. Extra Profits = 15/100 x 20,00, () Q x 6/12 = ₹ 1,50,000

(iv) Existing cost = marginal + fixed = ₹ 8 per unit. Existing profit = ₹ 4 per unit [excluding selling and distribution expenses overheads which are not given directly in the examples] At existing cost, the profit is ₹ 4 per unit, hence total profit = ₹ 4 x 50,000 units = ₹ 2,00,000

(v) Existing cost + portion of profit on the basis of preparing cost/total cost x unit profit ₹ 8/12 x ₹ 4 = ₹ 2.67 Existing cost ₹ 8 + ₹ 2.67 = ₹ 10.67 – existing marginal cost ₹ 4 = profit per unit = ₹ 6.67, Total profit = 50,000 x Rs 6.67 = ₹ 3,33,500.

(vi) Agreed market price = ₹ 8.50 – existing marginal cost ₹ 4.00 = ₹ 4.50 profit per unit Total profit = 50,000 units x ₹ 4.50 = ₹ 2,25,000

Problem 13 :

A company is organized into two divisions namely A and B. A produces three products, K, L and M. the relevant data per unit is given below.

Particulars	K	L	M
	Rs.	Rs.	Rs.
Market price	120	115	100
Variable costs	84	60	70
Direct labour hours	4	5	3
Maximum sales potential - units	1600	1000	600

Division B has a demand for 600 units of product L for its use. If division A cannot supply the requirements, division B can buy a similar product from market at ₹ 112 per – unit. What should be the transfer price of 600 units of L for division B, if the total direct labour hours available in division A are restricted to 15,000.

(ICWA, Final, Dec. 2002)

Solution :

Statement showing contribution per direct labour hour

Particulars	K	L	M
	₹	₹	₹
Market price	120	115	100
Variable cost	84	60	70
Contribution	36	55	30
Direct labour hours	4	5	3
Contribution per direct labour hours	9	11	10
Ranking	III	I	II

Statement showing utilization of labour hours

Product	Hours per unit	Max. sales / Production	Hours used	Balance hours
L	5	1000	5000	100000
M	3	600	1800	8200
K	4	1600	6400	1800

Transfer price of 600 units of L for division B

Balance hours available = 1,800 hours [15,000 – 13,200]

Hour per unit of product L = 5 hours

Number of units of L = 1,800 / 5 = 360 units

360 units of L can be produced by utilizing balance hours and this means that balance 240 units of product L will have to be transferred to B from existing production. Thus, there will be foregoing of contribution.

360 units of L can be produced by utilizing balance hours and this means that balance 240 units of product L will have to be transferred to B from exiting production. Thus, there will be foregoing of contribution.

As per the statement number one, contribution per hour for K is the lowest. Thus, 240 units of L can be produced by foregoing contribution on K.

Opportunity cost per hour [product K) = ₹ 9

Hours per unit of L = 5

Hence opportunity cost ₹ 9 x 5 = ₹ 45.

Thus price for 240 units = ₹ 60 + ₹ 45[opportunity cost]

= ₹ 105 Price for 360 units = ₹ 60

Transfer price for 600 units = [₹ 105 x 240 + ₹ 60 x 360]/ 600 = ₹ 78 per unit

Problem 14 :

A Co. has two divisions viz, Processing and Refining, Processing division produces 500 tonnes of product M from 1000 tonnes of a raw material per month. Refining Division produces 300 tonnes of product FM from 500 tonnes of M received from the processing Division. The cost data are:

Processing Division:

Raw materials	₹ 120 per tonne of input
Variable costs	₹ 80 per tonne of output
Fixed Costs	₹ 50,000 per month

Refining Division:

Variable costs ₹ 30 per tonne of output

Fixed costs ₹ 21,000 per month

The market price of product M is ₹ 500 per tonne and of product FM is ₹ 1,200 per tonne. Required:

(i) Compute the overall profit of the company for the month.

(ii) Compute the profit of each Division based on the following pricing methods;

(a) 200 % of variable costs of processing Division for M

(b) Market price of M

(iii) Which method will you recommend and why? **(ICWA , Final, Dec. 2000)**

Solution :

Processing Division	₹	Output of M = 500 t Cost/t ₹
Raw Material 1000 x 120	12,000	
Processing variable cost 500 x 80	40,000	
Total Variable Cost	1,60,000	320
Fixed Costs	50,000	
Total cost of processing	2,10,000	420

(i) Overall Profit of the Company:		₹	₹
Sales 300 x 1200			360,000
Processing Division cost transferred		120,000	
Refining Division:			
Variable cost 300 x 30	9,000		
Fixed Cost	21,000	30,000	240,000

(ii) Profit of each division :

Processing Division:	200% of variable Cost of Processing ₹	Market Price ₹
Selling price	640	500
Sale price	320,000	250,000
Sale of 500t	210,000	210,000
Costs	110,000	40,000
Profit		
Refining division	1,200	1,200
Selling price	360,000	360,000
Sale of 300t	320,000	250,000
Transfer price	30,000	30,000
Costs of Refining	10,000	80,000
Profit		

(iii) the transfer price based on 200 % of variable cost is ₹ 640 p.t while the market price is ₹ 500. If the division are organized into profit centres, the Refining Division is tempted to buy from the outside market.

If the processing Division has no alternative use for its capacity, its fixed costs of ₹ 50,000 will remain unrecovered. So, charging a price for the captive goods higher than the market price will be dysfunctional.

When market price method is used, Processing Division will be encouraged to reduce its costs to improve contribution. The Refining Division will also be encouraged to make the product competitive Assuming there is idle capacity in each Division, with the transfer price matching with the market price, both the Divisions will be eager to reap the benefit of larger scale of production. Individual Division's profits will increase and so will the corporate profit.

OBJECTIVE TYPE QUESTIONS

1. Transfer pricing is concerned with:
   (a) Inter-organizational transfer
   (b) Intra divisions of an organization
   (c) One multinational to another multinational
   (d) None of these.
2. Transfer pricing laid stress on
   (a) Maximum utilization of plant capacity
   (b) Optimum utilization of plant capacity
   (c) Average utilization of plant capacity
   (d) Excess utilization of plant capacity
3. Popular method of Transfer pricing is the
   (a) Cost-based pricing
   (b) Market-based pricing
   (c) Negotiated pricing
   (d) Opportunity cost pricing
4. Full cost plus is concerned with:
   (a) Cost-based pricing
   (b) Market-based pricing
   (c) Standard Costing
   (d) Marginal Cost pricing
5. Division under transfer pricing system is treated as :
   (a) Cost centre
   (b) Investment Centre
   (c) Profit Centre
   (d) None of these

Ans : 1. (b), 2. (b) , 3 (b), 4 (a), 5(c)

SHORT ANSWER QUESTIONS

1. What is transfer pricing ?
2. What do you mean by cost-based pricing?
3. What is negotiated pricing?

4. What do you understand by market-based pricing?
5. What do you mean by opportunity cost pricing?

LONG ANSWER QUESTIONS

1. What is Transfer price? Evaluate the importance of transfer pricing system.
2. What do you mean by Transfer Pricing? Examine its advantages and limitations.
3. Discuss the features and objectives of transfer pricing. Also examine the problem involved in it.
4. Discuss the nature of transfer pricing. Also examine the objectives to be kept in mind while setting transfer pricing by multinationals.
5. What do you understand by Transfer pricing? What are the objectives of the same?
6. Explain various methods of fixation of Transfer Prices'

EXERCISE PROBLEMS

1. The following information relates to budgeted operations of Division X of a manufacturing company.

Particulars	Amount in ₹
Sales - 50,000 units @ Rest. 8	4,00,000
Less: Variable Costs @ Rest. 6 per unit	3,00,000
Contribution margin	1,00,000
Less: fixed Costs	75,000
Divisional profits	25,000

The amount of divisional investment is ₹ 1,50,000 and the minimum desired rate of return on the investment is the cost of capital of 20 %

Calculate (i) Divisional expected ROI and (ii) Divisional expected RI

2. A large company is organized into several manufacturing divisions. The policy of the company is to allow the divisional managers to choose their sources of suppy and when buying from or selling to sister divisions, to negotiate the prices just as they will for outside purchases or sales.

Division X buys all of its requirements of its raw materials R from Divison Y. the full manufacturing cost of R for Division Y is ₹ 88 per kg at normal volume. Till recently Division Y was willing to supply R to Divison X at a transfer price of ₹ 80 per kg. the incremental cost of R for Division Y is ₹ 76 per kg. Since Division Y is now operating at its full capacity, it is unable to meet the outside Customers demand for R at its market price of Rs 100 per kg Division Y therefore threatened to cut off supplies to Division x unless the latter agrees to pay the market price for R.

Division X is resisting the pressure because its budget based on the consumption of 1,00,000 kg per month at a price of ₹ 80 per kg is expected to yield a profit of ₹ 25,00,000 per months and so a price increase to ₹ 100 per kg will bring the division close to break -even point.

Division X has even found an outside source for a substitute material at price of ₹ 95 per kg Although the substitute material is slightly different from R, it would meet the needs of Division X. Alternatively; Division X is prepared to pay Division Y even the manufacturing cost of ₹88 per kg.

Required :

1. Using each of the transfer price of ₹ 80 , Rs 88, ₹ 95 and ₹ 100 who with supporting calculations, the financial results as projected by the manager of Division X and Manager of Division of Y and the company.

2. Comment on the effect of each transfer price on the performance of th managers of Division X and Division Y.

3. If you were to make a decision in the matter without regard to the views of the divisional managers, where should Division X obtain its raw materials from and at what price?

3. A Company fixes the inter-divisional transfer prices for its products on the bais of cost plus an estimated return on investment in its divisions. The relevant portion of the budget for the Division A for the year 2010-11 is given below.

Particulars	Amount in ₹
Fixed Assets	5,00,000
Current Assets (other than debtors)	3,00,000
Debtors	2,00,000
Annual fixed cost for the division	8,00,000
Variable cost per unit of product	10
Budgeted volume of production ear (units)	4,00,000
Desired Return on Investment	28%

You are required to determine the transfer price for Division A.

Contribution from Department X to the Company (i.e, Universal Ltd) reduces by ₹ 1,40,000 resulting in the reduction in the profit of the Company by ₹ 1,40,000;

Department Y is able to contribute Rs 1,00,000 more (i.e., equivalent to saying in the purchase = 10,000 units × ₹ 10) and it, therefore, increases the profit of the company by ₹ 1,00,000 and

Consequent to the above, the company reports ₹ 40,000 lower profit that what it otherwise would have reported.

In the light of the above, it is advisable not to permit Department Y to buy from outside supplier.

❖ ❖ ❖

Chapter - 10
Activity-based Costing

Introduction

The main objective of any costing system is to determine scientifically the cost of a product or service. For facilitating the calculation the costs are divided into direct and indirect. Direct costs are the costs which are traceable to the products/services offered. On the other hand, indirect costs which are also called as 'overheads' which is not traceable to the products/services. Hence these costs are first identified, classified, allocated, apportioned wherever allocation is not possible, reapportioned and finally absorbed in the products/services. Charging the direct costs to the products is comparatively a simple procedure and can be done with remarkable accuracy. However, the indirect costs are the present problem in charging them to the products or services. There is a possibility of distortion of costs though the basis of charging them is quite logical. This is one of the limitations of the traditional costing system.

However, the increased technology and automation has reduced the direct labour considerably and so the indirect activities have assumed greater importance. Therefore, using the direct labour as a basis for absorbing the overheads can lead to distortions in the costs. Distortions in the costs resulting into incorrect cost calculations may lead to wrong decisions like errors in fixation of selling prices, product mix and ignoring customer orientation.

In order to overcome the limitations of traditional costing systems Activity-based Costing has been introduced. It is an upcoming and more refined approach for charging indirect costs to products and computing more accurate product costs. It provides a more accurate view of product cost, but companies typically use it as a supplemental costing system. The allocation bases used in activity-based costing differ from those used in traditional costing. Activity-based costing determines every activity associated with producing an item and allocates a cost to the activity. The cost assigned to the activity is then assigned to products that require the activity for production.

Traditional costing system

Traditionally, indirect costs are distributed to end products on the assumption that products consume resources in proportion to the production volumes. Distribution of overheads traditionally based on machine hours or direct wages, etc. The main steps in this approach is allocation and apportionment of overhead to various production departments and service departments. The next step is reapportionment of service departments overheads to production departments and finally absorption of production departments overheads by the end products.

Problem of under costing and over costing : In a traditional costing system, overheads, i.e., indirect costs are allocated, apportioned and finally absorbed in the cost units. There can be distortion in computing costs due to the basis selected for absorption. This approach uses average overhead rate, for all the activities to allocate cost to products or services. Charging overheads uniformly to products or services is known as cost smoothing or peanut butter costing. The cost smoothing leads to under costing of certain products and over costing of other products. It is known as product cost cross-subsidization. Activity-based Costing is suitable approach for charging indirect costs to products and computing more accurate product costs.

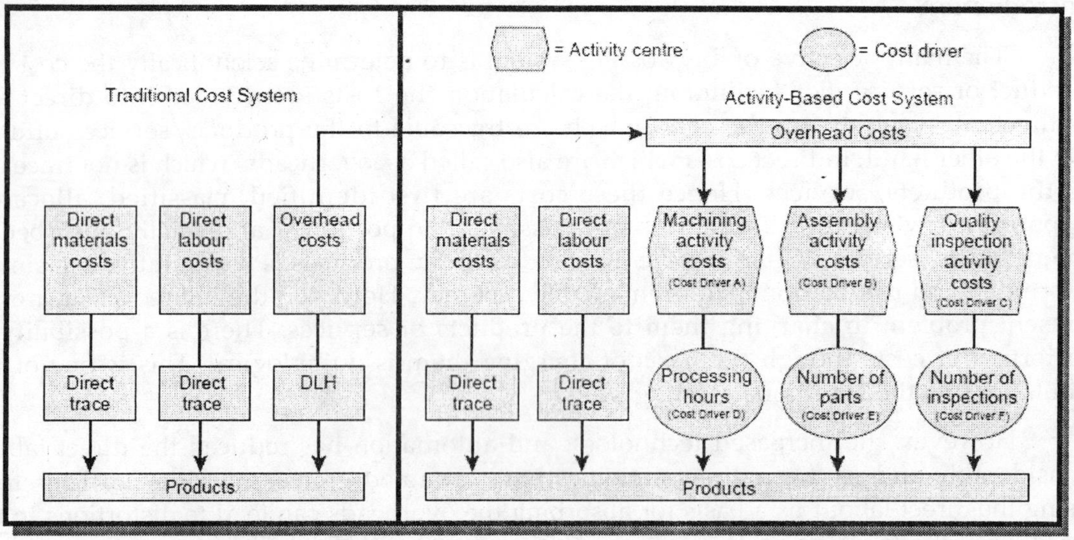

Figure 1 : Traditional and Activity-based Costing

Source : www.highered.mcgraw-hill.com

Activity-based Costing

Activity-based costing is a new and scientific approach developed by Cooper and Kaplan in 1998 for assigning overheads to end products, jobs and processes. This approach aims to rectify the problem of inaccurate cost information due to selection of wrong basis of indirect cost apportionment. ABC focuses on activities on a key assumption in activity-based costing is that overhead costs are caused by a number of activities and those different products utilize these activities in a non-homogeneous fashion. Usually, costing the activity is an intermediate step in the allocation of overhead costs to products, in order to obtain more accurate product cost information.

Definition

CIMA defines activity-based costing as, 'cost attribution to cost units on the basis of benefit received from indirect activities, i.e., ordering, setting up, assuring quality, etc.'

One more definition of activity-based costing is, 'the collection of financial and operational performance information tracing the significant activities of the firm to product costs.'

Objectives of Activity-based Costing

The following are the important objectives of activity-based costing.

1. To remove the under costing and over costing of total costs in the traditional costing system and bring more accuracy in the computation of costs of products and services.
2. To help in decision making by accurate allocation of costs and fixing price to products and services.
3. To identify various activities in the production process and further identify the value adding activities.
4. To distribute overheads on the basis of activities through cost driver rate.
5. To identify the opportunities for improvement and reduction of costs.
6. To eliminate non value adding activities.

Hierarchy of Cost

In activity-based costing, cost pools are often established for each level in a hierarchy of costs. For manufacturing firms, the following are identified:

Unit level costs : For any given product, these costs change in a more or less linear with the number of units produced. For example, fabric and thread are unit level costs for an apparel manufacturer: if the company wants to double production, it will need twice as much fabric and thread.

Batch level costs : These costs change in a more or less linear with the number of batches run. Machine set up costs are often batch level costs. The time required to prepare a machine to run one batch of product is usually independent of the number of units in the batch: the same time is required to prepare the machine to run a batch of 100 units or as a batch of 50 units. Hence, batch level costs do not necessarily vary linearly with the number of units produced.

Product level costs : These costs are usually fixed and direct with respect to a given product. For example, the salary of a product manager with responsibility for only one product. The product manager's salary is a fixed cost to the company for a wide range of production volume levels. However, if the company drops the product entirely, the product manager is no longer needed.

Facility level costs : These costs are usually fixed and direct with respect to the facility. For example: property taxes on the facility or the salaries of front office personnel such as the receptionist and office manager.

ABC provides more accurate product cost information compared with traditional costing systems. It allocates all overheads including batch level, product level and facility level overheads to unit level costs.

Terms used in Activity-based Costing

In order to understand ABC, one should be familiar with the analyzing manufacturing process and stages involved for installation of costing system. The following terms are important in ABC.

Activity : An activity may be defined as a particular task or unit of work with a specific purpose. This term is important on identification of activities. For example, a manufacturing company is purchase procedure may involve activities like receiving of purchase requisition for concerned departments inviting quotations from various suppliers, placing of an order, follow-up of the same and finally receiving and inspection of the goods. Whether in manufacturing or in service sector, activities are identified and the next step is to divide the activities into value adding and non value adding. The objective behind this is that attention can be focused on the value adding activities while non value adding activities can be eliminated in the future.

Cost Pool : Cost pool is defined by CIMA as, "'the point of focus for the costs relating to a particular activity in an activity-based costing system." For example, in case of a manufacturing organization, as regards to stores, cost of classification, cost of issue of stores requisitions, inspection costs, etc., can be pooled under the heading 'stores'. Thus cost pool concept is similar to the concept of cost center. The cost pool is the point of focus or in other words, it is the total cost assigned to an activity. It is the sum of all the cost elements assigned to an activity.

Cost Drivers : It is a factor that causes a change in the cost of an activity. Cost driver is of two types one is resource cost driver and another is activity cost driver.

Resource : A **resource** is an economic element needed or consumed in performing activities. Salaries and supplies, etc., are resources needed or used in performing manufacturing activities.

Resource Cost Driver : According to CIMA, "cost driver is any factor which causes a change in the cost of an activity, i.e., the quality of parts received by an activity is a determining factor in the work required by that activity and therefore, affects the resources required. An activity may have multiple cost drivers associated with it." In other words, cost driver means the factors which determine the cost of an activity. For example, if we repeat the example in stores, number of stores requisitions will be cost drivers, in customer order processing the number of customers as well as number of orders will be cost drive₹ Similarly, the number of times machines are set up will determine the cost of setting up of machines. Thus, a cost driver is an activity which generates cost. Activity-based Costing is based on the belief that activities cause costs and therefore, a link should be established between activities and product. The cost drivers thus, are the link between the activities and the cost.

Activity Cost Driver : Activity-based costing is a type of costing that identifies activities within the business and estimates the resources required to fulfill each activity. An activity cost driver is a factor that affects the costs associated with an activity. ABC allows managers to determine the costs to perform an activity as well as the costs associated with not performing the activity For example, when a production line has to wait for a certain part to arrive from an external distributor or other manufacturing line, the manager can quickly determine the true cost of waiting for the part. Activity cost drivers attempt to provide a more comprehensive view of the actual costs of an activity, such as a manufacturing process.

Cost Objects : The final stage in activity-based costing is to identify the cost with the final products which can also be called as cost objects. Cost objects include, products, services, customers, projects and contracts. As mentioned earlier, direct costs can be identified easily with the products but the indirect costs can be linked with the products by identifying activities and cost drive₹ Thus, activity-based costing is the process of tracing costs first from resources to activities and then from activities to specific products.

Steps in Activity-based Costing

The following are the steps in activity-based cost allocation:

Step 1 : Levels of Activities : First identify resource costs for various activities and then classify all activities according the consumption of resources.

1. ***Unit level activity :*** It is performed on each individual unit of product or service of the firm. For example, unit-level activities are direct materials, direct labour-hours, inserting a component, and inspecting every unit. A unit level activity is volume based. The required activity varies in proportion with the quantity of the cost object. The resource consumption driver and the activity consumption drivers are most likely to be the same for unit level activities.

2. ***Batch-level activity :*** Batch-level activity is performed for each batch or group of units of products or services. A firm incurs a batch-level activity for each batch or group of units of products or services scheduled to be processed together, rather than for each individual unit of the cost object. A batch has more than one unit of a product or service. Examples of batch-level activities are setting up machines, placing purchase orders, scheduling production, conducting inspections by batch, handling materials, and expediting production.

3. ***Product-level activity :*** It supports the production of a specific product or service. Examples of product-sustaining activities include designing products, administering parts required for products and engaging in engineering changes to modify products.

4. ***Facility-level activity :*** It supports operations in general. These activities are not caused by products or customer service needs and cannot be traced to individual units, batches, or products. Examples of facility sustaining activities include providing security and safety, performing maintenance of general purpose machines, managing the plant, incurring factory property taxes and insurance and closing of the books each month. Some firms refer to these activities as business or infrastructure sustaining activities.

   Unit level activity can always be traced to a batch (one of the units in the batch), and a batch-level activity can always be traced to a product (one batch of this particular product), and a product-level activity can always be traced to a manufacturing facility; but, the reverse is not possible.

Step 2 : Assign Resource Costs to Activities : Activity-based costing uses resource consumption cost drivers to assign resource costs to activities. Because activities drive the cost of resources used in operations, a firm should select resource consumption cost drivers based on cause-and-effect relationships. Typical resource consumption cost drivers include the number of labour hours for labour intensive activities; employees for payroll-related activities; setups for batch-related activities; moves for materials-handling activities and machine-hours for machine repair and maintenance.

Although a firm's accounting system is a good starting point to find information about the cost of resources, most accounting systems report the costs of different resources such as indirect labour, electricity, equipment and supplies but not report the cost of activities performed. New accounting systems are needed to obtain and track resource costs for activities.

The cost of the resources can be assigned to activities by direct tracing or estimation. Direct tracing requires measuring the actual usage of resources by activities. For example, power is used to operate a machine can be traced directly to that machine's operation by reading the meter attached to the machine.

When direct tracing is not available, department managers and supervisors need to estimate the amount or percentage of time (or effort) employees spend on each identified activity. Multiple resource consumption cost drivers often are needed to assign different resource costs to activity or activity center cost pools.

Main Activities and its Cost Driver

Activity	Cost Driver
Purchase of material	**Number of orders placed** Number of receipts of material Number of inspections
Personnel	**Number of employees recruitment** Number of employees
Research and development	**Number of research projects** Personnel hours on a project Complexities of projects
Customer service	**Number of products serviced** Number of service calls Number of hours spent on servicing
Customer order processing	**Order value** Order source
Production	**Number of machine set up** Number of units Number of machine hours

Production control	**No. of production process changes eng.** Number of engineering change orders
Distribution	**Number of items Distributed** Number of Customers Weight of items distributed
Power	**Number of kilowatt hours**
Marketing	**Number of Advertisements** Number of Sales personnel Sales Revenue

Step 3 : Creation of Cost Pool : Cost pool is grouping of individual cost items. A cost pool or cost bucket should be created for each activity. Cost pool is like a cost centre around which costs are accumulated. For example, the total cost of machine maintenance might constitute one cost pool for all machine, related costs.

Step 4 : Calculation of Activity Cost Driver Rate : In traditional costing overhead absorption rate is calculated in same way activity-based costing system cost driver rate is calculated.

$$\text{Activity Cost Driver Rate} = \frac{\textit{Total cost of activity}}{\textit{Cost drivers}}$$

Step 5 : Activity Costs to Cost Objects : The final step is to assign costs of activities or activity cost pools to cost objects based on the appropriate activity consumption cost drive₹ Outputs are the cost objects for which firms or organizations perform activities. Typical outputs for a cost system are products and services; however, outputs also can include customers, projects, or business units. For example, the outputs of an insurance company may be individual insurance policies sold to customers, claims processed, and types of policies offered.

Firms use activity consumption cost drivers to assign activity costs to cost objects. Activity cost drivers should explain why the cost of a cost object goes up or down. Typical activity consumption cost drivers are purchase orders, receiving reports, inspection reports or hours, parts stored, payments, direct labour-hours, machine-hours, set ups and manufacturing cycle time. Analyses should be conducted in determining proper activity consumption cost drive₹

Assign costs to the cost objects using the formula = Resources consumed × Activity cost rate.

Activity-based Management

The activity-based management is a tool of management that involves analyzing and costing activities with the goal of improving efficiency and effectiveness. Though it is closely related to the activity based costing, still it differs from the same in its primary goal. The activity-based costing focuses on activities with the object of measuring the cost of products/ services. It tries to compute the cost as accurately as possible. On the other hand, activity-based management focuses on managing the activities themselves. In activity-based costing resources are traced to the activities for the purpose of computing the costs while in activity -based management, resources are traced to activities for evaluation of the activities themselves. In other words, efforts are made to improve the activities further. Thus activity-based management is a set of actions that management can take, based on information from an activity-based costing system, to increase/improve profitability.

Activity-based Management attempts the Following Analysis

Cost Driver Analysis : The factors that cause activities to be performed need to be identified in order to manage activity costs. Cost driver analysis identifies these casual facto₹ For example, in a stores department, it may be observed that slow moving and obsolete stock is not disposed of in time, the reason being the staff in the stores is not trained properly in this area. Managers have to address this cost driver to correct the root cause of this problem and take proper action.

Activity Analysis : Activity analysis identifies value added and non value added activities. This analysis identifies the activities in the organization and the activity centers that should be used in activity-based costing system. In activity-based management, identification of activities into value adding and non value adding is made and efforts are made to eliminate the non value adding activities.

Performance Analysis : Performance analysis involves the identification of appropriate measures to report the performance of activity centers or other organizational units consistent with each unit's goals and objectives. Performance Analysis aims to identify the best ways to measure the performance of factors that are important to organizations in order to stimulate continuous improvement.

Activity-based Costing and Activity-based Management

Activity-based Costing is logical distribution of overheads, i.e., overheads are distributed on the basis of the consumption of resources. It helps to avoid distortion of costs of products/services. On the other hand, Activity-based management, is a discipline that focuses on efficient management so as to value of services rendered to custome₹ This focus on activities is being used effectively for cost reduction, business process re-engineering, benchmarking and performance measurement. Activity-based Management brings about a change in viewing at the objective by incorporation of financial perspective, internal business perspective, innovation and learning perspective.

Distinguish between Activity-based Costing (ABC) and Activity-based Management (ABM)

ABC	ABM
1. ABC refers to the technique of determining the cost of activities and the cost of output produced by those activities.	1. It refers to the management philosophy that focuses on the planning, execution and measurement of activities as a key to competitive advantage.
2. The aim of ABC is to generate improved cost data for use in managing a company's activities	2. ABM is a much broader concept and aims to use information given by ABC, for effective business processes and profitability
3. ABC is the operational segment of ABM	3. It is a conceptual aspect, i.e., management attitude.

Distinguish between Value Added and Non-Value Added activities

Value Added activities	Non-Value Added activities
1. These are activities necessary for the performance of the process	1. These are additional and extraneous activities, not fully necessary for the performance of the process.
2. These represent work that is valued by the external or internal customer	2. These represent work that is not valued by the external or internal customer
3. They improve the quality of function of a product. Hence, the customers are usually willing to pay for the service. VA activities result in "costs" and not in losses	3. NVA activities do not improve the quality or function of a product or service, but they can adversely affect costs and prices. NVA activities create waste, result in delay of some sort, add cost to the products or services for which the customer is not willing to pay.
4. Example: Making product more versatile for certain other uses	4. Examples : Expediting due to work delays, cost for re-work of defectives, etc.

ABC in the Service Sector

ABC is as important to companies in the merchandising and service sectors as to manufacturing companies. In fact, although the origination of ABC is generally prescribed to manufacturing companies in the 1980s, by then hospitals were already allocating overhead costs to departments and then to patient services using methods similar to ABC. Hospitals were required to implement relatively sophisticated allocation processes in order to comply with Medicare reimbursement rules. After its inception in the 1960s, Medicare established detailed rules regarding how overhead costs should be grouped into cost pools, and the choice of appropriate allocation bases for allocating overhead costs to departments and then to patients. Within these rules, hospitals were able to maximize revenues by shifting costs from areas such as pediatrics, labour and delivery, and maternity (which have low rates of Medicare utilization) to the intensive care unit, the critical care unit, and surgery (which have higher rates of Medicare utilization). Other non-manufacturing industries that have benefited from ABC include financial services firms and retaile₹

Installation of an Activity-based Costing System

Another refinement in product costing that often accompanies implementation of ABC focuses on identification of activities to allocation of indirect cost. The direct costs associated with the cost object. The company attempts to identify costs currently treated as overheads those that have not been traced directly to the cost object. In other words, costs are moved from the overhead cost pool to the direct cost category. For example, chartered accounting firm might take certain office-support expenses formerly treated as overheads, such as printing, copying, start tracking and assigning these costs to specific jobs (audits, tax engagements, etc.) for internal reporting and profitability analysis.

The successful implementation of ABC usually requires participation by managers from non-accounting functions, such as production and marketing. Because ABC focuses on activities but activities often cut across departments and functional areas, implementing ABC can improve lines of communication and cooperation within the company. On the other hand, more accurate cost allocation does not, by itself, reduce costs. The initial move from a traditional costing system to ABC usually shifts overhead costs from some products to other products, with some managers "winning" and some "losing." Some companies have found that hiring an outside consulting firm to assist with the ABC adoption facilitates obtaining "buy-in" by managers and employees throughout the company. Perhaps partly for this reason, ABC implementation has become an important consulting product for accounting firms and for many consulting firms.

The installation of an ABC system involves the following procedure :

1. **Specification of objectives :** The objective for pursuing ABC System generally involve to improve the product costing where it is believed that existing methods undercost or over cost the products and identify non-value adding activities in the production process which might be a suitable focus for attention or elimination

2. **Identification of costs for ABC :** Direct costs, like material and Direct Labour are easily assigned directly to products. Product specific indirect costs (eg. Specific advertising, dealer's commission), may be directly assigned to the product. Hence, the remaining indirect costs is the focus of ABC. Such costs are indirectly assigned to the cost object (i.e., product) through cost pools and activity drivers.

3. **Process Specification** : This involves identification of different stages of the production process, the commitment of resources of each process, processing times and bottlenecks. This provides a list of transactions which may be defined as activities at a subsequent stage.

4. **Activity Definition :** The list of transactions as identified in the previous stage is analyzed to ensure aggregation or grouping of common activities and elimination of immaterial activities. Activities are categorized into primary activities and support activities. The resultant cost pools will likely have a number of different events, or drivers, associated with their incurrence.

5. **Activity Driver Selection :** Activity cost drivers used to relate the overheads collected in cost pools to cost objects (products) should be determined. Generally a single driver is selected for every activity even through multiple and inter-related activity drivers may exist.

6. **Costing :** A single representative activity driver can be used to assign costs from the activity pools to the cost objects. Such linking of total costs to cost objects is based on the activity cost driver.

7. **Staff Training :** The co-operation of the workforce is essential for successful implementation of ABC. Staff training should be oriented to create an awareness of the activity, based costing.

8. **Review and Follow-up :** The actual operation of the ABC system should be closely monitored periodic review and follow-up action is necessary for successful implementation of the system.

Advantages of Activity-based Costing System

ABC system has the following advantages:

1. This is best system for accurate costing of products or services, customers and distribution channels.
2. It is good for understanding and analysis of overhead.
3. Decisions purpose it utilizes unit cost rather than just total cost.
4. It integrates well with six sigma and other continuous improvement programs.
5. This makes visible waste and non-value added activities.
6. ABC supports performance management and scorecards.
7. This system enables costing of processes, supply chains, and value streams.
8. Activity-based Costing facilitates benchmarking.

Limitations of Activity-based Costing

This system is effective but it suffers some limitations. These limitations are as follows:

1. Activity-based costing is a complex system and requires more records and deadly calculations.
2. Small organizations, traditional cost accounting system may be more beneficial than activity-based costing due to the simplicity of operation.
3. It is difficult to attribute costs to single activities as some costs support several activities.
4. Trained professionals are required but limited in number and more cost.
5. This system will be successful if and when total support is received from the top management.
6. More investment of time and money is required for the implementation ABC system.
7. Activity-based costing data can be easily misinterpreted.
8. Costs assigned to products, customers and other cost objects are only potentially relevant.
9. Taking any significant decisions by using activity-based costing data; managers must identify which costs are really relevant for the decisions.

Problem 1

A Company, manufacturing two products, furnishes the following data for a year 2011.

Products	Annual output (units)	Total machine hours	Total number of purchase orders	Total number of set ups
A	5,000	20,000	160	20
B	60,000	1,20,000	384	44

The annual overheads are as under : ₹

	₹
Volume-related activity costs	5,50,000
Set up-related costs	8,20,000
Purchase-related costs	6,18,000

You are required to calculate the cost per unit of each product A and B bases on:

(i) Traditional method of charging overheads

(ii) Activity based costing method (C.A.P.E. II)

Solution :

(i) Traditional Method

Total overheads = 5, 50,000 + 8, 20, 000 + 6, 18,000 = ₹ 19, 88,000

Total machine hours = 20,000 + 1, 20,000 = 1, 40,000

$$\text{Machine hour rate} = \frac{\textit{Total overheads}}{\textit{Total machine hours}} = \frac{\textit{Rs. } 19{,}88{,}000}{1{,}40{,}000 \textit{ hours}} = ₹\ 14.20$$

Traditional Method Statement of Cost

	Types of Products	
	A	B
(A) Output (units)	5,000	60,000
(B) Machine hours	20,000	1,20,000
(C) Overhead cost @ ₹ 14.20 per machine	2,84,000	17,04,000
(D) Overhead cost per unit (C ÷ A) ₹	56.8	28.40

(ii) ABC Method

1. $$\text{Machine hour rate} = \frac{\textit{Total overhead cost for volume related activities}}{\textit{Total machine hours}} = \frac{\textit{Rs. } 5{,}50{,}000}{1{,}40{,}000 \textit{ hours}} = ₹\ 3.93$$

(approx)

2. Total set ups = 20 + 44 = 64.

$$\text{Cost of one set-up} = \frac{Total\ \ Cost\ realted\ to\ setups}{Total\ number\ of\ set-ups} = \frac{Rs.8{,}20{,}000}{64\ set-ups}$$

= **₹ 12,812.50**

3. $$\text{Cost of one purchase order} = \frac{Total\ \ Cost\ realted\ to\ purchases}{Total\ number\ of\ purchase\ orders}$$

$$= \frac{Rs.6{,}18{,}000}{544\ Orders} = \text{₹ 1,136.03}$$

Total purchase orders = 160 + 384 = 544.

Activity-based Costing Statement of Cost

		Products	
		A	B
(A)	Annual Output (units)	5,000	60,000
(B)	Cost related to volume-related activities	20,000 @ ₹3.93 ₹ 78,600	1,20,000 @ ₹3.93 ₹ 4,71,600
(C)	Cost related to purchase orders	160 Orders @ ₹1,136.03 ₹ 1,81,765	384 Orders @ ₹ 1,136.03 ₹ 4,36,235.52
(D)	Cost related to set ups	20 setups @ ₹12,812.50	44 setups @ ₹ 12,812.50
(E)		₹ 2,56,250	₹ 5,63,750
	Total Cost (B + C + D)	₹ 5,16,615	₹ 14,71,586
	Cost per unit (E / A)	**₹ 103.323**	**₹ 24.526**

Problem 2

The budgeted overheads and cost driver volumes of ABC are as follows.

Cost Pool	Budgeted Overheads (Rs.)	Cost Driver	Budgeted Volume
Material procurement	6,80,000	No. of orders	1,300
Material handling	3,50,000	No. of movements	780
Set-up	5,15,000	No. of set ups	820
Maintenance	10,70,000	Maintenance hours	9,400
Quality control	2,76,000	No. of inspection	1,100
Machinery over heads	8,20,000	No. of machine hours	25,000

The company has produced a batch of 2,000 components of ZX-1, its material cost ₹ 1,20,000 and labour cost ₹ 2,10,000. The usage activities of the said batch are as follows.

Material orders – 30, Maintenance hours – 700, Material movements – 20, Inspection – 30, Set ups – 35, Machine hours – 2,200.

Calculate cost driver rates that are used for tracing appropriate amount of overheads to the said batch and ascertain the cost of batch of components using activity based costing.

Solution :

Calculation of Cost Driver Rate

Particulars	Details	Cost Driver Rate
Material procurement	₹ 6,80,000 / 1300	₹ 523
Material handling	₹ 3,50,000 / 780	₹ 449
Set up	₹ 5,15,000 / 820	₹ 990
Maintenance	₹ 10,70,000 / 9400	₹ 114
Quality control	₹ 2,76,000 / 1100	₹ 251
Machine over heads	₹ 8,20,000 / 25,000	₹ 33

Calculation of a Batch of 2,000 components of ZX - 1

Particulars	Details	Amount in ₹
Direct Materials		1,20,000
Direct Labour		2,10,000
Prime Cost - Direct Materials + Direct Labour		3,30,000
Add : Overheads		
Material Procurement	30 × ₹ 523	15,690
Material handling	20 × ₹ 449	8,980
Set-up cost	35 × ₹ 990	34,650
Maintenance	700 × ₹ 114	79,800
Quality control	30 × ₹ 251	7,530
Machine	2200 × ₹ 33	72,600
Total cost		5,49,250

Note : From the above calculations, it is clear that by using Activity-based Costing; there can be substantial accuracy in the overhead absorption. The overheads are charged on the basis of cost drivers and not on the basis of absorption rate.

Problem 3

ABC company manufactures two products X and Y. The product X is a low volume a n d i t ₹4,000 per year Product Y is high volume and labour intensive, its sales are 30,000 units per year.

X takes 8 labour hours to make one unit but Y requires 10 hours per unit.

Particulars	Product X	Product Y
Direct Materials - Rs.	250	150
Direct Labour -@ Rs.10 per hour	80	100
Total	330	250

Total overhead costs by the activities are as follows :

Particulars	Total Overheads	Details of Activity
Machine Set up	4,50,000	10,000 Set ups
Quality inspection	3,00,000	15,000 Inspections
Production order	1,80,000	600 Orders
Machine hours worked	6,25,000	50,000 Machine hours
Material receipts	1,95,000	1,500 Receipts
Total overheads	17,50,000	

The company works 1,00,000 direct labour hours per year. Total manufacturing overhead costs are ₹17,50,000 per year .You are required to compute per unit cost of each product using,

I. Direct labour hour rate method for absorption of overhead costs and

II. Activity Based Costing technique for absorption of overhead costs

Solution :

Calculation of the Product Cost based on Direct Labour Hour Rate.

Direct Labour Hour Rate = Total manufacturing overheads / Total direct labour hours ₹17,50,000/1,00,000 = ₹ 17.50

Absorption of manufacturing overheads:

Particulars	Product X	Product Y
Manufacturing Overheads	₹17.5 x8 Direct Labour Hours = ₹ 140	₹ 17.50x10 Direct Labour Hours = ₹ 175

Overheads based on Activity Based Costing

Identification of Activities and calculation of Cost Driver Rate :

Particulars	Total Overheads	Details of Activity	Rate per Activity [₹]
Machine Set up	4,50,000	10,000	45 per set up
Quality inspection	3,00,000	15,000	20 per inspection
Production order	1,80,000	600	300 per order
Machine hours worked	6,25,000	50,000	12.5 per hour
Material receipts	1,95,000	1,500	130 per receipt
Total overheads	17,50,000		

Allocation of overheads to Products on the basis of Cost Driver Rates

Particulars	Frequency of activity	Cost Driver Rate	Product X ₹	Product Y ₹
Machine Set up	10,000	45	6,000 x ₹ 45 = ₹2,70,000	4,000 x ₹45 = ₹1,80,000
Quality inspection	15,000	20	10,000 x ₹ 20 = ₹ 2,00,000	5,000 x ₹20 = ₹1,00,000
Production order	600	300	200 x ₹ 300 = ₹ 60,000	400 x ₹300 = ₹1,20,000
Machine hours worked	50,000	12.5	12,000 x₹12.5 = ₹ 1,50,000	38,000 x₹12.5 = ₹ 4,75,000
Material receipts	1,500	130	300 x₹ 130 = ₹ 39,000	12,000 x₹130 = ₹ 1,56,000
Total overhead costs			7,19,000	10,31,000
Units produced			4,000	30,000
Overhead costs per unit			179.75	34.37

Computation of Total Cost under Traditional Costing and Activity Based Costing

Particulars	Product X – Activity-based Costing	Product Y – Activity-based Costing	Product X – Traditional Costing	Product Y – Traditional Costing
Direct Material	250	150	250	150
Direct Labour	80	100	80	100
Manufacturing overheads	179.75	34.37	140	175
Total Production cost	509.75	284.37	470	425

From the above comparative analysis it is clear that, under Traditional Costing, Product X is charged with ₹ 140 per unit as manufacturing overheads while in case of Product Y, the share of overhead cost is ₹ 175. Under Activity Based Costing product X is ₹ 179.75 and product Y is ₹ 34.37 per unit. Thus due to activity based costing, the distortion in cost is avoided. From the above calculations under traditional method product X undercosted and product Y overcosted.

Problem 4

Naresh Limited has decided to analyse the profitability of its five new customers it buys bottled water at ₹ 100 per case and sells to retail customers at a list price of ₹ 120 per case. The rates pertaining to five customers are:

Particulars	Customers				
	Ax	Bx	Cx	Dx	Ex
Cases sold	5,000	20,000	1,40,000	70,000	9,000
List selling price	₹ 120	₹ 120	₹ 120	₹ 120	₹ 120
Actual selling price	₹125	₹ 110	₹ 107	₹ 115	₹105
Number of purchase orders	15	25	30	25	30
Number of Customer Visits	2	3	6	2	3
Number of deliveries	10	30	60	40	20
Kilometres travelled per delivery	20	6	5	10	30
Number of expedited delivers	0	0	0	0	1

Its five activities and their drivers are :

Activity	Cost driver rate
Order taking	₹ 500 per purchase order
Customer Visits	₹ 400 per Customer Visit
Deliveries	₹ 6 Per delivery km travelled
Product handling	₹ 4 per case sold
Expected deliveries	₹ 5per expedited delivery

Required :

Compute the customer level operating income of each of five retail customers now being examined (Ax, Bx, Cx, Dx and Ex) Comment on the results.

Solution :

Calculation of customer Level Activity costs

Particulars	Customers				
	Ax	Bx	Cx	Dx	Ex
1. Order taking costs (No. of purchase order × ₹ 500)	7,500	12,500	15,000	12,500	15,000
2. Customer visits costs (No. of Customer visits × ₹ 400)	800	1,200	2,400	800	1,200
3. Delivery vehicles travel costs (kms travelled by delivery vehicles x ₹ 6 per km)	1,200	1,080	1,800	2,400	3,600
4. Products handing costs (Cases sold x ₹ 4)	20,000	80,000	5,60,000	2,80,000	36,000
5. Cost of expedited deliveries (No. of expedited deliveries x ₹ 2,250)	-	-	-	-	5
Total cost of Customer level	29,500	94,780	5,77,500	2,95,700	55,805

Operating activities :

Calculation of Customer level operating income

Particulars	Customers				
	A	B	C	D	E
(A) Cases Sold (Units)	5,000	20,000	1.40,000	70,000	9,000
	₹	₹	₹	₹	₹
(B) Actual selling price	125	110	107	115	105
(C) Cost	100	100	100	100	100
Sales at actual price (A x B)	6,25,000	22,00,000	1,49,80,000	80,50,000	9,45,000
Less: Cost of goods sold (A x C)	5,00,000	20,00,000	1,40,00,000	70,00,000	9,00,000
Gross Margin	1,25,000	2,00,000	9,80,000	10,50,000	45,000
Less : Customer level activity costs	29,500	94,780	5,77,500	2,95,700	55,805
Customer Level operating income/loss	95,500	1,05,220	4,02,500	7,54,300	-10,805

Problem 5a

The budgeted overheads and cost driver volumes of Neptune Ltd. are as follows :

Cost Pool	Budgeted Overheads (₹)	Cost Driver	Budgeted Volume
Material Procurement	2,90,000	No. of Orders	550
Material Handling	1,25,000	No. of Movements	340
Set up	2,07,500	No. of set ups	260
Maintenance	4,85,000	Maintenance Hours	4,200
Quality Control	88,000	No. of Inspection	450
Machinery	3,60,000	No. of M/c hours	12,000

The firm has produced, a batch of 2,600 components of AXL-5, its Material cost was 1,30,000, and Labour cost 2,45,000.

The usage activities of the said batch are as follows :

Material Orders	– 26	Maintenance hours	–600
Material Movements	– 18	Inspection	–28
Set-ups	– 25	M/c hours	–1,800

Required :

(i) Calculate Cost driver rates that are used for tracing appropriate amount of overheads to the said batch; and

(ii) Ascertain the cost of batch of components using Activity Based Costing.

(ICWA June 2012)

(I) Cost driver rates =	Budgeted Overheads / Budgeted Volume	Cost Driver Rate (₹)
Material Procurement =	₹ 2,90,000 / 550	527
Material handling =	₹ 1,25,000 / 340	368
Set up =	₹ 2,07,500 / 260	798
Maintenance	₹ 4,85,000 / 4200	115
Quality Control	₹ 88,000 / 450	195
Machinery =	₹ 3,60,000 / 12,000	30

(II) Cost of Batch of Components		
Particulars		**Amount**
1. Direct Materials (given)		1,30,000
2. Direct Labour (given)		2,45,000
3. Overheads:		
Materials Procurement		
Material handling	=26 x 527 = 13,702	
Set up	=18 x 368 = 6,624	
Maintenance	=25 x 798 = 19,950	
Quality Control	=690 x 115 = 79,350	
Machinery	=28 x 195 = 5,460	
	=1800 x 30 = 54,000	1,79,086
Total Cost (1+2+3)		5,54,086
Of Batch of 2600 Components		

Problem 5

KLR. store wants information about the profitability of individual product lines: soft drinks. Fresh produce and packaged food. KLR Store provides the following data for the year 2011-12 for each product line:

Particulars	Soft drinks	Fresh Produce	Packaged food
Revenues	₹ 7,93,500	₹ 21,00,600	₹. 12,09,900
Cost of goods sold	₹ 6,00,000	RS 15,00,000	₹ 9,00,000
Cost of bottle returned	₹ 12,000	₹. 0	₹ 0
Number of purchase orders placed	360	840	360
Number of deliveries received	300	2,190	660
Hours of shelf - stocking time	540	5,400	2,700
Items sold	1,26,000	11,04,000	3,06,000

KLR. Store also provides the following information for the year 2011-12.

Activity	Description of activity	Total Cost (₹)	Cost - allocation base
Bottles returns	Returning of empty bottles	12,000	Direst tracing to soft drink line
Ordering	Placing of orders for purchases	1,56,000	1,560 purchase order
Delivery	Physical delivery and receipt of goods	2,52,000	3,150 deliveries
Shelf stocking	Stocking of goods on store shelves and on- going restocking	1,72,800	8,640 hours of shelf stocking time
Customer Support	Assistance provided to customers including checkout	3,07,200	15,36,000 items sold

Required :

(i) KLR. Store currently allocated support cost (all costs other than cost of goods sold) to product lines on the basis of cost of goods sold of each product line. Calculate the operating income and operating income as a % of revenues for each product line.

(ii) If KLR. Store allocates support costs (all costs other than cost of goods sold) to product lines using and activity-based costing system, calculate the operating income and operating income as a % of revenues for each product line.

(iii) Comment on your answers in requirements (i) and (ii) **(C.A.P.E II)**

Solution :

Traditional Approach

(i) Calculation total support cost (overhead) ₹

	₹
Bottles Returns	12,000
Ordering	1, 56,000
Delivery	2, 52,000
Shelf stocking	1, 72,800
Customer Support	3, 07,200
Total support Cost	9, 00,000

Total cost of goods sold = ₹ 6,00,000 + 15,00,000 + 9,00,000 = ₹ 30,00,000.

Total support cost as a% of cost of goods sold $= \frac{Rs. 9,00,000}{Rs. 30,00,000} \times 100 = 30\ \%$

Statement of operating income and operating income as a% of Revenues

	Soft Drinks ₹	Fresh Produce ₹	Packaged Foods ₹	Total ₹
Revenues (A)	7,93,500	21,00,600	12,09,900	41,04,000
Cost of goods Sold (COGS)	6,00,000	15,00,000	9,00,000	30,00,000
Support Cost (30 % of COGS)	1,80,000	4,50,000	2,70,000	9,00,000
Total Cost (B)	7,80,000	19,50,000	11,70,000	39,00,000
Operating income (A-B)	13.5	1,50,6000	39,900	2,04,000
Operating Income as a% of revenue	1.70%	7,17%	3,30%	4.97%

ABC Approach: Calculation of Cost Driver Rate

Activity	Total cost ₹	Cost drivers	Cost driver rate ₹
1. Ordering	1,56,000	1,560 purchase orders	100 per purchase order
2. Delivery	2,52,000	3,150 deliveries	80 per delivery
3. Shelf - stocking	1,72,800	8,640 hours	20 per stocking hr
4. Customer Support	3,07,200	15,36,000 items sold	0.20 per item sold

Statement of operating income and operating income as a % of Revenues

	Soft Drinks ₹	Fresh Produce ₹	Packaged Foods ₹	Total ₹
Revenues (A)	7,93,500	21,00,600	12,09,900	41,04,000
Cost of goods Sold (COGS)	6,00,000	15,00,000	9,00,000	30,00,000
Bottle return costs	12,000	0	0	12,000
Ordering cost (360: 840: 360)	36,000	84,000	36,000	1,56,000
Delivery Cost (300 : 2,190 : 600)	24,000	1,75,000	52,800	2,52,000
shelf stocking cost (540 : 5,400 : 2,700)	10,800	1,08,000	54,000	1,72,800
Customer support cost (1,26,000 : 11,04,000 : 3,06,000)	25,200	2,20,800	61,200	3,07,200
Total Cost (B)	7,08,000	20,88,000	11,04,000	39,00,000
Operating income (A-B)	85,500	12,600	1,05,900	2,04,000
Operating income as a % of revenues	10.78%	0.60%	8.75%	4.97%

Comments: From the above calculations under traditional approach and activity based costing results are different in the form of operating income as a % of revenue. The allocation of support costs under activity based costing is more reliable and accurate than under traditional method.

Problem 6

Matrix Limited trades Pharmaceutical products. It buys from the pharmaceutical companies and resells to each of the three different markets:

(i) General Supermarket chains

(ii) Drugstore Chains

(iii) Chemist Shops

The following data for the month of April 2012 in respect of Matrix Limited has been reported:

	General Super market Chains	Drugstore Chains	Chemist Shops
Average revenue per delivery	₹ 84,975	₹ 28,875	₹ 5,445
Average cost of goods sold per delivery	₹ 82,500	₹ 27,500	₹ 4,950
Number of deliveries	330	825	2,750

In the past, Matrix Limited has used gross margin percentage to evaluate the relative profitability of its distribution channels.

The company plans to use activity-based costing for analyzing the profitability of its distribution channels.

The Activity analysis of Matrix Limited is as under:

Activity	Cost driver rate
Customer purchase order processing	Purchase orders by customers
Line-item ordering	Line - items per purchase order
Store delivery	Store deliveries
Cartons dispatched to stores	Cartons dispatched to a store per delivery
Shelf - stocking at customer store	Hours of shelf- stocking

In April, 2012 operating costs (other than cost of goods sold) of Matrix Limited are ₹8,27,970. These operating costs are assigned to five activity areas. The cost in each area and the quantity of the cost allocation basis used in that area for April, 2012 are as follows;

Activity Area	Total Costs in April, 2012	Total Units of Cost Allocation Base used in April, 2012
Customer purchase order processing	₹ 2,20,000	5,500 orders
Line- item ordering	₹ 1,75,560	58,520 line items
Store delivery	₹ 1,95,250	3,905 store deliveries
Cartons dispatched to store	₹ 2,09,000	2,09,000 cartoons
Shelf - stocking at customer store	₹ 28,160	1,760 hours

Other data for April, 2012 include the following

	General Super market Chains	Drugstore Chains	Chemist Shops
Total number of orders	385	990	4,125
Average number of line items per order	14	12	10
Total number of store deliveries	330	825	2,750
Average number of cartons shipped per store deliver	330	80	16
Average number of hours of shelf stocking per store delivery	3	0.6	0.1

Required :

(i) Compute for April, 2012 gross margin percentage for each of its three distribution channels and compute Matrix Limited's operating income

(ii) Compute the April, 2012 rate per unit of the cost allocation base for each of the five activity areas.

(iii) Compute the Operating income of each distribution channel in April, 2012 using activity based costing information. Comment on the results. What new insights are available with the activity- based cost information?

(iv) Describe four challenges one would face in assigning the total April, 2012 operating costs of ₹ 8, 27,970 to five activity areas. **(C.A.P.E II)**

Solution :

(i) Statement of Operating Income and Gross Margin percentage for April 2012

	General Super market Chains	Drugstore Chains	Chemist Shops	Total
Revenues	2,80,41,750	2,38,21,875	1,49,73,750	6,68,37,375
	(330 x ₹ 84,975)	(825 x ₹ 28,875)	(2,750 x ₹ 5,445)	
Less: Cost	2,72,25,000	2,26,87,500	1,36,12.500	6,35,25,00
of goods sold	(330 x ₹ 82,500)	(825 x ₹ 27,500)	(2,750 x ₹ 4,950)	
Gross Margin	8,16,750	11,34,375	13,61,250	33,12,375
Less : Other Operating costs				8,27,970
				24,84,405
Operating Income	2.91%	4.76%	9.09%	4.96%
Gross Margin % of Revenue				3.72%
Operating income % of revenue				

ABC Approach

(ii) Computation of Cost Driver Rate for five activities

1. Customer purchase order processing ₹ 40 per order
   (₹ 2, 20,000 5,500 orders)
2. Line item ordering ₹ 3 per line item order
   (₹ 1, 75,560 58,520 line items)
3. Store delivery ₹ 50 per delivery
   (Rs 1, 95,250 3,905 Store deliveries)
4. Cartons dispatched ₹ 1 per dispatch
   (₹ 2, 09,000 2, 09,000 dispatches)
5. Shelf- stocking at customer store ₹ 16 per hour
   (₹ 28,160 1,760 hours)

(ii) Computation of operating cost of each Distribution channel

	General Super market Chains	Drugstore Chains	Chemist Shops
1. Customer Purchase order processing	15,400 (₹40 x 385 orders)	39,600 (₹40 x 990 orders)	1,65,000 (₹40 x 4,125 orders)
2. Line item ordering	16,170 (₹ 3 × 14× 385 Orders)	35,640 (₹ 3 × 12 × 990 Orders)	1,23,750 (₹ 3 × 10 × 4,125 Orders)
3. Store delivery	16,500 (₹50 x 330 deliveries)	41,250 (₹50 x 825 deliveries)	1,37,500 (₹50 x 2,7500 deliveries)
4. Cartoons dispatched	99,000 (₹ 1 x 300 cartoons x 330 deliveries	66,000 (₹ 1 x 80 cartoons x 825 deliveries	44,000 (₹ 1 x 16 cartoons x 2,750 deliveries
5. Shelf - stocking	15,840 (₹16 x 330 deliveries x 3hrs)	7,920 (₹16 x 825 deliveries x 0.6hrs)	4,400 (₹16 x 2,750 deliveries x 0.1hrs)
Operating Cost	1,62,910	1,90,410	4,74,650

(iii) Operating income statement for April- 2012 (using Activity based Costing)

	General Super market Chains	Drugstore Chains	Chemist Shops
Gross margin as per part(i) ₹ (A)	8.16.750	11,34,375	13,61,250
Operating Cost (₹) (B)	1.62.910	1,90,410	4,74,650
Operating income (₹) (A-B)	6.53.840	9,43,965	8,86,600
(operating income / Revenue) x 100	2.23%	3.96%	5.92%

Comments: The ABC shows that chemist shops use a large amount of company resources per rupee of revenue than general supermarket chains and drug store chains. Operating costs as a percentage of revenues for the three channels is shown below

1. General supermarket chains(Rs, 1,62,910 2,80,41,750) x 100 0.58%
2. Drug store chains (₹ 1,90,410 ₹ 2,38,21,875) x 100 0.80%
3. Chemist shops (₹ 4,74,650 ₹ 1,49,73,750) x 100 3.17%

(iv) Challenges Faced in Assigning Total Operating Cost

In assigning total operating cost of ₹ 8, 27,970 to different activities may face the following challenges:

(i) For each activity an appropriate cost driver has to be selected

(ii) For each cost driver, a reliable data base has to be developed

(iii) There may be certain costs that may be common for several activities. How to distribute these costs over activities may pose questions.

(iv) For computing cost driver rates, appropriate time period has to be selected.

Problem 7

Hinduja Health Centre (HHC) runs three Programmes: (1) alcoholic rehabilitation (2) drug addict rehabilitation, and (3) aftercare (counseling and support of patterns after release from a mental hospital) the HHC's budget for current year follows;

Professional Salaries		
4 physicians x ₹ 3,00,000	₹ 12,00,000	
18 psychologists x ₹ 1,50,000	27,00,000	
20 nurses x ₹ 60,000	12,00,000	₹ 51,00,000
Medical Supplies		3,00,000
General overheads (administrative salaries, rent, Utilities, etc)		8,80,000
		62,80,000

Dr, Anupam Verma, the Director of the HHC, is keen on determining the cost of each programme. He has compiled the following data describing employees' allocations to individual programs:

	Alcohol	Drug	Aftercare	Total Employees
Physicians		4		4
Psychologists	6	4	8	18
Nurses	4	6	10	20

Eight patients are in residence in the alcohol programme , each staying for about six months. Thus, the clinic provides 40 patient - years of service in the alcohol programme. Similarly, 100 patients are involved in the drug programme for about six months. Each. Thus, The clinic provides 50 patient - years of service in the drug programme.

Dr. Verma has recently become aware of activity based costing as a method to refine costing systems. He asks his accountant, Kulkarni, how we should apply this new technique kulkarni obtains the following information:

(a) Consumption of medical supplies depends on the number of patients – year.

(b) General overhead costs consist of

Rent and clinic maintenance	₹ 1,80,000
Administrative costs to manage patients charts, food, laundry	6,00,000
Laboratory services	1,00,000
Total	8,80,000

(c) Other information about individual Departments

	Alcohol	Drug	Aftercare	Total Employees
Square feet of space occupied by each programme	9,000	9,000	9,000	9,000
Patients - years of service	40	50	60	150
Number of labouratory tests	400	1,400	70	2,500

Required :

1. Using an activity- based costing approach to cost analysis, calculate the cost of each programme and the cost per patient- year of the alcohol and drug programme.

   What benefits can HHC obtain by implementation the ABC system?

2. What factors other than cost, do you think HHC should consider in allocating resources to its programme?

Solution :

1. Activity – based costs for each programme and cost per patient – year of the Alcohol and Drug progammes :

	Alcohol	Drug	Aftercare
Direct labour			
Physicians [₹ 3,00,000 x (0:4:0)	-	₹ 12,00,000	
psychologists (₹ 1,50,000 (x6:4:8)	₹ 9,00,000	6,00,000	₹ 12,00,000
Nurses labour costs	2,40,000	3,60,000	6,00,000
Direct labour costs	11,40,000	21, 60,000	18,00,000
Medical supplies [Rs 2,000 x (40:50:60)]	80,000	1,00,000	1,20,000
Rent and clinic maintenance [₹ 6 x (9,000 ; 9,000 ; 12,000)]	54,000	54,000	72,000
Administrative costs to manage patient charts food, and laundry[₹ 4,000 x (40:50:60)]	1,60,000	2,00,000	2,40,000
Labouratory services [₹ 40 x (400 ; 1,400 ; 7,000)]	16,000	56,000	28,000
Total Costs	14,50,000	25,70,000	22,60,000

Cost per patient = ₹ 14, 50,000 / 40 = ₹ 36,250 (alcohol)

= 25, 70,000 50 = 56,400 (drug).

- Allocated using patient years
- Allocated using square feet of space
- Allocated using patient years
- Allocated using number of labouratory tests

The ABC system allocates costs more accurately because it identifies better drive₹ It chooses cost driers for overhead costs that have a cause and effect relationship Between the cost drivers and the costs.

By implementing the ABC systems, Dr. Verma can gain a more detailed understanding of costs and cost derive₹ This is valuable information from a cost management perspective. The system can yield insight into the efficiencies with which various activities are performed. Dr. Verma can them examine if redundant activities are performed. He can study trends and work toward improving the efficiency of the activities.

In addition, the ABC system will help Dr. Verma determine which programmes are the most costly to operate. This will be useful in making long run decisions as to which programme to offer or emphasis on. The ABC system will also assist Dr. Verma in setting up those prices for the programmes that reflect their costs more accurately.

2. The concern with using costs per patient-year as the rule to allocate resources among its programmes is that it emphasizes "input" to the exclusion of "outputs" or effectiveness of the programmes. After-all, the goal is to cure patients while controlling costs. No to minimize costs per-patient year. The problem, of course, is measuring outputs.

Unlike many manufacturing companies where the outputs are obvious because they are tangible and measurable, the outputs of service organizations are more difficult to measure. Example are "cured" patients as distinguished from "processed" or "discharged" patients, "educated" as distinguished from "partially educated" students, and so on.

SUMMARY

Traditional product costing systems reports distort product costs whenever an organization produces a diverse range of low-volume and high volume products. Activity Based costing emphasizes the need to obtain a better understanding of the behavior of overhead costs, and thus, ascertain what causes overheads and how they relate to products. By emphasizing activities, ABC tries to ascertain the factors that cause each major activity, cost of such activities and the relationship between activities and products produced.

The design of ABC system involves identifying the major activities that take place in an organization, creating a cost pool/cost centre for each activity; determining the cost driver for each major activity and assigning the cost of activities to products according to the product's demand for activities.

ABC system is clearly superior in terms of accuracy of cost measurement than traditional cost systems. The benefits derived from implementing ABC are likely to be influenced by the level of competition faced, the number of products sold and the diversity of the product range and the proportion of overheads of a firm's cost structure. Companies operating in a more competitive environment have a greater need for more accurate cost information, since competitors are more likely to take advantage of any errors arising from the use of distorted cost information.

Glossary

- **Activity-based Costing** is that costing in which costs are first traced to activities and then to products. The ABC is a costing system which focuses on activities performed to produce products. Activities become the focal points for cost accumulation.
- **Total Quality Management** here, the management develops policies and practices to ensure that the firm's products and services exceed the customer's expectations in terms of reliability, durability, serviceability and product benchmarking.
- **Target Costing:** A target cot is the market determined price minus the desired profit. It is the difference between the sale price required to capture the desired market share and the desired profit per unit.
- **Back Flush Costing**: Here, the allocation of cost is delayed till the product is manufacture or sold. Once the production of the product is completed or it is sold, the allocation of materials and conversion cost is triggered
- **Benchmarking :** Here, the company continuously evaluates its performance in terms of its competitors who are the models to learn and improve in the critical areas
- **Cost Drivers** are the events or forces that are the significant determinants of the cost of the activities
- **Unit-level Activities** are performed each time a unit of the product or service is produced these activities consume resources in proportion to the number of units produced
- **Batch-related Activities** are performed each time a batch of goods is produced. The cost of batch – related activities varies with the number of batches made, but is fixed for all units within the batch.
- **Product Sustaining Activities** are performed to support different products line to enable individual products to be produced and sold, but the resources consumed by these activities are independent of how many units or batches of the product are produced
- **Facility-Sustaining Activities** are performed to sustain a facility's general manufacturing process. These activities are necessary to sustain the manufacturing process and are common and joint to all products manufactured in the plant.

Objective Type Questions

TRUE OR FALSE

1. Traditional method of costing may result in undercosting and overcosting of products.
2. Machine hour rate is used in traditional method of overhead costing but not in activity based costing.
3. Activity-based costing is one of the best tools for refining a costing system.
4. ABC system helps companies to better price their products.
5. An activity is an item for which separate cost measurement is required.
6. Cost pool is like a cost center.
7. Identifying less number of activities results is more accurate cost.
8. Purchasing of large quantity of materials is a cost driver.

[Ans. True – 1, 3, 4, 6, False – 2, 5, 7, 8]

THEORETICAL QUESTIONS

1. Briefly explain the meaning and purpose of activity-based costing.
2. Describe the main features of activity-based costing.
3. Do you agree that activity-based costing is a more refined system of charging of overhead cost to products that traditional method? Explain
4. Explain the steps in activity-based costing
5. Explain the following terms in ABC
   (a) Cost Object, (b) Cost driver , (c) Cost pool
6. Discuss the advantages and limitations of activity-based costing.

EXERCISE PROBLEMS

Problem 1

A company manufacturing two products furnishes the following data for a year.

Product	Annual Output (Units)	Total machine Hours	Total number of purchase orders	Total number of set ups
A	10,000	40,000	320	40
B	30,000	60,000	192	22

The annual overheads are as under

Particulars	Amount in Rupees
Volume related activity costs	7,50,000
Set up related costs	9,00,000
Purchase related costs	5,00,000
Total costs	21,50,000

You are required to calculate the cost per unit of each Product A and B, based on,

- Traditional method of charging overheads
- Activity-based costing method.

Problem 2

X Ltd company gives you the following information related to its products lines:

	Product Y	Product Z
Number of units produced	150	50
Machine set-up hours per product line	20	15
Direct labour hours per unit	3	2

Total budgeted machine setup related cost ₹ 15,000

Required :

(a) Allocate machine set up related to the product lines Y and Z using direct labour hour rate.

(b) Allocate machine set up related cost to the product lines using ABC system.

(c) Show cost per unit of Y and Z using (a) and (b) above.

Problem 3

Vijay Company gives you the following information related to its products lines producing three products:

(1) Budgeted Overhead expenses:	₹
Machine Depreciation and Maintenance	2,20,000
Receiving	90,000
Engineering	82,000
Machine Set-up	10,000
Inspection	30,000

Other particulars:

	Products			Total
	X	Y	Z	
Units produced and sold	30,000	20,000	7,000	57,000
Direct material cost per unit	₹. 40	₹. 30	₹. 26	
Direct labour cost per unit	₹. 24	₹. 28	₹. 20	
Machine hour per unit	1.5	2	1	84,000
Number per product line:				
Receiving orders	16	40	200	256
Production Orders	14	12	19	45
Production runs	4	8	22	34
Inspection	8	4	20	32

Required :

(a) Statement showing total cost per unit for each product using machine hour rate.

(b) Statement showing total cost per unit of each product using relevant activities for recovery of overhead expenses;

(c) Explain the reason for differences, if any in costs between (a) and (b) methods.

Problem 4

Sindhu company recently introduced product Y to complement its regular product X. the company accumulates all overhead in a single cost pool and allocates it using machine hou₹ The company wants to switch over to ABC. A study reveals that much overhead cost relates to machine set-ups and engineering changes. The number of engineering changes may be taken as the activity drivers for the two new cost pools. Machine hours may be continued to be the base for allocating all remaining Overhead.

The following information is given for the year ended 31.3.2012

	Product X	Product Y	Total
Units produced and sold	9,500	500	10,000
Direct material cost per unit	₹ 100	₹ 700	
Direct labour cost per	₹ 12,00,000	₹ 1,00,000	₹ 13,00,000
Machine hours	2,500	500	3,000
Machine setups	150	100	250
Engineering changes	90	110	200
Overheads:			
Machine setup related			50,000
Engineering related			1,50,00
Others			4,00,000

Required :

(a) Using traditional costing system, determine the total and unit cost for each product line.

(b) Using ABC, determine the total and unit cost for each product line.

(c) What percentage of total overhead did the two costing systems treat differently? By what percentage did the cost of product X change as a result of the change in the system?

Problem 5

XYZ CO. Ltd. Produces three products X, Y,Z it provided the following information.

	X	Y	Z
Output in units	5,000	15,000	22,500
Direct Material per unit	Rs. 100	180	60
Direct labour per unit	Rs. 60	80	100
Machine hours per unit:	4	4	7
Labour hours per unit	3	4	5
No. Of machine set-ups	130	120	150
No of Purchase requisitions	600	900	1,000

Production over head split by departments

Dept A ------ ₹ 5, 50,000 - it is labour intensive

Dept B ------- ₹ 7, 50,000 - it is machine intensive

Total hours in Dept. A --- 55,000

Total hours in Dept. B --- 1, 50,000

Production overhead split by activity

Ordering/receiving of material	₹	7, 00,000
Machine set up	₹	6, 00,000
No of Order placed/received	₹	2500
No of machine setups	₹	400

You are required to prepare a statement of cost under:

(a) Traditional method

(b) ABC method

Comment on the comparative results. (Adapted)

[**Ans.** Traditional method

Absorption rate: Dept A - ₹ 10 per labour hour

Dept. B - ₹ 5 per Machine hour;

Cost per unit: X - ₹ 210; Y - ₹ 220; Z-Rs 245]

ABC: Method

Cost driver rates - ordering/ inspection ₹ 280 per requisition

Machine set-up - ₹ 1500 per set-up

Cost per unit - X - ₹ 236.60, Y - ₹ 187.80, Z - ₹ 182.44

Problem 6

NEC Ltd produces three products X, Y, and Z. it provides the following information regarding standard cost per unit of its products.

	X	Y	Z
Direct Material per unit	₹ 49	43	32
Direct labour per unit	₹ 33	39	50
Labour hours per unit	3	4	5
Machine hours per unit:	4	4	7
No. of Purchase orders	1,200	1,800	2,000
No. of machine set ups	240	260	300
Output (units)	10,000	20,000	30,000

Production over head split by departments

Dept A ₹ 11, 00,000

Dept B ₹ 15, 00,000

Dept. A is labour intensive and Dept. B is machine intensive.

Total labour hours in Dept A	1,83,333
Total machine hours in Dept B	5,00,000
Production overhead split by activity	
Receiving and inspection	₹ 14,00,000
Machine set up	₹ 12,00,000
No of batches of material received/in spected =	5,000
No of batches of machine set ups	800

Prepare statement of cost under:

(a) Traditional costing and

(b) Activity based costing

Comment on the comparison of the result of the two. (Adapted)

[**Ans.** (a) Traditional method - Absopton rates.

Dept A – ₹ 6 per labour hr, Dept. B – ₹ 5 per Machine hr;

Cost per unit: X – ₹ 112; Y – ₹ 118; Z-Rs 133

(b) Activity based costing – Cost driver rates.

Receiving/ inspection – ₹ 280 per order.

Machine set-up – ₹ 1500 per set up,

Cost per unit – X – ₹ 152, Y – ₹ 127 , Z – ₹ 116

❖ ❖ ❖

Chapter - 11
Customer Profitability Analysis

Introduction

Over the past several years, companies have been tremendously focused on their customers, trying to enhance customer service, paying more attention to customer needs and measuring customer satisfaction. Customer profitability accounting is an important management accounting tool based on the recognition that each customer is different. Therefore, each dollar of revenue or each dollar of cost generated by the customer does not contribute equally to a company's profitability. Its value lies in its ability to improve strategic decision making. It can also be used to help companies to understand how dependent they are on the most profitable customers, what proportion of resources are used for different customers, the full cost of servicing a customer including advertising, service and returns, which customers are targeted by competitors.

Organizations use customer profitability analysis (CPA) to identify the most valuable customers or customer segments to prioritize marketing, sales and service investments. By studying profitability metrics such as lifetime value, repeat purchase rate and churn rate analysts can identify profitable segments and non value segments. Similarly retention programmes may be created for particularly profitable customers. Business intelligence provides the statistical and data mining capabilities to calculate lifetime value. It identifies product affinities for cross-sell campaigns and performs predictive analysis of profits resulting from additional marketing investment. Customer segments or individual customers may be further investigated through temporary analysis. It gives lists of customer segments that automatically notify by relationship managers when profitable customers have executed a transaction. In the global economic environment the main objective of each business represents the maximized profit. Customer profitability analysis influence strategic decisions and it have a significant impact on business's future results.

Definition

According to CIMA (2005) "analysis of the revenue streams and service costs associated with specific customers or customer groups" is known as customer profitability analysis.

Kotler (1997) defines; " A person, household or company that, over time, yields a revenue stream that exceeds by an acceptable amount the company's cost stream of attracting, selling and servicing that customer." is known as profitable customer.

The CIMA definition does not provide any guidance as to when the analysis of customer profitability should be undertaken. Good practice suggests that this analysis is undertaken over the lifetime of customers, so that a customer lifetime value (CLV) can be obtained. This is calculated on the basis that the profitability of customers can vary significantly over the life of their relationship to a company.

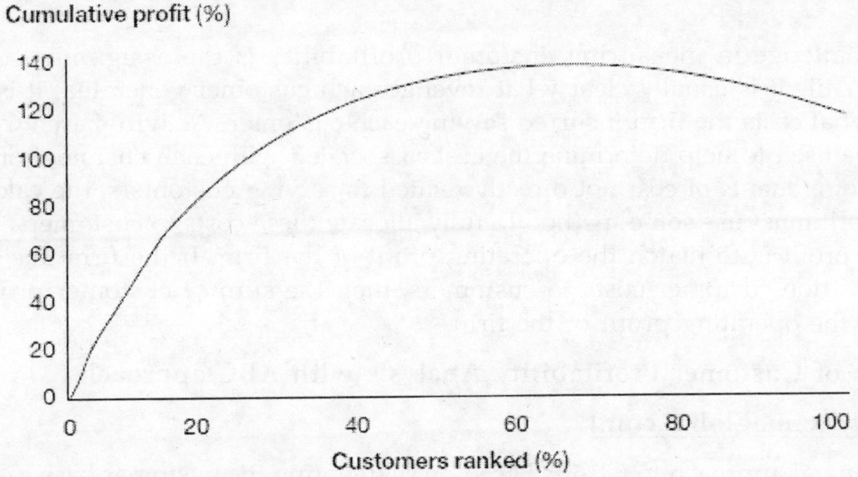

Source : CIMA Insider May 2003

CRM AND CPA

In recent years many firms have claimed to have moved from being "product-centric" to being "customer-centric". Customer relationship management (CRM) initiatives are usually at the forefront of their efforts. Their belief is that understanding customer behaviour and profitability is a key to gaining competitive advantage. CRM initiatives are associated with developments in both information systems and organization. For example, financial services companies have reorganized themselves so that one person is responsible for delivering all products to give customers. At the same time, they have set up databases holding information on the firm's dealings with particular customers.

CPA is intended to provide a guide for actions to be taken through CRM initiative. Its aim is to determine the profit margin generated by each customer. It found that a small number of customers generate a high proportion of the total profit, while the rest contribute little as explained by the simple graph (left). This ranks customers by order of profitability and shows that the first 20 per cent of customers account for 80 per cent of the firm's total profit, the next 40 per cent of customers generate a much smaller profit's and the last 40 per cent of customers actually lose money for our business.

Low-margin accounts can be treated in a number of ways that the sales to such customers can be routed via brokers or wholesalers. In extreme cases, some accounts can be closed. But the customer-centered view of a business associated with CPA and CRM must have a long-term, strategic dimension. The crux of this is that loyal customers are more profitable over time. It costs less to serve them and they probably refer others to your business. They may also pay a premium to continue dealing with you rather than switch to an unfamiliar supplier. You, therefore, need to take a life-cycle approach to dealing with customers and potential customers. CPA and CRM underpin a customer-centered, strategic approach to business but they do not themselves provide it. A company cannot simply install CRM database and expect the strategy to appear and start yielding results.

Challenges

The challenge in measuring customer profitability is the assignment of costs to customers. While it is usually clear what revenue each customer generated, it is often not clear at all what costs the firm incurred serving each customer. Activity-based Costing can sometimes be used to help determine the costs associated with each customer or customer group. For components of cost not directly related to serving customers, the calculation of customer profit must use some method to fully allocate these costs to customers, if the total of customer profit is to match the operating profit of the firm. If the firm decides not to allocate these non-customer costs to customers, then the sum of customer profit will be greater than the operating profit of the firm.

Application of Customer Profitability Analysis with ABC approach

(Source:www.cimaglobal.com)

The general approach to CPA is based on segmenting the customer base to determine the revenues and costs attributable to each segment. This is often combined with an activity-based costing (ABC) approach. Once the profitable and non-profitable segments are identified and profitable segments are maximized while non-profitable segments are reduced or eliminated.

Each of the key steps in this process is outlined below.

Step1 : Customer segmentation :

The basis for customer segmentation will differ across companies and across industries. Presently there are two basic approaches to customer segmentation:

1. *Demographic segmentation*: It is based on observable characteristics such as geographic area, customer age, sex and income level.
2. *Psychographic segmentation:* It is based on customer needs and behaviour such as customer values, attitudes and interests.

Step 2 : Revenue attributable to each segment

Once segments have been identified, the annual revenue is calculated for each segment this will depend on the products or services offered by the company. Adjustments to the price paid by the customer for a product or service, such as discounts, service fees or product enhancement fees, must be included to determine the true amount of revenue generated by each customer and the aggregated amount calculated for the customer segment.

Step 3 : Use ABC to determine the cost attributable to each segment :

The annual cost is calculated each segment. This will involve both directly attributable product or service costs and also customer costs including allocation of overheads, marketing, sales and distribution costs. These customer costs which are often hidden, such as quality control and inspection costs, order picking, order fulfillment and customer ordering costs. ABC is an effective way to assign both types of costs to customers.

Step 4 : Analyze the profitable versus the less profitable or unprofitable customer segments:

The profitable customer segments will be those whose annual revenues exceed annual costs. The profitability of customer segments is likely to vary from year to year. The accurate analysis could involve for calculating profitability over the lifetime of each customer segment, as noted below.

Step 5 : Develop strategies to maximize profits from profitable customers and reduce or eliminate less profitable or non-profitable customers :

This step involves detailed planning around the development of long-term customer relationships for increased revenues and hence, profitability such as customer retention and loyalty programmes. To address the least profitable or non-profitable customer groups, two main actions are used [Botten, N. 2007].

1. *Elimination* : Ceasing to supply these customers. This can be done by no longer marketing to these customers, changing the product or service so that it is no longer suitable, or raising prices.
2. *Re-engineering* : Turning the least profitable or non-profitable customer groups into profitable ones by either increasing revenue or decreasing costs attributable to these groups or both. Examples include charging additional fees for services or using differential prices and according to customer segment.

Step 6 : Review the impact of the new strategies on the performance of the customer segments :

The implementation of any new strategy first you should study the changes in pricing, cost reduction or customer service, and reviewed after an appropriate period to determine the impact on customer profitability.

Customer Lifetime Value (CLV)

This is the value generated by a customer over the lifetime of a customer's relationship to a company. This concept recognizes that the annual profitability of a customer group will vary from year to year. To calculate the CLV, companies need to make judgments about the duration of the company's relationship with the customer. This includes the likelihood, frequency and amount of expected purchases over the lifetime of the customer.

To determine the present value of these future income streams, a discount rate (usually the company's cost of capital) is used. CLV estimates are particularly useful to:

1. Companies with large variations in purchasing patterns by customers
2. Companies with high customer acquisition costs
3. Companies with high customer retention costs.

Source:www.cimaglobal.com

Advantages of Customer Profitability Analysis

The following are the advantages :

1. Eliminate non-profitable customers and maximizing sales or services to profitable customers.

2. An understanding of the true costs of each customer segment, including taking into account non-production costs when determining profitability.
3. Non-production costs can sometimes be more significant than production costs.
4. It provides a method of identifying customer groups who are of lifetime value to the company, and who are worth retaining or protecting.
5. Improved strategic decision making by providing useful information for customer related decisions, including pricing, discounting and marketing decisions.

Disadvantages of Customer Profitability Analysis

1. Companies may not have the data capture systems to produce an accurate estimation of customer segmental revenues and costs.
2. There may be practical difficulties in calculating costs attributable to each segment. Implementing ABC is often challenging for many companies.
3. CPA may overlook the combinations of products or services purchased by customers. Customer profitability depends on the mix of products or services bought. The danger is that the analysis will be used on specific underperforming products or services and will overlook the impact of sales of other products to the customer.
4. Annual profitability may not be representative of lifetime value. The costs of attracting and retaining a customer should be compared with the lifetime earnings and not just with the customer's annual earnings. For example, Taco Bell sells tacos at less than $1 each. However, the firm has estimated that a loyal repeat customer generates up to $11,000 over their lifetime [Kotler, 1997].

Key developments

1. **Advances in information technology :** This has allowed companies to improve the quality and quantity of information concerning customer profitability including information on revenue, costs, retention and lifetime value. Many companies have complicated customer profitability models and customer databases. These can be designed for any type of business and to accommodate different customer characteristics.

   Data can be aggregated by size of customer, size of order, service complexity, post sale service requirements, location and other factors. Information technology can provide detailed information and analysis on individual customers or groups of customers.

2. **Managing customer value :** Analyzing customer profitability has evolved into managing the overall value of customers. CPA now includes analysis of customer lifetime value and impact. It is also managing profitability through analysis of customer segments and margins. Customer lifetime value looks at the profitability of the customer over their lifetime. Customers have an impact on other customers, company employees and other groups through their transactions and communications. For example, they can refer other customers to company offerings.

Customer Cost in Service Companies (Hotel)

ABC Constructions for Customer Account Profitability Analysis : The implementation of customer account profitability analysis within a hotel environment necessitates a change in current accounting approaches to revenue and cost allocation. It requires an adjustment from the way in which revenues and expenses are traditionally recorded by operating and service departments and to identification by customer group. Which is designed to move from the way revenue and cost are traditionally recorded in accounting systems, by operating department and overhead categories to reporting each by customer group.

ABC activities have departmental origins and are more appropriately identified by analyzing the work of individuals within departments before cross functional groups can be formulated. The results of this study suggest that cross functional activities are actually groupings of logically related activities identified by analyzing work performed by individuals in separate functional areas.

ABC activities have a link to the mission of the company, possess a definite path to the cost object, process in nature and are observable and measurable. The revenue data by customer group can be sourced directly from many property management or yield management systems. The key to CPA lies in the selection of an appropriate method of matching costs with customer groups. Activity-based costing was the approach used to distribute the expenses from cost centres to activity centres. The way the expenses were distributed depends on the functional relationships or cost drivers in a hotel. Cost centres support specific activity centres and a given activity centre incurs costs for particular market segments. Measurement of the costs requires the distribution of expenses recorded by the financial accounting system to the appropriate market segments. The financial system records expenses according to cost centres, which include both operating departments and overhead items. The first group is directly incurred and includes operating expenses in rooms, restaurant, banqueting and telephone cost centres. The other group is attributed to overhead expenses from cost centres in finance, human resources, marketing, administrative and general occupancy. Classification is used for property operation and maintenance, energy, property taxes and depreciation.

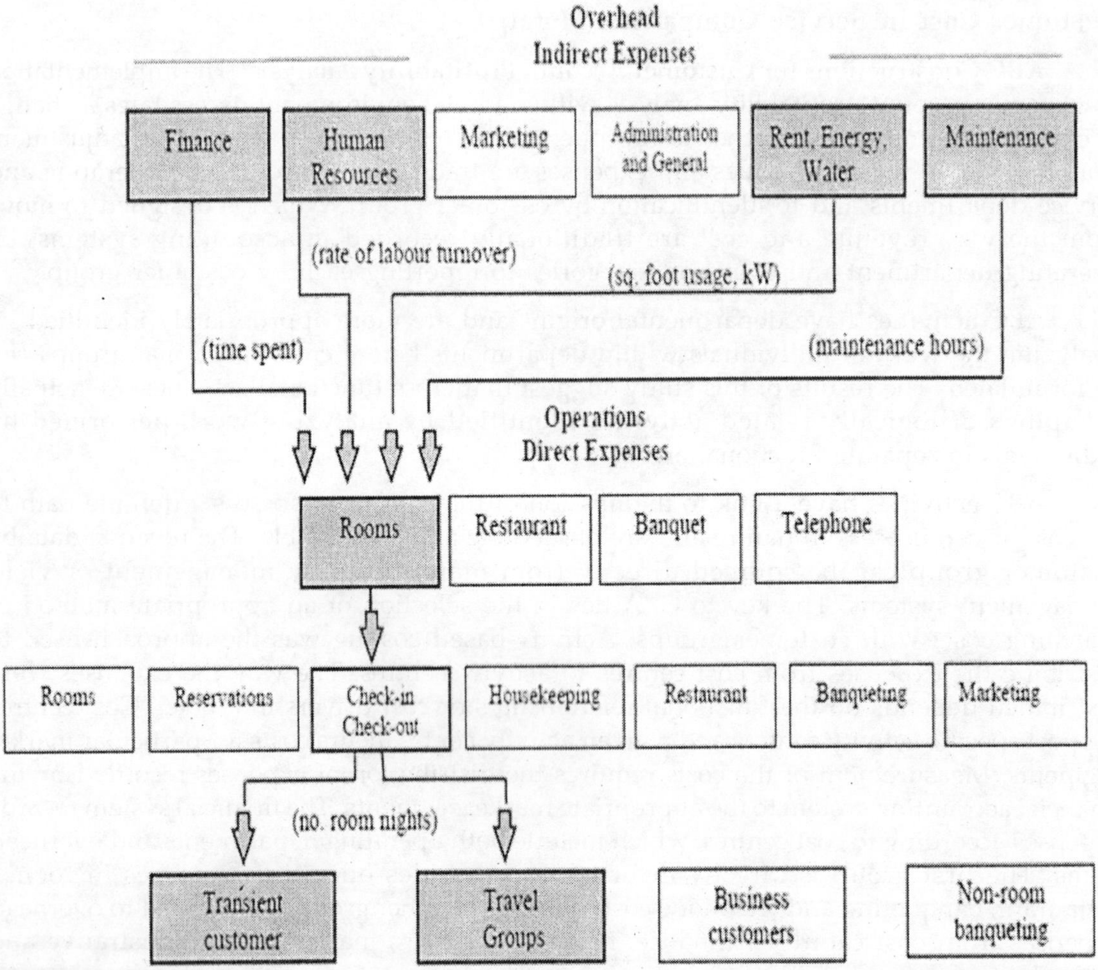

Source : *www. pc.parnu.ee/.../...(Vira Krakhmal)*

First, the expenses were distributed from the cost centres is called "activity centres". Activity centre costs were assigned to the appropriate market segment. The activity centres represent the functional costs of providing services to the guests e.g., administration, banquets, check-in and check-out, housekeeping, marketing, restaurants, reservations, rooms, and telephone. Breaking down the activity centres in this fashion makes the cost distribution more complex, but it also added accuracy to final expense analysis.

Noone and Griffin's (1997) mentioned that there may be more than one connection that is more than one cost driver, between a cost centre and the activity centres it supports. The cost drivers are identified according to the extent and proportion of the functional relationships between expenses. For instance, the finance and accounting department spends a substantial amount of time processing payroll and guest checks. The cost of running the payroll falls on all centres that use human resources, while the cost of guest accounting supports three activities: check-in and check-out, restaurant and banqueting. The cost driver used to assign costs from finance to payroll is the number of employees and the driver for finance to guest accounting was the number of checks. The remaining finance department costs were considered administrative so they were assigned to the administration activity.

Customer Cost in Service Companies (Banks)

In recent years banks have become increasingly aware of the need to measure the profitability of corporate customer relationships. Past emphasis on deposit size as a measure of rank has gradually given way to the realization that large banks are not necessarily the most profitable and those loans, not deposits, generate most bank earnings. At many larger banks, profitability analysis is essentially a sophisticated version of standard account analysis.' It has been introduced to assist in measuring individual customer profitability. *It describes the objectives of profitability analysis, discusses some of the general principles involve*d in constructing an analysis and considers the alternative types of profitability measures commonly used.

Account Analysis : The application of standard account analysis to both corporate and correspondent accounts became widespread in the mid-1960 when banks feared they might be caught in a profit squeeze. During that period the costs of providing bank services escalated rapidly as inflation became more pronounced and as the variety of bank services increased greatly. Corporate treasurers, while asking for larger loans and for highly specialized services were simultaneously reducing non interest bearing balances to invest the funds directly in the securities market. As a result interest rates rose; small-er banks began to sell large amounts of Federal funds, occasionally producing negative collected balances at correspondents. Mean while, bank liquidity was declining and li-ability management techniques were not proving fully satisfactory in meeting the demands for loanable funds when Regulation Q interest rate ceilings were binding. Under these circumstances larger banks initially developed account analysis techniques to ensure not only that adequate compensating balances would be maintained but also that the needs of the most profitable customers could be given priority.

In performing a standard account analysis, a bank determines the revenue from a customer's account by multiplying the average collected balance, generally adjusted for reserve requirements by an earnings credit or allowance. The expenses of servicing the account are by multiplying the number of times a given service is utilized by the cost (including allowance for profit) of providing the service. A typical account analysis schedule is shown in Table 1.

Table 1		
FIRST NATIONAL BANK		
Account Analysis for :		
Month of		
EARNINGS ALLOWANCE		
Average Ledger Balance		$
Less Average Uncollected Funds		$
Average Collected Balance		$
Less Legal Reserve of (17 1/2 %)		$
Average Balance Available for Investment		$
Earning Allowance (%)		
INVESTMENT VALUE		$
EXPENSES		
Account Maintenance		$
Credits		$
Debits		$
Deposited items		
Not Encoded	34 each	$
Encoded	24 each	$
Return Items	250 each	$
Stop Payments	$2.00 each	$
Wire Transfers	$1.50 each	$
Coupon Envelopes		$
Currency Transactions		$
Coin Shipped		$
Account Reconciliation %		$
Lackbox Services		$
Float Overdrafts		$
TOTAL EXPENSES		$
NET PROFIT (OR LOSS)		$

Source : *Federal Reserve Bank Kansas City, Monthly Review April 1975.*

While the account analysis represents an important step in determining the profitability of a customer relationship and it is not a measure of total profitability. For example, the analysis tends to focus on activity charges for which compensating balances are maintained account maintenance, items deposited, ledger entries, wire transfers, etc., but rarely makes allowance for other types of services such as loans, investment counseling, Federal funds transactions, trust services or data processing. Hence, the primary analysis the accounts of non borrowers with heavy activity charges, such as respondent banks for other customers. The omission of loan relationship has at times allowed the double or even triple use of compensating balances. Since cross-checking is frequently not automatic, a compensating balance required for a loan might at times be used to compensate for activity charges and also serve as a justification for a future call on credit. The primary objectives of account analysis are to measure the adequacy of compensating balances and to obtain an indication of the profits generated by an account relationship. The meaning of the profit figure obtained is generally uncertain and can rarely be related directly to the profits of the bank. Since the price of a service often includes a markup, a high volume customer is likely to be more profitable than a low volume relationship even though the computed profits are identical. Moreover, some banks build in an additional profit margin by granting earnings allowance on investable funds below the actual earnings value of those funds or by making a deduction for reserves which exceeds actual requirements. Increasingly, banks have sought to correct the double use of balances by deducting both the compensating balance for a loan and required reserves from the collected balances shown in an account analysis. While this approach represents a step in the right direction, it does not allow for an analysis of the profitability of the loan. Possible tradeoffs between interest rates on loans and compensating balances are not shown. Moreover, the costs of making loans, variations in risk, necessary return on capital, etc. cannot readily be handled in this framework. By comparison, profitability analysis seeks to determine the total relative profitability of a customer relationship. However, some bank services such as consulting, credit checks on accounts receivable, loan participations and security safekeeping are often not included in the analysis, with the result that the estimated profits could be biased upward. For these reasons, many banks avoid a listing for profits at the bottom of an analysis statement, preferring instead to show net revenue as the amount available to compensate for other non-listed services.

Profitability Statement of Banks

Profitability analysis seeks to overcome some of the shortcomings of regular account analysis by presenting detailed income statements for major customers. Multiple accounts for a single corporate relationship are consolidated including subsidiaries and perhaps even major officers. Losses on one account can be offset with profits on others. The earnings and expenses associated with loans and various fee services such as the purchase and sale of securities, not typically considered in an account analysis are likely to be included in a profitability statement. However, profitability analysis focuses on the commercial lending function of banks and is of the greatest use in determining the profitability of net borrowers.

In the profitability analysis, the net amount of funds borrowed is computed and the estimated profit or loss from the income statement is generally assumed to raise or lower the return on funds loaned. Since estimated profitability tends to be strongly influenced by the terms on loans compensating balances, interest rates and associated fees. The analysis has often been proposed as a means of determining the loan terms necessary to meet a minimum profit goal for a bank. It can also be a helpful guide in allocating bank resources since the analysis tends to highlight the most profitable types of customers and loans. In some banks the analysis is also used to evaluate the performance of lending officers.

As might be expected for relatively new techniques of computing customer profitability vary significantly among banks. In part these variations arise from differences in management philosophy about the types of services deserving emphasis and the appropriate base to which profits should be related. Other factors include the amount of effort a bank may wish to devote to a partially automated process, the degree of precision the bank expects from the figures and differences in concepts, judgment and sophistication in the measurement of certain variables. The more common methods of measuring profitability approach which demonstrates the general principles involved is shown in Table 2.

Sources and Uses of Funds : The first section of the profitability statement contains an analysis of the sources and uses of bank funds. Multiple loans to a customser are first consolidated to obtain average total loans outstanding [line1] is in the account analysis, average investable or loanable funds provided to the bank by the custom-er (line 4) are obtained by deducting cash items in process of collection and an allowance for reserve requirements from gross ledger balances. Some banks also make deductions for the compensating balances required to cover the activity charges in the account analysis. The deposit figure remaining after the various deductions have been subtracted is then net average loans outstanding to obtain the average net bank funds used by the customer (line 5). The customer in other words assumed to borrow his own funds first. For many banks the previous step completes the analysis of bank funds advanced to a customer. If the bank wishes to relate the profit on the relationship to the return on bank capital is the case in the example, the net funds loaned to the customer must be subdivided into at least two categories. The first is the proportion of funds supplied from the bank's capital account. Allocated capital (line 5a) is frequently a flat percentage of gross loans. Some banks assign capital in proportion to the estimated risk on loans, while others assume capital is also required.

Capital is also required to support the customer's deposits. Since profits will ultimately be related to the assigned capital, variations in its allocation can have a significant impact on the estimated profitability of a relationship. All other things being equal and higher capital allocation tends to reduce the profit rate. If the return on capital is to be a measure of actual profitability the capital assigned to a customer relationship should be selected in such a way that for the bank as a whole the total assigned capital is equal to the bank's actual capital.

The remaining category of bank funds supplied (line 5b) is a residual and represents funds obtained from sources other than the capital accounts. If the bank chooses to differentiate further among alternative sources of funds such as purchased funds and deposit funds, this entry could be subdivided. The use of multiple pools of funds is relatively uncommon.

Income

The second section of the profitability statement lists the major sources of income derived by the bank from the customer relationship. Most of the entries shown are self-explanatory. Gross interest income (line 6 includes the interest accruing on loans during the analysis period. Interest earnings on deposits 7) are imputed on the loanable funds supplied by the customer. This entry is required to give the customer income credit for compensating balances maintained. Service charges (line8a) represent any fees paid to the bank to cover deposit activity costs or any charges associated with obtaining loans such as points. Since these charges are most likely to arise when compensating balances are inadequate, provision must be made for their inclusion. Under the loan commitment entry (line a figure would be entered only if the customer had paid an outright fee for a commitment or a line of credit. If a compensating balance had been maintained instead, these funds would be reflected in the sources and uses section of the table and earnings accordingly imputed. In addition net bank funds used by the customer would be reduced, resulting in a lower charge for bank funds loaned in the expense section of the analysis. If the analysis and the charges were internally consistent either approach would have the same effect on estimated profits.

The inclusion of income from data processing services (line8c) is somewhat controversial). Some banks feel income should be included only to the extent it is related to regular bank services or loans. Under this view specialized services such as EDP or trust departments are treated independently of normal bank operations. These functions serve as separate profit centers but any income and expenses are not included in a profitability analysis related to loans. But it feels that an accurate picture of the profitability of a customer relationship can be obtained only if all income and expenses from services are included. Banks in this latter group often believe that customers are not likely to differentiate among different profit centers in considering the compensation for a bundle of bank services. Nevertheless, if a bank includes the funds received for a specialized service in the income portion of the profitability statement, the charge for providing that service should also be listed under expenses.

Table 2
FIRST NATIONAL BANK
Customer Profitability Analysis

Account	XYZ Manufacturing	Date:	July 20,1975
Affiliated Account		period	12/31- 6/30
		Type of Loan	

	CURRENT PERIOD		LAST 12 MONTHS	
SOURCES AND USES OF FUNDS				
1. Average Loan Balance		$		$
2. Average Collected Balance	$		$	
a. Investable Balance (17.5% Reserve)	$		$	
3. Average Time Balance	$		$	
a. investable Balance (3% reserve)	$		$	
4. Total loanable Funds(2a + 3a)		$		$
5. Bank Funds used by Customer (1 -4)		$		$
a. Allocated Capital (8% of 1)	$		$	
b. Funds Transferred from pool (5 - 5a)	$		$	

INCOME				$	
6. Gross interest income on Loans :		$		$	
7. Earnings on Deposits (xxx % of 4)		$	$		
8. Fees Paid:			$		
a. Service Charge Fees	$		$		
b. Loan Commitments	$			$	
C. Data Processing	$			$	
d. Total (8a + 8b + 8c)		$			
9. Total Income (6 + 7 + 8)		$			
EXPENSES					
10. Activity Costs from Account Analysis		$			
11. Interest Accuted on Time Deposits :		$		$	
12. Charge fbr Bank Funds Used:				$	
a. Allocated Capital (20% of 5a)	$				
b. Pool Funds (xxx % of 5b)	$				
c. Total (12a + 12b)	$				
13. Loan Handling Expenses		$	$		
14. Cost of Free Services		$	$		
15. Data Processing		$	$		
16. Total Expenses (10+11+12+13 + 14 +15)		$	$		
NET INCOME					
17. Net Income Before Taxes (9- 16)		$			
PROFIT ABILITY MEASURES			%		%
18. Allocated Capital Index (17 / 5a)			%		%
19. Net Profits/ Net Funds used (17 / 5)			%		%
20. Net Profits / Gross Amount Borrowed (17 / 1)			%		%
21. Gross Profits / Net Funds Used [(17 + 12c) / 5]					

Source : Federal Reserve Bank Kansas City, Monthly Review April 1975.

Expenses

The third major section of the profitability table derives the bank's total expenses associated with servicing the customer relationship. The first entry, charge for activity services (line10) could be approached two ways. The bank in the example has implicitly opted to assign any profit from activity services to general profits associated with loans. Thus, it has based the entry on the actual costs of providing services, ideally making sure that the charge includes the expenses of all services provided for compensating balances. To the extent a customer maintains compensating balances based on the price of services rather than the cost, the earnings on the compensating balances would exceed the bank's cost of services. Other banks often feel that it is inappropriate to allocate all profits to loans. According to these banks the users of services requiring much labour and equipment should be expected to contribute to the profitability of those services. The charges for the activity services performed by the latter group of banks are usually based on the prices used in the account analysis. The price approach allows banks to vary the profit margin on different services. Either option could be justified. Banks relatively confident that they have developed accurate cost figures for all important services would perhaps find the cost approach superior since the total profits on the relationship are made more explicit. On the other hand if a bank has not fully costed all services or if the accuracy of the cost figures is uncertain, the latter approach may be preferable.

The use of prices would tend to build in a margin for services not included in the account analysis. In recognition of these difficulties some banks compute profitability using both costs and prices and either method is capable of suffering from the same types of biases previously discussed in conjunction with the account analysis. In a similar vein, the charge for bank funds used (line 12) can be handled in a variety of ways. The example assumes the bank has established a specific pretax profit goal on capital. This target is simply built in as an expense. The target must be realistic given projected interest rates and earnings. Alternatively some banks do not establish a formal goal for return on capital. In these instances the total of net bank funds supplied to the customer is usually assumed to come from the general fund pool. Under this approach the computed profits are ultimately related to allocated capital but the expected return on capital is not built in as an expense. Variations can also arise among banks in the interest charge for pool funds (line some prefer to use an estimate of the bank's average cost of loanable funds, while others choose to use a measure of the cost of purchased funds).

The remaining items in the expense section are largely self explanatory. Interest accrued on time deposits (line 11) includes interest earned by the customer on any time and savings deposits listed in the sources and uses section of the table. Many banks include time deposits in the profitability analysis only if they are non-interest earning or carry interest rates well below market levels. Large denomination bearing competitive rates are often excluded from the analysis since these deposits are generally viewed as investments by corporate treasurers and are not likely to be bound to a bank by a customer relationship. Credit and loan handling expenses (line 13) are designed to cover the costs of making loans. Charges would be based on the operation and maintenance of the loan department salaries of loan analysts, an allowance for bank overhead, and any outright expenses the bank has incurred in making the loan, such as legal fees. The entry for fee services (line 14) should make allowance for the cost of any services included in the income portion of the statement which have not been classified elsewhere under expenses. Possible examples might be charges for account reconciliation, lockboxes, payroll preparation, and night depository services. Finally the inclusion of data processing expenses (line 15) is required as discussed earlier to ensure consistency in the treatment of income and expenses.

Net Income and Profitability

The last lines of the profitability statement are used to derive different indicators of the profitability of the customer relationship. Total profits or net income is shown in line 17. In line 18, the allocated capital index is computed by dividing profit by allocated capital. If greater than zero, this index indicates that the bank is actually realizing a higher profit rate on customer relationships than the goal previously established by the bank. A negative figure would suggest that profits were not sufficient to meet the target, while a zero figure would imply the goal had just been met.

The return on capital is by necessity an important criterion in judging the profitability of a customer relationship but it is not the sole concern. For example, it provides no indication of the size of the relationship. The index could be high but profits low. The amount of capital allocated to a relationship is also somewhat arbitrary possibly leading to distortions in the index number. These types of considerations have caused many banks to compute more than one profitability ratio. One possibility is to determine profits as a percentage of net bank funds borrowed by the customer (line 19).

While the specific methods of computing customer profitability differ greatly among banks, the general objectives are often quite similar. Not only does the analysis provide a guide to whether a customer is adequately contributing to the profits of an institution but it also formalizes the tradeoff between the terms on loans. For example, if the interest rate on a loan were to increase, income, net profits and the profitability indexes would all rise accordingly. Similarly, if larger compensating balances were to be maintained, profitability would also rise as the imputed interest on deposits increased and as the charge for net bank funds borrowed declined. Some profitability statements even contain a series of entries at the conclusion of the analysis specifying what interest rates on loans would be necessary to meet bank profit objectives given differing compensating balance requirements. Regardless, the applicability of profitability analysis tends to be limited largely to custom-ers which borrow. If the customer in the example were a non-borrower, the profitability indexes would be meaningless, although capital could perhaps be allocated on some basis other than gross loans.

Some caution must be exercised in analyzing the sample profitability statement. While the sample illustrates the general principles involved in computing customer profitability, the specific entries and the precise approach cannot be taken as representative of the analy-sis methods at all banks. There are wide differences among banks, not only in the approaches used to measure customer profitability but also in the items included in the analysis. Many banks exclude some deposits or some loans in measuring the sources and uses of funds. The range of services for which income and expenses are listed can also vary greatly.

Differences in the structure of an analysis can have a significant impact on estimated profits. Most banks determine only the total of investable funds represented by deposits, implicitly allowing those balances to serve as compensation for either loans or activity services but also make an explicit deduction from collected funds for the compensating balances required for activity services. The effect of this approach is to increase net funds borrowed. Thus lowering the estimated profitability of a given customer at those banks using a net funds borrowed ratio. Some banks allocate capital to borrowings while others assign an explicit expense charge for risk and loss.

Similarly, some banks charge customers the cost of money on the gross amount borrowed and give an interest credit on gross investable funds and others charge only for net funds borrowed. For these two methods to yield identical results the interest rates used for funds borrowed and supplied must be iden-tical and it is not always the case. Some banks compute the profitability of loan and investment services separately to avoid allocating all profits to loans and some use slightly different formulas for calculating the profitability of different types of customers. But these demonstrate a few of the differences that exist among banks in the techniques of com-puting customer profitability.

Indexes of Customer Profitability

Just as a bank has numerous options in designing a profitability analysis a wide variety of profitability measures could be computed. Nevertheless, all banks profitability is generally judged on the basis of a handful of standard indicators. These include the ratio of gross profits to net funds used; net profits to net funds used, net profits to gross amount borrowed, and net profits to allocated funds. While only one of these commonly used in-dexes makes any explicit reference to bank capital, the alternative ratios can often be re-lated in a fairly direct way to earnings on capital. As a result the desired return on capital can set minimum acceptable values to the noncapital ratios.

Gross Profits/Net Funds Used : One of the profitability measures least likely to be subject to sizable distortion. Therefore one of the most credible is the ratio of gross profits to net funds loaned. Gross profits are equal to total profits when the cost of money is not included in expenses. Under this approach customers are assumed to borrow their own funds first and funds supplied by a customer are implicitly granted an earnings allowance equal to the average rate on the customer's loans. In mathematical terms the standard formula is:

$$\frac{\text{Gross Profit}}{\text{Net funds Used}} = \frac{Y - E}{L - D}$$

Where Y equals gross income derived from the customer relationship; E equals all costs of servicing the relationship other than the cost of funds; L equals average loans attributable to the relationship; and D equals average loanable or investable funds provided by the customer. The behaviour of this ratio under varying circumstances can be readily seen. By eliminating the cost of funds from the analysis a bank can avoid a situation in which the profitability index for customers with fixed rate loans and compensating balances varies inversely as money market interest rates rise and fall. The index would be sensitive to changes in loan terms. Since the interest paid on loans is reflected in Y and the compensat-ing balances maintained are included in D, the index would rise if either of these variables increased. If net funds borrowed declines the ratio other things equal will approach infinity. This tendency implies that large borrowers unable to keep sizable compensating balances may have a comparatively low profitability ratio and that smaller borrowers are likely to rank higher. If the customer is a net borrower the value of the index can be compared directly to the bank's cost of funds or money market rates. As long as the ratio exceeds the bank's cost of funds the relationship would be profitable. To ensure that a target return on capital is realized however, the value of the index must exceed the bank's cost of funds by a sufficient margin.

The gross profits to net funds used ratio has two important limitations. First, it is of little use in analyzing the profitability of a net depositor. Since the denominator would be negative, the ratio would imply that a bank was losing money on net depositors, which, of course, is incorrect. Second, the index makes no allowance for the size of the customer rela-tionship. Among customers with identical rates of return on net funds used and relatively more funds are likely to be more important to the total profitability of the bank. While these qualifications are hardly unique to this particular measure they do demonstrate the need for examining the figures underlying the computation of an index number before drawing any conclusions. Not only is the value of the index importance but also the relative weight or significance that should be attached to it.

Net Funds Used

Despite the relative ease in computing gross profits, most banks prefer to base an analysis of customer profitability on net profits. Net profits are gross profits minus an allowance for the cost of funds loaned. The basic formula for this profitability index is:

$$\frac{\text{Net Profits}}{\text{Net Funds Used}} = \frac{Y - E - C}{L - D}$$

Where C equals the cost of net funds used. This profitability indicator differs from the gross funds used measure only in that the cost of funds (expressed as a per-centage of net funds used) is subtracted from the gross profit yield. If the gross profit index, for example, were 10 per cent, and the cost of funds were 6 per cent, net funds used would be 4 per cent. Obviously, a positive ratio implies the relationship is profitable. A zero ratio would suggest a break-even situation, and a negative one, losses. As a result of the parallelism between these two profitability measures, both have the same limitations and behave in a generally similar fashion.

Gross Amount Borrowed

A slightly different measure of customer profitability is the ratio of net profits to gross amount borrowed.

$$\frac{\text{Net Profits}}{\text{Gross Amount Borrowed}} = \frac{Y - E - C}{L}$$

The profitability index is applicable only to borrowers but unlike the previous measures does not require the borrower to be a net user of funds. While comparisons between the index value and money market interest rates are not meaningful the index varies directly with the average interest rate on loans. If the average loan rate rises 1 per cent, so would the profitability index. This measures the advantage of showing directly any change in loan interest rates necessary to meet minimum profit objectives. In general, a zero value for the ratio would imply a break-even situation. Banks utilizing this formula, though, generally seek a minimum return on gross loans of one and half to two and half per cent to realize a desired return on capital.

Net profit / Allocated Capital : The final commonly used profitability measure is the ratio of net profits to allocated capital. Since the example at the beginning used the capital allocation approach, little need be added about the general description of the mathematical formula is:

$$\frac{\text{Net Profits}}{\text{Allocated Capital}} = \frac{Y - E - C}{K}$$

Where K represents capital allocated to a customer relationship. If capital is allocated to both earning assets and deposits, this index is perhaps the most versatile of those widely used. The profitability of all customers, whether or not they are borrowers, could be analyzed.

Other Measures of Profitability : In addition to the four basic ratios, many banks have adopted additional indexes of customer profitability. These include such ratios as net or gross profits/total revenue, net profits/total expenses, total income/net funds borrowed, gross profits/total loans, actual income/target income and total revenue/total expenses. Some banks simply compute net or gross profits but don't relate the figure to any specific indicator of the size of a customer relationship. Although each indicator has unique properties and should be selected to reflect management objective, the choice of a particular indicator is not likely to be a crucial matter. Under normal circumstances, most indicators produce roughly the same ranking of customers.

Solved Problems

Problem 1

The new Controller of Tata Telecom (TT) has discovered that TT's customer differ greatly in their ordering pattern and interaction with TT's sales force. He feels that BT's costing system does not accurately assign marketing, distribution and selling expenses to customer. He has developed and ABC system to assign these expense to customers, He has identified the following marketing, selling distribution costs for two customers, X and Y.

	X	Y
1. Travelling by sales representatives	₹ 30,000	₹ 1,60,000
2. Services Customers	66,000	4,48,000
3. Handling customer Orders	14,000	58,000
4. Shipping to customers	86,000	2,78,000
	1,96,000	9,44,000
The following additional information is available		
1. Sales	18,50,000	15,30,000
2. Cost to goods sold	10,20,000	7,50,000

Required :

(a) Using the current costing approach of assigning marketing, selling and distribution expenses to customers using 30 percent of sales revenue, determine the operating profit of the two customers.

(b) Using the ABC information provided, determine their operating profit.

(c) Which of the two methods produces more accurate assignment of marketing, selling and distribution expenses to customers? Explain.

Solution :

(a) Customer Profitability Analysis (Current Costing Approach)

	X	Y
	₹	₹
Sales revenue	18,50,000	15,30,000
Cost of goods sold	10,20,000	7,50,000
Gross margin	8,30,000	7,80,000
Marketing selling and distribution expenses		
(0.30 x sales revenue)	5,55,000	4,59,000
Operating Profit	2,75,000	3,21,000
Profit (as percentage of sales)	14.86	20.98

(b) Customer Profitability Analysis (ABC Approach)

	X	Y
	₹	₹
Sales revenue	18,50,000	15,30,000
Cost of goods sold	10,20,000	7,50,000
Gross margin (A)	8,30,000	7,80,000
Marketing, Selling and Distribution expenses :		
* Travelling by sales representatives	30,000	1,60,000
* Service Customer	66,000	4,48,000
* Handling Customer orders	14,000	58,000
* Shipping to Customers	86,000	2,78,000
Total activity expenses (B)	1,96,000	9,44,000
Operating profit (A-B)	6,34,000	(-1,64,000)
	37.4	(-10.72)

(c) Y customer is more profitable than X customer according to the current costing system. Moreover, both the customer are profitable. But customer X emerges as hightly profitable and Y emerges as the most unfavourable customer according to the ABC approach. The ABC obviously produces more accurate assignment of marketing, selling and distribution expenses. As can be seen from the computations travels, customer services and shipping to customers, have huge demands on Y's marketing, selling and distribution resource in contract to X's But the current costing system fails to make this distinction between them.

Problem 2

Venu Limited has decided to analyses the profitability of its five new customers it buys at Rs. 80 per product and sells to retail customers at a list price of Rs 100 per product. The dates pertaining to five customers are:

Particulars	Customers				
	A	B	C	D	E
Products sold	4,500	20,000	1,35,000	72,000	9,000
List selling price	₹ 100	₹ 100	₹ 100	₹ 100	₹100
Actual selling price	₹105	₹ 108	₹ 90	₹ 110	₹104
Number of purchase orders	15	25	30	25	30
Number of Customer Visits	2	3	6	2	3
Number of deliveries	10	30	60	40	20
Kilometers travelled per delivery	20	6	5	10	30
Number of expedited delivers	0	0	0	0	1

Its five activities and their drivers are:

Activity	Cost driver rate
Order taking	₹ 750 per purchase order
Customer Visits	₹ 600 per Customer Visit
Deliveries	₹ 5.75 Per delivery km travelled
Product handling	₹ 3.75 per case sold
expedited deliveries	₹ 250 per expedited delivery

Required :

Compute the customer level operating income of each of five retail customers now being examined (A, B, C, D and E) Comment on the results.

Solution :

Calculation of customer Level Activity costs

Particulars	Customers				
	A	B	C	D	E
1. Order taking Costs (No. of purchase order × ₹ 750)	11,250	18,750	22,500	18,750	22,500
2. Customer Visits costs (No. of Customer visits × ₹ 600)	1,200	1,800	3,600	1,200	1,800
3. Delivery vehicles travel costs (kms travelled by delivery vehicles x ₹ 5.75 per km)	1,150	1,035	1,725	2,300	3,450
4. Products handing costs (Cases sold x ₹ 3.75)	17,550	73,830	5,13,000	2,68,313	32,906
5. Cost of expedited deliveries (No. of expedited deliveries x ₹ 250)	-	-	-	-	250
Total cost of Customer level Operating activities :	31,150	95,415	5,40,825	2,90,563	60,906

Calculation of Customer level operating income

Particulars	Customers				
	A	B	C	D	E
(A) Cases Sold	4,500	20,000	1,35,000	72,000	9,000
	₹.	₹	₹.	₹.	₹.
(B) Actual selling price	105	108	90	110	104
(C) Cost	80	80	80	80	80
Sales at actual price (A x B)	4,72,500	21,60,000	1,21,50,000	79,20,000	9,36,000
Less: Cost of goods sold (A x C)	3,60,000	16,00,000	1,08,00,000	57,60,000	7,20,000
Gross Margin	1,12,500	5,60,000	13,50,000	21,60,000	2,16,000
Less : Customer level activity costs	31,150	95,415	5,40,825	2,90,563	62,906
Customer Level operating income	81,350	4,64,585	8,09,175	18,69,437	1,53,094

PRACTICAL QUESTIONS

1. Explain customer account profitability analysis?
2. Discuss CRM and CPA?
3. How to implement the customer profitability analysis with ABC approach customer?
4. Explain the term lifetime value?
5. Discuss the advantages and disadvantages of customer account profitability analysis?
6. Explain key developments in customer account profitability analysis?
7. Discuss customer cost in service companies with reference to hotel?
8. Explain customer cost in service companies with reference to banks?
9. Explain the profitability statement of banks?
10. What are the indexes of customer profitability?

❖ ❖ ❖

Chapter - 12
Life Cycle Costing

Introduction

Globalization the manufacturing companies are required to produce a variety of products to satisfying individual customer needs with mass production efficiency in a shorter product lifecycle. On the other hand, customers are considering not only products cost but also after sale services. Recycling and disposal are also gradually forming part of company's responsibility. During the period of 1970s to the beginning of 1980s, the LCC analysis was mainly applied in the military field. After that period the applications of LCC analysis have spread to other industries such as aircraft, electrical power plants, oil, chemical industries and railway systems.

It is recent tool in costing that looks at a products entire value chain from a cost perspective. The concept of product life cycle takes into account different angles of marketing, elements of corporate strategy, finance and production. It is also called Whole Life Costing technique to establish the total cost of ownership. It is a structured approach that addresses all the elements of cost and can be used to produce a spend profile of the product or service over its anticipated life span. The results of an LCC analysis can be used to assist management in the decision making process where there is a choice of options. The accuracy of LCC analysis diminishes as it projects further into the future, so it is most valuable as a comparative tool for decisions.

Definitions

Life cycle defined as "time interval between a product's conception and its disposal".

Product life cycle defined as "the life span of a product from development, through testing, promotion, growth, maturity, decline and regeneration".

A new product is first developed and then introduced to the market. Once the introduction is successful, a growth period follows with wider awareness of the product and increasing sales. The product enters maturity when sales stop growing and demand stabilizes. Eventually, sales may decline until the product is finally withdrawn from the market or redeveloped.

Product life cycle cost (LCC) is defined as" the cost that incur through the whole life-cycle of a product including product creation, use and disposal".

Asset defined as "the total cost throughout its life including planning, design, procurement, support costs and any other costs directly attributable to owning or using the asset".

LCC consists of all direct costs plus indirect variable costs associated with the procurement and disposal of the system. Indirect costs may include linked costs such as additional common support equipment, additional administrative personnel and non-linked costs such as new recruiters to recruit additional personnel. All indirect costs related to activities or resources that are not affected by the introduction of the system are not part of LCC. Product life cycle costing costs accumulated for activities occurring during the entire life cycle of a product.

Importance of LCC

The LCC technique has accumulated costs for activities, occurring during the entire life cycle of a product. But not only the cost even sales or revenue related information also important in its entire life cycle. It is a planning tool and is a form of reporting in cost management systems. The product has finite life and passes through introduction, growth, maturity and decline. Product cost and profits varies as the product moves in its life-cycle. Each phase in the life cycle poses different threats and opportunities which give rise to different strategic actions. The cost and revenues of the product are traced throughout the period of the life cycle of the product. There can be extension of the life cycle through new user identification or increased usage by their existing users.

Product life cycle stages

The product life cycle stages explain the growth and decline of revenues and profits associated with a product or service. Many companies in addition to marketing and sales managers have product managers, who are responsible for specific products or services. The company has to develop appropriate strategies and tactics in each of these product life cycle stages in order to improve its market position and profitability which is called product life cycle management. Product life cycle management deals with different challenges at each stage and approaches the market with different strategies and tactics in each of these stages. Product life cycle has four stages but the life cycle for some products may differ.

The following are the stages of Product life cycle :

1. Introduction phase
2. Growth phase
3. Maturity Phase
4. Decline Phase

1. **Introduction :** This is the first stage started with research and engineering capabilities lead to product development. Product is launched into market after testing the business incurs R&D costs along with the testing costs. The product has been introduced with above average advertising and promotional investments by the company to introduce the new product to the target market. The demand for the new product has to be created and target customers are attracted to the new product. Generally during the market introduction stage the revenues are very low and the investments are very high. Most business do not generate any profits during this stage but use marketing and sales strategies and tactics to successfully position in the new product/service in the marketplace. Hopefully it generates profits in the next product life cycle stages.

After the initial acceptance, the sales rise slowly. Profit is low because the high unit cost that arises from low output, heavy promotional investments are made to encourage growth. As product launch costs have increased firm in order to have a general idea of the magnitude incurred are focusing on the product development and planning phase. The duration of introductory phase, for consumer goods is range between a few months to one year and for industrial goods it is more than a year.

2. **Growth Phase :** During this stage revenues and profits are increased. The product is accepted by the market, there would be mass sales. The target market is already familiar with the product and customers are purchase the product. There is a rapid sales growth and costs are much lower than the introductory phase. More competitors try to enter this business as they see the positive market trend development and increased profits generated by the companies.

   Due to economies of scale the overall cost of doing business is decreasing and the product profitability also increases. In order to ensure that there is a proper delivery of the product to the customer, much attention is given to the developing systems. Constant consumer satisfaction leads to a rapid growth in sales indicates that the product has been successful. Unit and promotion costs are low because of large scale production and wider area of marketing. Sometimes there is a shakeout period wherein competitors also have the market.

3. **Maturity Phase :** Maturity Phase is usually the longest phase of the product life cycle. In this stage market is saturated with the product and competition is very strong. The growth in revenues starts to decline and profitability decreases as competitors start to compete more on price and less through product differentiation since most of the competitors can offer the same product. At the same time strong competition requires more marketing and sales investments to keep the market share which increases the overall cost of doing business.

   This period can be extended through market segmentation and innovative uses of the product. Product reaches saturation and profits decrease, the potential customers and satisfied buyers decrease. The customers move to a new product with additional feature or alternative substitutes. The need for these replacement products is not enough to maintain the demand at the same level as before. Price starts to come down in the saturated market as small player struggle to find a foothold. Business withdraws unsuccessful brands from the market and the remainders continue with the customers of unsuccessful brands. Prices are stable in this period although profits decrease. Abandonment costs are incurred by the companies whose products are withdrawn.

4. **Product Decline Phase :** During this stage both revenues and profits were decline. New products are introduced in the marketplace and replace the old products. Customers changing tastes because of technological advancement it results the products decline. Many competitors will not be profitable and they withdrawn from the market. This phase may be a short or long duration.

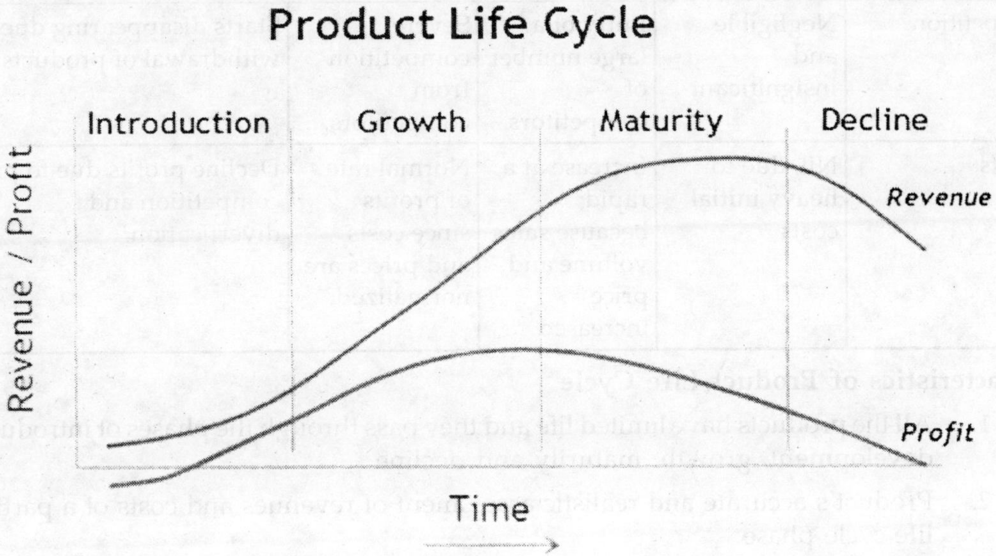

Source : excel4marketing.com

A comparative analysis of Product Life Cycle phases :

Particulars	Introduction	Growth	Maturity	Decline
Phase	I	II	III	IV
Sales Volumes	Initial stage hence sales are low.	Rise in sales levels at increasing selling price.	Rise in sales levels at decreasing selling price.	Sales level off and then start decreasing the selling price.
Prices of products	High levels to cover initial costs and promotional expenses.	Retention of high level prices except in certain cases	Prices fall closer to cost, due to effect of competition	Gap between price and cost is further reduced. In this stage price is less than cost also.
Ration of promotion expenses to sales	Highest, due to effort needed to inform potential customers, launch products, distribute to customers. etc.	Total expenses remain the same, while ratio of S&D OH to sales is reduced due to increase in sales.	Ratio reaches a normal % of sales. Such normal % becomes the industry standard	Reduced sales promotional efforts as the product is no longer in demand.

Competition	Negligible and insignificant	Entry of a large number of competitors.	Severe competition from competitors.	Starts disappearing due to withdrawal of products.
Profits	Nil, due to heavy initial costs	Increase at a rapid because sales volume and price increased.	Normal rate of profits since costs and prices are normalized.	Decline profits due to price competition and diverfication.

Characteristics of Product Life Cycle

1. All the products have limited life and they pass through the phases of introduction, development, growth, maturity and decline
2. Product's accurate and realistic assessment of revenues and costs of a particular life cycle phase.
3. It is relevant to most service contracts and equipment purchasing decisions.
4. Profit per unit varies as products evolve through life cycle.
5. Each phase throws a new challenge and calls for a specific strategic decision.
6. Finding new uses and new users, it is possible to extend life of a product.

Benefits of product life cycle costing

The following are the main benefits of product life cycle costing:

1. It gives good decision based on the accurate and realistic assessment of revenues and costs of a particular life cycle phase.
2. It results in earlier action to revenues or costs might be considered. There are a number of factors that need to be managed in order to maximize return from a product.
3. It provides framework for considering total incremental costs over the entire span of a product.
4. It can promote long term rewarding in distinction to short term rewarding.
5. LCC is simply a way-stop on the never ending journey for reducing costs.
6. It provides the tools to engineer maintenance budgets, ownership costs, and present decision making scenarios in a financial perspective to achieve the lowest long term cost of ownership.
7. LCC is the "laser guided missile" attack on important business problems for projects and processes.
8. LCC analysis allows for a cost trade-off to be made against the varying attributes of the purchasing options.
9. This analysis is relevant to most service contracts and equipment purchasing decisions.

10. It recognizes that maximizing revenue and minimizing costs at every stage might not maximize profits over the product life cycle.

Limitations of product life cycle costing

The following are the limitations of product life cycle costing :

1. The result of PLC is unpredictable because of uncertainty.
2. The period of each stage is unknown. Hence, it is not a useful planning tool.
3. There may be a change in PLC because of an alternative substitute product available in the market.
4. It is applicable at the industrial level rather than on individual products.

Figure 1 : Life Cycle Costing Process Task

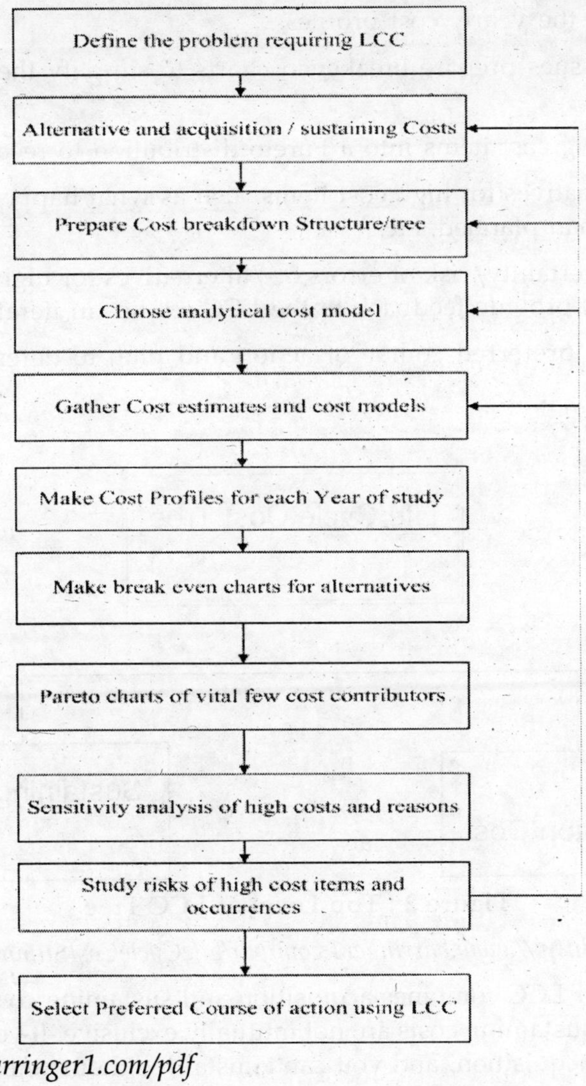

Source : http://www.barringer1.com/pdf

LCC follows a process (Fabryck, 1991) as shown in Figure 1 are :

Step 1 - Identify what has to be analyzed and the time period for the project life study along with the appropriate financial criteria.

Step 2 - Focus on the technical features by way of the economic consequences to look for alternative solutions.

Step 3 - Develop the cost details by year considering memory joggers for cost structures.

Step 4 - Select the appropriate cost model, simple discrete, simple with some variability for repairs and replacements, complex with random variations, etc. required by project complexity.

Step 5 - Acquire the cost details.

Step 6 - Assemble the yearly cost profiles.

Step 7 - For key issues prepare breakeven charts to simplify the details into time and money.

Step 8 - Sort the big cost items into a Pareto distribution to reconsider further study.

Step 9 - Test alternatives for high cost items such as what happens if maintenance cost is ±10% than planned, etc.

Step 10 - Study uncertainty/risk of errors or /alternatives for high cost items as a sanity check and provide feedback to the LCC studies in iterative fashion.

Step 11 - Select the preferred course of action and plan to defend the decisions with graphics.

The basic tree for LCC :

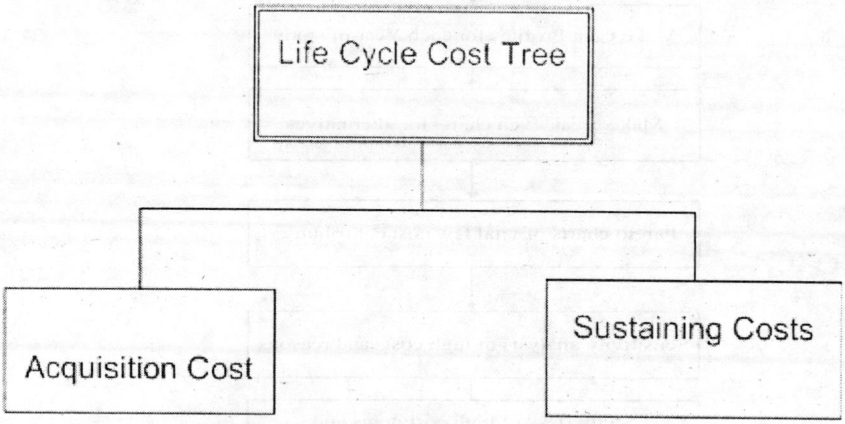

Figure 2 : Top Level of LCC Tree

Source: http://www.barringer1.com/pdf/LifeCycleCostSummary.pdf

The basic tree for LCC combines acquisition and sustaining costs as shown in Figure 2.The acquisition and sustaining costs are not mutually exclusive. If you acquire equipment, you must sustain the acquisition, and you can't sustain without someone having acquired the item.

Acquisition and sustaining costs are found by gathering the correct inputs, building the input database, evaluating the LCC and conducting sensitivity analysis to identify cost drivers.

Acquisition costs have branches for the cost tree shown in Figure 3 as a memory jogger. Sustaining costs have branches for the tree, which is also a memory jogger.

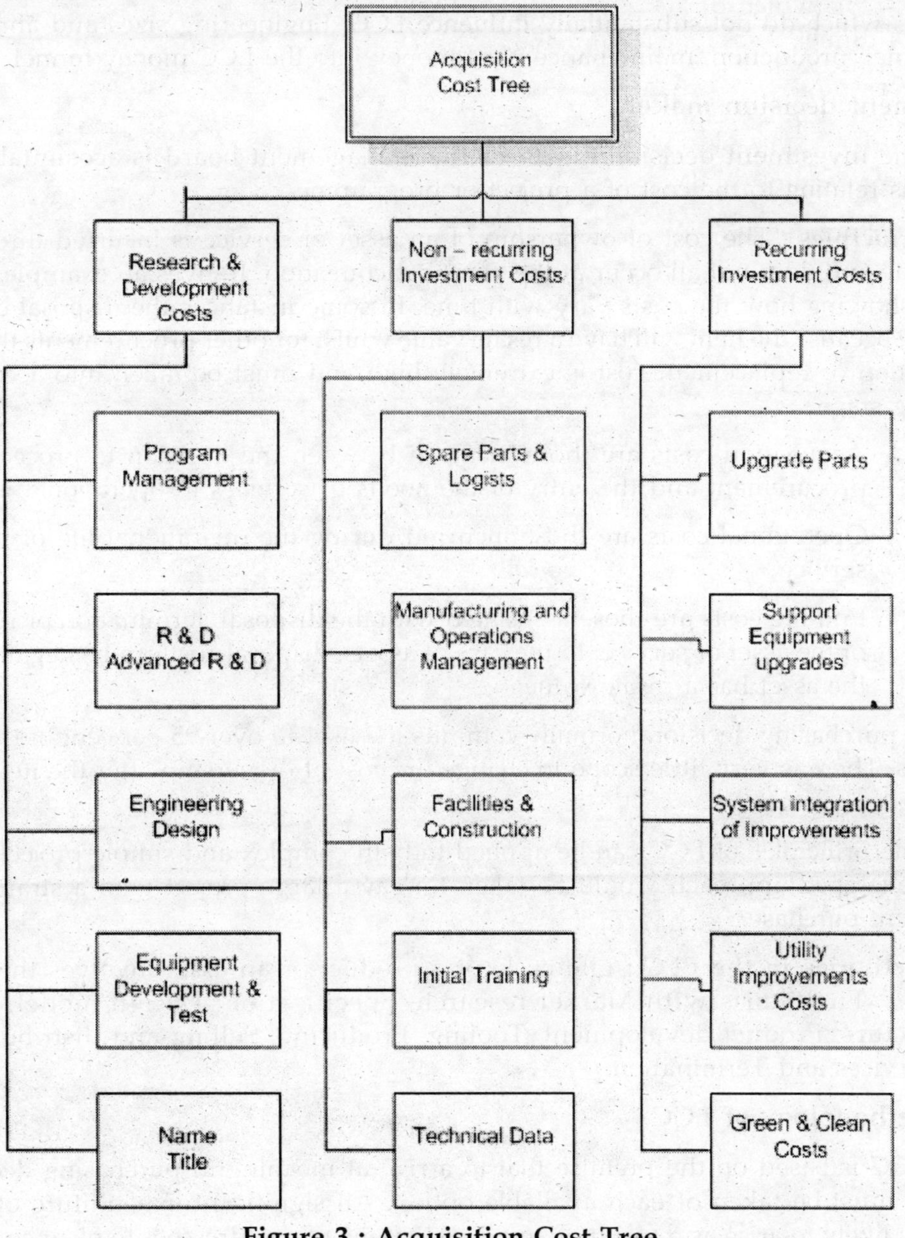

Figure 3 : Acquisition Cost Tree

Source : http://www.barringer1.com

What cost goes into each branch of the acquisition and sustaining branches? It all depends on the specific case and is generally driven by common sense. Building a nuclear power plant to generate electricity requires special categories under each item of acquisition cost and sustaining cost. Building a pulp and paper mill or modifying coke drums at a refinery to prevent characteristic over-stress which occurs during coke drum quench cycles have different cost structures. Include the appropriate cost elements and discard the trivial elements which do not substantially influence LCC. Engineering sizes and aims the LCC cost funnel; production/maintenance pour money into the LCC money funnel.

Investment decision maker

The investment decision maker or the management board is accountable for any decisions relating to the cost of a project or programme.

Principles : The cost of ownership of an asset or service is incurred throughout its whole life and does not all occur at the point of acquisition. It gives an example of a spend profile showing how the costs vary with time. In some instances the disposal cost will be negative because the item will have a resale value whilst for other procurements the disposal, termination or replacement cost is extremely high and must be taken into account at the planning stage.

- Acquisition costs are those incurred between the decision to proceed with the procurement and the entry of the goods or services to operational use
- Operational costs are those incurred during the operational life of the asset or service
- End life costs are those associated with the disposal, termination or replacement of the asset or service. In the case of assets, disposal cost can be negative because the asset has a resale value.

A purchasing decision normally commits the user to over 95 per cent of the through-life costs. There is very little scope to change the cost of ownership after the item has been delivered.

The principles of LCC can be applied to both complex and simple projects though a more developed approach would be taken for say a large project than a straightforward equipment purchase.

Activities in the PLC : Life cycle of a product or an asset involves the following activities. First starts with Market research, Specification, Design model, Prototype manufacture, Product development, Tooling, Producing, Selling and distribution, Offer sales services and Termination.

The Methodology of LCC

LCC is based on the premise that to arrive at meaningful purchasing decisions full account must be taken of each available option. All significant expenditure of resources which is likely to arise as a result of any decision must be addressed. Explicit consideration must be given to all relevant costs for each of the options from initial consideration through to disposal.

The degree sophistication of LCC will vary according to the complexity of the goods or services to be procured. The cost of collecting necessary data can be considerable and where the same items are procured frequently a cost database can be developed.

The following fundamental concepts are common to all applications of LCC :

- cost breakdown structure;
- cost estimating;
- discounting; and
- inflation.

Cost Breakdown Structure (CBS) : CBS is central to LCC analysis. It will vary in complexity depending on the purchasing decision. Its aim is to identify all the relevant cost elements and it must have well defined boundaries to avoid omission or duplication. Whatever the complexity any CBS should have the following basic characteristics:

1. It must include all cost elements that are relevant to the option under consideration including internal costs;
   - ➢ each cost element must be well defined so that all involved have a clear understanding of what is to be included in that element;
   - ➢ each cost element should be identifiable with a significant level of activity or major item of equipment or software.
2. The cost breakdown should be structured in such a way as to allow analysis of specific areas. For example, the purchaser might need to compare spares costs for each option; these costs should therefore be identified within the structure.
3. The CBS should be compatible, through cross indexing, with the management accounting procedures used in collecting costs. This will allow costs to be fed directly to the LCC analysis; or programmes with subcontractors.
4. These costs should have separate cost categories to allow close control and monitoring; and the CBS should be designed to allow different levels of data within various cost categories.
5. The CBS should be sufficiently flexible to allow cost allocation both horizontally and vertically.

Cost Estimating : Having produced a CBS, it is necessary to calculate the costs of each category. These are determined by one of the following methods:

1. *Known factors or rates* : These are inputs to the LCC analysis which have a known accuracy. For example, if the unit production cost and quantity are known, then the procurement cost can be calculated. equally, if costs of different grades of staff and the numbers employed delivering the service are known, the staff cost of service delivery can be calculated;
2. *Cost estimating relationships (CERs)* : These are derived from historical or empirical data. For example, if experience had shown that for similar items the

cost of initial spares was 20 per cent of the UPC; this could be used as a CER for the new purchase. CERs can become very complex but in general, the simpler the relationship the more effective the CER. The results produced by CERs must be treated with caution as incorrect relationships can lead to large LCC errors. Sources can include experience of similar procurements in-house and in other organizations. Care should be taken with historical data, particularly in rapidly changing industries such as IT where it can soon become out of date; and.

3. *Expert opinion :* It is a open to debate and the only method available when real data is unobtainable. When expert opinion is used in an LCC analysis it should include the assumptions and rationale that support the opinion.

Discounting : Discounting is a technique used to compare costs and benefits that occur in different time periods. It is a separate concept from inflation and is based on the principle that the people prefer to receive goods and services now rather than later. This is known as 'time preference'. When comparing two or more options, a common base is necessary to ensure fair evaluation. As the present is the most suitable time reference, all future costs must be adjusted to their present value.

Discounting refers to the application of a selected discount rate such that each future cost is adjusted to present time, i.e., the time when the decision is made. Discounting reduces the impact of downstream savings and as such acts as a disincentive to improving the reliability of the product.

Inflation : It is important not to confuse discounting and inflation: the discount rate is not the inflation rate but is the investment "premium" over and above inflation. Provided inflation for all costs is approximately equal, it is normal practice to exclude inflation effects when undertaking LCC analysis.

However, if the analysis is estimating the costs of two very different commodities with differing inflation rates, for example oil price and man-hour rates, then inflation would have to be considered. However, one should be extremely careful to avoid double counting of the effects of inflation. For example, a vendor's proposal may already include a provision for inflation and unless this is noted, there is a strong possibility that an additional estimate for inflation might be included.

Other Issues

Risk Assessment : Cost estimates are made :p of the base estimate (the estimated cost without any risk allowance built in) and a risk allowance (the estimated consequential cost if the key risks materialize). The risk allowance should be steadily reduced over time as the risks or their consequences are minimized through good risk management.

Sensitivity : The sensitivity of cost estimates to factors such as changes in volumes, usage etc need to be considered

Optimism bias : Optimism bias is the demonstrated systematic tendency to be over-optimistic about key project parameters. It can arise in relation to:

- Capital costs;
- Works duration;
- Operating costs; and
- Under delivery of benefits.

Optimism bias needs to be assessed with care, because experience has shown that undue optimism about benefits that can be achieved in relation to risk will have a significant impact on costs. A recommended approach is to consider best and worst case scenarios, where optimism and pessimism can be balanced out. The probability of these scenarios actually happening is assessed and the expected expenditure adjusted accordingly.

Life Cycle Assessment (LCA)

It is also known as life cycle analysis, eco-balance and cradle-to-grave analysis is a technique to assess environmental impacts associated with all the stages of a product's life from cradle-to-grave (i.e., from raw material extraction through materials processing, manufacture, distribution, use, repair and maintenance and disposal or recycling). LCAs can help avoid a narrow outlook on environmental concerns by:

- Compiling an inventory of relevant energy and material inputs and environmental releases;
- Evaluating the potential impacts associated with identified inputs and releases;
- Interpreting the results to help make a more informed decision.

PLC - Cost Assessment

The growing awareness about the need to protect the environment from any adverse effects of the PLC forms a major part of PLC assessment.

PLC assessment is a procedure by which product stewardship is made more effective. Product stewardship is the application of planning, producing, Conserving and recycling products so that there is not much harmful effect on the environment. This assessment provides a means of acquire knowledge about the effect of a product during the course of its life cycle, so that costs and benefits can be assigned to them.

Product Life Cycle – As per Environment Act

As per the Environment Protection Act product has four stages in its entire life:

1. Resource extraction
2. Product manufacture and packaging
3. Product use and
4. Recycling and disposal

A product may be recycled and used again in production, but it for any reason the product is unable to be recycled then it is disposed off and this is an issue of waste management. PLC assessment uses the cost accounting system by assessing and allocating the environmental costs which has been caused by the producer of each particular stage. This enables the manager to get a clear idea and compare the cost economics of a PLC regarding various competing designs.

Assessment Stages : PLC assessment comprises of 3 stages. They are as follows,

1. Inventory analysis
2. Impact analysis and
3. Improvement analysis

1. **Inventory Analysis :** This includes making decisions on the depth of the study. It gives details regarding the nature, proportion of resources, energy requirements and the resultant output e.g., manufacturing, packaging, distribution, use, and disposal. One step more detail would include extraction or production of the raw materials to produce the separate ingredients of plastic, paper, cotton, etc. Possibly you could spin off into even further subdivision such as cotton production and chemicals, energy, and equipment required for this. Thus a need exists to determine the boundaries of the LCA, within these boundaries, you need to decide what you will and will not gather data on in your environmental assessments.

   This output could be residue in solid, liquid or gaseous form. Inventory analysis is done throughout a products life cycle and is also an analysis of the recycle potential of the product and what the requirements for its disposal.

2. **Impact Analysis :** Impact analysis gives ranking to the competing designs through an assessment of their environmental effects. It analyses the meaning of the data values provided by inventory analysis and gives useful details regarding the various effects of inventory. Sometimes harmful effluents or gases are released during the life cycle of a product and hence this analysis helps to decide whether production of the product is feasible as regards the environment. For example is a pound of benzene in the air, a pound of herbicide in the water or loss of habitat for a threatened species the most important? As of now, no agreed upon method to do this type of ranking has been determined.

   Cost Assessment **:** Cost assessment is determination of the financial outcome of the environmental changes established in the first two stages of the life cycle assessment namely inventory and improvement stage. Assessment of costs is the first stage and it helps in measurement of the second stage. Environmental assessment helps to know what the costs are involved for recycling the particular product and whether or not it is economical. Assignment of costs can help prioritize the competing alternatives. Assignment of costs is through tracing of activities and activity of the following cost drivers:

   1) Trace and assign material costs
   2) Material consumed (per unit) x Material procurement price
   3) Assign energy costs and environment costs by driver tracing
   4) Assign private costs, recycling and disposal costs.

Calculation of environmental cost per unit

	Product
Material consumed	XXXX
Utilities	XXXX
Contaminant related resources	XXXX
Total Private costs	XXXX
Recycling benefits	XXXX
Environmental cost per unit	XXXX

3. **Improvement Analysis :** Improvement analysis having all the data pieces gathered from inventory and impact steps. It is the final step of PLC assessment and involves seeking new methods to decrease the environment impacts of the alternatives assessed. This step is directly related to the controlling mechanism of the organization. The main function is to enhance the products performance and procedure of the environment control system. Without this analysis, reductions in one aspect may result in increased pollution in other aspects of production

Pricing and Evaluation Criteria for Products at Different Stages of PLC

A management accountant comes across three pricing situations. One is special order decisions in which prices are fixed as per cost analysis. In second situation, firm uses the concept of target pricing in which firms prepares it by analyzing the market price and steps are taken to achieve costs necessary to make profits. The third pricing decisions involve all those situations which have not been covered under the two situations.

Pricing of products at different stages of PLC can be done as per the following two views:

1. Cost life cycle approach
2. Sales life cycle approach

1. **Cost life cycle approach :** This type of pricing is used in manufacturing and service firms, when competition is on the basis of cost leadership efficient producers set prices. This achieves cost reduction through usage of cost information resulting in operational efficiency. When competition is on the basis of differentiation a firm can set the prices as per their requirement. They may set a high price in the beginning and reduce it later all this to increase profits by catering to those who are willing to pay and those who are price conscious. This is skimming price strategy the firm may lower the price to increase the market share. This pricing system is known as penetration pricing strategy when competition is on basis of building customer relationship where value pricing evolving prices as per customer needs is set. Pricing could be as per seasonal demand, interest rates or other factors like new products or competitors pricing policies. If prices are difficult to set, web-based software is used to set the prices that are accurate for different customers. Pricing decision is based on cost information.

The following are the cost based methods :

1. Full manufacture cost plus markup
2. Life cycle cost plus markup
3. Full cost and desired gross margin percent
4. Full cost plus desired return.

1. **Full Manufacture Cost plus Markup :** The total manufacturing cost which is equal to the sum of the variable and fixed manufacturing cost and added the markup percentage. The markup percentage is set according to the firm's decision or as per the industrial standards or as per the profit level required.

   The following are the steps for calculating the price:

   Step 1 - Total manufacturing cost = Materials + Labour + Batch level costs + Plant overheads

   Step 2 - Total manufacturing cost x Markup percentage = Price

2. **Life Cycle Cost plus Markup :** In this method the total life cycle costs are used along with a markup percentage.

   Price = Total life cycle cost x Markup percentage

3. **Full Cost and Desired Gross Margin Per cent :** Price is determined based on full cost it may be total manufacturing cost or total life cycle cost with a gross margin per cent.

   $$\text{Price} = \frac{Full\ Manufacturing\ most}{1 - Required\ gross\ margin\ \%}$$

   OR

   $$\text{Price} = \frac{Full\ Life\ cycle\ Cost}{1 - Required\ life\ cycle\ gross\ margin\ \%}$$

4. **Full Cost plus Desired Return :** In this method the price is fixed based on full cost plus required return on assets. A margin percentage is determined using the full manufacturing cost or life cycle cost and then the price is determined.

   $$\text{Margin rate} = \frac{Desired\ before\ tax\ return}{Manufacturing\ life\ cycle\ cost\ of\ sales}$$

   Price = Manufacturing or Life cycle cost x Margin

2. **Sales Life Cycle Approach :** Life cycle is the cycle of a product or service and the sales of a product in the market through four stages i.e. introduction, growth, maturity and decline.

Stage 1 : Introduction : In this stage product was introduced but there is no competition and awareness of the product. At this stage expenses of research and development are high but invented with new technology of production. Generally during the market introduction stage the revenues are very low and the investments are very high. Most business do not generate any profits during this stage but use marketing and sales strategies and tactics to successfully position in the new product / service in the marketplace. Hence, this stage prices are set high because of high advertisement and research expenses. Profit is low because the high unit cost that arises from low output, heavy promotional investments are made to encourage growth.

Stage 2 : Growth : Slow then rapid increases in sales and increase in product variety. In this stage revenues and profits are increased. The product is accepted by the market, there would be mass sales. The target market is already familiar with the product and customers are purchase the product. At this stage expenses are still high for research, development and distribution channels and marketing. Hence prices are still high and competitors entered because of more demand.

Stage 3 : Maturity : The growth in revenues starts to decline and profitability decreases as competitors start to compete more on price and less through product differentiation since most of the competitors can offer the same product. At the same time strong competition requires more marketing and sales investments to keep the market share which increases the overall cost of doing business. Rate of sales are slow down, decline in product variety there is not much differentiation. Target costing used for setting price, according to competitive quality and functionality. Price starts to come down in the saturated market as small player struggle to find a foot hold. Business withdraws unsuccessful brands from the market and the remainders continue with the customers of unsuccessful brands.

Stage 4 : Decline : Customers changing tastes, because of technological advancement. It results the products decline, many competitors are not be profitable and they withdrawn from the market. This phase may be a short or long duration. Prices decrease with sales and there were no competitors. In this stage prices are set below the cost.

SOLVED PROBLEMS

Problem 1

TCS a computer software company developing a new accounting package "Ledger" the following budgeted information for Ledger over a 6-year product life cycle are given:

Year 1 and 2	
R & D costs	₹ 2,40,000
Design costs	1,60,000

Years 3 to 6		
	One- time setup costs	Costs Per Package
Product Costs	₹ 1,00,0000	₹ 25
Marketing Costs	70,000	24
Distribution Costs	50,000	16
Customer - Service Costs	80,000	30

Further, relevant data are given as under

Selling price per package	₹ 400	₹ 480	₹ 600
Sales quantity (in units)	5,000	4,000	2,500

Prepare a statement showing life cycle operating income for different levels, i.e., 5,000 Units 4,000 units and 2,500 units. You can ignore the time value of money for computing life cycle revenues and life cycle costs.

Solution :

Statement showing Budgeted Life Cycle Revenues and Costs for "Ledger" Software package of TCS

	Alternative Selling Price/ Sales - Quantity Combinations		
	1	2	3
Selling price per package	₹ 400	₹ 480	₹ 600
Sales quantity in units	5,000	4,000	2,500
Life Cycle revenues [₹ 400 x 5,000; ₹ 480 x 4,000; ₹ 600 x 2,500	20,00,000	19,20,000	15,00,000
Life Cycle Costs			
R & D	2,40,000	2,40,000	2,40,000
Design costs of product / process	1,60,000	1,60,000	1,60,000
Production Costs: ₹ 1,00,000 + (25 x 5,000); ₹ 1,00,000 + (25 x 4,000); ₹ 1,00,000 + (25 x 2,500);	2,25,000	2,00,000	1,62,5000
Marketing Costs: ₹ 70,000 + (₹ 24 x 5,000); ₹ 70,000 + (₹ 24 x 4,000); ₹ 70,000 + (₹ 25 x 2,500);	1,90,000	1,66,000	1,30,000

Distribution Costs : ₹ 50,000 + (₹ 16 x 5,000); ₹ 50,000 + (₹ 16 x 4,000); ₹ 50,000 + (₹ 16 x 2,500);	1,30,000	1,14,000	90,000
Customer - service costs: ₹ 50,000 + (₹ 30 x 5,000); ₹ 50,000 + (₹ 30 x 4,000); ₹ 50,000 + (₹ 30 x 2,500);	2,30,000	2,00,000	1,55,000
Total life cycle costs	11,75,000	10,80,000	9,37,500
Life cycle operating income	8,25,000	8,40,000	5,62,500

Problem 2

Sri Vinayaka supports the concept of life cycle costing for new investment decisions covering its engineering activities. The final side of this philosophy is now well established and its principles extended to all other areas of decision making. The company is to replace a number of its machines and the production manager is between the Tata Machine, a more expensive machine with a life of 12 years and the Beta machine with an estimated life of 6 years. If the Beta machine chosen it is likely that if would be replaced at the end of 6 years by another Beta machine. The pattern of maintenance and running costs differs between the two types of machine and relevant data are shown below:

	Tata	Beta
Purchase Price	₹ 19,000	₹ 13,000
Trade - in value	3,000	3,000
Annual repair costs	2,000	2,600
Overhaul Costs	(at year 8), 4,000	(at year 4), 2,000
Estimated financing costs averaged over Machine life	10% p.a	10% p.a

You are required to:

(i) Recommend with supporting figures, which machine to purchase and stating any assumptions made.

(ii) Explain life cycle costing and its benefits that are likely to occur from its use, Support your answers with examples of changes in practice that could occur from adopting this philosophy.

Solution :

	Year	Machine Exe - Life 12 years		
		Cost	Discount Factor	Discount Cost
		₹		
Purchase price	0	19,000	1	₹ 19,000
Overhead cost	8	4,000	0.47	1,880
Trade in value	12	-3,000	0.32	-960
Annual repair cost	1-12	2,000	6.81	13,620
				33,540

Annualised equivalent ₹ 33,540 ÷ 6.81 = 4,925

	Year	Machine Wye - Life 6 years		
		Cost	Discount Factor	Discount Cost
		₹		₹
Purchase price	0	13,000	1	13,000
Overhead cost	4	2,000	0.68	1,360
Trade in value	6	-3,000	0.56	1,680
Annual repair cost	1-6	2,600	4.36	11,336
				24,016

Annualized equivalent ₹ 24,016 ÷ 4.36 = Rs. 5,508

Recommendation : Purchase Tata

Assumptions

(i) Both the machine are same performance, capacity and speed

(ii) There is no inflation

(iii) The life time of machine Tata is 12-years and Beta is 6-years.

(iv) The annual cash flow at the year end.

SHORT ANSWER QUESTIONS

1. What is life cycle costing?
2. What is life cost analysis?
3. What is life cycle planning?
4. Explain the terms
   a. Growth Stage
   b. Maturity Stage

c. Introduction Stage

d. Decline Stage

ESSAY ANSWER QUESTIONS

1. What is the life cycle costing? Explain the stages in product life cycle?
2. State in benefits and limitations of product life cycle?
3. How life cost analysis is prepared, implemented and monitored?
4. What are the main steps in the application of life cycle costing model?
5. Explain basic tree of life cycle costing tree?
6. Explain various pricing and evaluation approaches of PLC?
7. What is product life cycle assessment? Describe the stages involved in life cycle cost assessment model?
8. Explain life cycle costing process?
9. Explain product life cycle profitability?
10. What is product life cycle? Explain its characteristics and stages of product life cycle?
11. Explain comparative analysis of product life cycle phases?

❖ ❖ ❖

Chapter - 13
Competitor Accounting

Introduction

Competitor analysis and accounting is a central issue in strategic management accounting. It is also called competitor focused accounting. It facilitates for collecting and analyzing accounting information with a competitive focus. The effectiveness of a central instrument of competitor accounting is the assessment of the competitor's cost examined. It reveals that cost leaders are aware of their cost lead and act differently from the cost leaders without such knowledge. Informed cost leaders implement their strategic decisions much more purposefully. They employ a far more expansive production quantity policy and a more aggressive pricing policy. Through pursuing these strategies aggressively, this knowledge of the competitive strengths at the cost level leads to better company performance.

Competitors need accounting information mainly for strategic purposes e.g. information on the strengths and weaknesses of their competition. They also use the information given in financial statements to compare their own performance with that of the other entity.

Process of competitor accounting

The following are the main steps in competitor accounting

1. Determine the customers and services of the company.
2. Identify current and potential competitors.
3. Gather basic information on each competitor.
4. Conduct in-depth research on each competitor.
5. Conduct a comparative analysis of the competitors.

Product price and quality are the concerns in competition. Hence company should conduct competitor accounting along with its competitor analysis to assess competitors' relative quality and price. The major concerns are comparing the position of the business with that of its competitors with regard to quality and price. If the industry is mature the competition is based on selling prices and identifies the key success factor to achieve a comparative cost advantage.

It is helpful for a company to conduct best practice benchmarking and compare its performance against the best competitor in the industry. This helps to increase company productivity and growth. Later the company can break through to a higher standard of performance. Value-chain analysis is also helpful for understand where and how it adds value. It helps the company determine its own sources of competitive advantage and it can then dissect strategically relevant activities so easy to understand the sources of competitive advantage through cost leadership or product specialization.

Companies practicing competitor analysis and accounting should also carry out competitive position monitoring. It analyzes competitor positions within the industry by assessing and monitoring trends in competitor sales. In addition the companies should conduct industry profitability analysis and it provides a measure for the nature and intensity of competition.

Competitor Analysis

In formulating business strategy, managers must consider the strategies of the firm's competitors. While in highly fragmented commodity industries the moves of any single competitor may be less important. In concentrated industries competitor analysis becomes a vital part of strategic planning.

Competitor analysis has two primary activities the first is to obtaining information about important competitors and finally using that information to predict competitor behavior. The goal of competitor analysis is to understand with which competitors to compete, strategies and planned actions, how competitors might react to a firm's actions and how to influence competitor behaviour to the firm's own advantage.

The knowledge about competitors usually is insufficient in competitor analysis. But competitors should be analyzed systematically; using organized competitor intelligence-gathering to compile a wide array of information so that well informed strategy decisions can be made.

Competitor Analysis Framework

Michael Porter presented a framework for analyzing competitors. This framework is based on the following four key aspects of a competitor:

- Competitor's objectives
- Competitor's assumptions
- Competitor's strategy
- Competitor's capabilities

Objectives and assumptions are what drive the competitor; strategy and capabilities are what the competitor is doing or is capable of doing. These components can be depicted as shown in the following diagram:

Competitor Analysis Components

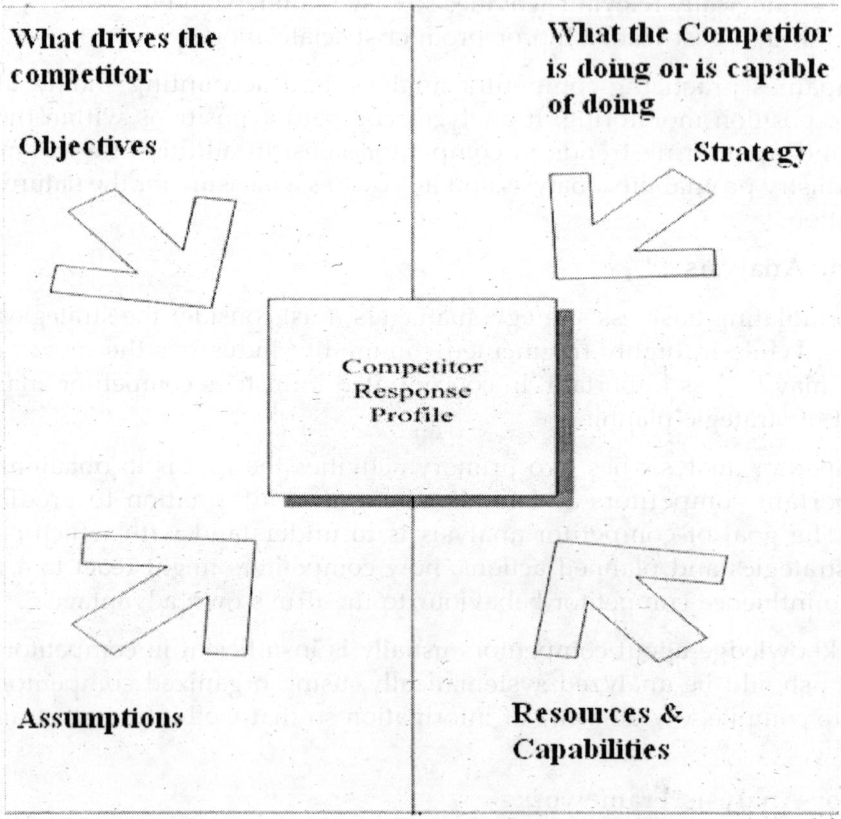

Source : Adapted from Michael E. Porter, Competitive Strategy, 1980, p. 49.

A competitor analysis should include the more important existing competitors as well as potential competitors such as those firms that might enter the industry for example, by extending their present strategy or by vertically integrating.

Competitor's Current Strategy :

The two main sources of information about a competitor's strategy is what the competitor says and what it does. What a competitor is saying about its strategy is revealed in:

- annual shareholder reports
- 10K reports
- interviews with analysts
- statements by managers
- press releases

However, this stated strategy often differs from what the competitor actually is doing. What the competitor is doing is evident in where its cash flow is directed, such as in the following tangible actions:

- hiring activity
- R&D projects
- capital investments
- promotional campaigns
- strategic partnerships
- mergers and acquisitions

Competitor's Objectives :

Knowledge of a competitor's objectives facilitates a better prediction of the competitor's reaction to different competitive moves. For example, a competitor is focused on reaching short-term financial goals might not be willing to spend much money responding to a competitive attack. But such a competitor might favour focusing on the products that hold positions and better can be defended. On the other hand, a company that has no short term profitability objectives might be willing to participate in destructive price competition in which neither firm earns a profit. Competitor objectives may be growth rate, market share and technology leadership. Goals may be associated with each hierarchical level of strategy corporate, business unit and functional level.

The competitor's organizational structure provides information to which functions of the company are deemed to be the more important. For example, those functions that report directly to the chief executive officer are likely to be given priority over those that report to a senior vice president. Other aspects of the competitor that serve as indicators of its objectives include risk tolerance, management incentives, backgrounds of the executives, composition of the board of directors, legal or contractual restrictions and any additional corporate-level goals that may influence the competing business unit. Whether the competitor is meeting its objectives provides an indication of how likely it is to change its strategy.

Competitor's Assumptions :

The assumptions that a competitor's managers hold about their firm and their industry help to define the moves that they will consider. For example, if in the past the industry introduced a new type of product that failed, the industry executives may assume that there is no market for the product. Such assumptions are not always accurate and if incorrect may present opportunities. For example, new entrants may have the opportunity to introduce a product similar to a previously unsuccessful one without acceptance because present firms may not take their threat seriously. Honda was able to enter the U.S. motorcycle market with a small motorbike because U.S. manufacturers had assumed that there was no market for small bikes based on their past experience.

A competitor's assumptions may be based on a number of factors including beliefs about its competitive position, past experience with a product, regional factors, industry trends and rules of thumb. A thorough competitor analysis also would include assumptions that a competitor makes about its own competitors and whether that assessment is accurate.

Competitor's Resources and Capabilities :

Knowledge of the competitor's assumptions, objectives, and current strategy is useful in understanding how the competitor might *want* to respond to a competitive attack. However, its resources and capabilities determine its *ability* to respond effectively.

A competitor's capabilities can be analyzed according to its strengths and weaknesses in various functional areas, as is done in a SWOT analysis. The competitor's strengths define its capabilities. The analysis can be taken further to evaluate the competitor's ability to increase its capabilities in certain areas. A financial analysis can be performed to reveal its sustainable growth rate.

Finally the competitive environment is dynamic, the competitor's ability to react swiftly to change should be evaluated. Some firms have heavy momentum and may continue for many years in the same direction before adapting. Others are able to mobilize and adapt very quickly. Factors that slow a company down include low cash reserves, large investments in fixed assets and an organizational structure that hinders quick action.

Competitor Response Profile :

Information from an analysis of the competitor's objectives, assumptions, strategy and capabilities can be compiled into a response profile of possible moves that might be made by the competitor. This profile includes both potential offensive and defensive moves. The specific moves and their expected strength can be estimated using information cleaned from the analysis. The result of the competitor analysis should be an improved ability to predict the competitor's behavior and even to influence that behaviour to the firm's advantage.

Benefits of Competitor Analysis and Accounting

Competitor analysis and accounting is regarded as a central element in business planning and control. There are four key benefits of competitor analysis and accounting:

1. **Industry benchmarking:** Companies compare themselves with similar companies in the same industry to identify their strengths and weaknesses.
2. **Learning from competitors:** Companies study their similar market experiments to those which they are planning. For example, BPO service companies compare plans of other BPO when planning a new promotion of BPO services.
3. **Positioning:** Companies try to identify their competitors' strengths when choosing competition methods, either by cutting the product price to exercise cost leadership or by launching a new product or service to achieve product specialization.
4. **Identifying opportunities and threats:** Competitor analysis and accounting links with the traditional strengths, weaknesses, opportunities and threats (SWOT) analysis for handling both business opportunities and threats.

The competitor analysis is critical for identifying opportunities and threats. In fact, competitor analysis helps decision makers understand who the competitors are and what the market structure is. It allows management to identify its competitors' making and selling strategies. By understanding who the competitors are and how they operate, managers can remove the issue of other companies making moves that are detrimental to their companies' health. Managers can also learn from their competitors.

Five Key Forces Affecting Industry Competition

Companies should consider the five key forces that affect industry competition.

1. **Entry barriers :** How many companies are there in the same industry? How easy is it for a new company to enter the industry? Is there legislation which would permit entry of a new company? Is there sufficient demand for a new entrant? For instance, 7-11 and Circle K dominate the convenience shop industry in Hong Kong. They provide a 24-hour convenience-goods retail service and make it difficult for others to enter the industry. Round-the-clock retailing is essential to the competitive ability of these two convenience shop chains.

2. **Competitive rivalry :** How many competitors are there in the industry? How intense is competition in the industry? In Hong Kong for example, there are three major supermarkets: PARKnSHOP, Wellcome and China Resource Vanguard. There are also some other higher or lower classes supermarkets of smaller size. However, if PARKnSHOP uses competitor analysis and accounting, it will only compare itself with Wellcome or China Resource Vanguard and not the various smaller supermarkets. Since these do not impose a direct threat on its operations.

3. **Substitute products :** What substitutes pose a threat to the company's profitability? Do other competitors offer a similar or alternative product? In recent years, young people prefer fast food to 'dim sum' food in Chinese restaurants. Chinese restaurants have clearly been replaced by fast food shops in both number and turnover.

4. **Supplier power :** How much bargaining power do suppliers possess? This will be determined by the number of suppliers in the industry, the other companies that they supply products to and the individual company's relationship with its suppliers.

5. **Customer power :** How much bargaining power do customers possess? Do the customers determine what the business is? For instance, a high-class boutique in Causeway Bay is not very susceptible to the bargaining power of buyers. But on the other hand, an outlet shop in Sham Shui Po, as the profit margin from an outlet shop is lower than that of a high-class boutique.

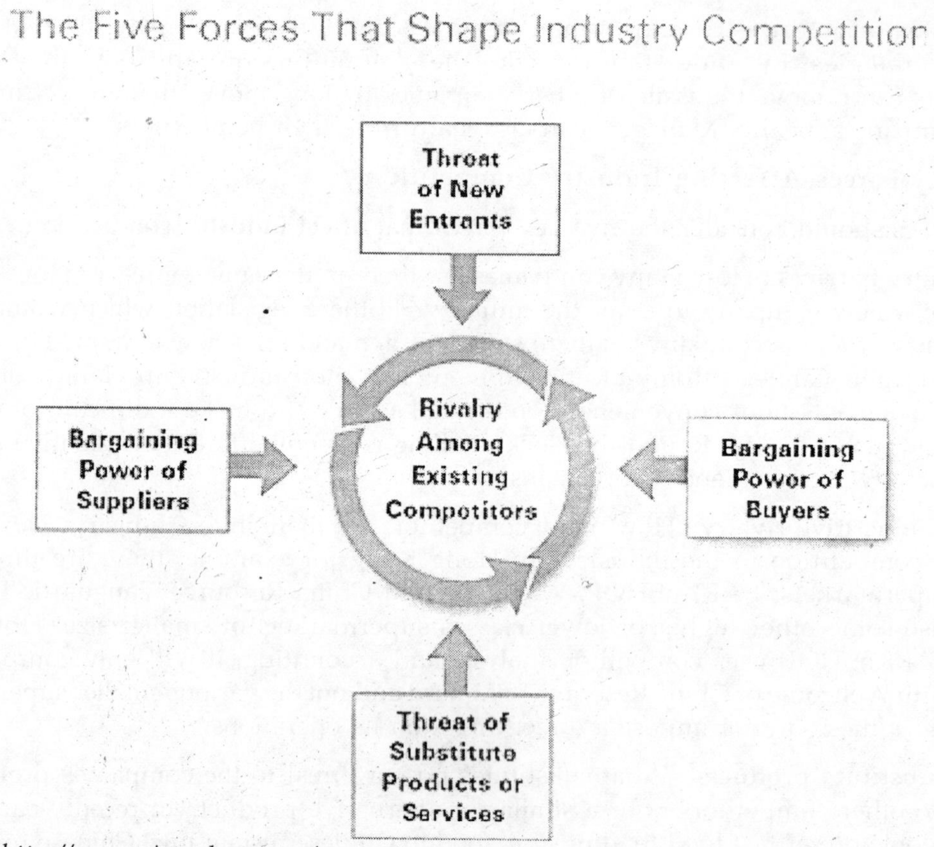

Source : http://www.virtual-one.org/competitoranalysis

Michael Porters Five key forces affecting industry competition :

The aim is to develop tactics designed specially to reduce the share of profits going to competitors.

For example :

1. To neutralize supplier power, standardize specifications for parts so your company can switch more easily among vendors.
2. To counter customer power, expand your services so it's harder for customers to have you for a rival.
3. To temper price wars initiated by established rivals, invest more heavily in products that differ significantly from competitor's offerings.
4. To scare off new entrants, elevate the fixed costs of competing; for instance, by escalating your R&D expenditures.
5. To limit the threat of substitutes, offer better value through wider product accessibility, soft-drink producers did this by introducing vending machines and convenience store channels, which dramatically improved the availability of soft drinks relative to other beverages.

Management Accountant's Role in Competitor Analysis

Management accountants perform three main roles in competitive analysis. The first role is collecting, analyzing and comparing competitors' relative costs and investments. The second role is assessing the quality of the information and finally predicting the future costs of competitors' products.

Competitor array

The following steps are required for competitor array:

1. Define the industry, especially the scope and nature of the industry.
2. Determine who the competitors are.
3. Determine who the customers are and what benefits they expect.
4. Determine what the key success factors are in the industry.
5. Rank the key success factors by giving each one a weighting (the sum of all the weightings must add up to one).
6. Rate each competitor on each of the key success factors.
7. Multiply each cell in the matrix by the factor weighting.

For example, two competitors are weighted using four key industry success factors: distribution network, customer focus, economies of scale and product innovation.

Competitor array - two dimensional matrix

Key industry Success factors	Weighting	Competitor 1 rating	Competitor 1 weighted	Competitor 2 rating	Competitor 2 weighted
1 - Distribution network	0.4	6	2.4	3	1.2
2 - Customer focus	0.3	4	1.2	5	1.5
3 - Economies of scale	0.2	3	0.6	3	0.6
4 - Product innovation	0.1	7	0.7	4	0.4
Totals	1.0	20	4.9	15	3.7

Competitor rating 1 – 10

Source : http://www.likiaat.org/images/uploads/articles

We can see that competitor 1 is rated higher than competitor 2 on product innovation ability (7 out of 10, compared to 4 out of 10) and distribution networks (6 out of 10). Yet competitor 2 is rated higher on customer focus (5 out of 10). Overall, competitor 1 is rated slightly higher than competitor 2 (20 out of 40 compared to 15 out of 40). But when the success factors are weighted according to their importance, competitor 1 gets a far better rating (4.9 compared to 3.7).

Prospector companies made greater use of and perceived greater usefulness in competitor accounting practices. Companies that build a strategic mission are more likely to use strategic pricing and strategic costing and to perceive these as being of greater helpfulness. Size is positively associated with greater use and perceived usefulness in competitor accounting practices. Logically, large companies can afford the resources to conduct competitor analysis and accounting. Hence, perceive its value for dealing with business competition. Business competition in new service industries such as the mobile phone business is supposed to be more severe than that in traditional production industries like furniture manufacture. The market potential and opportunity for new services are huge and dynamic.

Sources of Competitor Information

Davidson (1997) describes the sources of competitor information can be grouped into three categories:

1. **Recorded data**
2. **Observable data**
3. **Opportunistic data**

1. **Recorded data :** This is easily available in published form either internally or externally. Examples are competitor annual reports, product brochures, government reports and regulatory reports.
2. **Observable data :** It has to be actively sought and often assembled from several sources. Example is competitor pricing;
3. **Opportunistic data :** It data requires a lot of planning and organization. It is "subjective", coming from discussions with suppliers, customers and perhaps, previous management of competitors.

The table below lists possible sources of competitor data using Davidson's categorization:

Recorded Data	Observable Data	Opportunistic Data
Annual report & accounts	Pricing/ price lists	Meetings with suppliers
Press releases	Advertising campaigns	Trade shows
Newspaper articles	Promotions	Sales force meetings
Analysts reports	Tenders	Seminars/ conferences
Regulatory reports	Patent applications	Recruiting ex-employees
Government reports	Patent applications	Discussion with shared distributors
Presentations / speeches	Parent applications	Social contacts with competitors

In his book [Even More Offensive Marketing], Davidson likens the process of gathering competitive data to a jigsaw puzzle. Each individual piece of data does not have much value. The important skill is to collect as many of the pieces as possible and to assemble them into an overall picture of the competitor. This enables you to identify any missing pieces and to take the necessary steps to collect them.

Problems with competitor analysis

In general, it is difficult to collect information on competitors. Companies are reluctant to share information and to quantify the direct financial benefits of competitor analysis. Companies that undertake competitor analysis will perform better than those which do not. Clearly, though, smaller companies cannot afford to conduct competitor analysis.

Competitive Pricing

Competitor's price serves as an important reference point from which they set their price. In some industries, particularly those in which there are a few dominant competitors and many small companies, the top companies are in the position of holding price leadership roles where they are often the first in the industry to change price. Smaller companies must then assume a price follower role and react once the big companies adjust their price.

When basing pricing decisions on how competitors are setting their price, firms may follow one of the following approaches:

- **Below Competition Pricing** : A Marketer attempting to reach objective that require high sales levels (eg market share objective) may monitor the market to insure their price remains below competitors.
- **Above competition pricing :** Marketers using this approach are likely to be perceived as market leaders in terms of product features, brand image or other characteristics that support a price that is higher than what competitors offer.
- **Parity Pricing** : A simple method of setting the initial price is to price the product at the same level competitor's price their product.

Competitive Bid

As per Barron's Marketing Dictionary : Price quote from a prospective supplier in response to a request from a buyer. Competitive bidding is most often used by government agencies that are required by law to periodically open all contracts to bid and must award business to the lowest bidder. This is intended to ensure impartiality in buying decisions. However it also makes more difficult for the supplier to communicate value or quality advantages that may justify a higher price. The supplier must attempt to predict how competitors will bid in order to be priced competitively. The supplier may bid relatively low if excess capacity is available to be filled or it may bid relatively high if it has a significant competitive advantage. Competitive bids are also used to establish a market value for a product or service. For example, a long-term customer of a service business may request competitive bids from other suppliers to find out if the price they pay for their uniquely tailored service is still competitive. Competitive bids sometimes have a mandatory deadline and may require a deposit to establish the financial stability of the bidder.

Sealed Bid Pricing : Price quotes solicited by governmental and other public agencies to ensure objective consideration of competitive bids. Interested vendors are formally notified in advance of the request for a bid and must meet a bidding deadline as well as strict bid format requirements. Sealed bids are sometimes opened publicly in the presence of all bidders. The lowest bid is awarded the order.

Steps for Preparing a Winning Bid

Scott explained steps for small business firms should take when preparing to make a competitive bid on a project:

1. Contact the company's procurement officer and inquire whether or not the company has a current need for the type of services or products that your company provides.

2. If you are a minority or woman business owner, check to see if the company has any minority or women owned business programs in place. Also if you represent a minority owned business should be prepared to secure minority certification from a regional chamber of commerce or the National Minority Supplier Development Council.

3. Request an information package on the procurement process that is in place at the company. This package stated Scott, "will contain a supplier capability information from which routinely asks for information about your product or service, references, financial viability and past track record. Fill out the forms and send them back. The exact nature of these forms will vary from industry to industry; a company seeking to outsource three months of copyediting work will likely require somewhat different information than a company that is looking for a new supplier of electronic parts.

4. Once the above mentioned supplier capability information form has been completed and returned to the company. Scott noted that "your small business may be referred to different buyers within the agency or to different corporate offices throughout the country. Your company may also be placed on a data base that these buyers have access to."

5. Adopt a proactive business attitude. Many successful businesses that secure work through the bidding process remains aggressive though not unduly so even after taking care of all the necessary paperwork. "Don't rely on the buyers to offer contracts to you," cautioned Scott. "It is up to the small business owner to sell his business as an asset to each company or agency. That means calling constantly to inquire about opportunities, and showing real evidence that your company can do the job. You must be constant and may take months or years to win a contract."

"Winning proposals, regardless of the product, service, or organization have a number of characteristics in common. The unifying theme is that they all prove the case, demonstrate the wisdom of selecting a particular supplier by providing practical examples and clear evidence of the bidder's superior capabilities."

A good strategy should differentiate your company from competitors, emphasize your strengths while pointing out competitors' weaknesses and emphasize features that the customer wants and needs. The strategy should be translated into a proposal which demonstrates that your company should understands the problem at hand, is well-positioned to solve the problem, can perform the work successfully and provides value for the cost. "There is only one way to win in a competitive situation". "Provide the evidence that you are the best vendor with the best solution and the least risk at an acceptable price."

Negotiated Bids

Not all competitive bidding situations end with the customer's acceptance of one of the bids offered. In some instances a subsequent negotiation step may take place. "Some buying situations require the use of bids and the purchasing agent must take the lowest bid," said McCarthy and Perreault. "In other cases, however, the customer asks for bids and then singles out the company that submits the most attractive bid not necessarily the lowest for further bargaining. The list price or bidding price the seller would like to charge is sometimes only the starting point for discussions with individual customers. What a customer will buy if the customer buys at all depends on the negotiated price, a price set based on bargaining between the buyer and seller." McCarthy and Perreault go on to note that negotiated pricing, like simple bid pricing, "is most common in situations where the marketing mix is adjusted for each customer so bargaining may involve the whole marketing mix, not just the price level."

Summary :

Competitor analysis and accounting generates and monitors competitor costs and strategic information. Five key forces like entry barriers, competitive rivalry, substitute products, supplier power and customer power affect industry competition. An ideal technique to developing specific cost estimates are based on detailed analysis of the market, the competitors' cost structure, products and product costs. As a consequence, management accountants have to cooperate with their marketing and technical colleagues to conduct relevant competitor analysis and accounting.

SHORT QUESTION ANSWERS

1. Define Competitor Analysis?
2. Explain Competitor Accounting?
3. What is Competitor Array?
4. Explain term Competitive Bid?
5. How fix the Competitive Pricing?

ESSAY QUESTION ANSWERS

1. Define competitor accounting and process of competitor accounting?
2. Define competitor analysis and its framework?
3. Explain the benefits of competitor analysis and accounting?
4. Explain five key forces affecting industry competition?
5. What is the management accountant's role in competitor analysis?
6. Explain the sources of competitor information?
7. Define competitive bid? What are the steps for preparing a winning bid?

❖ ❖ ❖

Chapter - 14
TARGET COSTING

Introduction

Target costing is a system under which a company plans in advance for the product price points, product costs, and margins that it wants to achieve. If it cannot manufacture a product at these planned levels, then it cancels the product entirely. With target costing, a management team has a powerful tool for continually monitoring products from the moment they enter the design phase and onward throughout their product life cycles. It is considered one of the most important tools for achieving consistent profitability. Now a day's production process is quite complex and it needs a more inclusive approach about cost management. Cost information for the production and services are to be managed to suit the requirement of customers. There is need to maintain cost management to marketing management and finance. The traditional cost approach, i.e., 'cost plus pricing, is inappropriate for today's more competitive environment. In system, material, labour and overhead costs are measured and a desired profit is added to decide the selling price. At present Indian firms are compelled to be competitive in the global market, so the additive technique is no longer practicable. The need has increased to apply the technique of 'Target Costing'. It was introduced in the year 1960 but which has been widely used by Japanese firms since 1970s as a response to the challenge posed by customer demand for more diversity and shorter product was committed at the design stage.

Target costing developed as a multidisciplinary approach to managing costs from the earliest stages and was complimented by techniques such as process re-engineering and total quality management. At the same time increased automation and decrease labour cost made standard costing less improvement as main method of cost management within manufacturing companies. It emphasizes the reduction of cost during the planning and designing stage of the production life cycle of production cost is determined at this stage. In comparison to traditional product costing methods, target costing allocates more of the total cost to the development stage, simultaneously reducing cost during the production stage. It aims at profit planning, control cost and manage profit over a product's life cycle. Essentially, it is a part of a comprehensive strategic profit management system. At a time of entering a market, prices of the competitors product development and applies it throughout the product life cycle by actively involving the entire value chain in the product concept stage selling price and required profit are set after consideration of the medium term profit plans, which links the operational strategy to the long term strategic plans.

Definition :

According to the CIMA official Terminology a target cost is "a product cost estimate derived by subtracting a desired profit margin from a competitive market price".

Sakurai defines target costing as "a cost management tool for reducing the overall cost of a product over its entire life cycle with the help of the production, engineering, R&D, Marketing, and accounting departments". Cooper and Chew describe the value of target costing as its `ability to bring the challenge of the marketplace back through the chain of production to product designers.

Target Costing = Planning Selling Price - Required Profit.

A target cost is the maximum amount of cost that can be incurred on a product and with it the firm can still earn the required profit margin from that product. It is the estimated cost which enables a firm to remain and compete in the market in the long run. Target costing is driven by external market factors where market prices determine product costs. Under this system target market price is determined prior to designing and introducing of a product. The target price is set in such a way the firm is able to achieve a desired market share. Further, a desired profit margin is deducted from the target price to determine the target cost. Thus, target costing allows the profitability of a product to be determined before it is produced. It allows control over the cost of future products. If a firm says that costs are going to be higher than the target costs before it goes into the market, it is possible that adjustments can be made in design and process capability prior to production so as to resolve the problem. The firm can redesign product to use less expensive parts, components or materials. It may also change initial make or buy decisions and find cheaper alternatives by out sourcing or by producing vendor supplied items. The firm may also re-examine production process to introduce cost reducing efficiencies. It can ever opt to eliminate some non essential product features.

The procedure of target costing explained by Sakurai is as follows:

1. To plan and design high quality products that meet customer's needs. Hence this system attaches great importance to determining what features and level of performance the customer will want and it uses those preferences as the basis for allocating costs to major functions and group components.
2. To set a target cost for the products through the use of value engineering.
3. To attain the target cost at the production stage by use of standard costs.

Thus, the technique of target costing is 'before the fact' indicator that can keep a firm from getting more trouble in future. It is a powerful tool for reducing cost not only at the production stage but also at the planning and design stage of the product.

Steps in development of target cost

1. Ascertainment of customer requirements
2. Product planning
3. Concept design
4. Basic design
5. Detailed design
6. Manufacturing preparation

1. **Customer Requirements :** When determining the customer requirements, don't just rely on what they literally say. Dig deeper, use the opposite to understand what they are trying to say, and then test your assumptions. You may just find a new market you didn't know you had. Collect the market information about the perceptions of the customer regarding product characteristics and also his expectations about price, quality, product performance, technology etc. Data can be obtained through market research, customer survey, sales force feedback, comparison with competitors for existing product.

2. **Product Planning :** Product Planning is the ongoing process of identifying and articulating market requirements that define a product's feature set. Product planning serves as the basis for decisions about price, distribution and promotion. Net product planning is summarized in a document which defines and clarifies the design requirements. Usually it contains.

   - Outline the mission and concept of the product.
   - Primary performance specifications and design schedule, manufacturing and marketing activities for the products.
   - Cost target, selling price, sales volume and profitability of the product.

3. **Concept Design :** At this stage formulate the basic concept, normal selling price and attainable cost target of the new product on the basis of design requirements. Usually it consists of the following items:

   - Formulation of main functional areas.
   - Assignment of cost target to the top level functional areas.
   - Designing the basic concept of the product under the assigned cost target.
   - Ascertain whether or not the basic concept of the product is designed to fit the cost target by using rough cost estimation.
   - Profitability study of the product.

4. **Basic Design :** The focus of this stage is to construct a general drawing of the product based on the cost target. It is composed of the following items.

   - Assignment of the cost target to the top and middle function areas or main components.
   - Framing a general drawing under the cost target.
   - Ascertaining whether or not the general drawing of the product is designed to fit the cost target by making use of the rough cost estimation.

5. **Detailed Design :** At this stage draw up the manufacturing specification of the product on the basis of the framework of the general drawing and the cost target described in the earlier stage. Ascertaining whether or not the manufacturing specifications of the product are designed to fit the cost target by using detailed cost estimation.

6. **Manufacturing Preparations :** In this stage the manufacturing system is designed including production method, tools and processes of the product under the cost target. The detailed target cost structure is determined.

Features of Target Costing :

The following are the important features of target costing:

1. **Focus on the customer :** It focuses on the customer requirements for quality cost and time are incorporated into the product decisions. Definitely target costing forces firms to be specific about what customers want the prices they are prepared to pay. The process may also involve discussions with customers of different design options, making trade-offs between cost and value. This is a key difference from other cost management processes which tend to be disconnected from the value perceptions and requirements.
2. **Emphasis on cost reduction at early stages in development :** It starts at the earliest stage in new product development. In this a detailed financial analysis takes place from the outset and engineering changes are made before production beings. Hence the initial designers are simplified before manufacture, resulting in lower cost and time-to-market once the design is finalized.
3. **Consideration of the whole product life cycle :** In order to ensure that total cost are minimized for both the producer and the customer. Successful target costing examiner the full life-cycle cost of the product includes consideration of the purchase price, operating cost, maintenance and distribution costs.
4. **A multidisciplinary process :** Target costing is multidisciplinary nature of the process and it includes value chain analysis, life cycle costing and activity based costing. It also ensures the involvement of all functions in the analysis and decision making.

Techniques of Target Costing

1. **Value analysis :** It is a technique for performance improvement and improves the value in the particular product. It aims at cost reduction; investigate into economic attributes of value for increasing the value in a product. It is not an organized creative approach, which has, for its purpose, the efficient identification of unnecessary cost which provides neither quality nor use nor customer features. Value analysis serves all branches of an enterprise, *viz.*, engineering, manufacturing procurement, marketing and management. Value analysis exercise requires "brainstorming "with persons drawn from various multidisciplinary functions and it aims at import-substitution.
2. **Value engineering :** It involves the design of a product after gathering input from employees, various departments within a company and offering a different perspective on possible cost minimization tactics. It considers all aspects of the value chain and frequently involves outside of the firms such as suppliers in order to reach a decision that encompasses the most successful combination of price and quality. It is a systematic interdisciplinary examination of factors affecting a cost of a product or services. The aim of the value engineering is to achieve target cost by identifying improved product design and eliminating unnecessary functions. It requires the use of functional analysis involves decomposing the products into its many elements attributes.

3. **Just-in-time (JIT) :** It is an operating strategy that has significant effect on inventory control, purchasing and suppliers. It tries to reduce inventories to an absolute minimum and to eliminate safety stock. It provides information for delivery of components and materials as they are needed. Sometimes, suppliers very close to customer to achieve on time delivery. The suppliers' on the other hand, guarantee proper quality of materials as responsible prices as and when needed. Just-in-time ensures coordination and synchronization of all operations and material flows and thus excessive inventory cover is rendered unnecessarily. Just-in-time drastically reduces investment as well as total cost of operation. It also help the production process on demand pull basis If purchase price variances are used to evaluate the performance of the purchase management. The purchase management will be motivated to obtain material suppliers at lowest prices even if this results in use of many suppliers and more number of purchases and large quantity purchasing, resulting in higher inventories. It is useful for delivery of lower quantity of materials and indifference to attaining on time delivery. Just-in-time will focus on performance measures which will emphasis quality and reliability rather than material price variance.

4. **Total quality management (TQM) :** Total Quality Control is Japanese processes that initially develop in the United States as a method of Quality Control. It describes a management approach to long–term success through customer satisfaction. In a TQM effort, all members of an organization participate in improving processes, products, services, and the culture in which they work.

5. **Material requirement planning (MRP) :** It is a production planning and inventory control system used to manage manufacturing processes. Most MRP systems are software-based, while it is possible to conduct MRP by hand as well. The basic function of MRP system includes inventory control, bill of material processing and elementary scheduling. MRP helps organizations to maintain low inventory levels. It is used to plan manufacturing, purchasing and delivering activities. Manufacturing organizations, whatever their products, face the same daily practical problem - that customers want products to be available in a shorter time than it takes to make them. This means that some level of planning is required. Companies need to control the types and quantities of materials they purchase, plan which products are to be produced and in what quantities and ensure that they are able to meet current and future customer demand, all at the lowest possible cost. Making a bad decision in any of these areas will make the company lose money.

6. **Kaizen :** It is a Japanese word means continuous improvement. Kaizen costing focuses on obtaining small incremental cost reductions in the production stage of the product life cycle. Efforts are made to reduce the target costing and empower employees to make it happen. The Kazien costing views the system as dynamic in the cause of waste, excess and variation can be continuously reduced. Actual costs are compared with the target cost and necessary reduction is ensured in the Kaizen approach as the source of the solution.

7. **Activity-based costing and management (ABC/M) :** Activity-based Management is a further development on Activity Based Costing. Activity-based Management is a

discipline that focuses on the efficient and effective management of activates as the route of continues improvement in the value received and the profit received by providing this value. Activity-based Management is an analytic application that models business processes to determine cost, profitability and drivers. With this solution, organizations can make informed decisions that streamline processes, deliver revenue growth and reduce costs across the organization.

It utilizes cost information gathered through ABC. In this process the value added and non-value added activates are to be eliminated. It involves the identification of major activities area, assigning costs to cost pool for each activity, spreading of support activities across the primary activities and documentation of cost drives for each activity.

The target costing process

The stages in the process of target costing described by Gagne and Discenza (1995):

1. Establish a selling price for the new product and estimated sales volume from an analysis of the market and a target profit.
2. Determine the target cost by subtracting the profit from the selling price.
3. Perform functional cost analysis for individual components and processes.
4. Determine the estimated cost for the product.
5. Compare estimate with target.
6. If estimated cost exceeds target cost, repeat cost analysis/ value engineering to reduce estimated cost (an iterative process)
7. Make the final decision whether or not to product once cost estimate is on target
8. Manage costs during production of the product.

Impact of Target Costing On Profitability

1) Target costing improves profitability in two ways. First, it places a detailed continuing emphasis on product cost throughout the life of every product. Secondly, it improves profitability through precise targeting of correct prices at which the company feels it can field a profitable product.

2) It is part of a large concept called concurrent engineering which requires participants from many departments to work together on project team. Clustering representatives from many departments on a single design team can be quite a struggle. This problem can be solved by senior management.

3) The cost accountant should continue taking lead role in continuing review of supplier's cost.

4) A company, which issues a stream of new products should make target costing a central part of its strategy.

Implementation of Target Costing

(A) **Creating a project chart :** It is always good if target costing effort starts with a document approved by senior management, which describes its goal and what it is authorized to do.

(B) **Active participation and interest of top management :** There should be someone in corporate hierarchy, who strongly believes in the project outcomes. He supports fund sanctioning and solicits support of other members of the top management.

(C) **Funds approval :** It is necessary that funds should be got approved by higher management so that well-staffed design team can complete target costing tasks. The possible funding should be based on a formal allocation of money through the corporate budget.

(D) **Assign a strong team manager :** Implementation of target costing programme involves so many people with different background. It may become difficult to weld the group together into smooth functioning team focused on key objectives. A proper manager with leadership qualities should be asked to manage the team.

(E) **Full team participation :** It will always be in the interest of organization, if members of target costing team are fully focused on target costing. It is necessary that they should be relieved of all other responsibilities.

(F) **Uses of management tools :** Target costing may come out to be a complex effort. This specially hold true in case of high cost projects with many features and components. To ensure that the project stays on tracts, the team should use all project management tools.

Difference between Target and Traditional Costing

Target Costing	Traditional Standard Costing
1. It is focused on external.	1. It is focused on internal.
2. Target costing takes on a more proactive costing approach to pricing.	2. Compared to traditional standard costing approaches in which an estimate of product, general administrative, marketing and distribution costs is taken into consideration.
3. In comparison the marketplace directs target costing by first setting a selling price, then subtracting target income and finally reaching a cost.	3. Traditional costing determines cost based on the design of goods, adds a markup and establishes a price.

4.	Target costing utilizes costing information and focuses on the best possible price up front, preventing vested time on after-the fact discussion concerning design and redesigning of the product.	4.	Traditionally, a cost figure is obtained, implemented and once found to be poorly configured, sent back to management and engineers for reworking of production processes and cutting of costs.
5.	It is applied during the planning and design stage of the product's life cycle.	5.	It is applied during the production stage of the product's life cycle.
6.	It involves a proactive cost planning approach where pricing is considered prior to production.	6.	It involves a reactive cost control approach during production.
7.	This system used in assembly oriented industries (Variety, medium to small volume production).	7.	This system used in process-oriented industries (continuous production).
8.	In this method wastage is zero-defects.	8.	In this method astage is within the allowed limits

Advantages of Target Costing :

1. It ensures proper planning well ahead of actual production and marketing.
2. It improves the understanding of the costs of the products and services.
3. It is multidisciplinary and involves staff from all areas in the cost analysis and encourages them to take responsibility for managing the costs.
4. It can be used by service organizations to look at the impact which new services have on the existing ones.
5. It developed specific and real target which ensuré satisfactory financial performance.
6. Target costing ensures proper planning ahead of actual production and marketing.
7. It ensures a competitive atmosphere where ways and means are found to succeed in competition.
8. It focuses on customer's demand, there perceived value to the product and price they can pay for the product.
9. It promotes cohesive term spirit in the organization, which impels the members to attempt higher level performance.

Limitations of Target Costing

The following are the main limitations of target costing:

1. Design team generally requires a number of design iterations before it can devise a sufficiently low cost product. It helps the term to meets the target cost and margin criteria and development process needs larger time approach.

2. A large amount of mandatory cost cutting can result in finger pointing in various parts of the firm. Hence, employee generally resists the implementation of target costing.

3. Different representatives of design term from different departments may not see an eye to eye with each other and there may be a difficulty in reaching a consensus on the proper design, because there are too many opinions regarding design issues.

OBJECTIVE TYPE QUESTIONS

1. Pioneer of Target Costing is :

(a) Monio Suzuki

(b) G. Ford

(c) Akio Morito

(d) Ratan Tata

2. Target Costing is not useful in :

(a) Auto sector

(b) Consumer electronics

(c) Engineering

(d) Fast moving consumer goods

3. Best Example of target costing involves :

(a) Maruthi - 800

(b) Tata Safari

(c) Nano

(d) Innova

4. Target costing is concerned with :

(a) Procedures

(b) Rules

(c) Process

(d) Guidelines

5. Concept of target costing was originated in :
   (a) 1950
   (b) 1955
   (c) 1960
   (d) 1965

Ans : 1. (c), 2. (d) , 3. (c) , 4. (c) , 5 (c)

SHORT ANSWER QUESTIONS

1. What is target costing?
2. How does target costing affect profitability?
3. What are the advantages and limitations of target costing?
4. What are the features of target costing?
5. What is value engineering?

LONG ANSWER QUESTIONS

1. Explain target costing and the stages to the methodology?
2. Explain the steps involved in target costing approach to pricing.
3. What is target costing? How is it useful in assessing a product's total life cycle costs?
4. What is target costing? How does it different from traditional costing?
5. What do you mean by target costing? Does target costing require that profitability be viewed on a period by period basis or on a long term basis? explain
6. Explain difference between target costing and traditional costing?

❖ ❖ ❖

Frequently Asked Questions

December 2014

Section - A

Write short notes on

a) What is management control system?

b) State assumptions of break-even analysis.

c) Define responsibility accounting.

d) What is segment reporting?

e) What is activity-based costing?

f) CAP analysis.

g) State the stages in PLC.

h) Budget, budgeting and budgetary control.

i) What is performance budget?

j) What is target costing?

Section - B

2. a) Distinguish between management accounting and financial accounting system?

OR

b) There are two similar plants under the same management. The management desires to merge these two plants. The following particulars are available:

Particulars	Plant I	Plant II
Capacity operation	100%	60%
Sales	Rs 300 Lakhs	120 Lakhs
Variable cost	220 Lakhs	90 Lakhs
Fixed cost	40 Lakhs	20 Lakhs

You are required to calculate:

i. What would be the capacity of the merged plant to be operated for the purpose of break-even; and

ii. What would be the profitability on working at 75% of the merged capacity?

3. a) Discuss the various types of functional budgets in a manufacturing organization?

OR

b) From the following information, compute relevant material cost variances:

Material	Standard		Actual	
	Quantity (Tonnes)	Rate (Rs)	Quantity (Tonnes)	Rate (Rs)
Copper	700	40	600	50
Zinc	300	15	600	10
Output	960 tonnes		1056 tonnes	

4. a) Explain the significance of cost centre, profit centre and investment centre?

OR

b) Your company fixes the interdivisional transfer prices for its products on the basis of cost plus return on investment in the division. The budget for Division-A for 2010-11 appears as under :

Investments in Division – A :

Fixed assets	Rs 5,00,000
Current assets	Rs 3,00,000
Debtors	Rs 2,00,000
Annual cost of the division	Rs 8,00,000
Variable cost per unit of product	Rs 10
Desired ROI	28%

Determine the transfer price for Division -A.

5. a) Discuss the advantages and limitations of activity-based costing?

OR

b) Explain the significance of customer costs identification in a service organization?

6. a) Discuss strategic areas in product life cycle costing system?

OR

b) Explain the significance of cost analysis for competitive pricing and bidding process?

June 2013

Section - A

Write short notes on

a) Capacity Utilization.

b) Management Control System.

c) Budgetary Control.

d) Performance Budgeting.

e) Transfer Pricing.

f) Performance Report.

g) Cost Drivers.

h) Activity-based Costing.

i) Target Costing.

j) Competitor Accounting.

Section - B

2. a) Examine the nature, scope and importance of strategic management accounting?

OR

b) A factory engaged in manufacturing plastic buckets is working at 40% capacity and produces 10,000 buckets per annum. The present cost break-up for one bucket is as under:

Materials Rs. 10

Labour cost Rs. 3

Overheads Rs. 5 (60% fixed)

The selling price Rs. 20 per bucket

If it is decided to work the factory at 50% capacity, the selling price falls by 3%. At 90% capacity the selling price falls by 5% accompanied by a similar fall in the prices of material.

You are requires to calculate the profit at 50% and 90% capacities and also calculate break-even point for the same capacity productions.

3. a) What do you understand by zero-based budgeting? What are its advantages and disadvantages?

OR

b) A radio manufacturing company finds that it cost ₹ 6.25 to make each component X, the same is available in the market for ₹ 4.85 each, with an assurance of continuous of supply.

The break-down of cost is as under:

Material	Rs 2.75
Labour	Rs 1.75
Other Variables	Rs 0.50
Depreciation & Fixed cost	Rs 1.25
	Rs 6.25

The same component part is available in the market at Rs 4.85, should the firm make it or buy it?

4. a) What is meant by responsibility centre ? Outline the various types of responsibility centres?

OR

b) From the following data, prepare a flexible budget for production of 40,000 units and 75,000 units, distinctly showing variable cost and fixed cost as well as total cost. Also indicate element wise cost per unit. Budgeted output is 1,00,000 units and budgeted cost is as follows:

	Cost Per Unit (Rs)
Direct Material	95
Direct Labour	50
Production Overhead (Variable)	40
Production Overhead (Fixed)	5
Administration Overhead	5
Selling Overhead (10% fixed)	10
Distribution Overhead (20% fixed)	15

5. a) What is activity based costing systems? Explain.

OR

b) What is CAP analysis? Examine the need and importance of CAP analysis.

6. a) Explain the concept of product life cycle costing. Briefly write about process involved in assessment of PLC?

OR

b) What are the various sources of competitor information?

January 2013

Section - A

Write short notes on

a) Management Control system.

b) Variable costs

c) Standard costing

d) Performance Budgeting

e) Transfer pricing

f) Performance Report

g) Customer Costs

h) Cost Drivers

i) Competitive Pricing

j) Target Costing

Section - B

2. a) Discuss about the nature, scope and importance of strategic Management Accounting.

OR

b) From the following data, find out (i) Sales and (ii) New Break Even Sales, if selling price is reduced by 10%

Fixed Cost	Rs. 4,000
Break - even Sales	Rs. 20,000
Profit	Rs. 1,000
Selling Price per unit	Rs. 20

Solution :

Calculation of P/V Ratio :

$$\text{BEP Sales} = \frac{\textit{Fixed cost}}{\textit{p.v Ratio}}$$

20,000 = 4,000/ (P/V Ratio) : $\text{P/V Ratio} = \frac{4,000}{20,000} = 0.20 = 20\%$

Calculation of Margin of Safety (MOS) :

MOS = Profit / (P/V Ratio) = 1000/20% = Rs. 5,000

Calculation of Sales :

MOS = Sales – BEP Sales

5000 = Sales – 20,000

Sales = 5,000 + 20,000 = 25,000

i) Sales = ₹ 25,000

ii) **Calculation of new break-even point if selling price reduced by 10%:**

Variable Cost is 80% of sales (Because old P/V Ratio is 20%)

Variable Cost Per cent = Selling Price x 80/100 = 20 x 80/100 = Rs 16/-

New Selling Price (10% Decrease) = Selling Price - 10% Decrease of Selling Price = 20 – 20 x 10/100 = 20-2 = Rs. 18/-

New P/V Ratio = (C/S) x 100

Contribution = Selling Price –Variable Cost = 18-16 = 2

New P/V Ratio = $\frac{2}{18}$ x 100 = 11.11 %

New BEP = $\frac{Fixed\ Cost}{New\ p.v\ Ratio} = \frac{4000}{11.11\ \%}$ = Rs. 36,004/-

3. a) Do you support the concept of zero-based budgeting? Outline its advantages and disadvantages.

OR

b) The total costs of manufacturing a component part are as under:

Material	₹ 250
Labour	₹ 100
Variable expenses	₹ 50
Fixed expenses	₹ 100
	₹ 500

The same component part is available in the market at ₹ 450, should the firm make it or buy it?

3b Solution :

Calculation of Variable Cost

Particulars	Rs.
Materials	250
Labour	100
Variable Expenses	50
Total Variable Cost Per Unit	400
Product Available Market Price	450

Make or buy decision based on variable cost and market price of the product if the product market price is less than the variable cost then buy the product from market otherwise make the product. But in this problem total variable cost per cent is less than the market price. Hence make the product, it gives positive contribution and recover 50% of fixed cost.

4. a) What is a responsibility centre ? What are the types of responsibility centres ?

OR

b) The expenses for budgeted production of 10,000 units in a factory are furnished below :

	Per Unit (₹)
Materials	70
Labour	25
Variables overheads	20
Fixed overheads (10,000)	10
Variable expenses (direct)	5
Selling expenses (10% fixed)	13
Distribution expenses (20% fixed)	7
Administration expenses (Rs 50,000)	5
Total Cost per unit	155

Prepare a budget for production of 8000 units and 6000 units. Assume the administration expenses are fixed for all levels of production.

4b. Solution :

Flexible budget at Various Production Levels

Particulars	Per Unit (₹)	10,000 Units (₹)	8,000 Units (₹)	6,000 Units (₹)
A. Variable Cost:				
Materials	70	7,00,000	5,60,000	4,20,000
Labour	25	2,50,000	200,000	1,50,000
Variable Expenses	5	50,000	40,000	30,000
Variable Overheads	20	2,00,000	1,60,000	1,20,000
Variable Selling Expenses	11.70	1,17,000	93,600	70,200
Variable Distribution Expenses	5.6	56,000	44,800	33,600
Total Variable Cost	137.3	13,73,000	10,98,400	8,23,800
B. Total Fixed Cost:				
Fixed Overheads	10	1,00,000	1,00,000	1,00,000
Fixed Selling Expenses (10%)	1.3	13,000	13,000	13,000
Fixed Distribution Expenses (20%)	1.4	14,000	14,000	14,000
Total Administrative Expenses	5	50,000	50,000	50,000
Total Fixed Cost	17.7	1,77,000	1,77,000	1,77,000
Total cost (A+B)		15,50,000	12,75,400	10,00,800

5. a) What do you understand by CAP analysis? Discuss its need and importance.

OR

b) Discuss about activity based costing vs traditional costing.

6. a) What is competitor accounting? Evaluate the importance of competitor accounting.

OR

b) Outline the process involved in the assessment of product life cycle costing.

June 2012

Section - A

1. Write short notes on the following. All answers should be at one place.
   a) Define Management Accounting
   b) Key Factors
   c) Strategic Planning
   d) Performance Budget
   e) Investment Centre
   f) Transfer Price
   g) Activity-based Costing
   h) CAP Analysis
   i) Stages in PLC
   j) Target Costing

Section - B

Answer all Questions

2. a) Calculate the break-even sales from the following data for a company producing three products.

Products	Sales	Variable Cost
	₹	₹
A	10,000	6,000
B	5,000	2,500
C	5,000	2,000
	20,000	10,500

Total fixed costs amount to ₹ 5,700

2a. Solution :

Calculate the break-even sales from the following data for a company producing three products.

Particular	A	B	C	Total
Sales	10,000	5,000	5,000	20,000
Variable Cost	6,000	2500	2000	10,500
Contribution	4,000	2,500	3,000	9,500
P/V Ratio = C/s x 100	40%	50%	60%	47.50%
BEP Sales = F.C/Comb. P/V Ratio				5700/47.5% ₹ 12,000

Working notes : Calculation of combined P/V ratio

$$\text{Considered P/V Ratio} = \frac{\text{Combined Contribution}}{\text{Combined Sales}} \times 100$$

$$= \frac{9,500}{20,000} \times 100 = 47.5$$

OR

b) Explain the managerial uses of CVP analysis.

3. a) Discuss the merits and demerits of standard costing system.

b) The following is a summarized sales report of XYZ Ltd.

Products	Budgeted Sales (Units)	Actual Sales (Units)	Budgeted Selling Price
X	5,000	4,200	Rs. 4
Y	4,000	4,500	5
Z	1,000	1,300	10
	10,000	10,000	

Determine the sales mix variance

Solution :

Note : Actual and budget sales units are same and there is no need to calculate revised budget quantity of sales

Sales mix variance = Standard value of actual mix – Standard value of standard mix

Or (SP X AQ) – (SP x SQ)

A – (4 x 4,200) – (5,000 x 4) = 16,800 – 20,000 = 3,200 [A]

B – (5 x 4,500) – (5 x 4,000) = 22,500 – 20,000 = 25,000 [F]

C – (10 x 1,300) – (10 x 1,000) = 13,000 – 10,000 = 3,000 [F]

Total sales mix variance 2,300

----

4. a) State the need for divisionalisation and also explain various responsibility centres.

OR

b) The Hypothetical Ltd. has the following total operating results for the current year.

	Rs.
Sales revenue	56,00,000
Less : Variable Costs	37,20,000
Contribution	18,80,000
Less : fixed costs	10,00,000
Net Income	**8,80,000**

The following additional information concerning the performance of each of the firm's three operating departments has been provided:

	Departments		
	A	B	C
	Rs.	Rs.	Rs.
Sales revenue	24,00,000	20,00,000	12,00,000
Variable Costs	16,80,000	12,00,000	8,40,000
Direct fixed costs	3,20,000	2,80,000	2,00,000

Rank the three departments on the basis of their proportionate measure of relative profitability.

4b. Solution :

Calculation of Profit Margin and Ranks

Particulars	Departments			Total
	A	B	C	
	₹	₹	₹	
Sales Revenue	24,00,000	20,00,000	12,00,000	56,00,000
Variable Costs	16,80,000	12,00,000	8,40,000	37,20,000
Contribution	7,20,000	8,00,000	3,60,000	18,80,000
Direct Fixed Costs	3,20,000	2,80,000	2,00,000	10,00,000
Net Income / Profit	4,00,000	5,20,000	1,60,000	8,80,000
Profit Margin = (Profit / Sales)	16.67	26	13.37	15.71
Profitability Rank	2	1	3	

5. a) State the salient features of activity-based costing system.

OR

b) How to determine customer costs in service organizations.

6. a) Discuss the criteria's for cost assessment in product life cycle costing.

OR

b) What are sources for competitor information to present price biddings.

JAUARY 2012

Section – A

1. Write short notes on :
   a) Scope of Management Accounting
   b) CVP Analysis
   c) Standard Costing.
   d) Material Cost Variances.
   e) ZBB
   f) Cost Centre.
   g) Transfer Pricing.
   h) Cost Drivers
   i) CAP Analysis
   J) Target Costing.

Section - B

2. a) Explain the significance of strategic management accounting.

OR

b) ABC Ltd. manufactures and sells four types of products under the brand names of A, B, C and D. The sales mix in value comprises 33.33, 41.67, 16.67 and 8.33 per cent for products A,B,C and D respectively. The total budgeted sales (100 per cent) are Rs 60,000 per month. Operating costs are:

Variable costs as per cent of selling price: Product A 60, B 68, C 80, and D 40. Fixed Costs ₹ 14,700 per month.

Calculate the break-even point for the products on an overall basis.

2b. Solution :

Calculation of BEP on overall basis :

Average variable cost (%) = 62% $\left(\frac{60+68+80+40}{4} = 62\%\right)$

Hence contribution on (%) = 1 – Avg. V.C

P/V Ratio = 1-0.62 = 38%

$$\text{Overall BEP} = \frac{FC}{\text{Avg. P / V Ratio}} = \frac{14{,}700}{38} = \text{Rs } 38{,}684$$

3. a) State the significance of management control and operational control.

OR

b) The following is a summary statement of budgeted and actual sales of ABC Ltd.

Products	Budgeted (Units)	Actual (Units)	Budget Selling Price
A	5,000	4,000	₹ 4
B	4,000	3,200	5
C	1,000	800	10
	10,000	**8,000**	

Determine sales-mix variance

3a. Solution :

There is a difference between standard quantity and actual quantity, so this standard will be revised in proportion to actual quantity of sales.

Revised Standard :

Product A = (5000/10000) x 8000 = 4,000

Product B = (4000/10000) x 8000 = 3,200

Product C = (1000/10000) x 8000 = 800

S a l Variance = Standard Value of Actual Mix – Standard Value of Revised Standard Mix

Standard Value of Actual Mix

Product A = 4 x 4000 = 16,000

Product B = 5 x 3200 = 16,000

Product C = 10 x 800 = 8,000

Total = 40,000

Standard Value of Revised Standard Mix

Product A = 4 x 4000 = 16,000

Product B = 5 x 3200 = 16,000

Product C = 10 x 800 = 8,000

Total = 40,000

Sales Mix Variance = Standard Value of Actual Mix – Standard Value of Revised Standard Mix

= 40,000 – 40,000 = Nil

4. a) What is responsibility accounting and state its significance.

OR

b) The current year's operating results of the three divisions (A, B, and C) of Hypothetical Ltd. are given below (Amount in 000 rupees)

	Divisions		
	A	B	C
Sales revenue	400	400	2,000
Less : expenses	360	200	1,800
Segment Profit contribution	40	200	200
Segment assets	200	800	4,000

Determine the rate of return for the three divisions and rank these divisions assuming that the firm follows investment centre basis of performance evaluation.

4b Solution :

Calculation of ROI and Ranking

Particulars	Divisions		
	A	B	C
Sales revenue	400	400	2,000
Less: expenses	360	200	1,800
Segment Profit contribution	40	200	200
Segment assets	200	500	4,000
Return on investment (ROI)	20%	25%	5%
Ranking	2	1	3

From the above calculations Division 'B' Return on investment is more, hence its rank is division A is second and last rank is division C

5. a) Discuss the relative merits and demerits of activity-based costing with the comparison of traditional costing.

OR

b) Explain problems in managing Customer relationships.

6. a) How to assess costs in product life cycles?

OR

b) State the significance of cost analysis in pricing decisions.

June 2010

PART - A

Answer all questions serially

a) What is the revenue centre?

b) List out the assumptions of break-even analysis

c) Distinguish between standard costing and budgetary control.

d) Distinguish between cost centre and profit centre.

e) What is cost driver?

f) What is activity-based costing?

g) Explain the term variance.

h) Define target costing.

i) What are the uses of decision making?

j) What is zero-based budgeting?

PART - B

2. a) What is strategic management accounting ? Explain the scope and importance of strategic management accounting in a modern business enterprise ?

OR

b) During the current year AB Ltd showed a profit of Rs. 1,80,000 on a sale of ₹ 30,00,000. The Variable expenses were ₹ 21,00,000. You are required to work out.

1) The break-even sales at present

2) The break-even sales if variable cost prices increased by 5%

3) The break even sales to maintain the profit as at present, if the selling price is reduced by 5%

2b Solution :

Calculation of fixed cost with the help of marginal costing equation.

S – V = F + P

30,00,000 – 21,00,000 = F + 1,80,000

9,00,000 = F + 180000

9,00,000 – 1,80,000 = F

F = 7,20,000/-

Calculation of P/V Ratio

P/V Ratio = $\frac{C}{S}$ x 100

C= S – V = 30,00,000 – 21,00,000 = 9,00,000

P/V Ratio = $\frac{9,00,000}{30,00000}$ x 100 = 30%

Break even sales at present = $\frac{FC}{\frac{P}{V}\ Ratio}$

= $\frac{7,20,000}{30\%}$ = Rs 24,00,000

2. If variable cost is increased by 5%

(i) Calculation of new P/V Ratio

(Variable cost increased by 5%)

Variable exp = 21,00,000

+ 5% increased = 1,05,000

21,000 x 5/10

New total variable cost = 22,05,000

b) Contribution = Sales – V.C

= 30,00,000 – 22,05,000 = 7,95,000

New P/V ratio = C/S x 100 = $\frac{795000}{30,00,000}$ x 100 = 26.5%

(ii) New BEP (VC increased by 5%) New P/V Ratio

= $\frac{7,20,000}{26.5\%}$ = 27,16,981

3. Maintain some profit if selling price is reduced by 5%

Calculation of new sales and contribution

Total sales = 30,00,000

Then 5% selling price reduces = 15,000

30,00,000 x 5/100

New Sales = 29,85,000

Less: Variable cost 21,00,000

Contribution = 8,85,000

$$\text{Calculation of P/V Ratio} = \frac{Contribution}{Sales} \times 100 = \frac{8,85,000}{29,85,000} \times 100 = 29.65\%$$

$$BEP = \frac{Fixed\ Cost + profit}{\frac{P}{V}ratio} = \frac{7,20,000 + 1,80,000}{29.85} = \frac{9,00,000}{29.85}$$

= Rs 30,150,75

3. a) Explain the significance and objective of a break-even chart and state the factors which would cause the break-even point to change.

OR

b) A hypothetical company has prepared the following cost estimates for the manufacture of a sub component hitherto purchased from an outside supplier at ₹ 32 a unit; ordering and inspection cost are estimated at ₹ 2 per unit. The firm has spare capacity and no extra fixed costs will be required to be incurred.

Direct material	10
Direct labour	14
Variable overheads	6
Fixed factory overheads (Allocation)	6
Total cost per unit	36

Should the component be made or purchased from outside ?

3b Solution :

Since fixed cost are to be incurred whether manufacture they component or note the decision depends upon the marginal cost of making the component which is calculated as follows.

Marginal Cost of Component nether to per unit	Amount Rs
Direct Material	10
Direct Labour	14
Variable Overheads	6
	30

It is advisable to make the component itself if the marginal cost of making the component is lower than the purchase price because every component produced will give some contribution to the company. But in case, the marginal cost is higher than the purchase price, it is better to buy the component from outside than to make it.

In this problem the purchase price is ₹ 32 and ordering and inspection cost is ₹ 2. It is not advisable to buy the component from outside. We should rather make the component on our own because every component manufactured will give a contribution of Rs. 4

4. a) Explain the concept of product life cycle costing. How is it used in cost reductions?

OR

b) The following details are available from the record of Raj and Co. Ltd., engaged in manufacturing article "A" for week ended 28th September 2008, the standard labour hours and rates of payment per article A were as follows

	Hours	Rate per hour	Total
Skilled labour	10	3	30
Semi-skilled	8	1.5	12
Unskilled	16	1	16
Total			58

The actual production was 1,000 articles "A" for which the actual hours worked and rates are given below:

	Hours	Rate per hour	Total
Skilled labour	9,000	4	36,000
Semi-skilled	8,400	1.5	12,600
Unskilled	20,000	0.9	18,000
Total			**66,600**

From the above set of data you are asked to calculate

a) Labour cost variance

b) Labour rate variance

c) Labour efficiency variance

d) Labour mix variance

4b Solution :

Calculation of Standard and Actual Labour Cost

Category	Standard			Actual		
	Hours	Rate Per hours	Total ₹	Hours	Rate Per hour	Total
Skilled Labour	10,000	3	30,000	9,000	4	36,000
Semi-skilled	8,000	1.5	12,000	8,400	1.5	12,600
Unskilled	16,000	1	16,000	20,000	0.9	18,000
Total	34,000		58,000	37,400		66,600

a) **Labour Cost Variance** = Standard Labour Cost – Actual Labour Cost

= 58,000 – 66,600 = 8,600 [A]

b) **Labour Rate Variance** = Actual Time [Std. Labour Rate – Actual Labour Rate]

Skilled = 9,000 [3-4] = 9000 [-1] =	9,000 [A]
Semi-skilled = 8,400 [1.5 – 1.5] =	NIL
Unskilled = 20,000 [1-09] = 20,000 [0.1] =	2,000 [F]
Total Labour Rate Variance	7,000 [A]

c) **Labour Efficiency Variance** = Standard Labour Rate [Standard time – Actual time]

Skilled = 3 [10,000 – 9000] = 3 [1000] =	3000 [F]
Semi-skilled = 1.5 [8,000 – 8,400] = 1.5 [400] =	600 [A]
Unskilled = 1 [16,000 – 20,000] = 1 [4000] =	4000 [A]
Total Labour Efficiency Variance	1600 [A]

d) **Labour Mix Variance** :

Total standard time for skilled semi-skilled and unskilled = 34,000 hrs

Total actual time for skilled semi-skilled and unskilled = 37,400 hrs

When standard time of labor mix is different from the actual time of labour mix, the formula for calculating labour mix variance is:

$$\frac{Total\ time\ of\ Actual\ lab.Mix}{Std.time\ of\ Std.Lab.mix} \times \text{Std. Cost of Std.Lab. mix]} - \text{[Std. Cost of Act.Lab. Mix]}$$

$$= \frac{37,400}{34,000} \times [(10,000 \times 3) + (8,000 \times 1.5) + (16000 \times 1)] - [(9000 \times 3) + (8,400 \times 1.5) + (20,000 \times 1)]$$

$$= [(37,400 / (34,000)) \times 58,000] - [59,600] = 63,800 - 59,600 = 4,200 \text{ [A]}$$

5. a) Under what circumstances should activity-based costing system be used for increase in the competitiveness of the firm?

OR

b) What are various steps involved to install target costing approach within an organization

6. a) Disuss the merits and demerits of using profit centre and cost centre as ways of measuring managerial performance.

OR

b) Enumerate and briefly explain any three methods of determining transfer prices.

December 2009

Part – A

a) Characteristic of Management Control System

b) Capacity Utilization

c) Purpose of budgetary control

d) Variance analysis

e) Profit Centre

f) Transfer Pricing

g) Overheads

h) Need for Customer Profitability Analysis

i) Cost Apportionment

j) Target Costing

PART – B

2. a) Explain the importance, scope and characteristic of strategic management accounting.

OR

b) The following figures are extracted from the books of a manufacturing concern for the year 2003 :

Direct materials	2,05,000
Direct labour	75,000
Fixed Overheads	60,000
Variable Overheads	1,00,000
Sales	5,00,000

Calculate the break-even point. What will be the effect on BEP of an increase of 10% in

i) Fixed expenses?

ii) Variable expenses?

2b Solution :

Calculation of Total Variable Cost :

Total V.C = D.M + D.L + VOH

= 200000 + 75000 + 100000

= 3, 80,000

Contribution (c) = Sales – Variable Cost

= 5, 00,000 – 3, 80,000

C = 1, 20,000

$$\text{P/V Ratio} = \frac{C}{S} \times 100 = \frac{1,20,000}{5,00,000} \times 100 = 24\%$$

$$\text{BEP} = \frac{\text{Fixed cost}}{\text{P/V ratio}} = \frac{60,000}{24\%} = \text{Rs. } 2,50,000$$

Calculation of New Fixed Expenses (10% increase):

= 60,000 + 6,000 (60,000 x 10/100) = Rs. 66,000

$$= \text{BEP} = \frac{\text{New Fixed cost}}{\text{P/V ratio}} = \frac{66,000}{24\%} = \text{Rs. } 2,75,000$$

Calculation of Total Variable Cost (10% Increase):

= 3, 80,000 + 38,000 (3, 80,000 x 10/100) = 4, 18,000

New Contribution = Sales – New V.C = 5, 00,000 – 4, 18,000 = 82,000

$$\text{New P/V Ratio} = \frac{\text{New Contribution}}{\text{Sales}} \times 100 = \frac{82,000}{5,00,000} \times 100 = 16.4\ \%$$

$$\text{New BEP} = \frac{\text{Fixed cost}}{\text{P/V ratio}} = \frac{60,000}{16.4\%} = \text{Rs. } 3,65,854$$

3. a) What is "standing costing" and how you distinguish it from "budgetary control"? Explain.

OR

b) From the following data, calculate

(i) Labour Cost Variance

(ii) Labour Efficiency Variance

(iii) Labour Rate Variance.

XYZ Ltd. Sets five hours as labour as time standard for processing one unit of product A at a standard direct labour rate of ₹ 5 Per hour. During the month of May, the company used 6000 actual direct labour hours at ₹ 4 per hour to process 1000 Units of Products A

3b Solution :

Labour Cost Variance = Standard Labour Cost – Actual Labour Cost

= (1000 x 5 x 5) – (6000 x 4)

= 25,000 – 24,000 = 1000[F]

Labour Rate Variance = Actual Time [Std. Labour Rate – Actual Labour Rate]

= 6000 (5-4) = 6000 [F]

Labour Efficiency Variance = Standard Labour Rate [Standard-Time – Actual time]

= 5 [(1000 x 5) - 6000] = 5 x [-1000] = 5000 [A]

4. a) What is transfer pricing? Explain different methods of transfer pricing.

OR

b) A company is considering an outlay on new investments projects for its two divisions X and Y, the details about new investment projects are given below.

	Divisions	
	X	Y
Investment outlay (₹)	75,000	75,000
Expected return on new projects	14,000	10,000
Current ROI	16%	18%

The company's cost of capital is 12% You are required to give your opinion to the company regarding the investment in the above divisions.

4b Solution :

Calculation of ROI (Return on Investment)

Particulars	**Divisions**	
	X	**Y**
Investment Outlay (₹)	75,000	75,000
Expected return on new project	14,000	10,000
Current ROI	16%	18%
ROI = (Profit/Investment) x 100	18.67	13.33
Division X = (14000/75000) x 100		
Division Y = (10000/75000) x 100		

Division X expected ROI is more than the Current ROI but Division Y's expected ROI is less than the Current ROI. Hence, Division X is the Best Proposal for Future.

5. a) What do you understand by Customers Account Profitability Analysis? Explain.

OR

b) XYZ Produces Four products A,B,C and D for which the relevant cost information given below.

Particulars	Products			
	A	B	C	D
Direct material per unit (₹)	40	50	30	60
Direct labour per Unit (₹)	28	21	14	21
Direct labour per Unit	4	3	2	3
Machine hours Set ups	120	100	80	120
Number of purchase requisitions	500	700	400	400
No. of machine hours per unit	2	2	3	3
Output (Units)	10,000	20,000	5,000	15,000

Production overheads split by departments

Department I :	₹ 10,00,000
Department II :	₹ 12,00,000
Total :	₹ 22,00,000

Department I is labour intensive and Department II is machine intensive. Total labour hours in Department I is 1,00,000 hrs and total machine hours in Department II is 6,00,000 hrs.

Production Overheads split by activity.

Receiving and inspection =	Rs. 15, 00,000
Production scheduling/Set up =	Rs. 7, 00,000
Total	22, 00,000

No. of batches received/Inspected - 3,000

No. of batches for scheduling set-up - 3,500

Prepare cost statement under traditional costing and activity-based costing methods.

5b. Solution :

Traditional Method :

$$\text{Overhead absorption rate} = \frac{\text{Overheads of the department}}{\text{Hours}}$$

$$\text{Department I} = ₹\ \frac{10,00,000}{1,00,000\ \text{Labour}} = ₹\ 10 \text{ per Labour hour}$$

$$\text{Department II} = ₹\ \frac{12,00,000}{6,00,000\ \text{Machine Hours}} = ₹\ 2 \text{ per machine Hours}$$

Statement of Cost

Particulars	Cost Per Unit (Rs)			
	A ₹	B ₹	C ₹	D ₹
Direct Materials	40	50	30	60
Direct Labour	28	21	14	21
Overhead - Dept I A- 4 hrs @ ₹ 10 B- 3 hrs @ ₹ 10 C -2 hrs @ ₹ 10 D -3 hrs @ ₹ 10	40	30	20	30
Dept - II A- 2 hrs @ ₹ 2 B- 2 hrs @ ₹ 2 C- 3 hrs @ ₹ 2	4	4	6	6
Product Cost	112	105	70	117

ABC Method

$$\text{Cost driver rates} = \frac{\text{Overhead cost of the activity}}{\text{Cost drivers}}$$

$$\text{Receiving and inspection} = ₹\ \frac{15,00,000}{3,000\ \text{batches}} = ₹\ 500 \text{ per batch}$$

$$\text{Scheduling and set-up} = ₹\ \frac{7,00,000}{3,500\ \text{batches}} = ₹\ 200 \text{ per batch}$$

Calculation of receiving overhead percent

Product A = (₹ 500 x 500 requisition) / 10,000 units = ₹ 25

Product B = (₹ 500 x 700 requisition) / 20,000 units = ₹ 17.50

Product C = (₹ 500 x 400 requisition)/5,000 = ₹ 40

Product D = (₹ 500 x 400 requisition)/15,000 = 13.30

Calculation of Machine set up overhead percent.

Product A = (₹ 200 x 120 setups)/10,000 units = ₹ 2.40

Product B = (₹ 200 x 100 Setups)/20,000 units = ₹ 1.00

Product C = (₹ 200 x 80 Setups)/5,000 units = ₹ 3.20

Product D = (₹ 200 x 120 Setups)/15,000 units = ₹ 1.60

Statement of Cost under ABC Method

Particulars	Cost Per Unit			
	A ₹	B ₹	C ₹	D ₹
Direct Materials	40.00	50.00	30.00	60.00
Direct Labour	28.00	21.00	14.00	21.00
Overhead Receiving	25.00	17.50	40.00	13.30
Overhead Setup	2.40	1.00	3.20	1.60
Product Cost	95.40	89.50	87.20	95.90

6. a) Describe the life cost assessment model.

OR

b) What is competitive pricing and bidding? How do you evaluate target cost analysis for pricing decision?

May 2009

Section - A

(a) What is management control system ?

(b) Distinguish between fixed costs and variable costs.

(c) What is angle of incidence ?

(d) What is zero-based budgeting ?

(e) What do you mean by activity cost drivers ?

(f) Distinguish between traditional costing and activity-based costing.

(g) What is responsibility accounting ?

(h) What is variance analysis ?

(i) What is revenue centre ?

(j) What is margin of safety ?

Section – B

2. (a) What is strategic management accounting ? Explain scope and importance of strategic management accounting in a modern business enterprise.

OR

(b) There are two plants under the same management. The management desires to merge these two plants. The following particulars are available.

Details	Plant - I	Plant - II
Capacity Operation	100%	60%
Sales (₹ Lakh)	750	750
Variable Costs (₹ Lakh)	550	540
Fixed Cost (₹ Lakh)	100	120

You are required to calculate.

(i) The merged plant capacity to be operated for the purpose of break-even and

(ii) The profitability of working at 80 per cent of the merged capacity.

Solution :

(i) Working Notes

(a) Calculation of sales at 100% capacity plant - II

Sales at 60% capacity = 750 (in lakhs)

i.e., for 100 % = $\frac{100 \times 750}{60}$ = 1,250 (lakhs)

(b) Calculation of variable cost of 100% sales

Variable costs for sales 750 (in lakhs) = ₹ 540

Then for 1,250 = $\frac{1,250 \times 540}{60}$ = ₹ 900 (lakhs)

Break even point sales formula:

$$\text{BEP} = \frac{\text{Fixed Cost}}{\text{P / V Ratio}}$$

$$\text{P/V ratio} = \frac{\text{Contribution}}{\text{Sales}}$$

Contribution = Sales – Variables Cost

Calculation of P/V Ratio and Break-even point of merged plant

Particulars	Plant - 1 (lakhs)	Plant - II (Lakhs)	Merged (lakhs)
Capacity	100%	100%	100%
Sales (in Lakhs)	750	1250	2000
Less			
Variable Cost	550	900	1450
Contribution	Rs. 200 Lakhs	350 Lakhs	550 Lakhs
P/V ratio	200/750 = 0.26	350/1250 = 0.28	550/2000 = 0.275
Break-even point sales	100/0.26 = 384.615	120/0.28 = 428.571	220/0.275 = 800

(ii) Calculation of sales and variable cost at 80% capacity

At 80% capacity of merged plant

Sales are 100 % Capacity = ₹ 2,000 lakhs

Sales at 80 % = 1600 (Lakhs) $\left(\frac{80 \times 2,000}{100} = 1600\right)$

Variable cost 2,000 – 1450 at sales variable cost at sales 1600 lakhs

1600 – 1160 (Lakhs) $\left[\frac{1,600 \times 1,450}{2,000} = 1,160\right]$

Calculation of Profitability

Particulars	Merged Plant (In Lakhs)
Sales (in Lakhs)	1600
Less:	
Variable Cost	1160
Contribution	440
Profitability	440/1600 = 0.275

3. (a) XYZ limited had provided us with the following data

Particulars	Budgeted	Actual
Output per man hour	2.5	2.75
Overheads	₹ 1,66,000	₹ 1,92,000
Man hours per day	4750	5450
Number of working days in a month	24	26

You are required to find.

(i) Overhead cost variable

(ii) Expenditure cost variance.

(iii) Volume variance

(iv) Capacity variance

(v) Calendar variance and

(vi) Efficiency variance.

3 (a) Solution :

Calculation of standard overhead rate per-cent :

(i) Standard overhead rate per unit $= \dfrac{\text{Budgeted Overhead}}{\text{Budgeted Output}}$

$$= \frac{1,66,000}{(2.50 \times 4,750)}$$

$$= \frac{1,66,000}{11,875} = 13.9$$

Overhead cost variance

Actual Output × Standard Rate – Actual Overhead Cost

= [(2.75 x 5450) x 13.9] – 1, 92,000

= 2, 08,326.25 – 1, 92,000

= 16,326.25 [A]

(ii) Expenditure Variance

Budgeted Overheads – Actual overheads

= 1, 66,000 – 192,000

= –26,000 [A]

(iii) Volume Variance

Actual Output x Standard Overhead Rate – Budgeted Overhead Overhead cost

= [(2.75 x 5450) x 13.9] – 1, 66,000

= 208326.25 – 1, 66,000

= 42,326.25 [F]

(iv) Capacity Variance

Standard overhead rate x (Revised budgeted output - Budgeted output)

Workings :

= 13.9 x (11,875 – 12,864.58)

= 13.9 x (- 989.58)

= - 13.755.162 [A]

Budgeted production 2.50 x 4750 = 11,875 units

$$\text{Budgeted output for 24 days} = \frac{11,875}{24} \times 26$$

$$= 12,864.58$$

(v) Calendar Variance

Increase in production due to 2 more working days x Standard rate per unit, within 24 days, Standard output

24 days std. output = 11,875 units

Therefore, within 2 days, output will be increased by

$$\frac{11,875}{24} \times 2 = 989.58 \text{ units}$$

Calendar variance = 989.58 x 13.9

= 13,755.162 [F]

(vi) Efficiency Variance

Standard overhead rate (Actual production - Standard production)

= 13.9 x (14,987.5 - 15,964)

= 13.9 x (-977)

= - 13,580 [A]

Standard Production

Budgeted Production 11,875 units.

Add: Production increased

Due to 2 more working days.

For 24 days – 11,875 For 26 days ?

$$26 \text{ days} - \frac{11,875 \times 26}{24}$$

= 12864.56

= 12864 – 11875 = 989.58

3100

Production increased due to increase in capacity 989.58 + 3100 = 15964.58

OR

(b) A factory engaged in manufacturing buckets is working at 40 per cent capacity and produces 10,000 buckets per annum.

The present cost break-up for one bucket is as under,

Material	₹ 40
Labour Cost	₹ 12
Overheads	₹ 20 (60% fixed)

The selling price is ₹ 80 per bucket.

If it is decided to work the factory at 50 per cent capacity, the selling price falls by 3 per cent. At 90 per cent capacity the selling price falls by 5 per cent accompanied by a similar fall in the prices of material.

You are required to calculate the profit at 50 and 90 per cent capacities, and also calculate break-even point for the same capacity production levels.

3b Solution:

Statement showing the calculation of profit and break-even point at different capacity levels.

Particulars	40 % capacity	50 % capacity	90 % Capacity
Production	10,000	12,500	22,500
I. Selling Price (P.U)	₹ 80	₹ 77.6 * WN:1	₹ 76 × WN:2
II. Variable Cost			
1. Material	₹ 40	₹ 40	₹ 38 × WN: 3
2. Labour cost	₹ 12	₹ 12	₹ 12
3. Overheads (40 % variable)	₹ 8	₹ 8	₹ 8
	₹ 60	₹ 60	₹ 58
III Contribution	₹ 20	₹ 17.6	₹ 18
IV Fixed cost	₹ 12	₹ 12	₹ 12
Profit (III - IV)	₹ 8	₹ 5.6	₹ 6
Break even	₹ 12/20/80 Rs 0.6	Rs 15/17.6/77.6 ₹ 0.6818	Rs 18/18/76 ₹ 666.68

Contribution = Sales – Variable cost

Profit = Contribution – Fixed cost

$$\text{Break-even point sales} = (\text{Fixed cost/P/V ratio}) = \frac{\text{Contribution}}{\text{Sales}}$$

* 1. Given that, at 50% capacity, S.P. decreases by 3%

** 2. At 90% capacity, S.P decreases by 5%

*** 3. At 90% capacity, material price decreases by 5%

4. (a) Describe and compare the main performance measures that have been suggested to measure the divisional performance.

OR

(b) The operating performance of the three divisions of a standard mart for the year 2006-07 is as under,

Details	Divisions		
	AX (₹)	BY (₹)	CZ (₹)
Sales	50,00,000	2,40,00,000	2,60,00,000
Operating Profit	3,00,000	6,00,000	13,00,000
Investment	25,00,000	80,00,000	1,00,00,000

(i) Using the operating margin percentage as the criterion, which is the most profitable division?

(ii) Using the rate of return on investment as the criterion, which is the most profitable division?

(iii) Which of the two measures do you think gives the better indication of overall performance?

4b Solution :

Calculation of operating margin percentage

$$\frac{\text{Profit before tax}}{\text{Sales}} \times 100$$

Statement showing the calculation for operating margin and the profitable division ranking

Particulars	AX	BY	CZ
Sales	50,00,000	2,40,00,000	2,60,00,000
Operating profit	3,00,000	6,00,000	13,00,000
Operating margin	3lakhs/50 lakhs	6,00,000 / 2,40,000	13,lakhs/2,60,00,000
	0.06	2.5	0.05
Profitable division	II	I	III

(II) Calculation of Rate of Return on Investment or Return on Investment (ROI)

$$\frac{\text{Profit before tax}}{\text{Capital employed or investment}} \times 100$$

Statement showing the calculation of return on investment and the profitability ranking.

Particulars	AX	BY	CZ
Operating Profit	3,00,000	6,00,000	13,00,000
Investments	25,00,000	80,00,000	1,00,00,000
Return on investment	3lakhs/25lakhs	6lakhs/8lakhs	13lakhs/1,00,lakhs
(ROI)	0.12	0.075	0.13
Profitability division Ranks	II	III	I

5. (a) Describe the reasons for product cost difference between traditional costing systems and activity based costing system.

OR

(b) Discuss the meaning and need of customer account profitability analysis.

6. (a) Explain the pricing and evaluation criteria for products at different stages of PLC.

OR

(b) What is target costing? Describe how costs are reduced so that the target costs can be met.

December 2008

SECTION –A

(a) Define management accounting.

(b) Distinguish between product costs and periods costs.

(c) What is flexible budget?

(d) What is standard costing?

(e) What do you mean by activity-based costing?

(f) Cost driver.

(g) Define target costing/

(h) What is transfer pricing?

(i) What is responsibility center?

(j) What is responsibility centre?

(k) What is product life cycle costing?

SECTION - B

2. (a) Two firms A-Limited and X-Limited are identical and are under the same management. Their budgeted Profit and Loss Accounts for the year ending 31st December 2008 are as follows:

Particulars		A-Limited		X-Limited
Sales		Rs. 3,33,000		Rs.3,33,000
Less Variable Costs	Rs.2,44,000		Rs.2,00,000	
Fixed Costs	Rs.35,000	Rs. 2,79,000	Rs.79,000	Rs.2,79,000
Profit		Rs. 54,000		Rs.54,000

You are required to find.

(i) The BEP for A-Limited and X-Limited

(ii) The sales volume at which each of the two firms will make a profit of Rs.15,000

(iii) Which firm is likely to earn greater profits when the demand for the product is high and low?

2a Solution :

Formula's for Calculating B.E.P and Desired Sales

i. $\text{B.E.P} = \dfrac{\text{Fixed Cost}}{\text{p.v. ratio}}$

$\text{P/V ratio} = \dfrac{\text{Contribution}}{\text{Sales}}$

Contribution = Sales – Variable cost.

ii. Sales volume, when desired profit is given

$\text{Sales Volume} = \dfrac{\text{Fixed Cost + Desired Profit}}{\text{p.v. ratio}}$

(i) Calculation of BEP (In amount)

Particulars	A- Limited	X - Limited
Sales	₹ 3,33,000	₹ 3,33,000
Less:		
Variable cost	₹ (2,44,000)	₹ (2,00,000)
Contribution	89,000	1,33,000
P/V ratio	89,000/3,33,000 = 0.26	1,33,000/3,33,000 = 0.39
BEP	35,000/0.26 = ₹ 1,34,615	79,000/0.39 = ₹ 2,02,564

(ii) Sales volume at which two firms make profit of ₹ 15,000

$$\text{Required Sales} = \frac{\text{Fixed Cost + Profit}}{\text{P / V ratio}}$$

Calculation of Desired Sales

Particulars	A- Limited	X - Limited
Fixed Cost	₹ 35,000	₹ 79,000
Add:		
Profit	₹ 15,000	₹ 15,000
	₹ 50,000	₹ 94,000
P/v Ratio	0.26	0.39
Sales	50,000/0.26 = ₹ 1,92,308	94,000/0.39 = 2,41,025

(iii) With the fluctuations in demand there will be change in sales mix. In the given situation where for A-limited and X-limited even though sales are equal i.e., ₹ 3,33,000 but variable costs are more in case of A- ltd and fixed costs are more in case of X-ltd.

Variable costs are directly proportional to sales volume, so if we increase sales volume in case of A-limited variable cost will be more when compared to X-limited.

So, whenever demand is high X-limited is preferable and in case of low demand A-limited is preferable.

2. (b) The United Vision Limited is considering expansion. Fixed costs amount to ₹ 4,60,000 and are expected to increase by ₹1,40,000 when plant expansion is completed. The existing plant capacity is 32,000 units a year. Capacity will increase by 50 per cent with the expansion. Variable costs are currently ₹17 per uint are expected to go down by ₹ 1 per unit with the expansion. The current selling price is ₹ 40 per unit and is expected to remain same under either alternative. What are the break-even points under either alternatives? Which alternative is better and why?

Solution :

Calculation of BEP Points under either alternative.

Particulars	Before expansion	After expansion
Capacity Variable cost Fixed cost Selling price BEP Fixed Cost	32,000 units ₹ 17 per Unit ₹ 4,60,000 ₹ 40 Per unit 4,60,000	48,000 units ₹ 16 per unit ₹ 6,00,000 ₹ 40 per unit 6,00,000
Selling price - variable cost.P/V	40-17 = 4,60,000 23	40-16 = 600000 24
	=20000	=25,000

Capacity increased by 50% (32,000 + 32,000 x $\frac{50}{100}$)

Conclusion :

Hence, the United Vision limited, must go for an expansion alternative as it results in more break-even sales than before its expansion.

3. (a) Define Budgetary Control and distinguish it from Standard Costing. Discuss the interrelationship between Budgetary Control and Standard Costing.

OR

3. (b) Calculate Material Price Variance. Material Usage Variance and Material Cost Variance from the following information

Quantity of material purchased	3,000 Units
Value of materials purchased required	₹14,000
Standard quantity of material required per ton of finished products	20 units
Standard price of material	₹5 per unit
Opening stock of materials	100 units
Closing stock of materials	600 units
Finished product manufactured	100 tones

Solution :

Value of material purchased = ₹ 14,000

Quantity of material purchased = ₹ 3,000 units

Actual rate of material P/V = $\frac{14,000}{3,000}$ = Rs. 4.67

Actual quantity of material used,

Opening stock + Quantity purchased – Closing stock

= 100 + 3,000 – 600

= 2,500 units.

Standard usage for 100 tonnes of output @ 20 units = 2,000 units.

Material Price Variance,

MPV = Actual quantity (Standard rate – Actual rate)

= 2,500 (5-4.67)

= 2,500 (0.33)

= 825 (Favorable)

Material Usage Variace,

MUV = Standard Rate (Standard Usage – Actual Usage)

= ₹ 5(2,000 – 2,500)

= 5(-500)

= -2,500 (Adverse)

Material Cost Variance,

MCV = (Standard Usage x Standard Rate) – (Actual Usage x Actual Rate)

= (2,000 x 5) – (2,500 x 4.67)

= 10000 – 11,675

= 1675 (Adverse)

Verification :

MCV = MPV + MUV

-1675[A] = 825[F] – 2500[A]

- 1675[A] = - 1675[A]

4. (a) "Responsibility accounting is an important device for control". Evaluate the statement.

OR

4. (b) Varsha Limited is divided into three segments X,Y and Z. All the divisions were formed in the same year. Top the most profitable. The following data have been furnished for your analysis.

Details	Division		
Net income before taxes Investment	X(₹)	Y(₹)	Z(₹)
	1,00,000 2,50,000	1,11,000 3,00,000	1,60,000 5,00,000

Solution :

Calculation of Most Profitable Division

Particulars	**Division X**	**Division Y**	**Division Z**
Net Income before taxes i.e.(PBIT)	₹ 1,00,000	₹ 1,11,000	₹ 1,60,000
Investment	₹ 2,50,000	₹ 3,00,000	₹ 5,00,000
Capital Charge	14%	14%	14%

Return on investment (ROI)

$$\frac{\text{PBIT}}{\text{Capital employed}} \times 100 \qquad \frac{1,00,000}{2,50,000 \times 0.14} \times 100 \qquad \frac{1,11,000}{3,00,000 \times 0.14} \times 100$$

$$\frac{1,60,000}{5,00,000 \times 0.14} \times 100$$

Capital employed

= Profit ratio x investment

$$= \frac{1,00,000}{35,000} \times 100 \qquad = \frac{1,10,000}{42,000} \times 100 \qquad = \frac{1,60,000}{70,000} \times 100$$

	= 285.714	= 264.285	= 228.571
Ranking	I	II	III

Prepare ranking of the three division using ROI with a capital charge of 14 per cent that each manager might use to assert that his is the most profitable division.

5. (a) What are the dimensions of Activity- based Management (ABM) ? How do they differ?

OR

(b) What is activity analysis? How is this approach compatible with the goal of continuous improvement?

6. (a) What is life cycle costing? Describe the benefits of life cycle costing.

OR

(b) Define target costing. Examine the relationship between target costing and continuous improvement costing.

❖ ❖ ❖